The Politics of Dreaming

Regents Studies in
Medieval Culture

General Editor
Eugene Vance
University of
Washington

Editorial Board

Robert L. Benson
University of California,
Los Angeles

R. Howard Bloch
University of California,
Berkeley

Caroline W. Bynum
Columbia University

Brian Stock
University of Toronto

Paul Edward Dutton

The Politics of Dreaming
in the Carolingian Empire

University of Nebraska Press, Lincoln and London

© 1994 by the
University of
Nebraska Press.
All rights reserved.
Manufactured in
the United States
of America.
The paper in this
book meets the
minimum require-
ments of American
National Standard
for Information
Sciences-Perma-
nence of Paper for
Printed Library
Materials
ANSI Z39.48-1984.
Library of Congress
Cataloging-in-
Publication Data
Dutton, Paul Edward, 1952 –
The politics of dreaming
in the Carolingian
empire / Paul Edward Dutton.
p.   cm. – (Regents studies
in medieval culture)
Includes bibliographical
references and index.
ISBN 0-8032-1653-X
1. Carolingians.   2. Dream
interpretation – Political
aspects.   3. Charlemagne,
Emperor, 742–814 –
Influence.   4. France –
Politics and
government – To 987 –
Sources.   5. Political
poetry, Latin (Medieval
and modern) – France –
History and criticism.
I. Title.
II. Series.
DC73.D88   1994
944'.014 – dc20
93-38615
CIP

History, Stephen said, is a nightmare from which I am trying to awake.

Joyce, Ulysses

for Barbara

Contents

List of Illustrations   xi

Preface   xiii

Francia and Adjoining Areas in the Ninth Century   xvi

Carolingian Timeline   xviii

Introduction   1

CHAPTER ONE   The Sleep of Kings   5

CHAPTER TWO   The *Via Regia* of Dreams   23

CHAPTER THREE   Charlemagne and His Dream Critics   50

CHAPTER FOUR   Louis's Theater of Illusions   81

CHAPTER FIVE   Civil Wars and Worse   113

CHAPTER SIX   The Property of Dreams   157

CHAPTER SEVEN   In This Modern Age   195

CHAPTER EIGHT   Charles the Fat's Constitutional Dreams   225

EPILOGUE   Time to Wake   252

Notes   261

Index   320

Illustrations

Following page 160

Figure 1. The Stilling of the Storm at Sea

Figure 2. Psalm 3:6 (3:5): King David Rising from His Bed

Figure 3. Psalm 3:6–7 (3:5–6): Christ Replaces David

Figure 4. Psalm. 6:5–7 (6:4–6): David between Christ and the Sinners

Figure 5. Psalm 60 (61): King David on His Bed

Figure 6. Psalm 40:4 (41:3): The Overturned Bed of King David

Figure 7. Psalm 75:6–7 (76:5–6): Sleeping Riders and Vain Dreams

Figure 8. Psalm 75:6–7 (76:5–6): A Sleeping Rider and Whispering Demon

Figure 9. Psalm 72:14–20 (73:14–20): Dreamers Caught between the Saints and the Damned

Figure 10. The Cupola Mosaic of the Chapel of Aachen as Seen by Ciampini in the Late Seventeenth Century

Figure 11. Charles the Bald Gazing upon the Lamb of God

Figure 12. Charlemagne's Sight Lines in His Chapel at Aachen

Figure 13. Psalm 34:15 (35:15): David Being Lashed by His Enemies

Figure 14. Psalm 7:2–3 (7:1–2): David's Soul Attacked by a Raging Lion

Figure 15. The *Majestas Domini* Page of the Count Vivian Bible

Figure 16. The Shattered Sarcophagus of Louis the Pious

Figure 17. The Presentation Miniature of the Count Vivian Bible

Figure 18. An Outline Drawing of the Figures in the Presentation Miniature of the Count Vivian Bible

Figure 19. Count Vivian, a Detail from the Presentation Miniature of the Count
    Vivian Bible
Figure 20. Possible Representation of Audradus Modicus in the Presentation
    Miniature of the Count Vivian Bible
Figure 21. The Tomb of Hincmar of Rheims
Figure 22. Psalm 30:18 (31:18): A Sinner Being Led to Hell
Figure 23. Psalm 43:8 (44:7): A Bicameral World of Saints and Sinners
Figure 24. Psalm 1: David as King and Psalmist
Figure 25. Psalm 9:18 (9:17): A Noble Sinner Hooked
Figure 26. Bronze Equestrian Statue of a Carolingian King

Preface

The idea for this book was born over a dozen years ago, when I stood early one morning with my friend Edouard Jeauneau in a sun-washed square facing the Schatzkammer der Residenz in Munich. We had spent the previous hour examining, with Florentine Mütherich, the precious Prayerbook of Charles the Bald. With the beauty of one of its prayers, Alcuin's poetic plea for peaceful sleep, still stirring in my mind, I first began to think about the historiographical significance of sleep and dreams. It was, I confess, the image of King Charles holding in his hands that small book with its petitionary remedies against the dangers of night and its dark dreams that came to occupy a central place in my thoughts, instilling in me a desire, not yet fully satisfied, to understand the ninth century's politics of dreaming.

To have started down this long road with one friend reminds me of the many others who have helped along the way. Without the kindness and constant encouragement of Brian Stock this book would not exist. Throughout the years that I labored over Bernard of Chartres's glosses on Plato, Professor Stock never let me forget that I had earlier begun a study of political dreams to which I should someday return. I would also like to thank those individuals who kindly read drafts of the work in progress: Karl M. Morrison, John Shinners, John J. Contreni, Michael Fellman, Charles Hamilton, and Mary-Ann Stouck. Roger Reynolds twice went to some trouble to supply me with materials that I could not easily obtain here in Vancouver. I also need to thank Helen Davies for her research assistance, and Marjorie Nelles and Christine McConnell of the inter-library loan office of the W. A. C. Bennett Library for their persistence and good humor in hunting down books for my use. Jerald Zaslove, the director of the Institute for the Humanities at Simon Fraser University, with which I am proud to be associated, generously supplied me with research funding over two summers, and the Social Sciences and Humanities Research Council of Canada has supported my research over many years and many projects. Last, let me thank Eugene Vance, the principal editor of the Regents Studies in Medieval Culture, for his encouragement and active interest in this book over the last two years.

Unless otherwise indicated in the notes, all the translations in this book are mine. Psalms have been cited, where necessary, according to their respective psalm and chapter numbers in the Vulgate and King James versions of the Bible. I have cited in the notes only materials that bear directly on the points being made in the body of the book, but there is a vast literature on both dreams and Carolingian history that has shaped my investigations over the years and that I would encourage readers to explore. Indeed, in a synthetic work of this sort, the scrupulous reader is bound to come across mistakes and misjudgments, for which I beg forgiveness in advance.

Saint Augustine once thanked God for granting human minds the capacity to discern large truths in small things. For a time, these Carolingian dream texts have been the little things through which I hoped to view a larger world with its shifting sets of historical truths and the small gatherings of human beings who fervently pursued them.

ENGLAND

Dorestad

London ●

Nijmegen

Xan

Saint-Bertin

Meersen

Maastricht ● Aac

Saint-Vaast ●

Prüm

Saint-Riquier ●

Douzy

Corbie ● Quierzy ●

Compiègne ● Laon ● Attigny

Soissons ● Rheims ● M

Rouen ● Ver ● Verdun

Paris ● Meaux Châlons

Melun Ponthio

Chartres ● Sens

NEUSTRIA

Le Mans ● Ferrières Troyes

Orléans ● Auxerre

Angers ● Fontenoy

Tours Autun

BRITTANY

Nantes ●

Chalon

Bourges ●

Nantua

Lyons

Vienne

AQUITAINE

BURGUNDY

River

River

Saône River

Rhône

PROVENC

Cahors ●

Toulouse ●

SEPTIMANIA

Narbonne ●

MARCH OF SPAIN

SPAIN

Saragossa ●

Barcelona ●

Seine

Loire

100   200   300 KM

Francia
and Adjoining
Areas in the
Ninth Century

Hamburg

Bremen

SAXONY

Hildesheim

Paderborn

Corvey

THURINGIA

BOHEMIA

Cologne

Andernach   Fulda

Frankfurt   Seligenstadt

elheim

Mainz

Lorsch

River

Main

FRANCONIA

Rhine

Strasbourg

Danube   River

BAVARIA

Augsburg

Salzburg

CARINTHIA

PANNONIA

lmar

ALEMANNIA

Reichenau

Basle   Constance

Saint-Gall

ASE

RHAETIA

LOMBARDY

Vercelli   Pavia

Bobbio   Parma

PATRIMONY

Ravenna

O F

Spoleto

SAINT
PETER

DUCHY OF BENEVENTO

CORSICA

Rome

Monte Cassino

Benevento

Carolingian Time Line

Writers: Active Periods

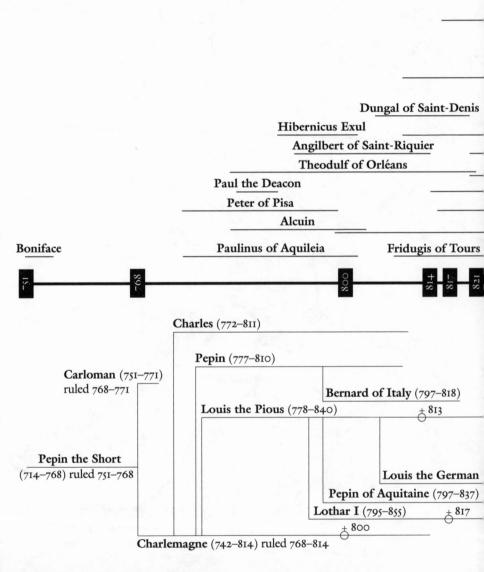

Dungal of Saint-Denis

Hibernicus Exul

Angilbert of Saint-Riquier

Theodulf of Orléans

Paul the Deacon

Peter of Pisa

Alcuin

Boniface

Paulinus of Aquileia

Fridugis of Tours

751   768   800   814   818   821

Charles (772–811)

Pepin (777–810)

Carloman (751–771)
ruled 768–771

Bernard of Italy (797–818)
✝ 813

Louis the Pious (778–840)

Pepin the Short
(714–768) ruled 751–768

Louis the German

Pepin of Aquitaine (797–837)

Lothar I (795–855) ✝ 817

✝ 800

Charlemagne (742–814) ruled 768–814

Princes, Kings, and Emperors: Lifespans

○ indicates the year that a king became emperor.

Freculf of Lisieux

Florus of Lyons

Engelbert

Hilduin of Saint-Denis

Moduin

Gerward

Audradus Modicus

Nithard

Dhuoda

Paschasius Radbertus

Prudentius of Troyes

The Astronomer

Thegan　　　　　　　　　Gottschalk

Lupus of Ferrières

Walahfrid Strabo　　　　　　　　　　　　　　Poeta Saxo

Heito of Basle　　Agnellus of Ravenna　　　　　　　Abbo

Jonas of Orléans　　　　　　　　Rimbert

Ermold the Black　　　Sedulius Scottus

Hrabanus Maurus　　　　　　　　　　　　　Notker

Agobard of Lyons　　　　　Eriugena

Einhard　　　　　Hincmar of Rheims　　　Fulk of Rheims

Rudolf of Fulda

830　833　840　843　855　858　875 - 81　881　888　900

Louis III (863–882)

Carloman (866–884)

Charles the Simple (879–929)

Louis the Stammerer　(846–879)

Charles the Bald (823–877)　　　　　　　± 875

Carloman of Bavaria (830–880)

Louis the Younger (835–881)

Charles the Fat (839–888)　　　　　± 881

06–876)

Charles of Provence (845–863)

Lothar II (835–869)

Louis II (825–875)　　± 850

Introduction

This book is about a series of short texts that haunted the intellectual history of Carolingian Europe in its *periculosa tempora,* its dangerous and troubled times. So habituated have we moderns become to the numbing pace of change that we have tended to think of the Middle Ages as exactly opposite, as a world so weighed down by the stubborn rigidities of place and tradition that men and women lacked even a passing awareness of historical change. Nothing could be further from the truth. Carolingian intellectuals may have been no more clever than we are at discerning the undercurrents and causes of contemporary change, but they were convinced that their society was being transformed before their very eyes, and the conception of a troubled age became an intellectual space into which they could pour their complaints about the dangerous turn of the times. Reaching out for a new level of literary discourse, some of them dreamed a different narrative of their times or, rather, they narrated a set of corrective dreams. This bumpy oneiric record, though dark with disturbing conviction and partisan interest, supplies us with a more intense, almost nightmarish, reading of ninth-century history, one that runs parallel to the annals of the age, casting at times a lurid, at times a splendid light on selected events. If in real life dreams often seem to represent the most subjective side of our nature, where we feel more than think, the political dreams of the ninth century must stand as the most intensely subjective statements of Carolingian political thought, for in them things that elsewhere remained unsaid were finally spoken, but with a clarity and conviction that real dreams rarely achieve.

In the century since Leopold von Ranke's seminal work on the *Royal Frankish Annals,* medievalists have worked diligently to separate fact from fiction, to unravel knotty names and dates, and to amass monumental prosopographies. Yet Richard E. Sullivan recently wondered whether "the generally accepted version of the Carolingian world is an 'imagined' world, existing only in the minds of modern historians."[1] That may be, but I have always been more concerned about our persistent neglect of another "'imagined' world," that storied realm conceived by the Carolingians themselves. What we have underestimated in our pursuit of the factual truths of the ninth century is the interpretive tale that the Carolingians told themselves about their time, for it may be the most captivating narrative of them all, one that occasionally possesses, as Ernst Kantorowicz once observed, the feel of a novel.[2] Until we have confronted the problem of Carolingian subjectivity, will we ever be sure that we have understood the whole record, the one that includes both events and actors, thoughts and their thinkers?

I have here, I confess, nothing as numerically rich to investigate as the 415 dreams of a sixteenth-century Spanish woman recently studied by Richard Kagan.[3] Indeed there are fewer than thirty dreams and visions from the ninth century that contain political matter. These texts were written in Francia in the period between the reign of Charlemagne and the proximate end of the reign of Charles the Fat, and all were composed in Latin, mostly by monks and clerics. Even the fitfulness of this dream record, however, has always seemed strangely appropriate, for its starts and stops, its episodes of searing intensity and its dramatic gaps, remind one of the features of a real dream, whose moments of profound and forgetful silence tell us almost more than the dream itself.

My plan is relatively straightforward. In the first chapter I shall explore what I have called the sleep of kings, not, I should add, the real sleep of the sovereign, but the meaningful metaphor of royal sleep. With this topic we enter into one of the many neglected rooms of historiographical thought, into what E. R. Curtius might have identified as another commonplace of good government. Next, in the chapter entitled "The *Via Regia* of Dreams," I turn to a consideration of the ancient and Christian backgrounds of royal dreams and why they have always been regarded as especially deserving of scrutiny. As they did in other fields, Carolingian writers were engaged in reinventing an older species of literary discourse, but what they discovered in a single century was neither the richness of the ancient dream nor the passion of the early Christian vision. It was their own oneiric voice. It is a voice we should listen to, for Charlemagne had hardly died before the political dreams started surfacing. After that I propose to proceed in more or less chronological fashion, placing each dream text in its proper political and literary setting. The reader will find that each of the last six chapters is organized around a principal theme, because one of the features of these texts was to concentrate on shared themes and clusters of contemporary concerns, which shifted as the politics did. Since I am investigating not just the dream texts but the times and ideas that gave rise to them, on occasion I shall have to supply a good deal of narrative and thematic background in order to tie all of this material together. Some texts that are not properly the records of dreams, such as Einhard's account of the demon Wiggo and the story of Charles the Fat's fit, seem to me to be of a piece with the dreams and will be treated alongside them. The reader should know that my concern here is not with the larger oneiric record of the Middle Ages, so well treated by Peter Dinzelbacher, S. Kruger, and others, but with a particular kind of dream, the political, and its specific meaning in its own time.[4]

The ninth century may not have been a golden age of political oneirocriticism, as some have claimed, but it was a time when dreams by kings and about kings came to hold a special place in the thoughts of some contemporaries. In this book I shall attempt to explore the myriad and crisscrossing connections of peoples, places, and written words that entered into and gave meaning to this dream work.

In my ear a voice whispers that none of this is possible. A celebrated anthropologist once doubted, after all, that Oxford dons could ever understand the thoughts of Charlemagne's poets or Louis the Pious's serfs.[5] That the immediate thoughts of Bodo and his crowd are largely lost to us must be true, but Charlemagne's poets and Louis the Pious's polemical churchmen devoted entire lifetimes to communicating their ideas. They would be disappointed to learn, I suspect, that we have so frequently turned our backs on their own interpretations of their time, and have dismissed their "imagined history" with such disdain. The thinkers of the Carolingian world attempted something that we can scarcely conceive of today: firmly grasping hold of what they knew of civilization, they embarked upon a program of reinforcement, reformation, and renewal. But from the outset they worried that spreading shades of disorder would swallow and destroy their small start. It remains one of the many ironies of Carolingian history that the so-called Carolingian renaissance flourished at a time when men and women thought they perceived their own historical decline. In fact, and unknown to the Carolingians themselves, these two crossing curves belonged together, just as they had in the Athens of Aristophanes, Euripides, and Socrates and in the Rome of Sallust, Catullus, and Cicero, for intelligent men and women set as their first problem the state of their own time, and the ninth century was a most intelligent age.

But, for all that, Carolingian intellectuals were, to rework a maxim of Thomas Carlyle, worse men in their dream texts.[6] Their collective dream diary is less than happy: it is filled with undisguised partisanship, with anxieties that gnawed at the soft underbelly of Carolingian civilization, and with an unsettling confidence in the correctness of the criticisms leveled. The men who wrote and circulated these texts were convinced that they *knew,* and they moved with the same conviction from a celebration of their kings to damning criticism of them, and back again. If there was a flaw to their view of the world, it was one born of royal patronage and propinquity, for they were centripetal thinkers caught in the vortex of a centrifugal age. If the dichotomy of their predicament prevented royal scholars from achieving a realistic reading of their time, and if it led them to a failure of perspective, it also led to creative success, for without Charlemagne there would have been no gathering of poets and without the poets no Charlemagne, at least not as the Western world has always imagined him. A king-centered view of Carolingian history must certainly be inaccurate, as we have been repeatedly warned, but we need to remember that the writers of the ninth century were royalists, and it is their imaginary world that we are about to enter. The greatest creation of ninth-century thought was not the wondrous *Periphyseon,* with its flights of digressive and enfolding genius, or the small and precious delights of Walahfrid's poetry, but the image we have of the kings themselves: of Charlemagne as *pater Europae,* of Louis the Pious betrayed by his wife, of three brothers bloodying the fields of Fontenoy, of Charles the Bald proudly staring out at us from his golden manuscripts. The royal dreams of the ninth century may have failed to move real kings to reform, but they remain another expression of the qualified confidence and commitment of their writers to the Carolingian world. Despite their steadily darkening doubts, these men held fast to their small world of court and king, resident wise men and monks, and in political oneirocriticism found another vehicle, perhaps the frankest of them all, to convey their deepest worries and highest hopes.

These, then, were the dream fragments they shored against their ruin.[7]

CHAPTER ONE

The Sleep of Kings

Si je dors, qui me donnera la lune?
        Camus, *Caligula*

Just outside the Great Hall of Hart House on the campus of the University of Toronto once hung a painting that busy students and hurrying professors seldom stopped to regard. It was painted by Hugh de Glazebrook at the end of the nineteenth century and was presented to the university in 1916 in appreciation of the ongoing war efforts of students and faculty on behalf of France. On a perimeter of faintly flickering campfires, during the darkest hour of a moonless night, a guard has fallen asleep while on watch. The painting captures the very moment when he awakes to discover that Napoleon himself has taken his place and now stands watch over the camp. In a state of drowsy stupor, the still recumbent sentinel cries out in amazement, "C'est l'Empereur!"

In the popular melodrama of this Napoleonic legend, we find ourselves in the presence of a very old and royal theme, for rulers are supposed to sleep less than other people. The king should watch while we sleep the sleep of the innocent, unaware of menaces in the night. "The watchfulness of caesar guards the sleep of everyone," said Seneca. Alexander the Great is reputed to have reminded his Macedonian soldiers after their mutiny in Asia that he shared their lot in all ways but one, for "this I know, that I wake before you and watch so that you might sleep soundly." According to Plutarch, neither wine nor sleep disturbed the vigilance of Alexander, who regularly slept with a poem and a dagger beneath his pillow. Thus, even in sleep, the two sides of Alexander's genius, the poetic and the violent, were close at hand. Ammianus Marcellinus went to even greater lengths to demonstrate the dynamic nature of this royal vigilance. He claimed that Alexander slept with his arm outstretched over a bronze basin and that he held in his hand a silver ball that would come crashing down should he slip into too deep a sleep. In the typology of royal biography sleep is a symbol: good and strong rulers resist its debilitating effects, weak and wicked rulers succumb. Livy claimed, for instance, that Hannibal only slept when all work was done and then not on some soft couch, but on the hard ground in the midst of his soldiers.[1] Great ones command and control sleep, or at least they do so in the stories told about them by the ancients.

Indeed sleep can serve as a measuring stick for sizing up Roman attitudes towards the powerful and the infamous. Some Romans suspected that sleep was a dead zone wherein people lost both identity and purpose. To live was to be awake, wrote Pliny the Elder. Three hundred years later Augustine transformed the same idea into a metaphor for spiritual conversion: "There is no one who wants to sleep forever, for with sound judgment all agree that it is better to be awake." Augustine confessed to God that he was unable to recognize his true self when asleep. This sense of the otherness of sleep and sleeper was not his discovery, of course, but the product of that high regard in which the ancients held consciousness and rationality. Epictetus, the earthy Stoic, considered the person who could not distinguish between the states of sleep and wakefulness to be worse than dead. Seneca, who must have seen too much of the twilight world of Nero's palace, charged that those people who lay snoozing while the sun was up were base churls, for they had turned upside down the offices of day and night.[2]

In Suetonius's *Lives of the Caesars* we find the same historiographical theme at work. The biographer parades before us a series of half-alive, indolent wretches who either could not sleep soundly because of their misdeeds or who slept too much and at all the wrong times. There is something of Seneca's upside-down world in the lives of Suetonius's caesars. Claudius, for instance, slept as he lived, foolishly. He would stumble from the dining hall to bed, where he would sleep with his mouth wide open in evident stupidity. Despite the drunken daze, he would wake by midnight and be unable to sleep again; yet the next day in court he would resume sleeping so soundly that the lawyers could awake him only with the greatest difficulty. Or take the case of the ill-fated Emperor Otho. Determined to commit suicide, he retired to bed for one last night of sleep with the words: "Let us add this night to life." When he awoke in the morning, after this final act of self-indulgence, he promptly stabbed himself to death. Caligula, for his part, could barely sleep at all, and wandered through the corridors of the imperial palace waiting for daylight to come.[3] Reading Suetonius's imperial portraits, the reader soon realizes that the chaotic sleep of the caesars mirrors the meanness of the men.

In Byzantium, slanderous Procopius gazed upon his emperor and empress in the same sullen light. Justinian, a ruthless ruler, had little need of sleep. In the enervating tautness of social life in Constantinople, with informers and intrigue the very air that people breathed, the emperor was the supreme watcher. But he was unable to obtain the repose of the just; night after night he roamed aimlessly through the palace, stalking his fellow demons. Procopius, who was telling tales out of school, had much, of course, to fear from imperial vigilance. But if the demon-emperor was wickedly watchful, his wife, the impressive Theodora, was malevolently somnolent: she slept for hours on end, from sunrise to sunset and sunset to sunrise, and still dominated the empire.[4] Again we find ourselves in an upside-down world with an evil emperor who could not sleep and an evil empress who would not wake.

In biographies sleep matches the ruler, for it is an external symbol of internal character. Livy, Seneca, Suetonius, and Procopius shared a system of mythic straitjackets that worked quietly, but effectively, to bind their subjects in ineluctable symbolic fetters. The sleeping habits of rulers have long been a part of this biographical typing and the historiographical pattern still persists. Dip into the biographies of most twentieth-century American presidents and you will find accounts of late nights and early mornings spent in the Oval Office. Ronald Reagan's election campaign in 1984 was curiously disturbed by only one troubling issue: was a president who frequently dozed off at cabinet meetings fit to rule? We possess a need, it would seem, to believe in the unceasing watchfulness of our rulers. Joseph Stalin apparently knew this, since he left a light burning at night in his Kremlin office so that passersby would think that he was still awake and working. No matter that the actual sleeping patterns of rulers are idiosyncratic! Augustus, after all, slept lightly, but did sleep until noon, and, during the Second World War, Winston Churchill expressly ordered that he was not to be awakened before eight in the morning, unless, of course, England had been invaded.[5] But biographers do not deal with the *reality* of royal sleep; instead, they employ silent symbolic codes according to which good kings refuse to succumb to the weakness of sleep and bad kings cannot wake or sleep too fitfully for the general good of their subjects.

The image of sleepless kings appealed to Carolingian writers, in part because the parallelism of king and Christ, the nocturnal protector par excellence, was so clearly drawn, and in part because the times were thought to be especially disordered and, therefore, in need of vigilant kings. During the paschal season of 837, while Halley's comet slipped slowly across the evening sky, Louis the Pious, ruler of the vast and sprawling Carolingian empire of continental Europe, remained awake and worried. Upon first seeing this dramatic violation of the evening sky, the emperor is reported to have stood rooted to the spot, gazing intently at the moving light.[6] He knew that tradition held that the appearance of a comet portended pestilence, famine, and war.[7] Indeed Einhard, his father's famous biographer, warned Louis that the frightening and furiously blazing star presaged the ruin that would fall upon the Franks if they were not penitent.[8] That very night Louis called upon his own biographer, the so-called Astronomer, to explain what the appearance of the star meant and, in particular, whether it portended a change in the fortune of the kingdom or the death of a king. As a good Christian and prudent courtier, the Astronomer answered that signs in the sky should surely not be trusted, since God was the final arbiter of the fates of both the stars and the Franks.[9] Nevertheless, Louis remained vigilant. After drinking with his men, he sent them home to bed while he spent the night scanning the sky. Duty demanded that he watch while his subjects slept. When dawn at last arrived with no disastrous consequences for the empire, himself, or his sons, the emperor prayed and praised God. In the comforting light of a new day, he ordered his servants to distribute alms, commanded masses to be celebrated, and then went hunting. For the Astronomer, the incident was yet another demonstration of Louis's royal nature: sleeplessness was both a royal function and a royal virtue, one that was Christlike. A good king was supposed to worry about the state of his kingdom, especially at night when mere subjects were succumbing to sleep.

Bad kings may have abdicated their real and symbolic responsibilities, but they paid an awful price for their neglectful natures. According to the Saxon Poet, it was when Attila the Hun was weighed down with wine and sleep, and the rest of the world was peacefully sleeping, that he was poisoned to death by his wife. Carolingian poets understood the code.

Ecce miser tandem potu somnoque sepultus
  Murman adest, oculos uix aperire ualens.

[Look! Wretched Morman finally appears, but so weighed down with
  Drink and deep sleep that he can scarcely open his eyes.][10]

This imagery of deadly sleep may have been lifted from Lucretius and Virgil, but the meaning was modern, for Ermold the Black and the Astronomer wanted to deny that Morman had ever been king of the Bretons, as he had claimed. The slackening of duty that wine and sleep represented would never have overcome a true king. Ermold reveled in the fall of this false king, mocking Morman even in death. So undistinguished was the severed head of the Breton pretender that a noble washed his face and combed his hair before presenting him to Louis the Pious.[11]

Louis was neither the first nor the last of his line to have endured sleeplessness in the name of his royal office. Carolingian kings thought of themselves as busy rulers, quite unlike the final Merovingian kings whose days were portrayed as drowsy and full of sloth. Some truth lay behind the image, for a king in the ninth century, when the administrative organs of the state were weak, found that his personal presence in turbulent parts of the kingdom mattered most of all. In October 841, for instance, Charles the Bald's half-sister Hildegard imprisoned one of his men at Laon. The young king and his best soldiers rode all night through extreme cold to secure the man's immediate release.[12] Charles's nocturnal ride, meant to impress his noble warriors as much as to correct his upstart sister, served notice that, though young, he was truly king and was ready to take up his royal duties, even at night. Thirty-five years later Charles once again demonstrated his capacity for royal exertion, but without the same success. In attempting to reunite the entire empire under his control, Charles led his troops at night through some perilous passes in eastern Francia. But this time the element of surprise failed, and Charles's forces, exhausted by the night march through incessant rain, were defeated at Andernach. Battles were seldom fought at night during the ninth century; instead, that time was reserved for collecting the bodies of the dead and dying.[13] Engelbert, a participant in the fierce contest at Fontenoy in 841, lamented in verse the too bitter and too cruel night that followed the battle and fell upon fields littered with fallen warriors and stained with Frankish blood.[14]

Night was a dangerous time for all Carolingians. On cloudy or moonless nights, darkness was almost unrelieved, and most men and women preferred to huddle around hearths and campfires with familiar faces. Lupus of Ferrières employed a messenger who was, he said, "still not able to sleep alone, presumably because of his terror of the night." The psalm warned, after all, that while humans labored in the light of day, night belonged to the creeping beasts of the forest, to bandits, to wolves, and to demons, who in the ninth century seemed to lurk just beyond the edge of the flickering firelight. Even armed Carolingians were reluctant to travel at night.

Latitant fures,   latrones uagi
Sole absente   siluis in densis.

[When the sun goes down, thieves and
Roving bandits lurk in the thick woods.][15]

A forested world must have made the fall of night an even more frightening prospect, one that would have precluded all but essential travel.

For the ruler, darkness threatened treachery and an assassin's sword. It was as darkness fell on 15 August 778 that the Basques ambushed the baggage train of Charlemagne in a pass of the Pyrenees; and in 833, on the Field of Lies, Louis the Pious's men slipped out of camp during the night and deserted to his rebellious sons. In 864 an assassin hid in a forest one night awaiting the opportunity to slay Charles the Bald and some of his men.[16] Yet Carolingian kings also employed darkness to cover their own escapes from danger. Princes found night the best time for fleeing from angry fathers, and dusk served to cloak the retreat of kings from conflicts that did not promise victory.[17]

Carolingian kings also must have found their nights filled with the irritation of a thousand administrative demands. Kings not only stood at the center of the state but at the center of the society of the palace.[18] Indeed, it would be more accurate to think of the ninth-century state as the king in his palace, for that was how contemporaries conceived of it. Hence, when Hincmar of Rheims thought about the fundamentals of the Carolingian state, it was in a work entitled *On the Governance of the Palace.* So preeminent a gathering place was the palace that it attracted guests, servants, petty officials, importunate advisors, and pleading petitioners, just as a light will draw even distant moths at night. In an age from which real urban civilization had fled, but not the Mediterranean longing for it, the palace became a kind of movable city, a *societas,* and its raison d'être was the king. Major state decisions, especially in times of crisis, could not be put off until morning.

Thus, early one morning Einhard found Hilduin, the powerful abbot of Saint-Denis, camped outside the royal bedchamber waiting for an audience with the emperor. Indeed, guards were posted at the doors of the king's bedroom to prevent the intrusion of unwelcome and frivolous petitioners.[19] Often, however, important state business could not be postponed until morning. In 830 Lothar, plotting rebellion against his imperial father, deliberated with his advisors through an entire night, and, after Louis the Pious was crowned emperor by Pope Stephen IV in 816, the two men, weighed down with their respective cares, could not sleep.[20] The nature of government in the ninth century, with its constant demand for the personal attention of the king, must have stolen sleep from many a sovereign.

We are not able, of course, to reconstruct with any accuracy what one of these bedrooms was like. Royal sleeping chambers were heated and no doubt less drafty than the single-room, wooden buildings in which whole families of peasant stock slept.[21] Even the relatively well-off monk Walahfrid Strabo complained that his new home, the monastery of Fulda, was bitterly cold:

In domo frigus patior niuale,
non iuuat cerni gelidum cubile,
nec foris lectoue calens repertam
    prendo quietem.

[In our house I suffer a snowy cold,
And the prospect of a freezing bed does not please me.
I am never warm enough, either in or out of my bed,
    To find restful sleep.][22]

Although royalty, too, must have felt the chill of night, it was privileged even within the confines of the monastery. Carloman, the tonsured and rebellious son of Charles the Bald, managed, for example, to hog more than his fair share of hearth and firewood at wintry Saint-Médard of Soissons. Furthermore, we know from official inventories that royal bedchambers were amply furnished with beds and couches, mattresses, pillows, and sheets. In the delicate sketches of the Utrecht Psalter, produced by 830 at Rheims, many beds and bedroom objects are shown, but they may reflect late antique rather than Carolingian models.[23] Nevertheless, kings were privileged sleepers and, unlike common folk, must have gone to bed with stomachs full of fine food and wine.

Whatever the actual sleeping habits of Carolingian kings, what emerges in the written record is a largely literary description, mixed of equal parts of myth and legend, the chief exemplar of which was Charlemagne. Alcuin, at his panegyrical best, envisaged his lord Charlemagne leaping from bed as a splendid day dawned and quickly rubbing the sleep from his eyes, before turning to the business of a new day. Peter of Pisa, meanwhile, reminded Charlemagne that Gideon had awakened a sluggish people from the burden of their sleep and had roused them to action.[24]

The fullest description of Charlemagne's sleeping habits is to be found in Einhard's biography of the emperor. Although the sketch is based in part upon Suetonius's account of how Augustus slept, the effect is different, for Suetonius meant to describe a man who slept poorly, Einhard a man who needed little sleep. The distinction is an important one for us to make, since it betrays the differing attitudes of the biographers towards their subjects. An overly zealous *Quellenforschung* has too often sold Einhard short.[25] There is no denying that he was deeply influenced by the patterns of Suetonius's language and construction, but Einhard eschewed the Suetonian weighing of his caesar on a set of moral scales. In contrast to Suetonius, who first credited the emperors with accomplishments and then piled up long lists of their misdeeds, Einhard provided a positive portrait from first to last, turning apologetic over delicate points in Charlemagne's career.

Augustus's sleep, for instance, had been irregular: he frequently had found it hard to fall back to sleep after waking in the night and would call for storytellers to read to him until he fell asleep. He abhorred the thought of sleeping alone in the dark and so would frequently stay over at friends' houses, but he slept incessantly when he could and often dozed off while his litter was being carried through the streets of Rome. For Einhard, Charlemagne was no "thirteenth caesar," but a new Constantine or, better still, another David. He slept as a Christian ruler should, casually, not compulsively. In the summer, after his midday meal, Charlemagne would undress as he did at night and rest for two or three hours. At night he slept lightly, often waking and getting out of bed as many as four or five times. Moreover, he was accustomed to conducting state business in his bedchamber. While dressing in the morning, the emperor would see friends and advisors, and disputes would be resolved on the spot, if they were urgent. Thus, for Einhard, the royal bedchamber was the solid center of the kingdom whenever the king occupied it. The little biographer imagined Charlemagne as an ever-energetic king whose sleep matched his life, for he slept as prudently as he reigned.[26]

The legend of Charlemagne's unceasing vigilance at night did not die with him, but grew richer in the telling. Notker the Stammerer, the author of an account of the deeds of Charlemagne and his heirs written for Charles the Fat late in the ninth century, related how one night, while on campaign against the Saxons, two young nobles were ordered to stand guard outside Charlemagne's tent. Thoroughly drunk, the two fell soundly asleep at their posts, whereupon the king, "who was, according to his custom, more often than not wide awake," slipped out of the tent undetected. He made his rounds of the camp and in the morning upbraided the two whelps in the full presence of his assembled nobles. This type of story was, as we have seen, typical; its point was to denote the royal attribute of watchfulness. Notker provided another revealing example of Charlemagne's sleeplessness and its advantages. A cleric, who had overheard details of a plot by the king's son, Pepin the Hunchback, to displace his father, came directly to the royal bedchamber at night and knocked at the door. *Vigilantissimus Karolus,* the ever-wakeful Charles, was surprised that anyone would dare disturb him at such an hour, but the door was answered and the conspiracy suppressed.[27]

The Saxon Poet, also writing at the end of the ninth century, imitated Einhard's description of a sleepless sovereign in his poetic annals:

Indulgere parum somno permiserat illum
    Mens semper magnis dedita consiliis,
Et res magnificas iugiter meditatio uoluens,
    Reddiderat curis multimodis uigilem;
Ob hoc nocte quater fertur uel sepius omni
    Somno depulso membra leuasse toro.
O quantum curis res publica creuerat illis;
    Quam conservatum floruit imperium!

[Charlemagne seldom succumbed to sleep,
    Occupied as he was with serious deliberations,
Constantly turning over in his mind great issues,
    He responded to his many cares with watchfulness.
For this reason, four times every night, or even more often,
    He shook off sleep and arose from bed.
O how greatly did the state prosper under his attention;
    How the safeguarded empire flourished!][28]

Charlemagne's sleep—or rather the lack of it—was a symbol of his special kingship. For the sake of the empire, he sacrificed his sleep. In this light, he was the true *pater patriae,* the father of his land, as praised by his poets, for like a father looking in on his children at night, Charlemagne oversaw the empire long after others had put the day's worries to bed. We need to remember that this paternal imagery, so unacceptable to twentieth-century sensibilities, sustained both ruler and ruled in a comfortable familial illusion during the ninth century.

The most charming tale of Charlemagne's sleepless vigilance is the Lorsch legend of the romance of Bertha and Angilbert. While serving at the palace, the poet Angilbert is supposed to have fallen deeply in love with Charlemagne's daughter. Since the couple did not wish to offend the emperor, they hid their love from him as long as they could. But one night, unable any longer to restrain his passion, Angilbert stole into the bedroom of the princess, where the couple made love. The greater part of the night slipped away with the lovers oblivious to their compromising situation. When finally Angilbert wished to return to his own bed, which lay some distance away in another building, he discovered to his great horror that a great deal of snow had fallen during the night, snow that would surely reveal to all the tracks of his retreat from the emperor's house. Bertha came to the rescue with a novel plan: she would carry Angilbert on her back so that only one set of footprints, and those female, would be visible in the snow, both coming and going (perhaps to a privy outside the royal apartments). The couple had, however, forgotten the famous watchfulness of Charlemagne, who even then lay awake in his bed. Rising, he chanced to peer out a palace window upon the rather ridiculous scene of his daughter lumbering across the yard with Angilbert perched on her back. He watched as she deposited her lover and then retraced her steps in the snow. At first Charlemagne remained silent about the incident, but later pardoned the sinners and granted them permission to marry.[29]

Such was the conviction of Charlemagne's extraordinary energy and unceasing vigilance that many refused to believe that he had passed from the world. "We feel half assured," Carolingians might have said with Marguerite Yourcenar's Hadrian, "that somewhere the white spring of sleep flows into the dark spring of death."[30] Sleep, as Alcuin had said in his riddling dialogue with Prince Pepin, is the image of death. Paschasius Radbertus wanted to stress the other side of this equation: that death was but a sleep in which men waited for the resurrection.[31] After Charlemagne's death stories arose that suggested he had not really died after all, but had only fallen into a deeper slumber than was his wont. In 829 Freculf, the bishop of Lisieux, completed the second volume of his world history and presented it to the Empress Judith for the education of her son. Looking upon Charles the Bald, then but six years of age, Freculf remarked that it was as if Charlemagne, "his grandfather, had not died, but rather, having roused himself from a deep and dark sleep, now lights up a new world."[32] To be sure, Freculf flattered the pretensions of Judith, who had encouraged the association of her young son with the memory of his grandfather. The shadow of great expectations was always to hang over the head of Charles the Bald, and his poets never let him forget after whom he had been named. But, at an even more resonant level, Freculf already reflected that sense of unreality that had begun to suffuse the Carolingian court in the late 820s and early 830s: could Charlemagne really be gone and had the promise of Carolingian power passed with him? Einhard's biography of the emperor was an attempt, however transparent, to recreate a royal circle that would restore a dead emperor to his rightful and memorable place among the living. The legend of the still-living Charlemagne, therefore, had its historiographical roots in that extraordinary period of Carolingian self-criticism that fell in the second quarter of the ninth century.

The legend was still alive in the year 1000 when the Emperor Otto III uncovered, to the great dismay of a contemporary chronicler, the remains of Charlemagne at Aachen.[33] The Count of Lomello claimed that he and the imperial party had found Charlemagne sitting upon a throne with a crown upon his head and a scepter in his flesh-covered hands. The tomb intruders were most amazed that the emperor's fingernails had continued to grow. They did not know, as we do today, that the fingernails of corpses only seem to grow as the flesh around them recedes; instead they thought this sure evidence that somewhere not too deep a living spark still burned in Charlemagne's body. Since to Otto and the assembled company, it seemed certain that Charlemagne was still alive, they merely repaired his vestments, cut his living nails, and reclosed the tomb.[34] It was as if they were readying the emperor for his reawakening.

Throughout the later Middle Ages, polemical rumors of the reappearance of Charlemagne, the last emperor of the world, circulated in a messianic context. Among these was the widely invoked imperial myth that the emperor was asleep inside a mountain, awaiting a call to return to the world, thus signaling the end of time.[35] Even in death, then, Charlemagne was not allowed to rest peacefully. People preferred to believe in his energetic insomnia, and the biblical blurring of the distinction between death and sleep opened up a domain wherein dead emperors might still breathe life into an old and troubled world.[36]

The theme of sleepless Carolingian kings gained added force from its association with the Christlike qualities of kingship. The Carolingians were fascinated by a disquieting episode in Christ's life, one the first three evangelists all treat in dramatic fashion: the stilling of the storm at sea. With Christ asleep in the stern of a small ship, the disciples were cast into a frenzy of self-doubt and worry, for who would protect them if God himself were asleep? Carolingian artists handled the theme a number of times, but preferred to depict the moment when the dilemma was resolved and doubt dissipated as the awakened Christ quieted the storm. A late tenth-century fresco from the northern nave wall of Reichenau depicts the two scenes side by side, with Christ asleep and awake at different ends of the same boat. In all these depictions the scene of Christ asleep is disquieting, that of Christ awake reassuring. The masterpiece of this developing iconography was finally achieved in the Ottonian Hitda Codex (Fig. 1).

There, in a swirl of undulating lines, Christ's ship threatens to take wing and burst through the very borders of the page. One of the apostles reaches out, with hesitant hand, to awaken Christ, for only with the Lord awake would the world once more cease to worry.[37]

For the Carolingians, there was a sense in which Christ, the perfect king, had never slept and would never sleep. It was Christ who had been prefigured by the psalm: "Behold, he that keepeth Israel shall neither slumber nor sleep." In the *Codex Aureus* of Saint-Emmeram, a magnificent book of Gospels made for Charles the Bald, Christ is represented by a plucky lion, while an encircling verse reminds us that the lion who smashed the gates of hell neither slumbers nor sleeps.[38] Alcuin combined the images in one of his night prayers:

> Qui uim uentorum, pelagi qui mitigat undas,
> Israel qui seruat, nullo qui dormiat aeuo,
> Fratribus hac requiem dulcem concedat in aula,
> Et quos inmittit somno uis nigra timores,
> Conpescat clemens domini, rogo, dextra potentis.

> [You who calm great winds and the stormy sea,
> You who watch over Israel and will not slumber in any age,
> Give sweet sleep to the brothers in this royal court.
> A dark power looses terrors in our sleep;
> I ask your merciful right hand to suppress them.][39]

Christ stood guard while others slept, according to Prudentius, and recalled them to life at cockcrow:

> Nos excitator mentium
> Iam Christus ad uitam uocat.
> "Auferte," clamat, "lectulos
> Aegros, soporos, desides."

> [Now Christ, the waker of souls,
> Calls us to life.
> "Away," he proclaims, "with beds
> Belonging to sickness, sleep, and sloth."][40]

Thus, Christ stood protective and merciful at the boundaries of sleep, and throughout its troubled passage.

This was the divine vigilance that Dhuoda contemplated when teaching her young son William how to pray at night. Though this noble woman might have despaired of the efficacy of prayer for herself, she taught her son to recite one last prayer before falling asleep at night:

> Guard me, O Lord, throughout the day; guard me also in this night, if it is your will. May I deserve to be hidden under the shadow of your wings, filled with the Holy Spirit, sheltered by royal defense, and encircled by the guardianship of angels, so that in this night, although I may find little rest, I may sleep the sleep of peace. If I occasionally wake, may I feel that you, who appeared on the ladder as Savior to the blessed Jacob, still stand guard over me in my sleep.[41]

The young man was to conclude the sequence by making the sign of the cross on his forehead and over his bed. "Fugiunt crucem tenebrae" ["Darkness and death flee from the cross"], Prudentius had said.[42] When they slept, the Carolingians did not sleep alone, for gathered around and over their beds were all the divine forces that the Christian world could muster for its never-ending, nightly battle.

The character of King David, who was, to Carolingian eyes, the best of all kings, reinforced this image of royal sleeplessness. In Psalm 3:5–6, the royal psalmist, in flight from his rebellious son Absalom and his thousands of supporters, laid down to sleep confident of God's protection. In the Utrecht Psalter, an angel can be seen here helping David up from his bed while Christ watches over and succors the king (Fig. 2). In the Stuttgart Psalter, painted at about the same time at Saint-Germain-des-Prés in Paris, a remarkable transference has taken place, for there we see Christ himself sleeping peacefully in David's place while the angry mob mills about his untroubled form (Fig. 3). This iconographic scene was carefully chosen to make the point that when Christians sleep soundly, they do so because Christ has filled their sleep with his presence. But David's sleep, like that of all Christian kings, was filled with worry: "I am weary with my groaning; all night I make my bed to swim; I water my couch with tears."[43] At this point in the Utrecht Psalter, the king is shown sitting bolt upright on his bed; he looks to Christ above, while below him the reprobate are being skewered in a pit (Fig. 4). In the Stuttgart Psalter, King David lies uneasily on his rumpled bed, his appearance that of a man weighed down with deep worry (Fig. 5). In another painting, the protective right hand of God has overturned the very bed of the troubled psalmist, trapping his scrambling form below (Fig. 6). Thus King David, the precursor of Christ and the very model of the Christian king, by his sleeplessness and constant vigilance worried for all.

Though kings might wish to say with Paul, "Let us not sleep as others do; but let us watch and be sober," they did sleep and sought special protection in it. In prayers Christ was besought to watch over the sleeping king. Indeed Carolingian kings were the patrons not just of churches and art but also of prayer. In a breviary dedicated to Charlemagne, Alcuin stressed that it was King David himself who had established the round of daily prayer. At the end of the day the Carolingian king was to say prayers: at vespers, compline, and, if his sleep should be interrupted, in the middle of the night. Alcuin called on the angels to stand guard over Charles while he slept. Later, in the *Chanson de Roland,* the archangel Gabriel would watch over the grizzled Charlemagne as he slept his troubled sleep.[44] But even when the angels were absent, Christ himself was still thought to be present, for somewhere in the heart of man, Christ was believed to hold constant watch. When we read Alcuin's enigmatic line—"If sleep closes your eyes, let the heart stand guard over you"—we need to remember that the Carolingians would have recalled the Song of Solomon 5:2, "I sleep, but my heart waketh," and would have instantly identified this wakeful heart with Christ.[45]

Charles the Bald possessed a private prayer book that is now kept in the Schatzkammer der Residenz in Munich. This extraordinary little book, so touching in its measured simplicity and humanity, was compiled by his court scholars and illuminated by his artists. The cycle of daily prayers designed for the young king included two night prayers. The second of these is an elegant poem of three elegiac couplets attributed to Alcuin:

Qui placido in puppi carpebat pectore somnum,
  Exurgens uentis imperat et pelago:
Fessa labore graui quamuis hic membra quiescant,
  Ad se concedat cor uigilare meum.
Agne dei, mundi qui crimina cuncta tulisti,
  Conserua requiem mitis ab hoste meam.

[With a calm heart, he snatched some sleep in the stern,
  Arising he commanded the wind and the sea.
Although my limbs rest here, weighed down with deep tiredness,
  Grant that my heart may keep watch with you.
Gentle Lamb of God, you who took away all the sins of the world,
  Guard my sleep from the enemy.][46]

Thus, each night before falling asleep, a young and vulnerable king could invite Christ into his heart to watch the whole night through. Kings were not supposed to sleep, but when they did they were replaced, according to the metaphor, by a higher king who inhabited their hearts and never slept.

The enemy who threatened kings threatened everyone. "A dark power," wrote Alcuin, "looses terrors in our sleep." At night, when bodies were bloated with food and reason was wrapped in sleep, the common enemy of all was thought to steal over the sleeper. Theodulf of Orléans warned the judges of the land, the *missi dominici,* to beware the excesses of food, wine, and sleep, for these things attacked the mind and left people exposed to dark forces.[47] The Devil stood waiting for the weak, said Peter: "Be sober, be vigilant; because your adversary, the Devil, goeth about like a roaring lion, seeking whom he may devour." For Alcuin, the terrors of the night through which the Devil worked were lust, fear, phantasm, and beguiling apparition.[48] In the Utrecht and Stuttgart Psalters, we once again can see these abstractions assume concrete form, as proud horsemen are cast into dead sleep, even as they ride, by winged demons, while sleepers with golden vessels at their feet are tormented by genii who whisper to them of vanities (Figs. 7–8). In the early Middle Ages, demons were believed to work their wickedness at night and in darkness, but hating light they fled at first cockcrow.[49]

In both the Roman and monastic breviaries, the *Te lucis ante terminum* was the evening prayer said at compline, that short and marvelous interval between sunset and all-embracing darkness. In the ninth century, these verses, long associated with Ambrose but probably dating from the seventh century, were universally popular. Quite likely every Carolingian king called nightly for the protection of Christ, "our guard and keeper," with this prayer:

> Procul recedant somnia,
> Et noctium phantasmata;
> Hostemque nostrum comprime,
> Ne polluantur corpora.

> [Let the dreams and phantasms
> Of the night depart to a distant place;
> Trample our enemy,
> That our bodies may know no pollution.]

In Dante's *Purgatorio,* one of the kings placed in the valley of the rulers begins to sing the *Te lucis* spontaneously at dusk.[50] His companions, also proud rulers once threatened by the all-too-worldly temptations of sleep, gently take up the hymn to nocturnal vigilance, for it was a prayer that held special meaning for kings who had known too much of compromise and not enough of purity.

The meaning of night was, in fact, somewhat controversial in the ninth century, for a strange debate broke out at the court of Charlemagne over whether nothingness and darkness actually existed. Alcuin's student and successor, Fridugis, had forcefully argued on grammatical and scriptural grounds that darkness and nothingness were substantial. He recalled that the darkness visited upon Egypt for its sins was so dense that it could be touched by hand. Darkness was not some deficiency of light for Fridugis, but an exterior object: tactile, sensible, and corporeal. "Darkness exists," he said, and God had named it night. Charlemagne read his short tract, but apparently found fault with its exegesis, for he called on Dungal of Saint-Denis to repair its weaknesses. The emperor urged Dungal to reconsider the question by returning to the truthful solidities of the Bible, without metaphorical flights of fancy, and he supplied the scholar with an additional set of biblical references to darkness that he should consider.[51] Thus, the nature of *tenebrae* mattered as much to Charlemagne as it did to his quibbling court.

We, who live just a switch away from the comforting rays of artifical light at all hours of the day, cannot fully appreciate what an overpowering reality night must have been for an earlier age. Even the biblical reminder "Ye are children of light and children of day; we are not of night, nor of darkness" must mean less to us, must carry less emotive force, than it did for the people of the ninth century. Night, darkness, and black clouds were, for early medieval men and women, more than just symbols of chaos; they were elemental aspects of the world's confusing disorder. "Night represents injustice, infidelity, and all misfortune," wrote Hrabanus Maurus in his encyclopedia, and Gottschalk knew nighttime to hold the hostile dangers of death and the black rivers of hell.[52] Eleven centuries ago darkness was an intruder that stole nightly over the Carolingian empire, threatening to sever the delicate fabric that bound small communities together, reducing the human community to its smallest units—to village, to family, and to the Carolingian cottage—and isolating people in their already isolated worlds.

Medievalists, in their understandable dislike of the disparaging label "The Dark Ages," have too often forgotten that the metaphor itself was a medieval one and that it had some Carolingian currency.[53] In the preface to his *Life of Charlemagne*, Einhard had charged that the very memory of the greatest man of his time was being swallowed up by the dark and enveloping shades of oblivion. A few years later, in his introduction to the same work, Walahfrid Strabo observed that his own time was descending into a darkness in which the light of reason could not shine. As the uproar of Louis the Pious's reign subsided, an unforgiving Paschasius Radbertus would look back and think that it was then that the Carolingian kingdom had passed from daylight into black night.[54] As darkness must succeed light in the solar day, so, too, in the realm of poetic images, and the starting point once again was Charlemagne. In his Latin name, CAROLVS, court poets had discerned a playful etymology, CARA LVX, "precious light," for, as the Saxon Poet said, the emperor had been "the shining light of the Franks," radiating wisdom over his people. Gottschalk may have called on Christ, the enduring light of the world, to banish confusing chaos and the dark abyss that led to hell, but most men and women looked more immediately to Christ's royal representatives for help.[55] Darkness was to be the imagery of political disappointment in the ninth century, brilliance a metaphorical reflection of patronage and, at times, of nostalgia.

Against this background of diurnal symbolism, where history met poetry and events were imaginatively reconstructed, the ninth-century political dream had its beginnings. For Carolingian intellectuals transport us through the magic of their art into an imaginary world of their own making, where they sometimes dreamed somber dreams of royal failure. The Carolingian awareness of the onset of troubled times was all the more heartfelt, because it registered a deep frustration. An all-too-brief moment of order seemed to be slipping away, and Carolingian thinkers wanted to know why. "We have driven order from our lives and we all struggle on in absolute confusion," Lupus said.[56]

Yet, despite this seeming pessimism, many intellectuals thought they knew why the kingdom was in trouble, and they collected the evidence and isolated its causes. They were, in short, on the lookout for signs of disorder and revelatory truth; in both cases, at the end of the day their attention focused upon their kings. For only kings, they thought, could bring about the renewal of the kingdom and peace to its people. Thus nighttime, with its special place in the imagery and ideology of rulership, was to come under close scrutiny. The royal bed, when occupied, was second to none in the kingdom, for pure potency of power seemed to reside in the figure of a divinely sanctioned, sleeping king. In the Utrecht Psalter, we gaze upon sleepers lying uneasily on unkempt beds, perched precariously between the separated worlds of the saints and the damned (Fig. 9). If kings were special sleepers, they also had always been privileged dreamers. At night a king was thought to see what other men could not: the unfolding design of history itself. Sleep seemed to carry him and the people who dreamed about him to that perilous fault line that ran between the blessed world of the saints and the infernal world of the damned forever stuck in some forbidding pit. It is into the circadian trough of this Carolingian dream that we must now slowly descend.

CHAPTER TWO

The Via Regia *of Dreams*

And the king said unto them, I have dreamed a dream, and my spirit was
troubled to know the dream.
                    Daniel 2:3

In a paradox that should alert us to the unsteadiness of the bed beneath us as we
slip from sleep to dream, Alexander the Great is supposed to have dreamt that
he did not believe in dreams. Neither, I might add, do historians. Gibbon once
groused:

> The philosopher, who with calm suspicion examines the dreams and
> omens, the miracles and prodigies, of profane or even of ecclesiastical
> history, will probably conclude that, if the eyes of the spectators have
> sometimes been deceived by fraud, the understanding of the readers has
> much more frequently been insulted by fiction.[1]

Like the elder Pliny, historians have been properly interested in the waking
lives of men and women, for history is made by actors, not by sleepers, dreamers, or the dead. Many historians have suspected, with Gibbon, that dreams are
fraudulent and fictitious historical sources, since they are seldom what they pre-
tend to be.[2] Indeed, it is natural to wonder whether any historical dreams are
genuine. As we encounter dream texts in the midst of our reading, the questions
come tumbling out: Was the dream actually dreamt or has the supposed dreamer
concocted it? Or is this dream simply a fiction that sprang from the writer's
brain utterly independent of any dream or any dreamer? And so on. Unable to

answer these questions, we most often read around the historical dream or throw it into our narrative as a patch of exotic native color.

Though we cannot long delay over the general problem of the authenticity of the historical dream, we need to recognize that historians have no acid test with which to distinguish between the real and fictive dreams of the past. Even in the present this would be an almost impossible task. Jung, for instance, claimed that when he was submitting to analysis by Freud he could not satisfy his mentor with his actual dreams, so he fabricated a series of free associations that would be more appealing to his master.[3] Freud never knew the difference or, perhaps, thought it unimportant. While some historical dreams have individuating features and a dream likeness suggestive of reality, others are ordinary and filled with common motifs. The former, we must admit, could be the products of sophisticated and deliberate composition, while the latter could be the culturally informed dreams of real individuals.

Even if common sense were enough to allow us to distinguish between true dreams and pseudodreams, we would still need to recognize that even the recollections of real dreams, and these must form some part of the whole, have been so substantially transformed by a wide variety of factors by the time they work their way into the historical record that they are far removed from any original act of dreaming. The unconscious itself, as Freud stressed, has already edited the remembered dream, cutting and pasting, excising and discarding, before the dream ever dares confront the hard strictures of narration.[4] But the awakened dreamer is also a storyteller, imposing a narrative structure upon the fragments of a recollected dream, seeking to make intelligible what was once chaotic. At its least sophisticated level, a beginning, middle, and end are given to what was once a mere episode in a dream continuum. Moveover, the little details that thread their way through our dreams are often lost in the retelling because they either seem insignificant or do not fit the story being told. Thus, we often end with dream narratives that have been tidied up and sanitized. Wide-awake dreamers are constrained by a consideration of personal, social, and political conventions that they do not often wish to break as they translate their dreams into the discourse of waking life. In the medieval world, for instance, monks and clerics occasionally dreamt of the ecstasy of reading classical authors, but when they awoke they explained away their flirtation with the enchanting elegance of ancient poetry and rhetorical rhythm as a stern reproach against pagan backsliding: the celebrated dreams of Jerome and Odo of Cluny come to mind here. In the case of political dreams, the issue of an acceptable interpretation is crucial. Ancient soothsayers might risk all if their readings

were either wrong or unpleasing to their powerful patrons. According to Suetonius, Tiberius very nearly threw his astrologer Thrasyllus over a cliff because
his rosy predictions had not been borne out by events.[5] Thus, a world of waking
concerns must intrude upon dream recollection, narration, and interpretation,
often shearing our woolly dream thoughts into pleasing and harmless shapes.

If even the real dream has been remade by the time of its first recounting,
then the historical dream record as a whole must be a radically edited one. In the
ancient world as well as the modern, most dreams belong in the first telling to
the realm of oral culture. They first enter history as spoken stories. Observe
how often in written records we encounter scenes of dreams being told and retold orally. In this type of scene, such as the oneiric encounters of Nebuchadnezzar and Daniel in the Bible, we are supposedly made witnesses to the first
narrative recounting of a dream. The written account merely testifies to that
first narration, which seems to stand closest in time and truthfulness to the
dream itself. How often dreams have survived only one or two tellings before
slipping out of recorded memory we cannot know, but this must have been the
fate of most. Those retold again and again, picking up and losing elements
along the way, became part of a larger cultural field. Divorced from the original
dreamer, they came to belong to the society that had taken an interest in preserving them. In oral cultures, these dreams might even serve as models of general
oneiric types. Thus, dreams that persist can, at one level, be said to reflect the
society that has bothered to remember them.

History, in short, sifts dreams. The historical record can contain but a tiny
fraction of all the dreams once recalled, in part because in the past dreams were
seldom considered to be equally and universally significant. Indeed, the truly
revolutionary aspect of Freud's work on dreams was his contention that every
dream was significant and meaningful, so long as he could talk to the awakened
dreamer soon afterwards. As Gregor Sabba put it, "You cannot psychoanalyze
a corpse." This belief in the importance of all "living" dreams ran against the
entire weight of tradition; it would have seemed absurd to a Greek or a Roman,
for, almost without fail, cultures have made an essential distinction between
significant and insignificant dreams. In imitation of Homer, Virgil contrasted
the two gates of dreams in a famous passage of the *Aeneid*. True dreams were
thought to come through a gate made of horn while false dreams flowed through
a gate of polished ivory.[6] To the extent, then, that individuals and societies have
distinguished between true and false dreams—a distinction made necessary by
the potential vastness of our dream lives—the surviving oneiric record of history is one already weighted towards "important" dreams. Royal dreams once

predominated in the record of historical dreams because they were deemed manifestly significant by virtue of the status of the putative dreamer or dream subject. By democratizing dreaming and dream interpretation, Freud in effect smashed the portals of selectivity that once protected the world from being overrun with dreams.[7]

What matters, given the historian's interest in living actors, is not the authenticity of the dream itself, but its meaning to the wide-awake world, and what matters most in the historical record is the meaning attached to dreams by their recorders and readers. For the historian, the dream really only enters history once it has been written down. Again we encounter the ongoing editorial process that had begun with the dreamer and the act of narrating the dream. In the ancient world, the instances in which writer and dreamer were one and the same figure were few. Frequently, indeed, it seemed more truthful if the dream was retold by an outsider, by a witness rather than an actor. Moveover, since most ancient dreams concerned the powerful, it fell to others to note their significance. Aelius Aristides, who fervently followed the curative incubation cult of Asclepius, recorded his own dreams, but even here we witness the overlaying of an editorial process. He claimed to have recorded at least three hundred thousand lines in his dream diary, but boiled them down to make the smallish and summary *Sacred Tales*.[8] Thus, the written account of Aristides, although it purports to record real dreams, must be a closely edited thing.

In the dream texts found in histories where the writer is not the dreamer and may not even have met the dreamer, dreams assume an even more problematic interpretive context. Dreams in these histories are already far removed from the original dream and are now given a new setting. Dream texts take on different meanings in conjunction with the material around them, for they are never placed there in absolute dissociation. Thus, in a larger text, the dream is both cut off from the dreamer and attached to another narrative flow.

But historians need to remember that they encounter dream texts and not real dreams or living dreamers, and that these dream texts are as much a part of the historical record as land transactions, personal letters, and the inscriptions on tombstones. We are not called upon to probe the subconscious minds of long-dead men and women, an impossible task in any event, but to study extant texts, how they arose, where they circulated, and what they reveal about their time. Another approach would be to assemble a series of comparative categories that would allow us to gauge the shifting elements of the dream literature of an age.[9] Here, however, I propose to study the historically important dreams of the ninth century, dreams that commented on, reflected, or even played some minor part in the political events of their time.

To return to Gibbon's salutary suspicion: it is exceedingly likely that most of the dreams and visions that the reader will encounter in the following chapters were the waking work of Carolingian monks and priests. That political dreams are not, for the most part, what they claim to be—the true visions of divinely inspired dreamers—does matter, because that disingenuousness works to reveal the author's purpose and the world of ideas and assumptions for which his text was designed. Indeed, these dreams often address the problem of their own credibility, asserting that they are genuine and providing proofs that, to critical eyes, surely undercut their authenticity. In seeking to persuade an audience of the rightness of some position, these dreams commented on and sought to influence contemporary political issues and personalities. For this reason, they properly belong to the study of the devolving Carolingian empire, and we shall need to investigate the circumstances of their creation and the shifting anxieties they express. But Carolingian royal dreams, even if they are most frequently fictions full of political purpose, also belong to a much older tradition of royal dreams, one with which we must begin, as the Carolingians themselves did.[10]

In the most famous statement of his theory, Freud said that "the interpretation of dreams is the *royal road* to a knowledge of the unconscious activities of the mind."[11] The very phrase *via regia* is, in the context of Freud's thought, a revealing psychoanalytic pun. In a theory of dream symbolism where everything stood for something else and where kings and queens represented the dreamer's parents, the kingdom became a subconscious symbol of the universal family. Thus, Freud's personal *royal road* was one that led him via dream interpretation to confront the royal person of his father.[12]

But it would be more helpful for us to return to the root meaning of this *via regia* of dreams, which must also have been rumbling around in the mind of the would-be classicist.[13] In the ancient world dreams were a royal road, for dreams by kings or about kings were considered to be of great importance to the success of the state.[14] Artemidorus of Daldis, the ancient oneirocritic, took it as an accepted fact that kings, magistrates, and nobles received dreams of universal matters: what they dreamt came true. Kings were, after all, divine dreamers, inasmuch as they stood closer to the gods than other men. They were thought by some to be conduits, divine pipes through which the powerful water of dreams and divination flowed. Even skeptical Cicero granted that in the Roman tradition augury and divining by dreams were thought to be especially becoming to a king. Fifteen hundred years later, Quevedo would still be advising the powerful that dreams should be heeded "when they touch upon affairs of importance, matters of religion, or are dreamed by great men and kings."[15] Only in the twentieth century can we speak of a personal history of dreams and of a sociology of dreams; the men and women of the ancient world had dream lives of their own, but dreams that mattered, dreams that touched the state, were the ones that survived in the historical record, and these mostly concerned kings.

The general attitude of the Greeks[16] and Romans[17] towards dreams is well known and need not be lingered over here. One important distinction has emerged, however. Many ancient Greeks emphasized the externality of dreams. In the highly stylized dream accounts of Homer, a dreamed figure appears to sleeping individuals at the ends of their beds. The word *oneiros* itself meant for Homer, as E. R. Dodds has pointed out, this dreamed specter and not the dream experience.[18] The dream was, thus, an objective fact outside the dreamer, who was its private and passive audience. Hence ancient Greeks generally spoke of seeing a dream or of being visited by a dream. Romans of the Hellenistic and post-Hellenistic worlds gradually came to believe in the internality of most dreams. Cicero simply doubted the prophetic value of dreams. Was there any silly thing, he wondered, that we could not conjure up at night in our dreams, and were not some of these vagaries bound to come true by chance alone? Romans were more likely to say that something had been shown to them in a dream. The shift in attitude, which was far from sharp or dramatic, was from dreams as objective facts to dreams as subjective fancies. Many Romans believed that dreams simply had their source in the mind of the dreamer: "each individual makes his own dreams," said Petronius.[19]

But there was one class of dreams that remained external and objective to the Roman mind: this was the appearance in a dream of a god or an ancestor. Popular belief, perhaps influenced by Pythagoreanism, held that the wandering soul of a dead parent could come upon and touch the soul of a sleeping Roman. In Cicero's *Dream of Scipio,* which imitates Plato's myth of Er the Pamphylian, the younger Scipio received a message from his ancestor. Probably this type of oracular dream, or *chrematismos* as Macrobius classified it, had such a powerful hold on the Roman mind because the Romans were always conscious of the need for subordination to state and parents.[20] Thus, when ancestors appeared to Romans in their dreams, their voices were to be heeded, for they were thought to impart objective and beneficial truths.

Indeed, it may be generally true that the oracular dream was more frequent in the ancient world than it is in our own. For ancient men and women hoped to look through such dreams to the future; Freud and his followers have wanted to probe dreams that would reveal something of a more immediate and personal past.[21] The shift in the attention to dreams paid by both dreamers and dream interpreters has necessarily shifted the nature of the dream record. Since it was the portentous side of dreams that engaged the ancient interest, Roman dreamers were on special lookout for the appearance of gods, parents, and ancestors. In the Roman world, this kind of dream achieved public force, for it spoke to the state as a whole. Virgil gave such a dream an important place in the very myth of Rome's foundation, for, after the conflagration of Troy, he imagined Aeneas receiving the foundational dream that sent him sailing towards distant Italy.[22]

But dreams on the whole were never formally embraced by the state religions of Greece and Rome, because they were, as Peter Brown has suggested, too "spasmodic" for systematic divination. Although they were considered an avenue of individual access to the gods, the dreams of common people were presumed to be largely free of political import. To interpret a dream, said Artemidorus, one must know the dreamer's identity, occupation, birthplace, financial status, state of health, and age. In his professional opinion, one could not dream of things beyond one's own state of affairs or capacities.[23] Thus, for the oneirocritic, the social context of the dreamer became an important element in dream interpretation. For instance, for a commoner to dream of being a king portended death, if the dreamer was sick at the time, since kings alone were like the dead in being subject to no one. Likewise, for a commoner in good health to dream of being a king signified the loss of his family and separation from his fellows, for monarchy was not shared. To dream of fighting with kings or powerful nobles portended that the dreamer would suffer greatly at their hands.[24] Thus, the lower classes dared not step outside accustomed roles even when dreaming, and the dream interpreter himself was required to interpret dreams within strict social boundaries.

Yet there was one way in which the dreams of common individuals might contribute to understanding the fortunes of the state. As Artemidorus put it:

> It has never happened that a dream that has meaning for the entire state has been seen by a single private citizen; it has been seen, rather, by many and in the same way—some of whom announce it publicly, while others do so individually and in private.[25]

The whisper of a thousand insistent dreams might in this way make the public over into a collective and prophetic eye. But Artemidorus either thought this kind of shared dream to be extremely unlikely or so exceptional as to be undeserving of further consideration, for he provided no examples. Victor of Vita, the author of a history of the persecution of North Africa by the Vandals in the fifth century, attempted to make a case for one such collective dream. Two years before the invasion, a great number of Christians began to suffer dreams of their imminent displacement. A priest was said to have dreamt of a crowd of people replaced by a multitude of swine and goats. Another dreamt of a Christian church, formerly bright and airy, suddenly filled with a choking and fetid odor. A bishop dreamt of a flock of sheep being systematically slaughtered and cast into cauldrons. Still another dreamt of a giant shouting from a mountaintop for Christians to flee.[26] Carl Jung also claimed to have witnessed a case of collective anxiety in the dream life of pre-1939 Germany.[27] But, whatever the meaning that collective dreams might have at the time that they are dreamt, their predictive patterns always seem to have been described much later in the insistent light of recognition.

If common individuals only infrequently had dreams that mattered to the state, kings regularly had them, or others dreamt of matters of importance to the king. It was by a principle of association that the latter came to have significance, for these dreams attracted the attention of the ruler and, therefore, at a practical level entered the orbit of royal concerns. The true *via regia* of dreams in ancient history is a persistent biographical theme that outlines the entire lives of rulers. Dreams such as Atia's famous encounter with a serpent seemed to the ancients to foretell the birth of great men like Octavian.[28] In Rome, future emperors also awaited dreams that would predict their rise to power, though some of these, like Galba's funny dream of the goddess Fortuna pounding at his door while he slept, ultimately delivered little.[29] But, in the ancient world, the interpretation of political dreams was deemed to be a respectable, if dangerous, avocation, one that might advance the career of a clever writer. Dio Cassius found, for instance, that his fortunes improved after he wrote a short work on the dreams and portents that had foretold Severus's rise to power. A copy of the book was sent to the emperor, who gladly received it and became the historian's patron.[30] Just as dreams anticipated the birth and success of a ruler, so, too, were they associated with his approaching death. Suetonius tells us that Caligula, on the day before his assassination, dreamt of standing in heaven before the throne of Jupiter. The god struck him with the toe of his left foot and hurled him to earth, thus literally booting him out of heaven.[31]

But the Carolingians would be more interested in another aspect of the *via regia* of dreams, one that was reinforced by the Bible: the warnings and punishments that fell upon kings in dreams. For the ancients, the exaggerated emphasis placed upon the portentous nature of dreams turned even dreamed absurdities into real events waiting to happen. Twice at the court of Claudius, according to Suetonius, men who merely dreamt of assassinating the emperor were executed for their treachery. Sir Thomas Browne was disdainful of a similar incident: "Dionysius was absurdly tyrannical to kill a man for dreaming that he had killed him, and really to take away his life who had but fantastically taken away his." Valerius Maximus, in his collection of historical anecdotes, gathered together a whole series of political dreams to illustrate the thesis that the fate announced in dreams could not be avoided. Fateful dreams thus provided a parallel to actual history; today's portentous dream was tomorrow's event. When Gaius Gracchus contemplated standing for the office of quaestor, his assassinated brother Tiberius appeared to him in a dream and told him that he too would die at the hands of an assassin.[32] The Carolingians were to be guardedly interested in the prophetic claims of royal dreams, but it hardly needs stating that in histories the prophecies of dreams, particularly political prophecies, are rarely left dangling: on papyrus and parchment, dreams almost always come true.

The class of political dreams that was to assume greatest importance for the Carolingians was the one in which rulers were shown suffering terrible punishments. The form itself was very old. In Plato's *Republic* the dead man Er had seen nobles tormented in the underworld for their worldly transgressions. In his *Morals,* Plutarch describes the vision of a certain Thespesius, who witnessed his father and friends suffering in the underworld. The visionary also observed the torment of Nero, who was being remade as a viper, but, since the emperor had paid for his crimes and had granted a measure of freedom to Greece, it was decided that he should be transformed into a gentle frog who would live in lakes and marshes.[33] Dream texts in the ancient and medieval worlds often assumed the character of tribunals; they were dead reckonings wherein the powerful of the world were finally judged and damned without the chance to crush their critics first. One thinks of Claudius's mock trial in the *Pumpkinification* as imagined by Seneca not long after the emperor's death.

Apparently it was not sufficiently satisfying for ancient authors to see kings and emperors condemned in the dreams of others. They imagined that wicked men would be visited by nightmares of their own misdeeds, as though the accumulated sins of their evil days had finally invaded their nights. Even Aeneas confessed that he had often dreamt of his father's ghost and was troubled in dream by the thought that he had deprived his son Ascanius of a kingdom. The Emperor Otho was haunted at night by Galba's ghost, whom he could in no way placate. Nero suffered most of all. After he had killed his mother he began to experience dreams and portents, though prior to that he had rarely dreamed at all. He envisaged himself steering a ship in his sleep when the tiller was suddenly wrenched from his hands. His wife Octavia, whom he had ordered executed, then appeared and dragged him into a black hole swarming with winged ants. Next statues in the Theater of Pompey circled him, preventing his exit, while he watched in horror as his horse was transformed into an ape. Finally the doors of the Mausoleum, the resting place of the emperors, flew open and Nero was told to enter. All of these dreams, reputedly dreamt by Nero himself, contain sharp and horrendous reversals of the laws of the state and nature; they were the mirror images of a murderous reign.[34] It is fascinating to watch the ancient author punish in sleep rulers who, full of confidence and charisma in real life, probably suffered little from remorse or the recrimination of nightmare.

Most melodramatic of all, Lucan imagined Julius Caesar and his troops collapsing in utter exhaustion upon a grassy bank after a break in the battle at Pharsalus against Pompey and his senatorial supporters. In maddening dreams, thoughts of the day's battle swept over the restless sleepers. Before their dreaming eyes marched the victims of the battle. Caesar himself saw each and every dead Roman and, in a vision of the future, saw hell and his own assassination, but he awoke to a radiant sun and plotted to fight again.[35]

Another, though less common, function of political dreams was consolation. I refer, in particular, to Cicero's famous account of the dream of Scipio. When worried about the fate of the republic, Scipio Aemilianus dreamt of his grandfather, the African, urging him to be brave and to listen carefully to his special message. The elder Scipio reassured the younger of his future successes and reminded him of the vastness of the cosmos and of the insignificance of human beings. He counseled his grandson to seek eternal truths and to work for the preservation of their fatherland. These were, of course, the virtues that mattered most to Cicero himself as the republic failed. The *Dream of Scipio* is wrapped in a mood of profound philosophical protest that had its roots in Cicero's own political reversals.[36]

If, in the ancient world, the destinies of the caesars were charted on colorful oneiric maps that foretold ascents to great power and forewarned of death and disaster, Carolingian writers inherited only a distorted and torn piece of that map. Of the various biographical functions of the ancient dream, they explored chiefly the admonitory, the one that highlighted crimes and punishments, and recommended remedies. What the Carolingians knew of the relationship between dreams and kings, they knew most directly from the Bible, but there they encountered an equivocal tradition.[37] In the Bible dreams frequently represent revelations of divine truth and, even better, direct contact with God. Yet the biblical dream has no automatic significance of its own; rather, it achieves importance as the vehicle of divine precept. The Israelites as a people do not seem to have believed, as the Romans did, that true dreams came from the world of the dead. Indeed the dead virtually never appear in biblical dreams. The symbolic dreams found in the Old Testament are for the most part replaced in the New Testament by simpler and more direct oneiric messages, often conveyed by an angel of the Lord. But the Bible, as richly evocative as ever, assumes no single position on the meaning of dreams. Although there are many examples of truthful dreams in both testaments, Deuteronomy 13:1–5 tells us that dreams lead people away from God and that the dreamers of dreams and false prophets should be put to death.

Kings are not, strictly speaking, privileged dreamers in the Bible, since true dreams depend upon the external agency of God, not upon the divine capacity of the king. God spoke to whomever he wished. Moreover, the dream itself is an inferior form of divine communication in the Bible. Christ himself never dreamt; his sleep was simple and untroubled by the weakness of human dreams. Being divine, Christ had no need to resort to limited forms of communicating with his Father. In the Old Testament, God often spoke through dreams to peoples distant from him. Pharaoh had a series of disturbing dreams, but he needed Joseph, who was closer to God's will, to interpret them. Daniel, too, was an oneirocritic to kings not of his faith. If God spoke to kings in the Bible, even to unbelievers, it was because they represented peoples he wished to correct; he spoke through them to wayward and hostile nations. Thus, the Christian *via regia* of dreams assumed an essentially corrective function: kings were chastised and warned in dreams; less often were they praised. Dreams were no longer exclusively about them, but about an even greater king, and the power of royal dreaming was shifting heavenward where it was to be the property of Christ's saints.

Thus early Christians were faced with the perplexing overlap of two different attitudes towards the interpretation of royal dreams. On the one hand, there was the tangled jungle of ancient oneirocriticism with its plethora of examples and confusion of classificatory systems;[38] on the other, there was the double-edged legacy of the Bible, which sometimes acknowledged the truthfulness of dreams and sometimes rejected them outright, which praised dream interpreters like Joseph and Daniel but damned false prophets. Christian thinkers attempted to reconcile the complex legacy of the Bible by distinguishing between true visions from God, which may occur in sleep, and dreams, which are products of one's own imagination and therefore false. Augustine's mother Monica, for instance, deftly distinguished between her vague and fanciful dreams and God's true visions, but she could not explain how; she simply said that she could smell the difference.[39] Only God's elite received visions of true things and even then infrequently; most men and women dreamt common dreams only fit to be forgotten. Thus a linguistic distinction came to cloak a hierarchy of visionaries at the summit and mere dreamers at the bottom. In this way the divergent opinions of the Bible could be incorporated and a hierarchy of Christian power preserved. In fact, Gregory of Nyssa chose to recognize only two classes of dreams: the normal and the divinely prophetic.[40]

In the early Christian world the power of public dreaming fell to the Apostles and their saintly successors. The apocryphal *Vision of Saint Paul* and the dreams of Perpetua moved right dreaming into the realm of the holy.[41] For almost three centuries kings did not join God's elite. If kings continued to dream political dreams, they did so in a world that did not much matter to Christians. God visited the martyrs with dreams that fortified them in the face of their persecution. Thus Maximian, before his martyrdom, dreamt of battling the agents of the emperor, which was a true foreshadowing of his passion. In the apocryphal tradition dependent on the *Vision of Saint Paul* these persecutors soon became "kings and princes" who were seen immersed in fiery rivers and baking in immense ovens.[42] In this way, the role of kings in early Christian dreams was being narrowed to but one of its many ancient functions. But these were pagan rulers who stood outside the world of Christian dreaming, and the centrality of the *via regia* of dreams was temporarily removed from the king's house.

Constantine opened the door once again. His dreams before the Battle of the Milvian Bridge returned kings and emperors to God's elite and restored some of their oneiric preeminence. As portrayed by Eusebius, Constantine's oneiric experience was the dramatic turning point in the emperor's conversion and in the history of Christianity, for the hard wall of pagan resistance had finally fallen because of the divine agency of a dream.[43] In Byzantium, a rich tradition of royal dreams followed in Constantine's shadow. The *via regia* of ancient dreams had persisted throughout the centuries of early Christian neglect, but in the eastern empire the two traditions were joined and so transformed. Both Theodosius the Great and Justin, Justinian's uncle, were said to have profited in their careers from divinely inspired dreams. By the time of Liutprand of Cremona's visit to Constantinople in the late tenth century, manuals for interpreting dreams were widely available and frequently consulted.[44]

But dreams cut both ways for rulers. Procopius, in his damning *Secret History,* related that a high-ranking citizen had once dreamt of Justinian drinking dry the waters that ran through the Bosporus Straits. For Procopius, the dream was a symbol of the beginning of Justinian's awesome avarice. In the crowded society of Constantinople, where informers flourished, Mercurius, "The Count of Dreams," was the most frightening of all. He used to worm his way into banquets and conferences, and if anyone let slip the details of a dream hostile to Emperor Constantinius II he would report it. Many individuals soon took to denying that they dreamed or even that they slept. Synesius of Cyrene, in contrast, wrote in his *On Dreams* that malicious governments would never be able to prohibit the oracles of dreams. A tyrant could only accomplish this, he said, by doing the impossible, by banishing sleep from the kingdom. His own dreams, he confessed, had given him the courage to consult the emperor.[45]

The successful reemergence of political oneirocriticism in the early medieval west was far from inevitable, quite unlike Byzantium with its late antique legacy or even Islam where Muhammad was a divinely inspired dreamer of things both political and religious.[46] For one thing, the emperor was in the east and saints continued to usurp the oneiric function of kings in the early medieval west: one thinks of the famous visions of Benedict of Nursia and Martin of Tours in this regard.[47] Between Constantine and Charlemagne, one looks in vain for the full historiographical reemergence of the *via regia* of dreams. Instead one glimpses only faint glimmerings of the theme, buried deep and almost unnoticed among the works of early medieval authors.

In Gregory the Great's *Dialogues,* which is filled with the heady air of the holy and the miraculous, we find but one striking example of political oneirocriticism. A hermit living on an island near Sicily had a vision of Theoderic the Great, naked and bound, cast into a volcano by two of his victims, Pope John I and the patrician Symmachus. Some visiting soldiers were surprised by the story, but returned home to find that the Ostrogothic king had indeed died during their absence.[48] Bede, despite his influential descriptions of the otherworldly voyages of Fursa and Drythelm, limited the *via regia* of dreams to the story of the exiled and hunted King Edwin, who spoke to a spirit in the dead of night about better days ahead.[49] Gregory of Tours informed King Guntram that he had seen his brother Chilperic tonsured and borne upon a throne draped with black cloth and illumined with lamps. Guntram, as if to confirm and explain the vision, had himself dreamt of three bishops leading Chilperic, bound in chains, into his presence. Two of them pleaded that he should be released after he had been mildly punished, but the third demanded that the fettered king be cast into a fire. In the distance Guntram saw a boiling cauldron into which Chilperic was thrown after his limbs had been broken. Gregory and Guntram agreed that these dreams had portended Chilperic's death.[50] Thus only a scattering of oneiric fragments survives from the sixth and seventh centuries. The ancient *via regia* of dreams, at least as Suetonius had known it, seemed almost on the verge of disappearing in the early medieval west, when the Carolingian age brought about the conditions necessary for its reappearance: a stronger central government and a literary revival. Royal poetry also experienced a similar cycle of neglect and rebirth, as Peter Godman has shown.[51]

On the chronological borderline between Merovingian and Carolingian Europe, a few royal dreams surfaced. Boniface, the great missionary to the continent and friend of the Carolingian royal house, wrote two letters about monastic visions concerning royalty. In one, a monk of Wenlock was said to have witnessed many awful and splendid things in the beyond, including the punishment of King Ceolred of Mercia. The visionary watched as a crowd of demons swept down upon the king to punish him for his wicked crimes. For a time angels shielded the king from the onslaught by holding a great book over his head, but they withdrew the shelter of their protection when they learned of the true nature of the king's sins. Then thousands of demons swarmed around the king, tormenting his fallen form. Boniface pointed out that Ceolred (who died in 716) was certainly alive when the monk saw him in the vision, but then he wanted the vision to be read as predictive rather than vindictive. Thirty years later he would remind King Aethelbald of Mercia that his predecessor had surely landed in hell for his destruction of monasteries and his sexual crimes.[52] Boniface's use of the image of Ceolred in hell should remind us that the real function of the royal dream in the early Middle Ages was to chasten kings, to call up before their eyes scenes so vividly horrible that they would avoid bad kingship at all cost. If the vision was not invented by Boniface, he was at the very least its literary recorder and disseminator, and he used the vision in the end to advise another king, not to chastise the dead Ceolred.

In a fragment contained at the end of one collection of Boniface's letters, we meet an unnamed visionary who once beheld people from all walks of life—counts and commoners, abbots and unbaptized children—all suffering or rejoicing in the otherworld according to their merits. There he saw the queens Cuthburga and Wiala tormented in pits by enormous demons for their carnal sins, their screams reverberating throughout the vast world beyond. Boniface and his contemporaries imagined the infernal regions as a place where men, women, and children were judged according to deed and misdeed, irrespective of their station in life. If the terrain of the otherworld often lacked specificity in the early Middle Ages, and if its sinners were frequently a faceless throng of fornicators and thieves set in "a seething maelstrom of fire and blackness," this was not true of the powerful of the world.[53] The only advantage to be won by kings and queens, a few nobles, and churchmen was to escape the anonymous horror of hell. They were named individuals who often suffered specific punishments for their famous crimes.

Although it survives in no manuscript predating the ninth century, the famous forgery popularly known as the *Donation of Constantine* seems to have been composed by a Roman cleric around 760, though his exact intention has always eluded scholars. At the heart of the document, perhaps bearing witness to older oral and written sources, is the story of a sick emperor and his revelatory dream. Gravely ill with leprosy, Constantine was supposed to have consulted pagan priests, who advised him to bathe in the blood of innocent children. Before this atrocity could be committed, however, the apostles Peter and Paul appeared to Constantine in a dream and ordered him to seek out the fugitive Pope Sylvester, who would wash away his leprosy in a pool of piety. The emperor, in turn, was commanded to build churches throughout the whole world, to abandon idolatry, and to cherish the one true God. Upon arising from his dreamy sleep, Constantine sought out the pope to discover whether he possessed paintings of the two apostles. When he saw the images of Peter and Paul, he exclaimed that these were indeed the men he had seen in his dream and, with this confirmation, he set out to fulfill their apostolic demands. The dream is the hinge on which the action of the *Donation* turns, for Constantine entered sleep as a pagan, but left as a man on the road to conversion; the dream, thus, explained the secret reason for his abrupt religious about-face. With the traditional account of Constantine's conversion, the *Donation* shared a belief in the divine agency and efficacy of dreams. At the same time, Pope Sylvester's role as archetypal papal intercessor and beneficiary of kings and emperors was divinely recognized and legitimized.[54]

But, for our purposes, the *Donation* confirms the special significance that dreams were thought to hold for kings. The dream sequence of the *Donation* was to be cited by a number of Carolingian councils, in the *Caroline Books,* and in the *False Decretals.*[55] Hincmar of Rheims and Walahfrid Strabo, who were to be prominent political oneirocritics, took special note of Constantine's dream.[56] Though modern historians have chiefly looked to the *Donation* for papal property and constitutional claims, Carolingian churchmen may more often have seen in it the correction of an emperor through the divine intervention of a dream. Boniface's visionary letters would also circulate widely, and Hincmar of Rheims would draw specific attention to them when circulating another dream text.[57] Though the kings and queens encountered in these mid-eighth-century texts were distant and even foreign to the Franks, examples of the oneiric criticism and correction of rulers did not go unnoticed by Carolingian writers.

Thus political dreams and visions reappeared in the mid-eighth century at precisely the time when the Carolingians were coming to official power. A sense of uneasiness and uncertainty washed over Europe in that delicate period around 750 when the Carolingians were displacing the Merovingians. The making and unmaking of kings and entire royal houses threatened the very underpinnings of a deeply traditional society. The Carolingians countered this temporary imbalance with supports that the Merovingians, who were manifestly royal, had not needed: oaths of allegiance, anointings, and papal sanction.[58] Perhaps the royal dreams that began to reappear in the disquieting mid-eighth century were a barometer of the rising anxieties of this changing world. After all, Boniface was a central player in the drama of the usurpation, and the *Donation* must reflect a Roman desire to achieve an advantageous stability in an unstable age. That it was God and not man who sanctioned, judged, rewarded, and damned rulers was the chief message of these mid-century dream texts.[59] Part of the Carolingian interest in them, if not the reason for their composition, was that these oneiric accounts seemed to offer another model for approaching the divine in a world suddenly without sure equipoise.

But the disquieting moment of the mid-eighth century passed and the Carolingians through to Charlemagne's time remained uncomfortable with dreams, which were variously viewed as either tainted with paganism or as too contentious. During the reigns of Pepin and Charlemagne, the official line was that popular dream interpretation was a form of pagan divination. The *Admonitio generalis,* Charlemagne's most influential capitulary, lumped dream divination together with soothsaying, augury, and sorcery as damnable practices.[60] Dream interpretation seemed to inhabit that demonic world of tree worship, spells, charms, love potions, and spirits that official Carolingians so fiercely rejected. The magical arts may have belonged to a synoptic structure of pagan beliefs that ran deep into the countryside and far into the past, but for Carolingian reformers they also challenged the superficial and incomplete Christian conversion of northern Europe. The condemnation of popular dream interpretation was therefore part of a package of all-embracing Christian reform that tended to label as magical anything that smacked of divination.[61]

Yet dreams lacking a Christian context and content and those possessing them were always to be considered very different things. For the Carolingians there was no apparent contradiction, since the referent was simply different: pagan dream interpretation belonged to a world of superstition while Christian dreams were the result of the divine will of God and could be carefully read. To have done otherwise would have been to have denied biblical precedent. Thus, the equivocation of the Bible on the status of dreams was, in the end, to keep the door to oneirocriticism ajar. The Carolingian world even knew a manual for interpreting dreams, the *Dreambook of Daniel,* but, despite its claim to biblical authority, the degree of its ninth-century popularity has never been determined.[62]

Yet if pagan oneirocriticism was easy to dismiss, Carolingian dreaming proved difficult, at first, to embrace. Charlemagne himself was exposed to a controversial case of dream interpretation. Sometime before 791, the king returned a wandering monk by the name of John to Pope Hadrian I. The monk had sought out the king and had apparently complained to him about a whole series of issues, including the involuntary imprisonment of men, probably in monastic life, and the abuse of spiritual power for temporal ends. The king must have been somewhat sympathetic, since he sent his agent, Duke Garamann, to Rome to investigate the case and to insure that the monk was not being mistreated. Hadrian, in a letter to Charlemagne, claimed that not only had John not been harmed, but he had been returned in perfect health to his monastery after receiving a lecture on proper obedience to the monastic rule. Hadrian was particularly worried by the contentious revelations that the wayward monk claimed to have received in his sleep. John said that he had seen the heavens open and the right hand of God appear. In another dream he, like Jacob, had seen angels descending from a great tower. One of these, with the likeness of a man but the wings of an eagle, was devouring a dead man while another, with a human body but the wings of a dove, declared that this corpse was the Christian faith.

Behind John's dreams as reported by the pope must stand vivid images not unlike those that survive in early medieval manuscripts today, especially the *dextra dei,* that downthrust hand of God dividing the heavenly clouds. But Hadrian was upset, not just because the second dream seemed to suggest that Christianity was dead, but because John's symbols were unorthodox. He observed that while one of John's angels seemed to fit the proper image of the Evangelist John, the dove was a symbol of the Holy Spirit and should not possess any human features. The pope was relieved that Charlemagne also recognized that John's dreams were apparitions or *phantasma.*[63]

Yet his uneasiness is palpable. Behind his anxiety lay the worry, which Charlemagne may have shared, that the free and unchecked interpretation of dreams would loosen established ecclesiastical authority and right order in the church. The incident with John had certainly given ample grounds for concern: the monk had charged that the church and its higher ecclesiastics were acting improperly, and he apparently attempted to bolster his position through the narration of two dreams. The first suggested, as the vaults of heaven opened and he saw the symbol of Christ, the *dextra dei,* that he had gained through his dreams special access to God and to divine truth, while the second conveyed heavenly criticism of the earthly church. But Hadrian claimed the right to declare John's dreams evil apparitions that lacked divine sanction; to do less would have been to have opened up a Pandora's box of free association and individual challenge to the church's right to interpret the divine. The official church as represented by the pope preferred revelation to be a finished thing, most safely stored within the determined dimensions of the Bible. At some profound level, dreams and visions promised or threatened, depending upon one's perspective, the uncertainties and intoxicating indeterminacies of continuing revelation: that somehow the divine story was not yet complete and that Christ might still visit the faithful with corrective visions of penetrating truth.

The problem of contentious dreams arose again during the events surrounding the western side of the Iconoclastic Controversy. At the Second Council of Nicaea in 787, Theodore, the bishop of Myra, sought to bolster the position of the iconolaters, the image worshipers, by invoking the dreams of his archdeacon. Pope Hadrian, who was represented at the council, received a hostile report of Theodore's use of dreams, but the pope recognized that in both testaments there were genuine examples of oneiric revelation.[64] With refreshing practicality, he asked the obvious: how could saints such as Ambrose have recognized the holy ones they had seen in their dreams if there had been no pictures of them? That same thought, of course, had figured in the *Donation,* where Constantine had asked to see pictures of the apostles who had appeared in his dream. Hadrian simply assumed that the dreams of saints were true and could be confirmed by means of Christian paintings. What the pope had charged earlier against the wayward monk was that the imagery of his second dream was inconsistent with orthodox iconography and, therefore, his entire revelation should be dismissed as spurious. Implicit in Hadrian's thought was the need to find some way to distinguish between true Christian dreams and false apparitions. Not surprisingly, the solution hit upon was conservative and traditional, since one test was whether the pictorial imagery of a dream matched the graphic symbols sanctioned by the church.

The so-called *Caroline Books* composed by Theodulf of Orléans, but with some minor contribution by Alcuin, contained the official response of Charlemagne's court to the Council of Nicaea, and consequently to Theodore's use of evidence based on dreams.[65] But the matter was delicate for Theodulf, because he wanted to dismiss most dreams as false, specifically the archdeacon's, and yet needed to grant that, in one part of the biblical tradition, exceptional dreams revealing divine mysteries were possible. Against Theodore and the iconolaters, he put forward a logical, if propositionally predetermined, solution. If the dream had been shown to the archdeacon by an angel, then it was right to worship images. Since, however, it was wrong to worship things lacking sense, such as images, an angel could not have revealed the dream to the archdeacon, but rather an evil demon had excited the sleeper's spirit. The dream, therefore, must be false. Moreover, Theodulf was quick to remind his audience that Constantine had come to verify the images of Peter and Paul, not to worship them. To support his contention that some dreams were false, Theodulf assembled a series of biblical readings, including Deuteronomy 13:1–3. He stopped short, however, of rejecting all dreams as false, since he acknowledged that Joseph, the prophets, and the three Magi had all experienced true dreams. For Theodulf, the best test of a dream's truthfulness was to examine the purpose to which it had been put. If it was used to buttress some dubious opinion, such as the worship of images, then it was clearly false:

> Whence, let no one insolently seek to use, follow, believe, or recite in gatherings these or similar dreams and let no one presume to affirm from these dreams contentious things in the manner of Theodore; this is, as we have said, outlawed by Sacred Scripture.[66]

Thus, as Hadrian had when faced with the dreams of a rambunctious monk, Theodulf rejected those idle dreams that claimed to supply divine sanction for controversial doctrines. Worried that marginal men might make a rebellious society centered on charismatic oneirocriticism, he condemned outright the contentious use of dreams.

Like others before him, Theodulf also sought to distinguish between true and false dreams by means of separative labels. *Somnia* were frequently false, because, though some sprang from genuine revelation, many were the products of purposive thought or temptation. In making this point, he doubtless recalled Gregory the Great's discussion of the causes of dreams, which were thought to arise from a full stomach, from an empty one, from illusions or our thoughts mixed with illusions, and from revelations or our thoughts mixed with revelations.[67] Carolingian thinkers partly subscribed to the "heavy supper" theory of the origin of disagreeable dreams. *Visiones,* however, were reckoned to be truer revelations. Here the *Caroline Books* and Alcuin, in a separate letter, followed the tripartite division of visions established by Augustine and repeated by Isidore.[68] Corporeal visions were thought to be received through the agency of the body; spiritual visions had their basis in remembered images stored in our memories; and intellectual visions, the best of all, were understood in the intellect without need of body or memory. Intellectual visions were preferred, not only because they were the most transcendent and therefore the closest to God, but also because they were the rarest. In adopting this Augustinian scheme, Theodulf and Alcuin properly belonged to that long-standing Christian drive to limit the this-worldly implications of discourse with the otherworld. If standards for the cautious acceptance of a few noncontroversial visions could be found, the disruptive potential of oneirocriticism could be contained.

The Carolingian use of the distinction between dreams and visions may seem odd to the modern mind, but we should remember that it was a linguistic solution to the perplexing problem of distinguishing between significant and insignificant dreams. For us, most Carolingian visions would be dreams, since they most often occurred in sleep. Paschasius Radbertus longed for "the sweet visions of a true dream," but even he was not sure that his ambiguous phrasing was appropriate. Moreover, the vision of Wetti took place while he was asleep on his sickbed, and the vision of Raduin began only after he "began to slip into sleep."[69] Macrobius, whose commentary on the *Dream of Scipio* was widely read, had named five categories of dreams: the prophetic (*uisio*), nightmarish (*insomnium*), apparitional (*phantasma*), enigmatic (*somnium*), and oracular (*oraculum* or revelation through an agent).[70] For the Carolingians, too, there was a sense in which both the dream and the vision were types of *somnia,* though in a few cases visions were experienced by wide-awake individuals. Often we are simply not told when a vision took place, a strategy of reporting that must have enhanced a vision's claim to superior status. In the *Caroline Books,* Theodulf admitted that the terms for dream and vision were freely mixed; the Carolingians were, after all, inextricably tied to a biblical vocabulary that employed both types of experience in a positive sense.[71] For purposes of the present study, I have employed the word "dream" in the modern sense to cover all things envisaged in sleep.

But we need to remember that, though the distinction between dreams and visions is admittedly artificial and phenomenologically inaccurate, Carolingian writers meant something by it. They meant, above all, to designate a divinely inspired dream by labeling it a vision. Many Carolingian intellectuals became the patrons of these special dreams; they protected the interpretation of the dream they deemed true and they recommended it to the attention of their fellow Christians. Hence, the very use of the term *uisio* became a first and favorable statement, an advertisement, as it were, of the genuineness of the dream. Neither the sober prudence of Theodulf and Alcuin nor the specific prohibitions of the capitularies mattered to the promoters of special dream texts, for the true dream had its own compelling claims and it had patrons.

For the Carolingians, true dreams were most often dreamed by holy men and by kings, but the borders between these two types of dreamers were far from fixed. When one of Saint Richarius's disciples lay in a hut with the body of his master, he dreamt, for instance, of the saint still alive and standing "in a splendid royal palace that shone like the sun and was adorned with gold and jewels." Paschasius may in his time have condemned soothsayers, but he too believed in the possibility of divine dreams and in the superior vision of the saint:

> If souls still clinging to bodily chains, as if bound tight in a prison of limbs, can in the still of the night perceive higher things and things separated from their appearances, how much more do they see who are free from all earthly corruptions, for, as one of the saints said, they see with a sense both pure and ethereal.[72]

Thus dreaming, in this golden light, was a next-to-saintly activity that a pious Christian might hope to emulate. Indeed, a largely unstudied aspect of Carolingian hagiography is the function of dreams and visions, for the power of divine dreaming was assumed in the eighth and ninth centuries to have belonged specially to saints. But some of the functions of the holy dream remind us of those that once belonged to the high society of the Roman emperor. Alcuin, for instance, described how Willibrord's mother had seen a vision in her sleep of her saintly son's birth.[73] Dreams also warned the saints of betrayal and danger, foretold their martyrdoms, and, above all, connected them to the court of Christ, binding them tight to the circle of those privileged to receive messages from above.

Despite their caution, both Theodulf and Alcuin used dream materials in their own writings, seemingly sanctioning the occasional truthfulness and poetic possibilities of dreams. Theodulf concluded his poem on his favorite books with Virgil's image of the two gates of dreams, for he had found the act of reading a difficult negotiation between theology and poetry, Christian truth and the enchanting fictions of myth. At the end of this poem, we find the poet searching for the means to separate true things from false, horn from ivory, vision from speech. Although Theodulf may have cast a cautious eye on the river of dreams, it seems that he once wrote a poem on sleep and dreams. That poem, however, has not survived.[74]

Jean Devisse thought that the starting point for any history of the Carolingian imagery of the descent into hell should be Alcuin's poetic rendering of Bede's account of Drythelm. Alcuin's account is wonderfully picturesque, as he imagined Drythelm, a common man, first dying, then being led out of his body by a radiant figure. He was transported to a valley raging with fire and pelted with hail, where he was left alone to watch the wicked suffer and to worry about his own fate. When his guide returned, he led Drythelm up through the air onto an impossibly high wall, which looked over a splendid and fragrant plain where the saints dwelled in holiness. Before returning him to his body and to life, the guide informed Drythelm that he should not think that he had seen either heaven or hell, but a holding space in between, beyond which lay those absolute realms.[75] At the end of his long poem on the history of York, Alcuin claims that he had personally encountered in his boyhood a young man who had several times been visited by visions of a tall man, dressed in white, who had spoken to him of the future. Shortly after his death, Alcuin's own hagiographer adorned the story of his master's life with accounts of dreams and nightmares.[76] Despite his own experience and Bede's examples, however, Alcuin's attitude towards dreams and visions always remained stubbornly cautious. In his commentary on Ecclesiastes 5:7, he reminded his readers that the Hebrews had advised people not to believe too easily in dreams. For Alcuin it was a mistake for the average person to put much faith in them:

> If while you rest at night you should see a variety of things and if your mind should be disturbed by terror or excited by promises, condemn those things since they are only dreams. Fear God instead. For those who believe in dreams give themselves up to vanity and folly.[77]

Even those who believed in the divine voice of some dreams knew that others were to be dismissed as dangerous and misleading. Wetti had one of those bad dreams, but quickly rejected it. The funniest account of a silly dream surely belongs to Walahfrid Strabo. He dreamt, or feigned to have dreamt, that one night while deep in sleep the eagle of Jove swept down and snatched him up. As the dreamer flew upwards, imagining that he was some new Ganymede or Daedalus soaring towards the heavens, he suddenly became dizzy and then nauseous, for his insides wanted, he said, to return to mother earth. A comic scene ensued in which the eagle invited the dreamer to hold tightly onto his tail and vomit quickly over the side. When this unpleasant business was done, the eagle informed the dreamer that he could not possibly think of taking such a filthy creature to heaven. Wake up, he told the dreamer, and take a good look at your mess. When Walahfrid, now a fallen Icarus, did so, he found that he had vomited all over his bed. The lesson the poet learned was not that all dreams were wrong, but that he was at that time too earthbound, too heavy and bloated in spirit, to dream of soaring to the heavens.[78]

But the true skeptics could be answered, even in dreams. The monk of Wenlock, for instance, had been told by his angels to relate his vision to all believers, but to refuse to talk to scoffers. In the *Deeds of Dagobert,* the saints told the young king that they would protect him if he cherished their tombs. They promised to supply him with a sign of their power, "lest you think that you are deluded by the fantasies of a dream." Wetti himself heard in his vision about a bishop who maintained that "the nonsense of dreams ought to be ignored," but an angel reassured the dreamer that this was not the case. The doubting bishop, a certain Adalhelm, received his comeuppance since Wetti heard that he was now stuck on the side of a purgatorial mountain where the elements lashed him mercilessly. Walahfrid, in the preface to his poetic version of the *Vision of Wetti,* knew for certain that there were men who judged this vision to be merely a vain dream, but he did not want his patron, Grimald the court chaplain of Louis the Pious, to be counted among them.[79] Walahfrid had little to fear. The *Vision of Wetti* became the most famous of all Carolingian dreams, and there was a flowering of dream literature in the ninth century. Even Alcuin had admitted that what mattered in the end was the truth of the dream: "the outcome of things establishes true dreams," he said.[80] Thus, even the skeptics lived in a world where it was difficult to deny the existence of powerful and probative dreams.

Finally, not long after Christmas in the year 800 when Charlemagne had been crowned emperor in Rome, the Carolingians entered upon their own royal road of dreams. An author, who may have been Einhard, wrote a major epic poem, popularly called *Charlemagne and Pope Leo,* from which one book now survives.[81] In its original form, the poem must have celebrated the events that led to Charlemagne's assumption of the imperial title; one of these was the rescue of Pope Leo III by the king. In language and imagery deeply influenced by the *Aeneid,* the poet described how, after a day of pomp and procession, hunt-

ing and feasting, an exhausted company of royal retainers had finally succumbed to sleep. But the king's rest was not to be peaceful.

> Portentum rex triste uidet monstrumque nefandum
> In somnis, summum Romanae adstare Leonem
> Urbis pontificem mestosque effundere fletus,
> Squalentes oculos, maculatum sanguine uultum,
> Truncatam linguam horrendaque multa gerentem
> Vulnera. Sollicitos gelidus pauor occupat artus
> Augusti . . .

> [In his dreams the king sadly sees a monstrous
> And execrable sign: Leo, the supreme pontiff of the city of Rome,
> Stands before him shedding sorrowful tears.
> His eyes are damaged and his face is stained with blood,
> His tongue is mutilated and he bears many horrible wounds.
> A cold fear lays hold of the restless limbs
> Of the emperor . . .][82]

In April 799 the enemies of Leo had, in fact, seized the pope and, in the
church of San Silvestro in Capite, had torn from him his pontifical vestments.
As part of this act of deposition, the rebels had decided to blind the pope and rip
out his tongue, but for some reason they never carried out their full plan, although they seem to have wounded him. Ever after, said Notker, Leo bore "a
snow-white scar that ran across the line of his turtledove eyes."[83] Later in the
year, the pope traveled to Paderborn to seek Charlemagne's help, and the next
year, in response, the king went to Rome in order to restore Leo fully to his high
office, and to become emperor himself.

The poem achieves dramatic force with its image of the sleeping Charlemagne seized by a cold chill. Upon awaking, he immediately dispatched three
representatives to Rome to see "what his sad dreams might mean." They returned to Paderborn with the pope in tow and full of details about the plot
against his person. As Charlemagne then gazed upon the mangled face of Leo,
setting it beside the remembered image from his dream, he realized that his
dream had been a true one; the outcome of things had, indeed, proved it true.[84]
Thus, the validated dream drew attention to the legendary perspicacity of an
omniscient king.

In the dream sequence of *Charlemagne and Pope Leo* the several legacies of
the Carolingian *via regia* of dreams were finally brought together. The very

lines in which the poet carved out the scene were creatively adapted from Aeneas's speech to Queen Dido and the banqueters gathered in the royal halls of Carthage. As Troy fell, Aeneas told them how Hector had appeared to him in his sleep; he was weeping, his hair was matted and his beard bloodied, as he counseled the dreamer to flee the burning city and seek out the promised land. But Charlemagne is more than another Aeneas in the poem, for he has the royal capacity of a Christian king to interpret his own dreams. Carolingian exegetes knew that pagan kings needed the assistance of holy men to understand their dreams, but in *Charlemagne and Pope Leo* the king could dream and then directly act, because God had not hidden his message in symbols.[85] Instead he had given Charlemagne a simple representation of Leo's cruel fate. The dream dramatically demonstrated that God had communicated specially and directly with a favored king, aiding him, even in sleep, in keeping watch over a sprawling empire and its vulnerable church.

Charlemagne's dream occupies a point of dramatic fissure in the poem, a decisive break in the pleasant flow of pastoral detail and church building that had come before, and the monumental march to Rome, with its awaiting imperial crown, that must have followed. The dream both foreshadowed and documented actual events, alerting the king to a flagrant flaunting of his authority and to a dangerous assault upon the Catholic church. Royal dreams, even in the panegyric of an epic poem, were often to represent ruptures in the troubled world of the Carolingian kings. More than that, they demanded royal action, some redress for wrongs committed. Looking back from late in the ninth century, readers would have been amazed at how satisfying this dream was, for it led, unlike more recent royal dreams, directly to royal action and to triumph. The poem was the first important example of a Carolingian royal dream, and it was one closely connected to the very idea of the rebirth of the Roman empire.

But we cannot leave this remarkable oneiric episode behind without one final, somewhat Gibbonesque observation. Charlemagne's dream does not take us inside the king's head but the poet's, and we must wonder what liberties he took in imagining a dreaming king. So panegyrical in purpose and so familiar with court history was the poem that it must have been composed for and read aloud to Charlemagne and his court. Could the poet have expected Charlemagne to understand a poetic device borrowed from the *Aeneid* or one that belonged to the ancient and decrepit road of royal dreams? Since Leo was never, in fact, blinded, and managed to retain his tongue—and since by the time of his visit to Paderborn the whole Carolingian court must have known that, no matter what rumors they had previously heard—listeners must have understood Charlemagne's dream to predict what would have happened had he not been warned. Thus, because of the dream, he was able to thwart the plot against the pope and to change the course of unfolding history. The epic poet conjured up, therefore, just the kind of divinatory dream that Charlemagne had denied to everyone else in his capitularies. What must the emperor have thought in 801 as he sat listening to someone like Einhard digging in his dreams? Whatever he thought, royal and saintly dreams must have regained some measure of respectability at the court of Charlemagne or the poet never would have dared to think his way into the king's dreaming head.

Thus behind Carolingian writers stretched a vast and colorful cloth of dreamed and dreaming kings. On it were embroidered the imperial dreams of Virgil and Suetonius, Daniel at the court of dreamy Nebuchadnezzar, Paul's visionary voyage through an awesome otherworld, Drythelm's towering wall, Constantine's cross in the sky and his dream of the apostles, and King Theoderic, hungry and thirsty, standing in pitch-black hell with his cronies Pharaoh, Pilate, Nero, and Julian.[86] We need to remember that before the Carolingians began writing their own dream literature, they had been exposed to a limited world of possible dreams and dream types. Their literary response to that literature is everywhere evident. The most famous of all Carolingian dreamers would call from his sickbed for his brother monks to read to him from Gregory's *Dialogues*. After listening to that work with its oneiric episodes and its dusky Ostrogoth, Wetti would lapse into sleep and instantly be transported into the awesomeness of the world beyond.[87]

Early in the ninth century Carolingian intellectuals began to construct their own *via regia* of dreams. It was, one must suppose, no coincidence that this development paralleled, or rather belonged to, that revival of letters that began to transform certain segments of the Carolingian world late in the eighth century. These men and a few women were both readers and writers; they were the recipients of the fundamental educational reforms introduced by Charlemagne and his court. Moving across a wide frontier of literary genres, ranging from Latin poetry to annals, these writers explored older types of literary expression and shaped them anew. Ironically, Charlemagne was to be the first royal target of the rediscovered road of dreams. Literary dreaming in the ninth century was to be an exercise in focusing attention on royal figures, and the figure of Charlemagne, that rich repository of images, would prove to be the first in a series of shifting royal focal points. Nor was it coincidental that the *via regia* of dreams reemerged alongside the rebirth of an empire, for the imperial ideal, which is so poignantly expressed in *Charlemagne and Pope Leo,* raised hopes of unity and

Frankish brilliance that could only be disappointed by the ninth century's politics of fragmentation.

But such was the underlying suspicion of dream divination, and so piecemeal was the reception of historical dream literature that Carolingian writers still approached political oneirocriticism hesitantly. The fuller development of royal dreams awaited the death of Charlemagne. While he lived, the emperor never appeared in a negative light in any dream text; his presence was too powerful and the official attitude towards dream interpretation too cautious for the true return to the *via regia* of dreams. The dream sequence in *Charlemagne and Pope Leo,* however promising and however elegant, would also be unique: it would be the only royal dream that portrayed a Carolingian king positively and in epic dimension. The door to full-blown royal dreaming would, with persistent pressure, open slowly, but Charlemagne would be discovered standing behind it, blocking the way.[88]

The *via regia* of dreams, for both the ancients and the Carolingians, was a textual by-product of a general concern with the meaning of power. But the royal dream was to be, for the Carolingians, even more focused than it had been for the ancients, for it was not merely to be a commentary on power or the more facile praise of a ruler but a specific tool designed to shift the massive weight of recalcitrant royal power in a new direction. It would not do to neglect these semiprecious dreams, for in their reflected light we may chance to catch the edges and bold outlines of a world of meaning.

CHAPTER THREE

Charlemagne and
His Dream Critics

He is catholic in faith, king in power, prelate in preaching, judge in justice, philosopher in the liberal arts, distinguished in his habits, and excellent in all good character.[1]

With these words, Alcuin praised Charlemagne as the Frankish world's summit
of human accomplishment. He was joined by virtually every court scholar who
lived during the king's long reign. Charlemagne, as they saw him, and perhaps
as he saw himself, was a living example to the kingdom and a paragon of vir-
tuous kingship. Angilbert and Theodulf, Einhard and Paul the Deacon all wrote
similarly exaggerated praises of the man who bestrode their small world.

But, in dying, Charlemagne did the one thing that he had always avoided doing while alive, the one thing that had seemed impossible for the rock-hard
builder ever to do: he shook that small and fragile world of king and court that
he had spent a lifetime constructing. If anything, those at some remove from
Aachen registered an even deeper sense of shock, for to them Charlemagne
must have seemed almost superhuman. In a famous lament for the emperor, a
Carolingian monk described how profoundly his life had been shaken by Charlemagne's death and interment at Aachen. Worry, he said, had now invaded his
sleep:

Nox mihi dira iam retulit somnia,
Diesque clara non adduxit lumina.
   Heu mihi misero!

[Night now brought me ominous dreams,
And daytime delivered no bright light.
    Alas for wretched me!]²

With images of night, dire dreams, and the absence of light, the monk sketches his sadness in a language of familiar symbols. But his personal grief stands at the middle of the poem. He had begun by acknowledging the profound sense of loss felt by the whole world, for all races and Christian peoples must now lament the loss of the emperor. But proceeding inward towards his own heart where the pain was sharpest, the poet, at his lowest point, began to turn upward towards thoughts of salvation, not his own, but Charlemagne's. He scolded himself for his incessant weeping and self-pity: better by far, he thought, to pray for Charlemagne's soul, and better to ask Christ, the Lord of heaven and hell, to grant the king a splendid seat among the saints. Later Dhuoda, the countess of Septimania, would observe that people who had lived as much in the world as she and her embattled noble family needed prayers more than most people in order to gain entrance to heaven. The monk's dirge has the same idea behind it. Yes, the poet seems to say, the world has lost its great protector, but what had it cost him to protect them? Yes, the souls of all people need prayer because no one's salvation is sure, but kings are more exposed to the world's corruption than most men and women and are more in need of prayer. He called on Christ to give Charles peace at last and on the Holy Spirit to lift up the emperor's soul to final, relaxing rest.³

We should not underestimate the central place that royal figures held in the imaginative lives of their subjects, especially in those of monks far from court and conscious of the welcome weight of royal power and patronage. Charlemagne's death provoked a visionary dream in another monk. Rimbert, the late ninth-century archbishop of Hamburg and Bremen, described his predecessor Anskar as one who "had from infancy been inflamed by spiritual revelations from heaven and who had frequently been advised, by the grace of the Lord, through celestial visitations." In 814, when he was only thirteen years old, Anskar had just become a newly tonsured monk of Corbie. Walther Lammers once wondered whether Anskar's Marian dreams might have been the product of his early separation from his parents.⁴ But, in describing what must have been a frequent personal crisis in the Middle Ages as young men and women replaced familial security with extrafamilial commitment, Rimbert presented Anskar's adolescent anxieties as the fitting battleground for a saintly monk: he was setting aside his human weaknesses and growing cold towards the world.

At this critical juncture in his life, Anskar learned of the death of the emperor. He had once personally seen Charlemagne and had heard people praise him for his skillful governance of the kingdom. "And so, overwhelmed with terror and horror at the death of the emperor," Anskar began to pray to Mary, his special guardian. As Rimbert describes it, the monk took this crisis as a signal that he should redouble his efforts to lead a holy life by putting aside all frivolity and lightness. As a servant of God and battler against vice, the world was becoming completely dead to him. After prolonged prayer, vigil, and abstinence, Anskar had an awesome dream during the night of Pentecost, four months after Charlemagne's death. In it a young, bearded John the Baptist and an elderly, grizzled Peter appeared to Anskar and led him to a place raging with purgatorial fire, where they left him for three days. Rimbert reports the next stage of the dream in what he claims were Anskar's own words. After retrieving him, Anskar's holy guides ushered him into a radiant and wonderful place where he gazed upon a long line of saints stretching to the east and the twenty-four elders of the Apocalypse sitting upon thrones. The elders, looking further east themselves, chanted ineffable hymns to God while a light of sublime purity and color shone down from on high. The dreamer could not see what lay at the center of this intense radiance; he could perceive only the surface from which the light shone, flooding the elders and looking like an arc of clouds. Anskar instantly realized that Christ himself, the *Majestas Domini,* must exist at the center of this impenetrable light, and a voice whispered to him that his own martyrdom would one day recall him to this radiant place.

In part, this visionary dream was his summons to become a missionary, for only missionary work might normally lead to martyrdom in the ninth century. Indeed, Anskar did become the first great Carolingian missionary to Sweden and Denmark, but he died peacefully in his own bed in Bremen in 865.[5]

The most striking feature of Anskar's dream is its visual force. Julius von Schlosser was so impressed by the vision that he included it in his pioneering collection of materials on Carolingian art history.[6] Beyond the mere vividness of the dream is an interesting correspondence, for Anskar's vision reads for all the world like a walk through Charlemagne's palace chapel at Aachen. Even today the visitor enters the church through the west entranceway with its formidable Wolf's Door. As in the vision, the visitor is then looking east. Walking towards the octagonal space that lies at the center of the building, one passes under the sturdy vaults of the ambulatory. Upon arriving in the central octagon and looking up, the viewer finds that he is gazing upon a row of saints, executed in mosaics, that are placed above the arches but below the curve of the dome.

Above the saints, along the rim of the dome, are the twenty-four elders of the Apocalypse. Although today the icongraphic scheme of the cupola mosaics is a nineteenth-century reworking, we know from a seventeenth-century drawing made by Ciampini that the elders of the original Carolingian mosaic were depicted in the act of rising from chairs to offer their crowns to the enthroned Christ (Fig. 10). The *Codex Aureus* of Saint-Emmeram may depict Charles the Bald looking upwards upon a similar scene in the same church a half-century later (Fig. 11). Today the mosaics portray the elders standing and without their thrones, but in the ninth century the twenty-four elders were shown moving in two lines around the dome towards the east, where Christ in majesty could be seen sitting upon a throne. Although the subject of considerable debate, Christ's position in the original mosaic was full of meaning, for he was situated on a vertical axis that cut through the altars placed on two levels below and on a diagonal axis that rose up from Charlemagne's stone throne in the west tribune.[7] Seated upon his throne high up in the cathedral with the two altars facing him, and looking upon the worshipers gathered below and on Christ directly across from and above him, Charlemagne occupied a special place of symbolic power in the chapel of Aachen (Fig. 12). His position was a visual confirmation of that Carolingian belief in the superimposed and overarching presence of the divine order above the human, and of the king's powerful and perilous place on the unmoving borderline between the worlds. Alluding to this intersection of royal and divine natures, Lupus of Ferrières would later ask the young King Charles the Bald: "Who is unaware that you have taken up the place of God?"[8]

Rimbert does tell us that Anskar had once seen Charlemagne, but could this have been in Aachen? The palace chapel was not only an extraordinary building, one that made an overwhelming impression on all who saw it, but it was also the site of legendary dreams. Notker told the story of a miserable cleric who once had fallen asleep in the chapel while waiting for Charlemagne; he had dreamt of a giant who intended to lead the royal steward Liutfrid to hell on a camel for embezzling the king's resources.[9] But to speculate on the real connections that might lie behind saintly dreams and saintly dreamers is an idle activity. The most that we can say is that the living Charlemagne, seated on his stone throne in Aachen, and Anskar, the dream voyager of Rimbert's history, both looked out upon starry heavens that glimmered and shone like glass towards Christ enthroned in transcendent glory. Thus another Carolingian monk had fallen to dreaming after receiving news of the mighty Charlemagne's death. So politicized were the monks of the ninth century that the king, no matter how distant in fact, seemed close at hand and a solid reference point in their imaginations. Like the saints who loomed so large in their thoughts, Charlemagne had also come to hold an imaginable place in the monastic mind.

Before confronting the dream critics of Charlemagne, we shall need to spend some time in the first twenty years of the ninth century, when a different opinion of Charlemagne was taking shape. At his death in 814, Charlemagne's reputation stood very high indeed, but a powerful undertow of roiling criticism had begun to drag it down. In administrative terms, the last decade of the emperor's life has been characterized as disastrous. The emperor was old and had settled his court permanently at Aachen, which he rarely left. But power in the early Middle Ages was far too personal for a king to be able to rule his kingdom from one fixed point for very long. It was his personal presence in the far-flung corners of his land that commanded respect, for he carried justice about in his person and his word was literally law. When Charlemagne ceased to move throughout the land, he was forced to rely on his agents, and they could not always be trusted. Thus, although the administrative agencies of the Carolingian court were precocious for the early Middle Ages, they remained weak. Even the *missi dominici,* the cornerstone of the Carolingian administrative edifice, were often corrupt in Charlemagne's last years.[10]

When Louis the Pious succeeded Charlemagne in early 814, he immediately informed his nobles that he was keenly aware of the injustices that had been committed in his father's time. At his first assembly as sole emperor, Louis sent out envoys to dispense justice throughout the land and to relieve the oppression of the people. Behind this act of reform lay the complaint that had been so slow to surface: that Charlemagne had done much that was wrong and had allowed even worse to be done in his name.[11] The process should be a familiar one, since throughout history new rulers have often begun their reigns by blaming their predecessors. On occasion this natural drive towards reform goes further, since the very reputation of the old governors must sometimes be discredited before new governors feel free to step forward, untrammeled, into their own moment in time.

Now, if Charlemagne's administrative capacities at the end of his life were weak, his personal life was downright messy. In high dudgeon, Gibbon surveyed this negative reputation:

> Without injustice to his fame, I may discern some blemishes in the sanctity and greatness of the restorer of the western empire. Of his moral virtues, chastity is not the most conspicuous; but the public happiness could not be materially injured by his nine wives or concubines, the various in-

dulgence of meaner or more transient amours, the multitude of his bastards whom he bestowed on the church, and the long celibacy and licen-
tious manners of his daughters, whom the father was suspected of loving
with too fond a passion.[12]

The indignation expressed here was not Gibbon's invention, for he, too, was a
reader of a Carolingian dream text.

But if Wetti supplied Gibbon with the tone of his moral disapproval, Einhard
proved to be an insufficient counterweight and may have unwittingly furnished
the historian with inside information. Writing in the mid-820s, Einhard was, I
believe, attempting to answer Wetti and the other dream critics. One only needs
to look at his emphasis. For Einhard, Charlemagne was, above all else, a family
man: a good brother, dutiful son, attentive husband, and loving father. The biographer confessed, and others confirmed, that the very reason for his right and
duty to compose the biography was his special intimacy with the royal family at
court.[13] It should not, therefore, surprise us to find Einhard striving to cast the
emperor's domestic life in a positive light, obscuring its occasional blemishes
where necessary. For instance, he claimed that, despite Carloman's quarrel-
some and jealous nature, his brother Charlemagne had endured his animosity
with such patience that it seemed marvelous to all.[14] He had treated his sister
Gisela and his mother Bertrada with the greatest respect. The vocabulary with
which Einhard described these relationships—*patientia, in magno honore,
colebat, cum summa reuerentia, magna pietate*—reveals the warm and effu-
sive nature of his domestic portrait of Charlemagne.

Yet the biographer turned laconic when dealing with Charlemagne's bed-
mates, a purposeful vagueness that is reminiscent of the summary treatment of
genealogical materials found in Paul the Deacon's *Acts of the Bishops of Metz*,
which Einhard knew and Thegan was to adapt in wonderful fashion later.[15]
Feigning ignorance, for instance, Einhard passed over the marriage and repu-
diation of the Lombard princess sometimes known as Desiderata without remark.[16] He described the marriages to Hildegard, Fastrada, and Liutgard in
terms of the royal children they produced. The four concubines who succeeded
these wives were listed in even more cursory fashion, for, whereas the wives
had had their origins and, in the case of Hildegard, a noble lineage outlined, the
concubines and their children were merely named. The lack of much detail
about any of Charlemagne's companions should not go unnoticed by the reader,
for it has the effect of reducing the women with whom Charlemagne shared his
bed to mere childbearers.

Thus the reader is carried rapidly towards the compassionate relationship that existed between Charlemagne and his children. Both his sons and his daughters were trained in the liberal arts as their father had been. He taught the boys to ride and hunt while the girls were educated in the domestic arts. Charlemagne loved his children so much, we are told, that he could not bear to be parted from them. They rode beside him on journeys under the watch of select guards and at home they dined with their father. His daughters were so beautiful, said the biographer, that Charlemagne always kept them close to him and would not, despite some unfortunate incidents, allow them to marry and leave home. This natural affection was also bestowed on his grandchildren, whom he gathered near him at court, and on friends like Pope Hadrian, whom he cherished like a brother. But what touched this proud father most, according to Einhard, were the deaths of his children, three of whom preceded him to the grave. Despite the greatness of his spirit, Charlemagne could not contain his grief; he wept openly.[17]

An impression of fatherly affection pervades chapter 19 of the *Life of Charlemagne* and is followed, quite naturally, in chapter 20 by an account of Charlemagne as the unfortunate and suffering head of a family. Pepin the Hunchback, the illegitimate eldest son of Charlemagne, rose against his father with a group of Frankish nobles at his side. Pepin was ultimately captured, tonsured, and bundled off to the monastery of Prüm. An earlier conspiracy had also ended in death, exile, or blindness for the conspirators. In neither case was Charlemagne at fault, according to his biographer:

> The cruelty of Queen Fastrada is believed to have been the cause and source of these conspiracies, for in both cases men rose against the king because, in consenting to the cruelty of his wife, he seemed to have deviated excessively from the goodness of his nature and from his usual gentleness.[18]

Einhard here echoed the apologetic tone of the *Royal Frankish Annals,* noting that after these incidents Charlemagne returned to his gentle ways and forever after gained praise at home and abroad.

But Einhard went too far in extolling the domestic character of his emperor. He came to the rescue of Charlemagne's reputation at all its most vulnerable points, because he must have been aware of the widespread criticisms of Charlemagne's domestic life that had surfaced in the 820s. What has been too little appreciated about Einhard's biography is that it was not a first and favorable portrait of the emperor—for surely that had been painted earlier by his own poets Angilbert and Theodulf, and perhaps by Einhard himself—but an apology, and Einhard, like all apologists, overreaches.

To blame Fastrada for the conspiracies against her husband was to shift to the queen blame that properly belonged to the king. She was simply a safer target, as both Einhard and the royal Frankish annalist must have known.[19] Indeed, there was much in Charlemagne's personal life that wanted apology. Even in his own lifetime, Charlemagne must have heard the complaints. His mother Bertrada, try as she might, could not heal the rift between her two sons. When Carloman died prematurely, his wife and children, probably fearing (with good cause) the old mayoral trick of shipping enemies and relatives off to monasteries, fled to the king of the Lombards, Charlemagne's enemy. Bertrada herself, with very little honor indeed, was unceremoniously relieved of her matriarchal position in Charlemagne's house after the death of Carloman. The divorce of Desiderius's daughter also brought forth criticism from Adalhard, Charlemagne's cousin, but Einhard ignored it.[20]

After Liutgard's death in 800, Charlemagne declined to remarry, probably so as not to complicate the matter of his succession. The emperor had more than enough legitimate sons to succeed him, or so it must have seemed when he divided up his lands between his three living sons in 806.[21] But this bold, if informal, strategy for managing his family was bound to call forth ecclesiastical censure, since it led Charlemagne to live in open sin with a series of concubines.

By the same token, his treatment of his daughters was also subordinate to dynastic needs. Charlemagne feared that legitimate children born to his royal daughters would lead to trouble for his direct male line. His bitter enemy Tassilo had been the product of just such a marriage with one of Charles Martel's daughters.[22] Charlemagne wished, we must suppose, to keep his own daughters close by and preferred to have them bear (if it was unavoidable) illegitimate children who could not easily establish rival royal dynasties. Thus, Charlemagne's domestic life was untidy and left wide open to criticism, because he had deliberately subordinated it to his deeper dynastic designs.

But the churchmen of the early ninth century can have only half guessed the reasons for Charlemagne's improprieties. They were, after all, not the best observers of royal politics, being both too close to the court and too distant from the counts of the countryside. If Einhard understood why Charlemagne remained unmarried at the end of his life, he never stopped to provide an explanation. We need to recognize that a king as powerful as Charlemagne had no need to explain his dynastic strategies to bookish clerics and royal servants, especially if these plans offended ecclesiastical mores. Indeed, these men did not fully share in Charlemagne's world. They rarely seem to have seen the world of aristocratic excess—of banquet halls, goblets overflowing with wine, beautiful serving girls, and vainglorious Germanic poems—to which Charlemagne also belonged, or at least they never described it, but the noble Thegan would, albeit cursorily.[23]

While Charlemagne lived, direct criticism of his family life was almost never voiced by his court scholars; he was, after all, their patron, and they provided only official portraits.[24] Yet these scholars were not without strategies of indirection, as the attack on Fastrada revealed. If Charlemagne could not be criticized safely, his court could be: it was frequently characterized as a place of loose values. Hibernicus Exul urged the girls of the court to pursue chastity, because he must have known of the temptations in the palace. Alcuin's critical attitude can be inferred from his condemnation of the lustful kings of Britain. In 797 he urged Osbert to warn King Offa about the dangers of adultery, lest he insult God and lose his throne. His letters to Charlemagne contain no reproach, but he did urge young King Pepin to be happy with the wife of his youth and to avoid other men's women, for in this way the blessing of God would lead to a long line of descendants.[25] To Gundrada, Adalhard's sister, who was at court in 802, he wrote:

> Let the maidens be as noble in character as they are in parentage. Let them not serve carnal desire, but the teaching of Christ. Let them live honestly in the sight of men and worthily in the sight of God. Let them do penance for past deeds and beware future ones . . . for all things that we do in secret are known to God and, even if they are not voiced, conscience cannot hide them.[26]

The scandals of Charlemagne's court can hardly have been a secret to Alcuin, even in distant Tours. Clerics, he came to believe, risked losing their spiritual lives amidst the excesses of the court. But Alcuin died without seeing the scandalous last decade of the emperor's life, with its string of concubines and illegitimate offspring.[27]

But what Alcuin missed Louis the Pious could not ignore. In 814 the new emperor arrived in Aachen convinced of the need to reform the empire. German scholars have called the first phase of this reform program *die Säuberung der Pfalz,* the cleansing of the palace, for Louis was shocked by the reputation of his father's court. He believed that his sisters' activities had stained his father's house, yet he, too, feared the prospect of having them marry powerful nobles. His solution to the problem was very different from his father's: after an investigation conducted by his agents, he banned the entire female company from court. He sent his sisters to the royal lands and monasteries bestowed on them by their father, and personally provided for those who lacked properties.[28] Thus, the beloved daughters of Charlemagne, in whom he had taken so much delight, were cast off very quickly by their reforming brother.[29] Indeed, only those sisters "conceived by his father in just matrimony" were allowed to share in Charlemagne's treasure. Finally, before he would divide the empire among his own sons, he enjoined them to enter into legal marriages.[30] Thus, at a practical level, Louis found a technique for interpreting his father's will to his own advantage and for controlling property and dynastic power. But at a moral level he seemed to draw a devastating, if widely shared, conclusion about the moral failings of his father's domestic life.

Louis followed the banishment of the ladies from court with a general investigation into the moral condition of the palace and of Aachen. Officials were dispatched to discover if any prostitutes or *igroti homines* were kept at court.[31] Even members of the imperial family were to be investigated. His agents pursued their inquiries at Aachen in the homes of nobles, Jews, merchants, bishops, abbots, counts, and even men who were not Louis's vassals. Prostitutes and other sexual offenders were to be whipped in the marketplace of Aachen. The emperor received weekly reports from his agents about their findings. With this extensive investigation of behavior in the capital, Louis, in effect, continued his condemnation of the moral slide of the kingdom during Charlemagne's last decade. But if the official line was that the "naughty princesses" had been the only blemish on his father's house, then Louis could have stopped after they had been banished. Indeed, he could have shifted blame from his father to his sisters, as Einhard was later prepared to do. But the continuing investigation suggests that Louis thought otherwise and intended to go further.

By making the cleansing of the palace the first stage of a larger reform of the empire, Louis seemed to suggest that the moral health of Francia as a whole depended upon the behavior of those resident at the royal court, especially members of his own family. If the sexual customs of Carolingian kings and Frankish nobles had once existed behind drawn curtains through which censorious clerical eyes had rarely dared to peek, Louis threw those curtains open, baring the noble bedroom to the cold stare of public scrutiny. The writers of the *Fürstenspiegel,* those advice manuals written for princes, would soon state that it was the king's first duty to preserve his own purity and that of his household.[32] If Charlemagne had been born into a world that had been little concerned with the domestic side of his public persona, his reputation would be judged by a posterity that expected a great deal. Although even Charlemagne's own poets had flattered him with images of his splendid family, there is, in Einhard's emphasis on his domestic perfection, a note of anachronism and deliberate distortion. What lay behind this was, I think, the work of the dreamers, for they lived in that reforming world made by Louis, a world in which public criticism of the private lives of Carolingian kings had become possible.

Yet Louis's criticism of Charlemagne remained cautiously indirect; his father's crimes were never specifically cited and his name had not, in fact, surfaced in the charges. If Louis had opened the curtains leading to his father's bedroom, it was to be the dreamers who dared to enter. In a series of dream texts that appeared in the 820s, Charlemagne's domestic reputation came under critical scrutiny. Without that oneiric examination, Einhard's apology need never have been written, or, at least, its emphasis on Charlemagne as a superior family man might have been different in tone.

These dreams will transport us to an infernal world that will seem familiar at first. But a word of caution is in order here: the Carolingian conception of the otherworld was not Dante's. It was a roughly horizontal landscape, with features such as rivers and mountains that remind us of terrestrial topography. But the dramatic verticality of Dante's otherworld, with its multidimensional and hierarchical character, did not figure in Carolingian dreams. Even purgatory was not yet a well defined space or a rigid category of experience. Hence, as Jacques Le Goff has stressed, we find talk of purgatorial fires and the adjective *purgatorius* rather than a sharply delineated idea of purgatory itself. But the Carolingians knew that before the Last Judgment men and women must occupy some intervening space between heaven and hell, just as Drythelm had.[33] This was, however fluid and however provisional, the awesome otherworld of the Carolingian dreamer.

Romans would have felt themselves to be in a familiar, if strangely distorted, landscape in a Carolingian dream; Virgil, on the other hand, should have collapsed in disbelief at the exotic physical world into which Dante placed him. Carolingian dreamers imagined an infernal world constructed on a small scale, where the distance between destinations was short and walkable. Thus even the world of dreams was as highly localized, as the early Middle Ages was. Indeed, the dream traveler could often look from one state of purgation to another, or smell the sweet fragrance of flowers drifting over from a nearby place. But if the visionary landscape of the Carolingian dreamer was one of intimate dimensions, where both sinners and saints could be seen with a sweep of the eyes, it was still a perilous terrain. Dream travelers climbed small mountains, descended into dark valleys, and fought off suffocating heat, but at least they were on the move. The residents of this otherworld were stuck, according to their merits, in purgatorial versions of paradise and hell. For sinners, the proximity of the blessed added immeasurably to their suffering and remorse. Caught in between in a purgative state of being were those who had sinned, but not mortally, and those who could receive the benefits of intercession.[34] Charlemagne was one of these, for his sins seemed to demand purgation and intercession. Carolingian writers, at this point in the 820s, ceased to speak solely of the dreams of ancient, long dead, and distant kings; political oneirocriticism was pulled closer to the concerns of their own time and their own kings, and Charlemagne had been the most important of these.

The simplest of the three dreams, although its date of composition remains unknown, is the *Vision of Rotcharius*.[35] Its monastic writer claimed that he was repeating exactly what Rotcharius had reported and was sending it to his abbot for the edification of their fellow brothers. On the morning of 6 May of some unknown year, the monk Rotcharius had been lying ill in an infirmary when he fell into a deep sleep. An angel shimmering with light appeared to him, casting his brilliance over the monastery and church of Saint Benedict. Without the exchange of a single word, the angel led Rotcharius along a road of wondrous scenery until they came to an immense and beautiful mansion. Rather than resembling a stone or wooden house, the mansion was fashioned in the form of a throne. There he saw the multitude of the saints gathered, radiating a reddish glow so intense that he could barely gaze upon them. Among the saints, he saw Charles, shining brilliantly. The king was not the last of the saints, but stood somewhere in the middle of the host. He spoke to Rotcharius, saying: "Son, know that I am Charles and that, on account of the most devout prayers of those faithful to God, I was rescued from punishment and placed in this glory."[36] The dreamer declared that he had also seen another mansion in which Christ himself, the *Majestas Domini,* was known to live, but he could not look upon Christ's beauty because of an overpowering light that blazed forth. In a third mansion, placed lower than the others and filled with deformity and darkness, the dreamer saw a crowd of clerics and other people who were being tormented by a black demon. The demon set fires under the sinners that ran from their feet up to their chests. To add to their misery, he continously poured boiling water over their heads, which he drew from a bubbling pot. Three of Rotcharius's brothers were suffering these endless tortures, and the dreamer heard their horrible screams.

The *Vision of Rotcharius* contains a series of stark opposites: light and dark, blessedness and deformity, the ordered company of the saints and a chaotic crowd of sinners. The great mansion the dreamer saw was that heavenly house foreseen by Paul. In the otherworld men and women were thought to live in common dwellings (*domus*) according to their merits, or so Gregory the Great had supposed.[37] Charlemagne, we are meant to understand, had moved from one mansion to the other, for prior to attaining his present place within the circle of the saints, he had undergone some form of punishment. Neither Rotcharius nor Charlemagne tells us why the king deserved this penalty, but they never denied his guilt. Indeed, one wonders if it were not just this sort of scenario that lay behind the unknown monk's funeral dirge for Charlemagne: he had prayed for Charlemagne to take up his proper place among the saints, because he must have worried that the emperor had found a less-blessed place of repose.

Rotcharius's dream, however, is not primarily about Charlemagne, but about monastic rectitude. The dreamer may have begun by visiting Charlemagne and the saints, but he finished with his true audience: the monks of his own monastery who needed to know what awaited their evil brothers in the beyond. Thus, his dream concluded with three specific monks—Isachar, Gaudius, and Winemundus—who were, he said, still alive at the time. Rotcharius saw them being foully tormented in the otherworld, two while sitting, the other while standing. Another monk, while later tending to one of the three in the infirmary, fell asleep and heard a voice say that this sick monk was to be perpetually beaten with switches, thus confirming Rotcharius's dream and suggesting that the monk's crime may have been of a sexual nature. In the marketplace of Aachen, sexual offenders had been whipped just a few years before, and Wetti would see the same punishment in his dream (see Fig. 13). The king's appearance in the dream is exemplary, however, for the fate of Charles demonstrated the promise of redemption and the efficacy of prayer. If even the greatest of men could suffer otherworldly torment for the sins he had committed, then surely anyone could. The sequence also suggested the corollary: that if even the greatest of sinners could be released from punishment because of prayer, then anyone might. Charlemagne's place in Rotcharius's dream, therefore, depended to some degree upon his preeminence as king—"I am Charles," he had announced, even though the monk already knew who he was—and upon his special standing as sinner.

Wilhelm Wattenbach thought that the monastery mentioned in the dream text might have been Saint-Benoît-sur-Loire (Fleury), which is not impossible. The monks of Fleury were interested in the *Dialogues* of Gregory, and Adrevald, later in the century, would dabble in dream literature. But one can find the names Rotcarius, Isger, Gaudius, and Winimunt in the rich ninth-century necrologies of Reichenau.[38] Given the similarities between the *Vision of Rotcharius* and other dream texts associated with Reichenau, we must now turn our attention to the world of Wetti.

Early in November 824, Wetti, a monk of Reichenau, died. Several days before, he had fallen into a stupor after drinking a medicinal potion and had had a very strange dream in which he saw evil spirits dressed like clerics, good spirits dressed like monks, and an angel enrobed in shockingly unangelic purple garb. Wetti lectured this unlikely angel: "you ought to work even harder now, because we humans are weaker in times such as these."[39] The dreamer seemed to know that something was seriously wrong with his drug-induced dream, which had the delusional makings of what people in the 1960s might have called a "bad trip." He woke abruptly, cutting short the dream, and told the monks at his side what he had just seen and heard.

But Wetti was not finished, for after asking the monks to read out the beginning of the last book of Gregory's *Dialogues* he fell asleep again, and this time entered into a vast and panoramic dream of the otherworld. The same angel appeared to him once more, but he was now properly dressed in white and led Wetti along a wondrous path where he saw towering mountains and rivers of fire. There he noticed many priests and the women they had defiled, both groups standing in raging fire up to their genitals. Every third day, he was told, their genital organs were lashed with switches. The angel explained that these priests had wantonly pursued worldy advantage and had devoted themselves to the concerns of the palace. Surrounded by the distracting delights of court, they had taken up with prostitutes.

After passing a place where monks were undergoing purgation, the dreamer came upon a suffering Charlemagne:

> Wetti said that he had seen standing there a certain prince, who had once ruled Italy and the Roman people, and his genitals were being mangled by the teeth of a beast, although the rest of his body remained free from injury. Wetti was struck with violent bewilderment, wondering how so great a man, who had appeared almost alone among others in this modern age in defense of the Catholic faith and direction of the holy church, could have been inflicted with such a hideous punishment. His angelic guide quickly answered that although he had done many wonderful and praiseworthy things accepted by God, for which he would not be deprived of his reward, nevertheless, alongside these other goods offered to God, he had

given himself up to the delight of debauchery and had chosen to end his long life in this state. It was as though [he thought] the small obscenity and license allowed to human weakness could be covered over and completely hidden by the weight of his great goods. Nevertheless, said the guide, he is predestined to [eternal] life in the company of the elect.[40]

In Scandinavian sagas, dreamers are often chased by savage animals who represent their enemies, and in Carolingian art animals can be seen attacking men (Fig. 14). But the symbol of the animal gnawing at the genitals of Charlemagme is apparently unique, a specific punishment for the crime of lust.[41] There was some general precedent in the *Vision of Saint Paul* for particular punishments to be assigned for specific sins, but it must have been shocking and unexpected for a ninth-century reader to encounter Charlemagne suffering in this hideous fashion. The symbolism of the punishment is transparent: when Charlemagne gave into his lust, he gave into his animal nature and should suffer accordingly. He was being punished by the sin itself. The Carolingians seem to have admired animal strength, and even monks continued to use names like Wolf (Lupus), but no one wanted to be associated with animal behavior. As other noble Carolingians did, Charlemagne apparently wore his fur jacket with the hairside turned inward toward his skin so as not to look to the outside world like a savage beast. That Charlemagne could be punished at all was, of course, sanctioned by the Bible: "for there shall be a most severe judgment for them that rule . . . : the mighty shall be mightily tormented."[42] In Wetti's oneiric preoccupation with sexual sin, Charlemagne may not be the most outrageous sinner, but he certainly was the most famous. He stood alone on an illumined plain, all attention focused on him and his frightening plight. Thus, a moral spotlight isolated him and his sin for all to see.

After leaving Charlemagne, Wetti immediately came upon a great stash of stolen loot, mounds of silver vases and horses covered in shining cloth, which recall the scenes painted in the psalters (see Figs. 7–8). His guide informed him that these riches had belonged to the counts of the kingdom. The angel charged that the counts were no longer the defenders of justice but the doers of injustice; they were the cause of much of the bribery, thievery, and persecution at work in the world. Next the angel led Wetti to a place where he saw the ineffable light of Christ in the presence of the ranks of saints, and there his own fate was discussed. The angel informed Wetti that he must try to correct the abuses that existed in the world, particularly sodomy and concubinage. When Wetti protested that he was unsuited to proclaim this message in public, the angel informed him that he must do what God had commanded. He also must speak out against abuses in monasteries, notably against the excesses of gluttony, drunkenness, elaborate dress, and pride. Greed, too, needed to be condemned, for there were men who had an unquenchable thirst for earthly riches. Wetti's dream was one that called for a fundamental reform of the vices that polluted all the orders of the Carolingian world. When the new day dawned and monastic rounds permitted, Wetti told his abbot Erlebald, the senior monk Heito, and some others the details of his great dream. He insisted that it be written down and circulated, which both Heito and Walahfrid Strabo did within the next two years.

But Heito, formerly abbot of Reichenau and bishop of Basle until 822 or 823, declined to report everything Wetti told him. The angel had given the dreamer the names of the bad counts, priests, and monks, but Heito dropped almost all of these from his prose account. Such shrewdness suggests that Heito was conscious of the practical advantages and plasticity of political oneirocriticism, since he could reveal some things and hide others. There was, of course, only one recently dead *princeps Italiae*, a title that designated the emperor, but Heito chose not to name Charlemagne directly. Even the details of his sin remained unspecified, though its sexual nature was unmistakably represented in symbol. Thus, the pieces of Charlemagne's sordid domestic life—its illicit affairs, concubines, bastards, and wanton daughters—were blended together in a lumpen mass of sexual debauchery. Not even Charlemagne's good deeds could hide the disgusting manner in which he had ended his life.

The guide assured the shocked dreamer of the ultimate redeemability of the emperor. He must suffer proper purgation, but he would finally reap the reward for his good deeds. In the 820s, both Einhard, who was writing a biography, and Ermold, who was writing a poem in honor of the new emperor, wanted to remind Louis of the good deeds of Charlemagne and of his deserved place in heaven.[43] Theirs was a response, one fervent, the other muted, to the charge that Wetti had laid and Heito had begun to circulate.

But the dream assault on Charlemagne's reputation was still somewhat vague, since no one as yet had dared to name him. Walahfrid Strabo was fourteen or fifteen years old in 824 and already a monk at Reichenau. He had, in fact, spent a few hours with the dying Wetti after his great dream, acting as his secretary. But it was in 827, as a young monk newly arrived at the monastery of Fulda, full of ambition and poetic genius, that Walahfrid decided to rewrite Wetti's dream in verse. His poetic version was, therefore, to reflect a mixture of sources. Heito's prose version was to stand at the core of his poem, but he would mix in his own independent witness and some new information. And there at last, in Walahfrid's first great poem, Charlemagne was named, but in a fashion that was, for spoken poetry at least, still silent. Walahfrid informed Grimald, to whom he sent the poem at court, that he who looked carefully at the text would find hidden names. Indeed, at the point where the fate of the *princeps Italiae* is being described, the first letter of each line spells out, in acrostic fashion, CAROLVS IMPERATOR.[44]

In Walahfrid's sophisticated rendering of the scene, which follows Heito's details, we once again meet Charlemagne, the ruler of Ausonia (that is, Italy) and the Roman people, on an illumined plain, rooted to the ground, as an animal tears at his genitals. Wetti, in a state of profound shock, wondered how this great man, who had in this modern age promoted learning, defended the faithful, and upheld justice, could suffer so.

> . . . In his cruciatibus, inquit,
> Restat ob hoc, quoniam bona facta libidine turpi
> Fedauit, ratus inlecebras sub mole bonorum
> Absumi et uitam uoluit finire suetis
> Sordibus. Ipse tamen captabit opimam,
> Dispositum a domino gaudens inuadet honorem.

> [He remains in these agonies, [the angel] said, because
> He fouled his good acts with disgusting lust.
> He was convinced that his pleasures would be buried
> Beneath the great weight of his good deeds and
> Chose to end his life in habitual squalor.
> Yet, even so, he will attain the blessed life and
> Joyfully enter into the honor laid up for him by the Lord.][45]

Thus, in Walahfrid's version, the dream image of Charlemagne had finally achieved exactness, and the connection between sinner and sin was finally nailed down. By supplying in this secret fashion the names previously withheld, Walahfrid may have hoped not to interfere with the main outlines of Wetti's narration as reported by Heito, but he may also have retained some of the old reluctance to name Charlemagne outright. Still, he wanted no one to mistake the identity of this *princeps Italiae*. No longer could the court or the princesses be blamed for the sexual excesses of the palace. Acrostics, which had so often been employed by Carolingian poets for fun and for panegyrical purposes, allowed Walahfrid to leap across the yawning chasm of social division that must have separated an eighteen-year-old monk from the great Charlemagne and from the startling truth, for though Charlemagne had done many good things, he had ended his life in sexual squalor.

Wetti had dreamed that a man could not escape in death the evil deeds that he had done in life. Walahfrid wanted no one to misundertand this cautionary truth, so he added an explanation not to be found in Heito's version. The angel, he said, meant to signify that people who spend their lives following good habits should beware lest they lose everything through some single crime and all their good works slip away in utter ruination. Men such as Charlemagne, he explained, carefully collect water, but they store it in a cracked pot. What they gather with great care will pour out through a hole if the vessel of their lives is not whole. The image was Jeremiah's. Then, in an ironical thrust at King Charlemagne, Walahfrid wrote:

Omnibus in rebus uitam moderetur in aruis,
Qui cupit in caelis regnum retinere perenne.

[Let him who wishes to hold an enduring kingdom in heaven,
Govern his life in every respect while here on earth.][46]

Thus, Charlemagne remained, as he had been in the dream of Rotcharius, a symbol of the high brought low; he was an everyman or, at least, all people could learn from his example a truth about the danger of a mismanaged life. The faithful, through alms, prayers, and masses, could intercede for sinners, even famous ones such as Charles, but it was the living who learned through these dreams the hard lessons of the dead. Perhaps part of what worried the Reichenau monks about Charlemagne's case was that he may never have repented his sins; it fell, therefore, to Wetti and the other dreamers to investigate, to report, and to warn other powerful people to do penance before it was too late.

But if Rotcharius and Wetti lead us to the central example of Charlemagne, the poor woman of Laon will lead us via Charlemagne to Louis the Pious. While rapt in ecstasy, this unnamed woman was supposed to have seen many remarkable things, which she was able to describe when she returned to a normal state of being.[47] A man in the habit of a monk had led her to a place where she saw the peaceful bliss of the saints and the awful punishment of the wrongdoers. There she observed the *princeps Italiae* (that is, Charlemagne) in torment and saw other famous people placed either in triumphant splendor or in a state of punishment. When she asked her guide if that prince would ever be given eternal life, he answered that he would indeed be released from his torment if his son, the Emperor Louis, charitably arranged for seven memorial services for the dead on his behalf.[48] Pico, who had been the friend of the king, was seen lying on his back writhing in agony while two black demons poured boiling gold into his mouth. They told him, as they poured, that because he had been unable to satisfy his thirst while in the world, he must now drink his fill. Next the poor woman came across Queen Ermengard (the first wife of Louis, who had died in 818), also placed in torment: three toothlike rocks had grasped her head, chest, and back and were violently pulling her into the depths. The queen shouted out to the poor woman that she should seek out the assistance of her lord, the emperor, so that she might be released from the wretched condition in which she found herself. That the emperor might know that she was truly sent by Ermengard, the queen gave the poor woman a sure proof, something which until then had been known only to Louis and to herself. The queen said that, in the crisis of her deposition, she had spoken to Louis privately in a garden. He would immediately recognize this event, since until then the conversation had been hidden to all.

The poor woman and her monastic guide continued on until they came to a wall that ran straight up to heaven. In front of it there was another wall that was entirely covered with golden letters. When the woman asked what this was, her guide informed her that beyond it was the terrestrial paradise, and that people could not enter there unless their names were inscribed on the wall. When the guide commanded the poor woman to read, she protested that she had never learned her letters. Nevertheless, he said, she must read. When she did, she found the name of Bernard, once king, written in brilliant letters and shining more splendidly than any other there. King Louis's name, however, was so faint that it could scarcely be read. Why, the poor woman asked, had that name been erased? The guide explained that before Louis had brought about the murder of Bernard, no name had been brighter than his. But the murder of Bernard led to the erasure of Louis's name. The guide ordered the poor woman to report these things to the king, but she failed to carry out her mission. After this the guide urged her once again to perform the task that had been assigned to her, but she kept her silence and would not approach her king. Finally, on a third occasion the guide returned to ask why she had not carried out God's command. When she protested that she was a common person and dared not publicize such things, the poor woman was told she would be deprived of her sight until she had related everything in the presence of the king. Many days later, the blind woman came before the king, told all, and was rewarded with the return of her vision.

The *Vision of the Poor Woman of Laon* transports us to the years between 814 and 824 and to the first great crisis of Louis the Pious's crisis-ridden reign. Once again we encounter Charlemagne waiting for his rightful intercession and redemption. As in the *Vision of Rotcharius* and the *Vision of Wetti*, he was the first named individual seen in the otherworld. Indeed, Charlemagne had become something of a way station, the first important stopping point for the political dream traveler of the 820s. Here, however, the nature of his sin was left entirely unspecified, though the author of the vision has left us with the distinct impression that everyone already knew what it was, that it was so familiar that it was unnecessary to raise the matter again. What lay behind this tone of familiarity was the fame, I think, of Wetti's vision. But something had changed, for Charlemagne's rescue now depended upon his son, who was the true subject of the poor woman's vision.

Even the characterization of Charlemagne here as the *princeps Italiae* may take on another and more suggestive association. For the title may refer to Charlemagne's direct and inheritable possession of the kingdom of Italy, which he had placed under the control of his son Pepin, who had died in 810. From Pepin the land had passed to the legal control of his son, Charlemagne's grandson, Bernard, and the vision of the poor woman chiefly concerns his fate.

But if the poor woman learned about Bernard, the message she bore was one designed for Louis. Indeed, the afterlives of Charlemagne, Ermengard, and Louis himself all depended, according to the vision, upon the actions of the emperor. Only he could set right what had gone terribly wrong. On behalf of Charlemagne, he needed only to offer seven memorial services in order to secure eternal life for his father. All the other suffering wrongdoers were set in such dire straits that no easy remedy seemed at hand.

Every person in the vision had been contaminated in some way by Louis's imperial policy, except for innocent Bernard, who was destroyed by it. When Louis assumed independent control of Francia upon his father's death in early 814, he was suspicious of the old guard, men like Theodulf who had seemed to be too personally attached to Charlemagne and the old order of the empire. Relatives like his cousins Adalhard and Wala, whose positions had grown stronger in the later court of Charlemagne and who had had a special attachment to Pepin, the king of Italy, and then to his son Bernard, were sent to monasteries. Bernard's five sisters, who had become a fixture at Charlemagne's palace, were also sent away from court with the rest of the company of women.

The imperial title and, in fact, the concept of empire meant something different for Louis the Pious, something all at once more Christian—hence the recrowning of Louis as emperor by the new pope in 816—and more emphatically unitary. But the constitutional document known as the *Ordinatio imperii,* which was issued in 817, finally brought into conflict two parties of thought on the nature and inheritability of Carolingian power. In naming Lothar as co-emperor and dividing Francia between his three sons, Louis did not mention the fate of his nephew Bernard. This was no oversight, since it continued Louis's policy of not recognizing illegitimate offspring. Despite Charlemagne's recognition of Bernard, Louis must have thought of him as the illegitimate son of his brother and, therefore, without a legal claim to hold Italy as a kingdom.[49] But then it could be argued that the *Ordinatio* itself flew in the face of Charlemagne's own political and personal designs, which had been to treat the imperial title as largely personal and only by happenstance inheritable—that happenstance being the survival of just one of his sons—and to recognize the Italian legacy of Bernard, son of his dead son. Thus, many lords and court churchmen, who retained a certain loyalty to Charlemagne's policies and promises or who had been associated with the government of Italy, probably considered the new division of territories and powers to be an unjust act. Reared with the idea of the ancestral precedence of Germanic partition, they cared little for Louis's amorphous idea of imperial unity. They saw only the unjust abandonment of Bernard and, perhaps worse, the overturning of Charlemagne's own wishes.

Not surprisingly, Bernard and his defenders resorted to open resistance, but their machinations were quickly quashed, and on 17 December 817 they submitted to Louis. The conspiracy stretched into the highest ranks of court and church, as Theodulf of Orléans, Anselm of Milan, and Wolfold of Cremona were all sent into exile. Early the next year, Bernard was blinded for his treachery and died shortly afterwards from his injuries. But we need to remember that blinding was not only a punishment for treason; it was also a developing dynastic strategy for removing forever the prospect of kingship from blood relatives without having to kill them. For, in the politics of the Carolingian world, where noble factions collected around different parts of the royal family, a king risked alienating powerful nobles if he murdered members of his own family. Moreover, the Carolingians had always prided themselves on not practicing the politics of Merovingian assassination. The last thing that Louis the Pious would have wanted was the death of Bernard, but he did want him out of the way.

The *Vision of the Poor Woman of Laon* is a particularly partisan document, one that implicitly criticized the new empire and new imperial tendencies of Louis the Pious. It also testified to the intense politicization of the Carolingian world early in Louis's reign, during the transitional years. Hubert Houben has suggested that Heito was the most likely author of the text, given his interest in dreams, his version of the *Vision of Wetti,* and the close correspondence between the two texts.[50] Heito's attachment to Charlemagne and his court must have been very strong and personal. Notker remembered the relationship as an intimate one. For instance, the emperor had appointed Heito to lead the mission sent to Emperor Nicephorus in Constantinople in 811–12. Perhaps of greater significance, he was one of the witnesses to Charlemagne's will as recorded by Einhard.[51] Thus, Heito may well have seen himself as one of the guardians of Charlemagne's legacy. But even he could not refrain from reporting Charlemagne's one great sin, perhaps one that, as a visitor to the late court of Charlemagne, he knew more about than most. The first time he had heard that public charge, however, had been at the bedside of Wetti; he was not its inventor. Yet in the poor woman's vision Charlemagne has been displaced as a figure of central importance. He leads the reader to Louis and Bernard, not to a more penetrating examination of his own sexual excesses. We also need to recall that Reichenau, where Heito retired after 823, had always had a particular loyalty to Charlemagne's son Pepin: the abbot Waldo, whom Heito and Walafrid were to remember in their versions of the dream of Wetti, had been Pepin's tutor in Pavia, and Gerold, Queen Hildegard's brother and Pepin's uncle, was to be richly remembered in the *Vision of Wetti.*[52] Thus, the sympathy for Bernard expressed in the text of the poor woman's rapture fits with what we might have expected of Heito of Reichenau's personal experiences and partisanship. In the memorial list of Reichenau compiled around 824, some of the men associated with Bernard's resistance were still listed as benefactors of the monastery.[53]

The *Vision of the Poor Woman of Laon* holds fast to a singular set of political concerns, declining to wander from place to place, topic to topic, as even Wetti had. On its polished surface, one can see the settling of old scores and the intimation of secret information. Pico, for instance, is better known to us as Count Bego of Paris. In the 780s, he was ordered by Charlemagne to assist young Louis in governing Aquitaine, but he was, in fact, to become Louis's friend, with all the power and all the resentment that such close friendship brought in the Carolingian world. He married one of Louis's daughters, and his death on 28 October 816 was said to have greatly disturbed the emperor. All that was remembered of him in the poor woman's vision was his greed, the legend of which must have already been spreading by the 820s and which was later to surface in texts associated with Rheims.[54] Heito himself may have witnessed some example of Bego's agressive pursuit of his own interests, but he was to punish him in the poor woman's vision with an ancient torture, one anticipated by

Wetti's image of nobles who were thirsty for riches.[55] As with Charlemagne's mauling by the beast, Bego's punishment matched his crime; it shared a certain symbolic identity with the sin.

Heito's purpose was not to rail against avarice, however; it was to damn the people closest to Louis, those who were deemed to be the architects of Bernard's fall. For one must suspect that Heito thought that Bego, this friend of the king, this *secundus a rege,* somehow stood behind the plot to rob Bernard of his kingdom, a plot hatched out of greed. Hence Bego's punishment in the vision supplied one explanation for Bernard's overthrow: Louis had been misled by an avaricious advisor. We need to recognize the political dynamic at work here, for the Carolingian elite was a rivalrous body of nobles jockeying for position around the king, but there was a price to be paid. In a moment of existential morosity, Northrop Frye once observed that "to participate in anything in human society means entering into a common bond of guilt. . . . Whatever we join contains evils and . . . what we accept is the guilt of belonging to it."[56] Perhaps men and women in the ninth century would not have fully appreciated the idea of the guilt of human association, but they would have understood its practical meaning. In the compromising and criss-crossing nature of top-heavy political power in Carolingian Europe, to make one powerful friend was to spawn a hundred jealousies. The resentment that percolates through the poor woman's vision is the rejection of the new court of Louis and of its powerful magnates, men like Bego.

Ermengard, who had died six months after Bernard, suffers in the vision as a member of that guilty gathering of selfish interests. As the mother of the beneficiaries of the *Ordinatio imperii,* Ermengard had a vested interest in the imperial neglect of Bernard, and her family seems to have had a role to play in encouraging Louis's imperial designs.[57] The vision seems to suggest that Ermengard, by greedily seeking power for her own sons, had set in motion the events that led directly to the murder of Bernard. Hence, the vision, like the earlier charge against Fastrada, implied that an evil queen might secretly enjoin her husband to perpetrate an unjust deed against his better nature. Did Heito once see, either in 817 when the *Ordinatio* was being framed or in 818 before Bernard was punished, Louis and his wife talking in some garden and from this fashion the secret sign that we encounter in the text, or was it merely a convention? Secret conversations of this sort were supposed to be a queenly tool; Saint Leoba, for instance, was said to have been called to court once for a secret meeting with Queen Hildegard, but she fled when she learned of the queen's purpose.[58] Ermengard spoke to the poor woman about her deposition in a time of crisis. Had she given witness against Bernard and the conspirators or does the reference to the deposition in a time of crisis refer to Bernard's overthrow? In either case, Heito had set Ermengard squarely in the middle of the horror of Bernard's murder. Thus, he supplied another explanation for Louis's awful action: he had been deceived by a wicked wife who was pursuing her own familial interests. The queen had been dragged down by her three sons who are symbolically represented by the three rocks pulling her deeper into the purgatorial pit. In the vision Ermengard is offered no assurance of escape from her torment, no release from her guilt.

In shockingly bold terms in the vision, Louis himself was directly tied to the murder of Bernard, but the vision would not tell him how he could atone for an act that could not be undone. The very imagery of the golden characters on the wall leading to paradise doubtless reflected Reichenau's preoccupation with commemorative lists of the dead, as though one could never gain entrance to heaven unless one were properly remembered in prayer on earth.[59] But dream literature cut deeper. Through its inner vision of the workings of the otherworld, it canceled any false notions about the pleasant reception the powerful might expect in heaven. The only individual in the vision sure to go to heaven was Bernard, whose name shone ever brighter on the wall leading to the security and comfort of the terrestrial paradise. Heito had combined two images here: the wall that demarcated paradise in Drythelm's vision and the golden columns recording the names of those destined for heaven in the *Vision of Saint Paul*.[60] The questions that loomed over the text were: What could Louis do to restore his name? What could he do to win the place in heaven that he had so meanly squandered?

Heito did not hesitate to back Louis into a dream corner from which the only means of escape was proper penance. The poor woman was thrice commanded to report the contents of her vision to the emperor. The fact that she was a poor woman, a *uilis*, with no involvement in the lives of the people she saw or in politics in general, was meant to establish her as a disinterested and believable witness. Indeed, she shared with Wetti an unwillingness to report controversial dream messages to the powerful in the waking world. That she claimed not to be able to read is a marvelous touch, for it must suggest that Heito was aware that this vision would be dismissed as a literary fabrication. Heito must have hoped his audience would believe that an unlearned woman would be unable to tell literary lies. Even the woman's reluctance to assume the roles of visionary and messenger was supposed to reinforce the idea that she had no personal interest in the high politics of the vision. But there was another theme at work here, since the very choice of a poor peasant woman, the most powerless of all people in the ninth century, was meant to suggest how deformed the time was and how obdurate the king's heart. Only a hard wall of wicked human resistance could have prevented God from speaking directly to the king in his own dreams, as he had once warned Charlemagne of mischief abroad in the land. Louis was like Pharaoh, needing others to dream divine things on his behalf. What God wanted from his king was penance, and he was prepared to blind the poor woman in order to convince her to carry his message to the king.

In the years between 817 and 825, Louis suffered from an ever-rising crescendo of criticism. Men like Heito did not forget the death of Bernard, nor would they let others forget it. The *Vision of the Poor Woman of Laon* stated boldly and anonymously one set of criticisms, but we cannot be sure that Louis ever learned of its contents. It may have merely reflected the devastating opinion of some men, but it was an opinion that Louis himself came to share, at least in part. For it is striking that the vision's call for royal action on behalf of Charlemagne and Louis matched what had happened at Attigny in 822. There the emperor performed public penance for the wrongs that he had inflicted upon Bernard and his followers, specifically Adalhard and Wala, who were recalled to their former positions of trust. More remarkably, Louis openly admitted at Attigny that he and his father had perpetrated injustices, for which he sought atonement and forgiveness.

If Louis was, as his churchmen claimed, a new Theodosius undergoing penance for his sins in 822, he was never able to wipe the slate clean.[61] When Louis read out the penitential statement prepared for him by his rebellious bishops in 833, the murder of Bernard would still be counted as one of his outstanding misdeeds. Thegan, in his biography of Louis, tried to absolve him of great guilt in the matter, since he said that Bernard had been in the clutches of wicked advisors and that Louis had not been fully informed about the plan to blind his nephew. According to Thegan, when the emperor heard that Bernard had died, he wept for a long time; then he performed penance in front of his bishops and gave charity to the poor "in order to cleanse his soul."[62]

It was in the refractory light of Louis's difficult first decade in power that the dreams of Rotcharius, Wetti, and the poor woman were published. If these texts shared themes, images, and language, it was because they belonged to what Brian Stock has called a textual community.[63] Heito must have stood near the very center of that gathering of readers and writers. In the devolving Carolingian political world after the death of Charlemagne, he had something special to say and an audience at Reichenau ready to listen. Wetti, too, properly belonged to that textual community. In other words, he may have had a dream, but what mattered were his actions upon waking, and these all had to do with publication: "obvious facts were imposed on me by a resounding voice," he said, "and must be directly and immediately shouted to the whole world." On waking, he first related the dream to those monks at his side, then he had them record the dream narrative on wax tablets, and finally he narrated the account again to senior monks, relying in part on the wax tablets. Moreover, Wetti spent the last day of his life sending out letters to acquaintances, which Walahfrid copied out, although he wished that, for clarity's sake, he had been allowed to improve them.[64] We need to remember, too, that Wetti's second dream was induced, in part, by his own desire to hear once again the visionary sequences from Gregory's *Dialogues*.

In the ninth century, Reichenau became a monastic laboratory for the collection, creation, and adaptation of dream texts, and Wetti, Heito, and Walahfrid were all workers in it. Between 835 and 842, Reginbert, a scribe of Reichenau, made a list of the books he had either donated or copied for the monastery. In the fifth volume noted on his list, he had gathered together a variety of vision materials, including Julian of Toledo's three books of prognostications, the fourth book of Gregory's *Dialogues,* the separate visions of Furseus and Barontus, material from Bede, and finally; "the book of the vision of Wetti, our brother, which Bishop Heito copied out and which Walahfrid, our brother, following that account, adorned with poetic verses."[65] Thus, Reginbert's dream collection can be described as an official one.

Heito himself, also a collector of dreams, went so far as to insert one of those dream stories into his account of Wetti's dream. Walahfrid was an obvious member of this dream factory, not only reworking Heito's prose account of Wetti's dream but probably later editing it as well. Houben compiled a fascinating graph of nine codices containing the *Vision of the Poor Woman of Laon;* all of these codices also contain Heito's version of Wetti's dream, and two contain Walahfrid's version. In the ninth century, Reichenau itself possessed a codex with the *Vision of Wetti* (presumably Heito's version) back to back with the *Vision of the Poor Woman of Laon.*[66] At about the same time, the nearby monastery of Saint-Gall acquired copies of the visions of Wetti and Barontus; today it possesses a ninth-century copy of the Latin version of the *Vision of Saint Paul,* one of the oldest in existence.[67]

If Reichenau became the first systematic purveyor of dream texts in the ninth century, it was not to be the last.[68] But the reasons for producing and spreading this kind of literature were not simple. Walahfrid, for instance, may have composed his *Vision of Wetti* at the request of Adalgis, another monk of Reichenau, but he sent the finished poem to Grimald, the court chaplain of Louis the Pious and his former teacher at Reichenau. In his preface, Walahfrid sought to secure Grimald's support and, perhaps, the greater patronage of the emperor. Indeed, late in the poem Walahfrid directly addressed Louis, appealing to him to end the practice of appointing widows as abesses.[69] What Walahfrid wanted, therefore, was one of the things that Wetti had warned against, attachment to the court. Within two years Walahfrid was at Aachen and was appointed tutor to the young Charles the Bald.

Heito's involvement in the production of the *Vision of Wetti* raises complex issues. He was a man who seems to have been interested in the stuff of dreams even before Wetti's experience. But one has to wonder about the degree of his interference with Wetti's story. He dropped the names of the famous people given to him by the sick monk and parenthetically inserted another dream text into Wetti's story. The *Vision of the Poor Woman of Laon* reflects the *Vision of Wetti* and not the reverse; the scene with Charlemagne is very similar, but less passionate in the poor woman's account; in both he is called the *princeps Italiae;* in both the visionaries were reluctant to carry messages of reform; and while Wetti had merely seen some nobles who were thirsty for riches, the poor woman saw Bego drinking gold. The progression of this imagery may suggest that Heito had learned from Wetti the conventions of dream literature, but the *Vision of the Poor Woman of Laon* was also informed by the politics of the late 820s, particularly Louis's penance. The text seemed to call for an already accomplished act, in part because Louis had not yet been forgiven. The *Vision of Rotcharius* is more difficult to place. If it was not a product of Reichenau, it was surely shaped by the other dream texts. Yet the many mysteries and the exact nature of the filter of narration that existed at Reichenau in the 820s are never likely to be revealed to us. The one certainty is that the monks of Reichenau and their friends worked towards opening an oneiric door on otherwise indeterminate and inaccessible truths. Together they uncovered what they must have thought of as a divinely inspired vehicle for carrying their particular reading of the world out from behind monastic walls to distant friends and a curious court.

Thus, in a complex and cumulative fashion, the door to full-blown political oneirocriticism opened at Reichenau, and Charlemagne was the first king discovered standing behind it. In his case, the point of these texts was straightforward: even the mightiest of men, king or noble, was not beyond correction. The politics of dreaming was, in the 820s, a politics of penance. The dreamers had come to warn misguided rulers of the risks they took in not repenting their sins straightaway. If Charlemagne had been deserving of clerical censure in the years following his death, surely Wetti and his reporters finally said what Louis the Pious himself had encouraged them to say. But by the time the *Vision of the Poor Woman of Laon* was written, Charlemagne had ceased to be the central focus of attention for political dreamers. His role was now exemplary and introductory. He leads the reader to other kings and to fresher sins, to wicked counts and to a murderous son.

The texture of these dream texts was essentially monastic: Rotcharius and the redactor of his dream, Wetti, Heito, Walahfrid, and the poor woman's guide were all monks. In a world filled with *homunculi,* with ordinary people living unenlightened lives, the monk, because of his special and self-styled closeness to God, felt called upon to humble the mighty. He had the ear of God. It was this conviction that must have given someone like Heito the confidence to pass off as God's word those things that his own heart told him were true. The divine posturing of these dream texts may unnerve the modern reader, who may wonder how a former bishop could have invented such stories, but a good deal of invention was necessary in order to sell these texts even in the ninth century. We should not think that Heito and the others lacked artifice. Not only did they know a good deal about available dream literature, but they worked to perfect their own strategies of indirection: diverting our attention from their own work by means of dream voices that were different and more credible, and dropping signs, like Ermengard's secret, that seem to usher readers into private worlds packed with dramatic truths. We need to notice, too, that the Bible is almost never quoted in dream texts, probably because readers were meant to understand that God himself stood behind these new revelations and had no need to quote himself.

Monks must have believed that God had given them glimpses of the otherworld, pellucid images with which they could reform the world in which they lived. "To imagine the otherworld was to wield a political weapon," Jacques Le Goff has observed.[70] But the dream was a rather small lever with which to attempt to budge what must have seemed the massive weight of an almost immovable political world. We need to realize, before we proceed much farther, that dream texts were never to be the chief tools of political discourse. They were to appear during periods when other forms of change seemed to have been blocked off and when resentments had reached a critical level. Monks like Heito, Walahfrid, and Wala found it difficult to put down their pens. With no small touch of arrogance, they styled themselves the consciences of their world—its ever watchful, moral eye; hence their emphasis upon the impossibility of concealing sin. It fell to churchmen, as Jonas of Orléans said, to admonish kings, to counsel them so that they might achieve salvation.[71] But, if the *Fürstenspiegel* or mirror of the princes was an official species of political literature designed to shape the character of young princes by supplying examples of good and bad rulers in history, the royal dream in the ninth century was an unofficial type of literature that sought entrance through the back door, not the front.[72] Yet dream advice was more direct than that found in the advice manuals, since it dealt not with the dusty stuff of ancient kings but with the misdeeds of the recently dead or still living Carolingian king. The royal dream punched a hole through what at times must have seemed the sealed envelope of a frustratingly static world, supplying an image of the recent past with which to reform the immediate present.

Ironically, it had been Louis the Pious who opened the door to political oneirocriticism. By sanctioning criticism of his father, he had engaged early on in a kind of patricide of reputation. Hence, Louis had cleared the way for the criticism of Carolingian kings. While Charlemagne had been alive, criticism had been forced underground by a combination of brute force and firm patronage. The emperor was too important as the *pater patriae, pater regni,* and *pater Europae* for Carolingian conceptual architects like Alcuin, Angilbert, and Theodulf to worry overmuch that he left a great deal wanting in his personal fatherhood. Perhaps Charlemagne himself worried more about the state of his soul in his last years than even his scholars cared to admit.[73] But it was Louis who broke apart the bonds of patronage that had protected Charlemagne from written criticism.[74] He had his own supporters, men like Benedict of Aniane, who urged him to reform the empire and its monasteries, and he feared his father's old supporters. Louis not only disapproved of his father's infamous domestic life, but he may have supported the revelation of his father's criminal behavior as a way of undermining the old guard that still clung to Charlemagne's name and greatness. Heito and Walahfrid were able to condemn Charlemagne's criminal lust openly, because Louis had encouraged them to do so. Twice Louis publicly apologized for his father's wrongdoings, he banished his sisters from court, and he put a stop to the sexual license of the palace. Thus, Walahfrid had little to fear when he sent his poem to Grimald at court; it was his calling card, one that a reforming emperor could only accept.[75]

In the thirteen years between the cleansing of the palace in 814 and Walahfrid's *Vision of Wetti* in 827, the criticism of Charlemagne's infamous personal life was finally and firmly made. The monks of Reichenau may have been hesitant in their approach at first, but that had been because of the immensity of Charlemagne's reputation. Yet once the charge was made public, Charlemagne's long unutterable sin lost its appeal to ninth-century dreamers, though the rumor of the emperor's insatiable lust would linger in legend. By the end of the ninth century, the Saxon Poet and Notker had entirely forgotten or preferred to ignore the stories of Charlemagne's animal nature.[76]

Yet it was the example of Charlemagne undergoing purgation that set Carolingian royal dreaming free for the rest of the century. Not until the end of the empire, when that particular Carolingian connection of court scholars and kings ceased to have the same cultural cohesion, was the door to be closed again. Despite its unmanageable size, the Carolingian empire was a place of central gathering points: palaces, monasteries, and cathedrals. There the learned and powerful men of the realm gathered to discuss the only subjects of real interest to them: religion, politics, and property. In its topical consistency and its shared vocabulary, the dream imagery surrounding Charlemagne testifies to an ongoing cultural conversation among these men. If I am correct in thinking that Einhard's portrait of Charlemagne's domestic life was a response to the emperor's dream critics, especially to Wetti, then people must have been listening to what the dreamers had to say.

Moreover, the clerics of the realm had learned a lesson in these years, one that marked a new direction for their participation in public affairs. A king, in fact the greatest of all the Frankish kings, had been criticized candidly, but stains will spread. What Louis had unloosed soon overtook him personally, for Heito finally dared to bring a suffering father and his sinful son together in a daring dream text.

The *Vision of the Poor Woman of Laon* remains a remarkable political document, bringing together a crowd of the controversial dead as a way to chastise a living king. Thus, Heito and the monastery of Reichenau dragged political dreams into the present. The still living Louis became, willingly or unwillingly, the target of a contemporary dream text. It was a precious moment. Students of Carolingian thought frequently find themselves in this remarkable situation as they watch the Carolingian intellectual make a quantum leap forward in form and thought: from minor annals to major annals, from collections of decretals to collections of false decretals, from philosphical glosses to masterpieces like the *Periphyseon,* and from dreams about dead kings to dreams that involve the living. The last of these leaps occurred because of a deep-seated awareness of troubled times. The events of 817–18 had disturbed some Carolingian intellectuals profoundly, for they thought they saw that most worrisome of medieval phenomena: an unjust king. Beyond the injustice of Louis in his treatment of Bernard and the legendary lechery of Charlemagne, these dream texts called bad kingship itself into question. "A king is a king by right ruling," the Council of Paris was soon to say.[77] Royal dreams made public what had long been hidden; and what had once been whispered in the corridors of the royal palace and in hushed cloisters was now, as the clamorous monk had said, to be "shouted to the whole world."

CHAPTER FOUR

Louis's Theater
of Illusions

The palace became a theater, formerly one of straight talking, where the
illusions of fortune-tellers now kept bubbling up.[1]

Thus Paschasius Radbertus, monk of Corbie and reader of Terence, looking
back from the middle of the ninth century, characterized the court of Louis the
Pious around 829. In a book rich in pseudonymous association and the unsettling banter of monks about their kings, Paschasius imagined recent royal history as a black comedy of distraction and delusion. His hero Wala had wanted to
drive all the soothsayers, diviners, seers, mutes, dream interpreters, and readers of entrails from their nest in the palace, but the court was too spellbound, too
mired in a confusing morass of strategem and sorcery, to follow his wise lead.

But the enchantments of Louis's court were never magical; they were hermeneutical. Paschasius's exaggerated image conjures up not the black arts but
the dark waters of opinion and advice that constantly washed round the emperor. How, people wondered, had Louis lost his royal way? In condemning
false fortune-tellers, however, the monk of Corbie never acknowledged that his
man, Wala, had also, in his time, been a purveyor of gloomy forecasts. Louis's
world was far more interesting than most of his moralizing critics ever suspected, but then so were they: for through their criticisms these men were
searching for a true reading of contemporary history, one that would explain its
seemingly disastrous design.

Despite all his intellectual gifts, Paschasius had failed to comprehend completely the dynamic forces of this historical hermeneutics. Behind the scenes, the intellectuals of the new empire of Louis the Pious were struggling to understand the unfolding crises of his reign. Convinced that something had gone terribly wrong in the kingdom, these intellectuals began to search for the divine plan hidden behind the intersecting events of the physical and political worlds. As they surveyed the natural world, they looked for signs that would reflect their disastrous drift as a Christian society. No one dared any longer to face the Carolingian scene with the cheerful optimism of Hibernicus Exul, who, sounding like a young Ovid celebrating the coming of the *pax Augusta,* had once written to Charlemagne: "We prefer the present age to the past." Instead, remarked Paschasius in full funk, "Our minds now invent monstrosities."[2]

Indeed, he claimed that by 829 everyone could call off a long list of the kingdom's festering sins: "disasters, disease, famine, bad weather, and even the warnings of visions."[3] For us this may seem a simple catalogue of disasters, but for Paschasius something more was understood: for him, sin and calamity had become synonymous. Since God does not punish without purpose, the very existence of horrible happenings in the physical world must reflect some indwelling deformity in the people, and so the surest proof of sin was calamity. Jonas of Orléans matter-of-factly assumed that the disasters oppressing the Franks were sent by God as divine punishment for their wickedness. His real worry, though, was that today's troubles were merely a warning of worse to come. He observed that the stubborn Egyptians of the Old Testament, who had ignored all the signs and portents given to them by God, were chastened with blows of adversity.[4] The mood lingered late into Louis's reign. After seeing Halley's comet in 837, Einhard wrote to Louis:

> This star supplied, I believe, a suitable indication of our standing and demonstrated the coming calamity that we deserve. For what does it matter whether God's threatening wrath is foretold to humans by a man, an angel, or a star?[5]

For almost all the fortune-tellers at Louis's court, including Einhard, the purpose of carefully observing what went on in the natural world was to collect clear evidence of the dangers facing the kingdom. This bad news was designed, almost exclusively, for the eyes of Louis and those who might influence him. It must have seemed to writers like Einhard that to shape the emperor's understanding of the general drift of the empire was to gain some measure of control over the nature of change itself. These thinkers shared the Socratic conceit that to know the good was to do the good; thus, in troubled times, the power to raise the emperor's awareness of the true state of affairs in the empire was critical.

Why Louis would have listened is another matter. His problems may not have arisen from some weakness in his personality, as was once supposed, but they were certainly made worse by his willingness to listen to endless advice.[6] A good king, sang the mirrors of princes in unison, welcomed the counsel of trusted and wise advisors. If Charlemagne seemed to have succeeded without any deep dependence on advisors, his son never would. Indeed, Louis's life, as we look back at it, was a bumpy ride that led him from one chief advisor to the next, with the resulting shifts in policies and personalities that each brought to court. In 822, Louis in essence conceded that his problems had arisen because of his failure to heed the advice of trusted counselors. But at Attigny the guards were being changed once again, as Benedict of Aniane passed from the scene and Adalhard of Corbie was recalled from exile. Louis himself, as Benedict's influence over him proved, had always been willing to heed strong advice, especially if it came from one who possessed the convincing charisma of a saint.

The one individual from whom Louis probably received less than his fair share of advice was his own father. When still a boy, Louis, like all of Charlemagne's heirs, had been sent from court to a distant land in order to learn how to be a king. Thereafter, he met his father only infrequently, usually on state occasions when Charlemagne, the all-powerful emperor, must have seemed even more distant and unapproachable. Louis had spent all but three of his first thirty-six years in Aquitaine. It was Charlemagne himself, therefore, who shaped the pattern of his son's reliance on advisors, as in those early years Louis must have been utterly dependent on his father's men, individuals like Count Bego. Moreover, Louis's independence may never have been encouraged, for before 813 he was never Charlemagne's first choice as successor; he was God's, or so Thegan thought.[7]

It is down this twisted and forever-forking path into Louis's world that we must turn for the moment, for it is along this path that we shall find a few more royal dreams. The reader should be forewarned, however, that these new dreams represent only a small part of the searching spirit of the age; we cannot understand them without carefully considering their wider setting in an age preoccupied with crisis and desperate to find a way back to its right and royal path. We need to spend some time in Louis's theater of recurring illusions, because the men who wrote and circulated its dream texts were dedicated theatergoers.

Let us enter this hermeneutical age in the company of Theodulf of Orléans, who in exile had turned melancholy and reflective. Once he had stood, as we have seen, near the very summit of Charlemagne's court and had been the bishop of Orléans since 788. But in 814, as the new emperor approached Orléans on his way to Aachen to assume full power on his father's death, a delicate moment occurred, one that suggests the already difficult nature of Theodulf's new position. The bishop simply did not know whether he should meet Louis outside the walls of the city or wait for him inside, and the matter had to be negotiated through messengers. The concord between the two men was not to last long. We shall never know with any certainty just how Theodulf became implicated in Bernard's revolt of 817. Whether he was culpable or was "framed" by the count of Orléans cannot be determined definitively, but that he suffered a mighty fall from royal grace cannot be doubted.[8] Theodulf and his friend Moduin preferred to portray the poet as another Ovid, falsely accused and wrongly exiled.[9] In 818, deprived of his bishopric and confined to monasteries, first in Angers and finally in Le Mans, Theodulf wrote plaintively to his friends.

In an undated poem, modeled on Cyprian's famous letter to Demetrian and containing allusions to Ovid's exile poetry, Theodulf once argued that the end of the world was not far off.[10] The world now sang of its coming ruin through not-so-subtle signs: the seasons were out of joint and the earth had become sterile. Nor was society as fixed and firm as it once had been. Everyone and every virtue had become unhinged: the farmer in his fields, the soldier in his castle, the sailor on the seas, justice in the courts, and piety in the marketplace. Harmony had faded in friendship and learning in art, and dreadful old age now devoured all things. The world was succumbing to physical exhaustion, thought Theodulf, as the sun grew fainter, trees became gnarled with age, fountains dried up, and walls split wide. All these were nature's signals announcing ruin; sweetness was abandoning a weary world and was being replaced by vice and decrepitude. The nagging thought that now "nothing stands as firm as it stood before" must have whispered constantly to Theodulf after that day in early 814 when his world, with the stilling of a heartbeat, had changed.

Beyond the familiarity of the apocalyptic imagery and the febrility of the pessimism, one does find in the final poetry of Theodulf a cultivated and self-consciously Ovidian awareness of changed times. Like Ovid, he pleaded in melancholy poems for sympathetic understanding. His present life, he wrote, without study, teaching, or worship, was worse than death. In a poem of lamentation to Moduin, he charged that at the hands of Louis he had not received a trial, only condemnation, and he protested that the pope surely should have judged his case.[11] In the middle sections of this poem, he undertook to chronicle some recent strange events. In the first, he described how the river running under the walls of Le Mans had dried up in February 820 and was, for a time, fordable. The citizens worried that walls of water were about to come crashing down, but Theodulf remembered Joshua remembering Moses as he passed through his own separated waters. This curiosity, he concluded, was a *noua res* signaling some change in the wider world.[12]

Theodulf claimed that "many strange things" were to be seen during his last years, including a magnificent battle of birds.

> Rebus et exemplis quaedam bene nosse ualemus,
> Cum non diuinem, haec scio res quid agat.

> [In events and patterns, we can certainly comprehend some things,
> And though I am not a diviner, I know what this event means.][13]

Like Virgil's bees, Theodulf's birds mirrored men: they gathered in armies to fight against each other, wing to wing, talon to talon. A few birds flew from side to side as though on missions of peace, much as the Romans and Carthaginians used to send messengers back and forth on the field of an impending battle. But the search for peace was in vain. For six days the birds whirled high in the air and fought. Thousands died, falling from the sky like leaves from oak trees with the coming cold of winter. In an ironic ending to this portion of his somber set of verses, Theodulf imagined the local people asking the bishop of Toulouse if they might be allowed to collect and eat the dead birds. Hence, the poem ends with human appetites, with the sound of carts heaped high with avian carcasses rolling back through the fields to distant villages, and with an unanswered question. For Theodulf never tells us what the incident meant to him or whether he saw in it a sign of Bernard's civil war. Instead he set it in the midst of his own exile and his allusive reflection on ancient history. As he turned to the last section of his poem, he connected another battle of birds with the civil wars experienced by the Romans and stopped to ponder the ancient practice of augury.

Theodulf may not have been a traditional diviner, as he properly protested, but he was certainly a learned Carolingian symbol-maker. By collecting accounts of irregular natural phenomena, setting them in the context of his exile days, and publicizing his account of them, Theodulf showed himself to be one of the new wave of fortune-tellers. His poem contains the features commonly found in the works of the worried interpreters of Louis's reign: indirection and allusiveness. They contain what I would call a studied and deliberate ordering of disorder. If, as T. F. X. Noble has argued, Theodulf once wrote an acerbic set of verses against Louis's constitutional arrangement of 817, and if it was this that threw him into disfavor, then the reasons for Theodulf's final obliquity would be understandable. His poetry needed to imply, not to state, to suggest rather than to specify what he thought had gone wrong in the land. Not everyone was quite as gloomy. Ermold the Black, also in exile, tried to win his way back into the good graces of Pepin of Aquitaine and then Louis by writing playful panegyric in an older vein.[14] But Theodulf was a man with a foot in two worlds, the old world of Charlemagne and the new world of Louis, and his sense of disabling dislocation must have run deep. He knew, in a way that Ermold can never have appreciated, how much had changed. In Theodulf and the other fortune-tellers, a synoptic awareness of a disordered world was born. They came to discern in nature a mirror image of the history of their own failing empire.

The reader of the *Royal Frankish Annals,* the house history of the Carolingians between 741 and 829, confronts the same design. The transition from the straightforward style of the annals between 788 and 795 to the more sophisticated style of the later entries is marked. But the impression that the modern reader has of increasing disorder in the 820s is less a product of forces at work in the outer Carolingian world than in the inner one, forces that included improved reporting, an expanding worldview, and the changing attitude of the annalist towards his king. A new annalist, either the Archchaplain Hilduin or the Chancellor Helisachar, was responsible for the entries between 820 and 829, and he was less than happy.[15] Where before the royal annalists had wholeheartedly supported the king, the new annalist became increasingly critical of Louis. To his dismay, for instance, the rebellious Prince Ceadrag of the Obodrites, although guilty of countless misdeeds, was not only allowed to go unpunished but was rewarded with gifts by the emperor. Louis slipped into the same trap when he believed the promises of the treacherous Breton Wihomarc, who, also regaled with gifts, returned home to resume molestation. In 826, according to the annalist, Louis was infuriated by the continuing treachery of the Saracens, but chose to do nothing for the moment. The very next year, due to the incompetence of the dukes whom he had put in charge of the Frankish army in the Spanish March, the villages around Barcelona and Gerona were pillaged and destroyed.[16] Thus, the royal annalist laid responsibility for a series of political misfortunes at Louis's doorstep. In effect, he continued that policy of criticism that had helped to bring about Louis's public penance in 822. Perhaps the annalist felt that these continued criticisms would lead, in time, to a chastened and better ruler.

The last annalist was convinced that he and his fellow watchers of the empire were witnessing troubled times, and he meant to alert the emperor to them. His language swells with words describing treachery, violence, and defeat.[17] This descriptive vocabulary and the flexible structure of the annals allowed him to create almost impressionistic montages of annual adversity. What allowed him to compose his entries in this way, as opposed to recording events in a strictly chronological fashion, was the particular nature of annual composition. The annalist rarely saw the events that he recorded; instead, he gathered reports of these events throughout the year and fashioned them into a single annual entry in February. Working according to a fairly standard pattern, he would note the date, make some comment on the weather of that winter, and then describe in a roughly chronological and regional progression the main events of the year. Last, the annalist would place information of general interest at the end of the entry. There was no necessary order to this last section of random events, except one imposed by the annalist, and here we find him ordering disorder.

The most striking of the annalistic montages is the one for 820. The annalist began with a description of the assembly held at Aachen to consider the issue of Ljudovit's rebellion and the extended campaign against him that followed. But then, in quick succession, he reported that a treaty with Abul Aas had been broken, Italian pirates had sunk eight merchant ships off Sardinia, and Northmen had raided Flanders, the mouth of the river Seine, and Aquitaine, where a village was plundered. Immediately following this report of incursions, the annalist assembled a list of physical disasters:

> In this year, on account of constant rain and air enfeebled by too much moisture, great misfortunes occurred. For a pestilence harmful to both men and cattle raged so savagely, far and wide, that scarcely any part of the entire Frankish kingdom could be found uninjured and untouched by this disease. Grain and beans, rotting because of the continual rain, could not be gathered or went bad when they had been collected. Even the wine, the yield of which was small in that year, became bitter and unpleasant for lack of heat. In certain places the fall planting was so hindered by the overflow of rivers and water standing in the level land that almost no grain was sown before springtime. During the second hour of the evening of 28 January, there was an eclipse of the moon.[18]

Although after 795 the annalists had been increasingly fascinated by details of the physical world, this was the first disasters report. In gathering together in one entry a series of what he called great misfortunes, the annalist had made a reflective comment on the condition of his times. Like Theodulf, he adumbrated the collapse of a weary world, but he went further, for he linked these

natural *incommoda* to a series of political and military reverses. Thus, an annalist convinced that the empire was in crisis found in the physical world another
indication of God's judgment on the land.

As readers of the royal annals, we need always to keep in mind just how
much of the described disorder was a product of the annalist's special presentation of events. After 820 he assumed a regular approach to these physical details. Where before they had been scattered throughout the yearly reports, they
were now most frequently gathered together at the end of an entry. Freed from
chronological limitations when it came to treating events in the natural world,
the annalist patched together a quilt of random events, which, when encountered last in an entry, creates a powerful impression of a chaotic and backsliding
world. The long cold winter of 821, with its disastrous fall planting season, was
followed by a round of miraculous happenings collected at the beginning of
the annal for 822. At the end of the entry for the next year, the annalist gathered
together a lengthy list of that year's prodigies: among these was the case of the
girl who fasted for ten months, the destruction of twenty-three villages set on
fire by a bolt of lightning from heaven, the case of a church painting that had
long been faded but now shone forth brightly for two days, crops destroyed by a
hailstorm, lightning that destroyed houses and killed men, and a furious disease
that killed both men and women. In the entry for 827 the annalist reported that
the Franks, losing a battle to the Saracens and Moors around Saragossa, had
seen battle lines and shimmering lights in the night sky, which were believed to
be "presentiments of this disaster." Finally, the entry for 829 opened with a report of an earthquake that had struck Aachen and a violent storm that had damaged the chapel of Charlemagne.[19]

After 829 the *Royal Frankish Annals* stops, its cessation being, in hindsight,
its final annalistic statement about disorder. The last annalist had transformed
these annals from a house journal and record of official views into an early
warning system. He no longer considered himself a simple recorder of events
but another reader of patterns of disorder in the Carolingian empire. A careful
and understated pessimism lies behind the tone of the final entries, but it should
not be mistaken for resignation, for the annalist was both interested and involved in events. Indeed, the annals may have stopped because the annalist
himself, like Hilduin, had taken the side of the sons against their royal father in
the revolt of 830. Open revolt was the logical step for one who had become as
disenchanted with Louis as the royal Frankish annalist had.

He was not alone. Throughout the 820s, thinkers continued to collect evidence of oncoming calamity, and Einhard was one of these. He knew a copy of

the revised *Royal Frankish Annals,* and with it in hand made a further assemblage out of the moments of disorder gathered there.[20] In chapter 32 of the *Life of Charlemagne,* written around 826, Einhard brought together a striking series of portents that were supposed to have foreshadowed the death of Charlemagne. In composing his own Suetonian pastiche of imperial portents, Einhard cleverly rewrote history: "There were many prophetic signs of Charlemagne's approaching end, so that not only others but even he himself could sense that the end was near."[21] First, in three successive years near the end of Charlemagne's life, there were eclipses of the sun and moon, and a dark spot was seen on the sun for a period of seven days. In the annals, Einhard actually found reports of eclipses spread over six years, but he chose to render them more portentous by squeezing them into a tighter time frame.[22] The second portent—the collapse of the portico that joined the chapel and palace at Aachen—may also have been taken from the *Royal Frankish Annals,* but from an entry three years after Charlemagne's death. On Maundy Thursday 817, a wooden portico at Aachen collapsed on Louis, nearly killing him and some of his companions. F. L. Ganshof's defense of the accuracy of Einhard notwithstanding, Einhard knew from Suetonius that collapsing buildings portended the deaths of emperors, and in the annals he found a dramatic example of the type, albeit three years too late to have concerned Charlemagne.[23]

Einhard also noted that one of the emperor's greatest building projects was the construction of a bridge, five hundred feet long, over the Rhine River at Mainz. The bridge, however, had burned down in May 813, just eight months before Charlemagne's death, so that, although he had planned to replace the wooden bridge with stone, he did not have enough time to carry out his plans. Among Einhard's collection of fateful portents, the incident of the burned bridge is presented as remarkable, for that bridge had "seemed capable of lasting forever." Set on fire by accident, it burned down in just three hours; the only wood that survived was under water. Although even Charlemagne seems to have thought of the bridge as temporary and inadequate, Einhard regarded it here as a structure that gave the impression of great permanence. Louis Halphen's comment that Einhard had forgotten that the bridge was made of wood overlooks the deliberate way in which the biographer was assembling examples of failure.[24]

Heinrich Fichtenau made much of the next portent, though it again belongs to Einhard's special ordering of disorder. On his last campaign into Saxony in 810 against Godefrid, king of the Danes, Charlemagne set out one morning before sunrise, when a meteor suddenly flashed overhead. While everyone stared at it and wondered what it might portend, the emperor's horse suddenly lowered its head and fell, throwing Charlemagne to the ground with such violence that the buckle holding his cloak broke and his sword belt was ripped off. The emperor's spear was found a full twenty feet from where he had fallen, and he himself had to be helped to his feet by attendants.[25] The royal annalist did not report the incident, though he did note the outbreak of an epizootic in Saxony that year that inhibited the campaign. The epizootic of 810 attracted much attention within the empire. Charlemagne himself ordered a fast that year to expiate sins and to aid men and cattle, and Agobard of Lyons complained that many people had believed that Duke Grimoald of Benevento, an enemy of the emperor, had sent men to spread poisonous dust in order to kill Carolingian cattle. Even Einhard may have suspected that the emperor's horse had been sick, but in the context of his collection of evil omens and with the addition of the mysterious meteor, he made the incident a dramatic portent of Charlemagne's death.[26]

Next he noted that tremors had shaken the palace and that the golden apple atop the cathedral of Aachen was struck by lightning and fell.[27] Last Einhard recalled that the red inscription in the royal chapel, which ran below the horizontal molding separating the upper and lower arches (see Fig. 12), contained the words KAROLVS PRINCEPS as well as the name of the architect. Certain people had noticed that in the very year the emperor died, in fact only a few months before his death, the lettering of the word PRINCEPS had become so faded that it was hardly visible. Suetonius had told a similar story: lightning melted the C from CAESAR inscribed below one of the statues of Augustus, and this was interpreted to mean that the emperor would live only one hundred days. Einhard concluded this section of the *Life of Charlemagne* with a statement that seems to contradict the one with which he began "Charlemagne ignored all of these portents or spurned them as if none of them had anything to do with his affairs."[28] If Charlemagne was a disbeliever, so was Einhard, or at least his heavy-handedness in creating a history of the portentous suggests that he also knew how to wrestle disorder into suggestive shapes. In Louis the Pious and his librarian Gerward, Einhard had a natural audience at court for this reading of the times as calamitous.[29]

His carefully constructed pattern of portents would have lifted those readers beyond Charlemagne himself to a wider world of dramatic change, for collectively the portents forecast even greater failure. Men like Gerward would have moved through those pages in a twilight world of fading light and obscure signs, while around the dying Charlemagne buildings collapsed and golden apples toppled from the pinnacles of glorious churches. Marino Marini, the great

Italian sculptor of the twentieth century, might have appreciated the image of an imperial rider and his mount crashing to the ground, for he spent some thirty years imagining the breakdown of the once solid contact of horse and rider; it was his metaphor for the widening divide between modern man and the natural world. Einhard's purpose may at first seem simpler, to document as Suetonius had the majestic significance of the little things that precede an imperial death, but Einhard's were the complex thoughts of a man of the 820s. Like Theodulf, Einhard constructed patterns of disorder that take their meaning from the time of their construction and not from Charlemagne's time. Thus, in ordering moments of imperial disorder, Einhard met his readers in the late 820s and confronted them with his conviction that Francia faced desolation. For if the portents prefigured Charlemagne's literary death in the biography, Einhard transformed them into the proper prelude to their own disturbed times. The emperor's death thus became another portent, the first in a new series, alerting the people of his own time to their impending ruin.

But, by 826, the saints were rushing north to rescue the kingdom of Louis the Pious. The royal Frankish annalist reported that in that year Hilduin of Saint-Denis, with the permission of the pope, had translated the relics of Sebastian from Italy to Saint-Médard of Soissons.[30] To encounter saints in the pages of the royal annals, after the usual parade of ambassadors, legates, kings, counts, and hostages, is to find the fixed borders between the living and the divine dead somehow suspended. These saints were being translated into the Frankish world not only physically but politically, and the architects of the Carolingian cult of the saints were actively engaged in transforming their unseen heroes into royal advisors.

In 827, by means of a shady and unscrupulous dealer in holy bones, Einhard secured the translation of the saints Marcellinus and Peter from Rome. He wanted to enshrine the relics in one of his churches, but while being carried from Rome some of the bones were quietly stolen by one of Hilduin's men and carried to Saint-Médard of Soissons.[31] The primary cause of these translations of relics is not hard to find. Northern Europe, having missed the great age of the martyrs, lacked its own relics. Moreover, life in the ninth century was necessarily so localized and travel so limited that the Carolingians rarely went on pilgrimages to far-off places such as Jerusalem and Compostela. Instead they traveled to local churches like Saint-Médard of Soissons, where relics were richly housed in golden reliquaries set in chapels lit by candlelight. Thus the Carolingians internalized the act of pilgrimage within the empire, and churches were architecturally designed to accommodate within their walls a form of miniature pilgrimage.[32] But the intense and competitive pursuit of divine drawing cards for churches led otherwise honorable men like Hilduin and Einhard to send their men out to skulk around in the dark, stealing dust from pouches and paying men to rob graves in decaying Roman cemeteries. If these translation histories occasionally remind us of tawdry spy stories, they must have struck ninth-century men and women otherwise—as truly suspenseful—because even holiness in the ninth century was forced to struggle against the wicked and obstructive devices of a sinful world. In Einhard's case, after Hilduin's conspiracy had been uncovered, he was able to reunite the relics, and he wrote an account of the translation, in part, to confirm his complete possession.

Yet his book has still more ambitious designs, both private and public. Among the many miraculous cures of the blind, sick, and crippled, Einhard counted his own recovery from a serious illness. In the environs of Aachen and the imperial palace to which he carried the relics, word of the curative power of the martyrs' bones began to spread, and even members of Louis's court successfully sought cures. When Gerward returned to Aachen after a short absence, he found that everyone was talking about Einhard's saints, and he managed to confirm one case of a miraculous cure. He related this to the emperor in the presence of Einhard and the court, and Louis responded by publicly acknowledging the divine mercy and power of the martyrs.[33]

Einhard and Hilduin wanted the patronage of the powerful for their saints, for from patrons flowed privileges and properties that mattered. In 828, Einhard himself was a man seeking to withdraw from the rigors of public life, pleading that his own service to the saints was a better investment for Louis than his attendance at court. "I believe that these holy martyrs will intercede for you with God, if you are willing to put their needs before your own," he wrote to Louis. He sought specially to secure the help of the Empress Judith as he attempted to shift his service from Louis to the saints.[34] The relics of Marcellinus and Peter thus achieved an instrumental efficacy for Einhard: they helped him to hoard prestige and served as a holy lever with which to lighten the load of royal demand.

But Einhard also hoped that his saints could cure an ailing empire. He wrote to the emperors Louis and Lothar that, by the secret judgment of God, the saints had come to Francia to glorify and protect the empire. Amidst the confusion of contemporary politics, Einhard believed that his saints might shine a beam of revealing light onto an otherwise confused landscape. Everyone knew that the saints and angels frequently worked their cures through the divine agency of dreams, and in late 828 they wanted to speak to the emperor himself.[35] Einhard related how a blind man by the name of Aubrey from Aquitaine had persuaded some merchants from Mainz, who happened to be sailing along the Main River in search of grain for sale, to take him to Einhard's church at Mulinheim. Aubrey had been blind since birth and suffered from limbs that shook so violently that he had difficulty feeding himself. But he had the power of prophetic dreaming and, although he had been at Mulinheim for only seven days, he received a dream from Marcellinus that cured his trembling. For two years he remained at Einhard's church, and not a night went by that he did not dream of the martyrs.[36]

One night after evening mass, Aubrey approached Ratleig, Einhard's assistant and secretary, and whispered that he wished to speak to him in private. The two men withdrew into Ratleig's bedroom, whereupon Aubrey related a miraculous story. That very night, shortly before the bells had rung to waken the brothers, a man with white hair, dressed in a white garment and bearing a golden rod in his hand, had spoken to the blind man:

> Aubrey, understand everything that I am about to tell you and hold it fast
> in your memory, so that you can repeat it to those who will write it down.
> For I wish these things to be written down and shown by your master to
> the Emperor Louis, who should read them. This is extremely important
> business and must not only be understood by the emperor, but must be ac-
> ted upon by him into whose kingdom the martyrs, by divine command,
> have come.[37]

The oneiric messenger then dictated a dozen or so chapters and ordered Aubrey to relate them to Ratleig and to four others, whose names we never learn. After that, Ratleig was supposed to make a little book and carry it to Einhard, who was at the time resident at court. Ratleig was to command Einhard, on the authority of the martyrs, to present the book to the emperor as quickly as possible.

Although Aubrey at first had believed that he was talking to Saint Marcellinus, he soon learned that he was, in fact, in the presence of the archangel Gabriel, who had taken on the saint's form because God had placed him in charge of all things concerning the saint. His present mission, he confirmed, was to communicate with Louis. But Aubrey told Gabriel that he doubted that anyone would believe that he had spoken to an angel about such matters. The archangel promised to provide proof. He told Aubrey that if he stood in front of the altar and held a candle in each hand as he dictated Gabriel's message to the witnesses, the candles would be miraculously lit without anyone lighting them.

Ratleig confirmed that the miracle had taken place just as promised, and he immediately carried the dictated book to Aachen. Without hesitation, Einhard received him and the booklet:

> I took the little book from him and read it completely, and after I had corrected it and made a new copy, I presented it, as commanded, to the emperor. And, in truth, he received and read that little book, but of the things that it commanded or advised him to do, he bothered to accomplish few.[38]

Einhard fails to tell us, though, what Louis did or did not do, or even what the little book was about. He was satisfied to record the circumstances of Aubrey's vision, but not the contents of its special message to the emperor. In particular, he did not think he should pass over the miraculous lighting of the candles caused by the outstanding merits of his martyrs. The criticism of Louis's lack of action (and, earlier, of Hilduin's duplicity) suggests that Einhard may have circulated the *History of the Translation* during the revolt of 830.

Gabriel stands out as the one solid feature of Aubrey's dream and it is not an unimportant one, for the Carolingians regarded Gabriel as the archangel specially called upon to interpret dreams that concerned kings and their struggles. They knew that Daniel had once had a great and political vision of a horned he-goat, whom Gabriel had identified as the future king of Greece (Alexander the Great) who would defile the sanctuary. "And I Daniel fainted, and was sick for days; afterward I rose up, and did the king's business; and I was astonished at the vision, but none understood it."[39] Charlemagne was told by a court cleric:

> Since the vision was one concerning battles, the conflicts of kings, and the successions of kingdoms, it was appropriate for Gabriel, who is the overseer of battles, to be given this task.[40]

Moreover, it was Gabriel who was specially charged with announcing the birth of Christ and, hence, the beginning of the war against the rebel angels.[41] Perhaps it was for that reason, among others, that so many Carolingian churches had massive towers at their west ends dedicated to Gabriel and Michael; those mighty bulwarks, protected by combative archangels, were designed to block the entrance of all evil spirits. Gabriel was also known to have called on the Jews to finish with transgression and make an end of sin.[42] In the figure of Gabriel, then, the dreamer Aubrey had found the great, angelic reformer of wayward kings. He had also found the archangel of the Annunciation and thus the special bearer of royal messages from God.

What Gabriel wanted, with a certain pounding and precise insistence in Aubrey's dream, was to speak to Louis. But, as Stuart Airlie has observed, even

Gabriel understood that the Carolingian court had proper procedures; Gabriel did not appear to Louis directly, but sought out a go-between to deliver his message.[43] Yet an obdurate king, who listened but would not act, revealed himself, as he had to the poor woman of Laon, to be the source of the kingdom's intransigence. That Gabriel was forced to work through Aubrey, Ratleig, and Einhard was itself, in the context of Einhard's history, a comment on Louis and the obstacles placed in the way of divine truth ever penetrating the imperial heart. Louis had grown too distant from God.

At almost the same time, another booklet was brought to Einhard from his church at Mulinheim, and he described its origins immediately following Aubrey's dream. A sixteen-year-old girl from the area around Frankfurt had been brought before the saints' relics at Mulinheim because she was possessed by demons. Before their tomb, a priest read the words of exorcism over her and then entered into a conversation with the demon inside her. This demon, who called himself Wiggo, answered in Latin, though neither the girl nor her parents understood the language.

> I am an attendant and disciple of Satan. For a long time I was the gatekeeper of the infernal regions, but for some years now I have ravaged the kingdom of the Franks with eleven of my mates. We destroyed, as ordered, grain, wine, and everything that grows from the earth and is useful to man; we wiped out herds of cattle with disease; we let loose plague and pestilence among men themselves; and we caused and inflicted on them all the misfortunes and evils that they have suffered for so long now because of their sins.[44]

When the priest wondered why such power had been granted to the demon, Wiggo answered that it was "because of the maliciousness of this people and the manifold injustices of those who are placed above them." He condemned these superiors in stark terms: they loved profit not justice, feared men more than God, oppressed the poor, and ignored the anguished cries of widows and orphans. Moreover, both rulers and the people at large daily committed countless other sins: perjury, drunkenness, adultery, murder, theft, and rapine. No one, he charged, prohibited these acts and, when they were done, no one punished them. Instead, the powerful in the kingdom chased after filthy lucre, vainglory, and pride. They directed hatred and malice not against those outside the realm but against those inside and even against their own relatives. Worse still, he said, now "friend does not trust friend, brother hates brother, and father loves not his son." Among the people, few paid tithes and fewer still gave alms, since they counted the money given to charity as lost. Against the law of God, people employed unjust weights and measures to cheat each other. They deceived one another with fraud and feared not to give false witness. The Lord's day and feast days were not observed, since many preferred to work as usual. The very promises made at baptism had been broken. Wiggo informed the priest that he had been commanded to create chaos throughout the land, because the people were guilty of defying God's laws and, therefore, deserved to suffer for their sins.

The priest then commanded the demon to come out of the girl's body. Wiggo announced that he would depart, not because of the priest's order but because of the power of the saints. He threw the girl down on the pavement and made her lie there as if asleep. With Wiggo expelled, the girl awoke to the amazement of all the gathered witnesses, but she could no longer speak Latin.

Whether Einhard circulated this second strange little book around the royal court or not, he does not tell us. In December 828 he was at Aachen, but he was unhappy to be there, longing instead to stand in the compassionate presence of his saints. Despite issuing from one of the twelve satellites of Satan, the story of Wiggo and his unholy antiapostolic mission contained a corrective message, one more informative than Gabriel's unrecorded program. Einhard lamented that his own time had fallen so low that it was not good men but evil demons who lectured them about their crimes and the need for reform.[45] He took small comfort from the fact that it had been the powerful presence of his saints that had produced this revelatory exorcism.

What the demon told Einhard was frighteningly familiar, for surely it was what he already knew. With Wiggo and his gang of fiends, hell seemed to have spilled over into the waking world of the Carolingians. It walked among them and its name was calamitous sin. Why else would the infernal gatekeeper have been called from his post, except that the Franks now deserved special punishment? Thus, in Wiggo's demonic speech, one theme dominated, a theme that we have seen developing throughout the 820s: calamity was thought to be the direct consequence of sin. Indeed, in the annals, that tidy little Latin phrase, *peccatis nostris exigentibus,* became a formulaic explanation for calamity. Those writers who had ordered disorder—Theodulf, the royal annalist, and Einhard—were engaged in documenting the physical effects of Carolingian sin. But if Gabriel had provided a positive set of injunctions for reform, Wiggo looked after the negative, supplying the Carolingian reader with a rare view of the malevolent causes and effects of continuing calamity. Wiggo's shocking statement helps us to understand what the royal Frankish annalist meant when he lingered over his reports of failing crops and unchecked disease. The woes of the world were a Carolingian creation, a consequence and proof of the continuing corruption of fallen mankind and its unreformed rulers.

Einhard had also, therefore, shaped another textual community, albeit smaller than the dream factory at Reichenau. Ratleig, who had carried the relics back from Rome and who had written up Aubrey's dream, was a key agent of the group. Someone, too, must have written up the little book about the exorcism that Einhard received at court. These works of Einhard's circle, which were all filtered through him, are neither simple nor without literary effects. In the histories of the incidents with Gabriel and Wiggo, for instance, we encounter devices of verification similar to those found in the *Vision of the Poor Woman of Laon:* a blind man who could not write, and so needed the services of writers and witnesses; and an ignorant and disinterested country girl who knew no Latin. Moreover, in both cases Einhard was conveniently at court and, therefore, seemingly, not involved in the primary actions. But he was their presenter, in some sense, their Daniel. He not only corrected and rewrote Aubrey's vision, but made the accounts of Gabriel and Wiggo the central panels in his *History of the Translation.* Moreover, he had a clear conception of his imperial audience. Louis the Pious himself, as auditor and reader, was made part of Einhard's textual community; he was supposed to have read Gabriel's special message and must have seen or heard about the *History of the Translation.* So popular and so public was Einhard's history of the relics that it is difficult to believe that he could have fabricated Louis's role as the reader of Aubrey's dream text. Later in the century, as we shall see, it was remembered that Louis had read Gabriel's booklet and that one of the things that it may have contained was a condemnation of clerical concubinage.[46] We are also allowed, I think, to imagine other readers of Einhard's work at the imperial court: women like Judith and men like Gerward and Hilduin, who also must have encountered the archangel and the demon in Einhard's pages.

Gabriel and Wiggo were invisible messengers—albeit one light, the other dark—to a worried court. Even Einhard never seems to have doubted the truthfulness of the demon's words. Moreover, Gabriel's insistent and emphatic elaboration of the precise means by which his message was to be passed to the emperor works to heighten the reader's impression of its great importance. This message alone would make all the difference for Louis and his crucial reform of the empire. But this belief in secret truths and hidden designs was a symptom of the times and of its general malaise. Many critics of Louis believed that they had, through their newly discovered art of historical hermeneutics, seen inside a calamitous age to its corrupt core. Wala, too, was supposed to have written a little book in 828 or 829 on the evils rampant in the kingdom, which he explained to the emperor and all who would listen in Aachen.[47] Like the books of Gabriel and Wiggo, Wala's booklet called for fundamental reform. Alongside these three reform programs, we need to remember that Heito's prose account of Wetti's dream, with its vision of a corrupt church and wicked counts, had been written in 825 and that Walahfrid's poetic version had been sent to Grimald at court in 827. In his poem, Walahfrid had addressed Louis directly about abuses in the church and how the emperor could correct them. By 828, then, the voices calling for reform had reached an importunate pitch, and among the shouting could be heard the cries of dreamers, angels, and the garrulous gatekeeper of hell. When Paschasius recalled in the middle of the century that Louis had been warned by visions, he was doubtless alluding both to Wetti's famous dream and to Aubrey's dream of Gabriel.[48]

If during the heady early years of his reign Louis had suppressed evil and put an end to the Devil's oppression of the land, as Ermold the Black claimed, by the late 820s many were convinced that he had unloosed a new set of misfortunes on the empire.[49] In beginning his reign with reform, Louis had sanctioned and promoted reforming bishops and abbots who would not now forgive him for the kingdom's apparent slide back into crisis and confusion. Committed churchmen believed that they had uncovered the real road to salvation. What Einhard had found in his saints' relics and in voices from the beyond were auxiliary supports that carried an insistent demand for reform to an opinionated and drifting court.

In late 828, amidst this reformist rhetoric, Louis announced that he would hold four councils during the next year. The emperor and his eldest son Lothar circulated a general letter calling for the councils, but it exists in two forms. The major one called for general reform, a period of fasting, and the mobilization of armies to fight the enemy. The minor one, which was probably reworked and falsified by an unknown bishop the next year, is, for our purposes, more interesting.[50] In this letter, Louis and Lothar ask:

> Is there anyone who does not feel that God has been offended and roused to anger by our wicked deeds? In the kingdom committed to us by him, his wrath has been at work for many years in the form of many disasters: by ongoing famine, the deaths of animals, pestilence attacking men, the almost complete sterility of crops, and, as I might have put it, by the various scourges of sickness and great poverty that have vexed and misera-

bly assaulted the people of this kingdom and, thus, completely stolen from them all prosperity.[51]

The letter writer lamented, in Louis's name, the outrages committed in the kingdom by tyrants who worked to undermine the peace of a Christian people and to tear apart the unity of the empire. Even the invasions in 828 by the enemies of Christ—the Northmen—who burned churches and cruelly killed and captured Christians were a result of sin. In this letter, Louis and Lothar accepted full blame, confessing that they had sinned more than others, for it fell upon their imperial shoulders to correct evil men, to care for all their people, and to provide a healthy example to the kingdom.[52] Both forms of this imperial letter, the true and the false, agreed that the kingdom had suffered many blows from an angry God, who remained propitiable, but the legitimate letter was more activist, calling for the councils to correct bad behavior, for soldiers to resist the invaders, and for prayer. The episcopal letter eschewed collective blame and the need for steady action, preferring to point a finger directly at the sinful source of the trouble.

Wiggo's words, in fact, reflect the language of the reformulated epistle. Indeed, the extant decrees of the Council of Paris, convened in June 829, attempt to address some complaints almost identical to those made by Wiggo: against those who failed to observe the Lord's day, against both clerics and laymen who robbed the poor, against the oppression of the poor, against usury, against those who took advantage of the king, and against lay injustice, especially as it affected widows and orphans.[53] In a supplementary letter, the bishops condemned many of the same things again, including those who employed false weights and measures to cheat people. The bishops were convinced that the land was being punished by famine and disease because of criminal wrongdoing. But they reminded Louis, in the official letter of preface to their report, that God had canceled the overthrow of Nineveh because the people had repented and that Ahab and Manasseh, once wicked kings, had been saved by God because they had repented and refound God.[54] Moreover, the second book of the council's doctrines was centrally concerned with good kingship. A king, as the council agreed and Jonas of Orléans was to repeat later, was a king by acting rightly, but he forfeited the title if he committed injustices. Indeed, the peoples of older times used to call all kings tyrants, though for Christians a king now meant someone who ruled piously and justly. The bishops felt called upon not only to define kingship but to rescue a wandering people: "to free men from the darkness of infidelity and transport them to the light of faith, and to transform sons of rage into sons of adoption.'' They worried that if priests did not vigorously preach against iniquity, they themselves would be complicitous sinners.[55]

But the Council of Paris was convened in that unsettled year which had opened with Wala's demand for reform. The clamor of Gabriel and Wiggo could still be heard amidst the winds that blew through Paris.[56] The bishops gathered there demanded greater power in order to reform the church, for they had come to believe that the reform of a Christian empire and the correction of the emperor were one and the same thing. If men like Einhard hectored Louis, it was in order to show him, through their sophisticated ordering of disorder, the severity of the situation. They wanted to open the emperor's eyes to a catastrophic sequence of events:

> How can anyone be faithful to you if, seeing and understanding the danger that you are in, he does not do as much as he can to point it out and make you aware of it, so long as an occasion and opportunity to do so are not entirely denied him?[57]

In the heady days of his revolt against Louis, Agobard justified his boldness in these terms; the truly faithful subject must speak his mind to the emperor. A decade earlier, men like the royal Frankish annalist had also sought to alert Louis to the dangers all around, but they did so by intimation, not proclamation. Even a supportive subject like Walahfrid Strabo was still working within the old model of allusive advice in 829 when he wrote his exceedingly rich and complex poem *On the Statue of Theoderic*. There we find him still searching for enlightenment, for some way to understand how, beyond the avarice and evil represented by Theoderic and still polluting his own world, a new deliverance by a new Moses might be achieved.[58]

The death of Bernard, the public penance of Louis, his marriage to the ambitious Judith, and the birth of a new son were all events that had unsettled courtiers like Einhard, but worse was to come. Late in 829, at the behest of the new chamberlain, Bernard of Septimania, Lothar and his supporters were driven from court and young Charles was given the previously allotted territories of Rhaetia, Alsace, and a portion of Alemannia and Burgundy. Thus, it was believed that Louis had begun to break his own constitutional arrangement of 817 in order to make room for his new son. Louis was abandoned by his army on his way to suppress a rebellion in Brittany in early 830, and his sons Lothar and Pepin rose in revolt against him. The emperor and his son Charles became virtual prisoners of Lothar, while Judith was held in an abbey at Poitiers and the chamberlain Bernard fled for his life to the Spanish March. By October 830,

Louis, still emperor, managed to reassert his authority at Nijmegen and to settle old scores with rebels such as Hilduin and Wala. With order restored in 831, Louis set out a new partition of the kingdom, the *Division of the Kingdom*, modeled on his father's *Divison of Kingdoms*.[59] Lothar was not mentioned at all; the kingdom was to be divided among Pepin, Louis the German, and Charles the Bald, and the imperial title was seemingly to die with Louis, or so it must have appeared to some contemporaries.

But in 832 the sons began to plot once more against the seeming injustice of their father. Again they rebelled. Utterly deserted by his supporters on the "Field of Lies" near Colmar in June 833, Louis became their prisoner; Charles and Judith were dispatched to monasteries. At Saint-Médard of Soissons in the autumn of that year, Louis, in the presence of a huge gathering, laid aside his crown, his imperial robes, and his sword, and in their stead put on the sackcloth of a penitent. He then proclaimed a long list of his crimes, prepared for him by his accusers, and prayed for forgiveness. Thus, Louis the Pious, son of Charlemagne and sole emperor of Francia for almost twenty years, was deposed.

The rhetoric of the 820s, which had laid the groundwork for Louis's deposition in 833, changed during the period of revolt. The criticism of men like Agobard of Lyons, Hilduin, and Ebbo of Rheims now took a more direct line. They had no need to advise Louis indirectly or subtly when they could participate in his deposition and chastise him openly for what they considered his many misdeeds. Louis was criticized by name, and treatises were written on behalf of the three sons who felt that they had been betrayed by Louis when he had tried to undo his former promises to them. They moved the debate to a level that should have been familiar to Louis, for they justified their revolt on the grounds that they only wanted to cleanse their father's palace. The supporters of the elder sons charged that Louis's court was full of moral and sexual improprieties; that indeed Bernard, the powerful chamberlain, had committed adultery with the Empress Judith. Since Louis was Bernard's godfather, some had claimed that incest was involved. A later medieval legend charged that Charles the Bald was really the issue of Judith's adultery and that, when he later killed Bernard, he committed patricide. According to the Astronomer, from whom we possess a fairly full account of the rumors of the 830s, some critics said that Louis was so blinded by delusions that he could neither see nor avenge these sordid deeds.[60] Paschasius Radbertus, as we saw, thought of Louis as a stone-blind emperor stuck in his theater of illusions.

Louis's opponents tried to account for his misrule in these terms: the man himself seemed both devout and sincere, but he had made so many errors of judgment that he must have been deluded. The supporters of the rebellious son Pepin urged him to rebellion, because "they said a good son ought to bear paternal dishonor indignantly and ought to restore a father to reason and dignity."[61] From the perspective of the sons, it was the duty of a good son to correct a wayward father. Had it not been Louis himself who had set this example after his father's death? The sons claimed that they did not want to increase their own earthly kingdoms, but they felt that they must open Louis's eyes to the outrages committed all around him, especially in his own house. In a passage rich in sexual double meanings, Paschasius accused Bernard of plunging headlong into filthy pig troughs like a wild boar; he had occupied the imperial bedchambers and penetrated all things.[62] The monk believed that royal dignity had been destroyed when Bernard had sundered and defiled the imperial household. Worst of all, he had turned sons against their father and the father against his sons: that had been one of the horrors anticipated by Wiggo.

Louis's critics were still writing booklets, but the criticisms were no longer hidden behind any false fronts: stategies of indirection were less necessary during a time of open revolt. Agobard of Lyons, who was one of Louis's harshest critics, composed a statement approving of Louis's deposition. Under Louis, he said, the kingdom had tottered and been driven to ruin.[63] He invited Louis to look into the little book produced by the bishops as into a mirror in which he would see the foulness of his crimes. But in this work he attributed the decline of the kingdom principally to Louis's negligence and idleness. In the same year, he published two short books in which he openly attacked Judith, whom he believed to be the source of the kingdom's problems. In one he demonstrated, with biblical examples, how evil women had frequently led good men astray. Samson had so suffered, and Louis himself was now deceived by a wicked woman; murder, adultery, and incest had followed her to court.[64] In the other more striking work, Agobard openly announced:

> Listen all peoples! Let the whole world learn and reflect at the same time on the fact that the sons of the emperor, Lord Louis, have been and are justly outraged and that they properly plan to cleanse their father's palace of its filthy crimes and foul factions and to cleanse the kingdom of its most bitter and turbulent disturbances.[65]

At one time, Agobard protested, Louis had stayed peacefully at home and had fulfilled his marital duties, but, as time passed, this right relationship had waned and grown cold, and Judith had turned to open wantonness. Soon not only a few in the palace but the whole world knew of Judith's indiscretion:

young men laughed, old men mourned, and esteemed men deemed it unbearable. The sons of the emperor were moved by a reasonable outrage, since they had looked on as

> the bed sheets of their father were stained, the palace disgraced, the kingdom confused, and the name of the Franks, which up to that point had been brilliant throughout the whole world, was darkened.[66]

As one they rose up to reform the palace and restore their father to quiet dignity. Thus, the rebellious sons of Louis justified their action as a restoration rather than a deposition.

Behind Agobard's thinking lay a coldly rigorist and self-serving appraisal of how a father ought to treat his sons. In a letter sent to Louis in 829 or 830, he had suggested that if Louis had cared to lead a peaceful life with his sons, as Charlemagne and Pepin had with theirs, he would have obviated the many evils assaulting the land.[67] For Agobard, then, it was precisely the disruption of the royal family that had produced disorder in the land. But this game could be played by both sides. Both Jonas and Einhard had reminded Louis's sons in 831 of the honor a son owed his father and of how God was displeased with contumacious and disobedient sons.[68] In 834, after the alliance of his rebellious sons had dissolved, Louis reclaimed the imperial throne. In a treatise written in that year for the emperor, Hrabanus Maurus dealt with the question of the filial respect all sons owed to their fathers. Hrabanus marched out a whole series of scriptural injunctions to prove that sons and daughters not only should obey their parents but should never dispossess them of their goods and honors. But Hrabanus was writing after Louis's true restoration to power, and so he urged him to forgive the sons who had done him wrong. The work reinforced Louis's impression that he had been the injured party. Rudolf, a monk of Fulda, later described the book as a work of consolation. Yet Hrabanus's work continued to have some relevance for Louis, who was haunted until his death by the specter of filial revolt. In 836, Louis put the book to good use; he sent legates to his eldest son Lothar, who was then confined to Italy as though under house arrest, reminding him of the obedience and reverence owed to a father. The biblical injunctions that were read aloud to Lothar corresponded exactly to those in Hrabanus's treatise.[69] Thus, in the shadows of a divided family, Louis's supporters turned to erect a defensive wall of biblical precept and paternal priority around the emperor.

The argument over right behavior also turned on questions of faithfulness, since both sides believed that the other had broken oaths. Ironically, because of

the *Ordinatio imperii,* which had attempted to preserve imperial unity, the supporters of Lothar and his rebellious brothers in 830 and 833 could use the notion
of unity to condemn Louis. Pope Gregory IV, under the patronage of Lothar,
had accused Louis of working against peace and unity. Agobard believed that,
by abandoning the inspired earlier agreements, Louis was a breaker of oaths,
while at the same time he had made men swear countless and contradictory
oaths to himself and Charles.[70] Moreover, Carolingian monarchs, who had actively encouraged the vassalage of their powerful subjects, saw the oath of fealty as a bulwark against rebellion. Louis the Pious apparently reproached his
rebellious sons in 833 with the words: "Remember that you are also my vassals
and that, with an oath, you confirmed your fealty to me." The sons swore, in
turn, that they were indeed his *fideles* and had never yet abandoned their military duty.[71]

Between 830 and 833, when revolt was in the open and discontent manifest,
the subterfuge of royal dreams seems never to have surfaced. It must not have
been necessary. When the first rebellion broke out, Einhard was traveling to
Aachen. With great good luck or cunning convenience, he fell ill and was
forced to take refuge at Saint-Bavon. In a letter, Einhard urged an unnamed acquaintance at court to explain to the emperor what had happened to him, because he did not want his loyalty to be doubted in this time of widespread dis-
loyalty. But Einhard also pleaded with his friend for information about events at
court. He signed off with a note of sad resignation: "Everything that is now happening in this kingdom was foretold two years ago through the agency of the
martyrs of Christ."[72] Thus, during the Lenten rebellion of 830, Einhard recalled the recent warnings of Gabriel and Wiggo and must have wondered why
Louis had not paid heed. Still, that was the stuff of old dreams, and not long lingered over.

Royal dreams had always had functions other than the merely corrective and
admonitory, even if they were, for the most part, neglected by the Carolingians.
One of these was consolation, and Walahfrid Strabo was, in 833–34, a monk in
need of otherwordly comfort. As the tutor of Charles the Bald and the client of
the Empress Judith, Walahfrid had lost his place and position when they fell into
rebel hands. Hence, the poem in which he celebrated the rescue of Judith from
imprisonment in Italy is one of excitement and high drama, for it was rumored
that Lothar's agents had planned to murder Judith before she could be freed. But
Walahfrid imagined the young noble Ruadbern, to whom he sent the poem,
stealing through narrow passes in the Alps and fording violent rivers. At every
turn, he encountered the oppressions of hunger, darkness, and death. But Ruad-

bern was a clever servant, the master of a thousand clever tricks, and overcame all adversity as he wended his way to the empress with news of her release and recall.[73] That the obstructive and oppressive forces were now found on the rebel side allowed Walahfrid this once to imagine epic heroism. Had Ruadbern died en route, Walahfrid could have made of him a Roland in the rough. Indeed, the character of the great king Carles in the *Chanson* fits Louis better than Charlemagne, for it was Louis the Pious who needed defending and his men who suffered overthrow and oppression.

Yet Walahfrid could fight back in his poetry, and in his dreams. In 834, after Ruadbern's mission and Judith's return, he presented the empress with a dream poem. During the rebellion, Walafrid said that he had looked on in sadness as the holy faith, the people, and their father (Louis) had experienced hatred, violence, exile, jail, and irons:

Solaque per gremium regni nutantis ineptos
Perfidia exeruit feruore tyrannidis ausus.

[And a singular treachery vehemently spread the improper designs
Of a faithless tyranny throughout the heart of the kingdom.][74]

Tyrants—those men who had lost the name of king according to Jonas—had not only invaded the body politic, they had invaded Walahfrid's sleep. During those dark days, "no comfort came to me through prophetic dreams," the poet wrote. But God finally came to his rescue in a dream, driving away the dark clouds of his fear and advising him to look forward to a bright new day.

As sleep stole over his restless form, a beautiful book appeared before Walahfrid's eyes. When he examined it closely, he saw that it was filled with alternating sections of poetry and prose, and observed that it spoke of events affecting the king and kingdom. Under a picture of the emperor, he noticed the name EQVITATIVS inscribed rather than LVDOVICVS. The unusual nature of the epithet did not bother Walahfrid, since he knew at once that in this wondrous book of history people and events were described according to their familiar and manifest characteristics. As he read, therefore, he encountered a summary and categorical vocabulary: impiety and the double violation represented the rebel side, while victorious patience and the retrievable glory of the king stood for Louis's side. But as he looked into this book of truth, his eyes burning from reading it over and over again, a monk appeared and, like some librarian looming over an innocent reader at closing time, took the book away. Before going, he reassured the reader:

Tristior ex oculis humor, quam tota decebat
Pectora, non longae passuri damna ruinae.

[Tears sadder than it was right for any breast to bear fall from the eyes
Of one who will not suffer the misfortunes of a long overthrow.][75]

When the dream dissolved and the dreamer awoke, he could scarcely remember anything except the two lines and the unusual name for Louis. He knew that the name Equitatius stood for the good works and virtue of Louis, but left the rest of the dream for Judith to interpret.

There is more, of course, to Walahfrid's dream poem than the vague recollections of a still sleepy poet, for this poet's vision was deliberately Boethian. Indeed, in the manuscripts this poem generally follows the verses on the statue of King Theoderic, where Walahfrid had alluded to the *Consolation of Philosophy,* especially to the idea that men who, through lack of self-knowledge, turn their backs on their true and human natures fall lower than the beasts. Near the end of that poem, Walahfrid had remembered Boethius, in colloquy with Lady Philosophy, recalling the Platonic truth that the best states are those in which kings are wise and where the wise reign.[76] In the poem to Judith, Walahfrid was also looking for prophetic reassurance and philosophical revelation. Indeed, the book into which he gazed was a Carolingian *Consolation* constructed with the Boethian bricks of matching prose and poetry. Like Boethius, Walahfrid presented himself as one over whom events had swept and like him he was unsure about what the future held or what recent history meant. He had become, for the moment, Boethius in his own dark prison of doubt. The rebels remind us of his image of Theoderic as avaricious and tyrannical.[77]

His dream poem was also an allegorical exercise: the tyrants were not identified as individuals, but as the evil impulses impiety and greed. Louis himself was designated by an inscription that suggested that, in the conflict with his rebellious sons, fair dealing, justice, and equanimity (*aequitas*) stood with him, not with them.[78] Louis's tears, according to the angel, flowed because of the injustice and injurious insults he had received. Walahfrid's royal dream was one of the few ninth-century examples that supported rather than undercut a king, offering the dreamer consolation and reassurance. Indeed, the dreamer was so taken with his dream book of Frankish history that he wanted to continue reading it forever. Instead, in case he had missed the point, his monastic messenger left him with words of final reassurance: Louis was sad and had suffered greatly, but he would be restored. In Plutarch's *Morals,* Thespesius once had spied a similar snatch of verse about the suffering of a good emperor.[79] But Walahfrid's poem belonged to 834 and to Judith, supplying divine confirmation of the justice of Louis's certain and inevitable restoration and proof of Walahfrid's unwavering loyalty in the dark days of the previous year, when he had dared to dream about his fallen father.

What the poem in part said to the empress was that she and Louis had truly been the injured parties in the recent debacle. The true book of Frankish history had already been written, for it was this thick book that the dreamer perused, and it not only foretold the future, it rendered sure judgment on the present. This should remind us not only of Reichenau's fascination with the fixity of the written word, but also of those names written on the wall leading to the terrestrial paradise in the poor woman's vision. In the overriding confusion of a recently disrupted kingdom and a still severed royal family, men like Walahfrid welcomed divine confirmation of their all-too-earthly partisanship. Still, with Louis at his most vulnerable, political oneirocriticism had fulfilled one of its many functions. But in addition to offering consolation, this dream still criticized—now not kings, but tyrants who would overthrow the *pater patriae*. In this way, the politics of dreaming shifted as power shifted; with its corrective mandate, it was not bound exclusively to the criticism of kings, but to the chastisement of all the world's wicked, especially those who would be king.

If much of this politics of dreaming was carried on outside the king's awareness and if he was not a player in its too subtle game, then we should stop to consider the case of King Aethelwulf. In 839, the new king of the West-Saxons and Kentishmen and father of Alfred the Great was hoping to make a pilgrimage to Rome and he sent legates to Louis the Pious to obtain free transit through Francia. On this occasion,

> he also advised the emperor to be even more concerned and anxious about the welfare of the souls of his subjects, since a vision shown to one of his subjects had terrified them a great deal. The king took the trouble to send an account of this vision to the emperor.[80]

Thus Prudentius of Troyes, the continuator of the so-called *Annals of Saint-Bertin* after 835, introduced the dream into his annal for 839.

A man appeared to an English priest one night while he slept, not long after Christmas, and ordered him to follow. He was led into a strange land filled with remarkable buildings and entered a church where he found many boys engaged in reading. With trepidation, the priest approached the boys and saw that they were reading books with alternating lines of black and blood-red letters. The guide explained that the bloody lines represented the many sins that Christians had accumulated because they cared to do little of what was commanded in holy books. The reading boys were the souls of the saints who daily deplored the sins and crimes of Christians and who attempted to intercede for them and to lead them to penance. You will remember, the guide informed the priest, that in the present year there had been an abundance of fruit in the fields and trees, but because of the sins of many men a great deal of it had perished. He warned him that if men did not quickly repent and observe the Lord's day, great danger would fall upon them. For three days and nights a great mist would cover the land and out of it would sail the Northmen (*homines pagani*), who would randomly murder men and destroy property with fire and sword. Only through proper penance for their sins would they escape this disaster, for their prayers and fasts might bring about the intercession of the saints.

Aethelwulf's pilgrimage to Rome by way of Francia was postponed until 855, but the implications of his message to Louis are fascinating. For Aethelwulf, the dream seemed to carry a divine and universal warning that should be shared with a fellow king. Like an ancient haruspex looking into a liver, the king read in the priest's dream not a local meaning but an extended one, a meaning that matched the rhythms of the wider world of a Christian commonalty locked in a feverish and sinful flux. For again, in this dream, calamity was a consequence and reflection of sin, and the remedy was religious. Wiggo would have understood. The Frankish and Anglo-Saxon kingdoms shared problems with Norse invasions and failing crops; they also required the same remedies of penance and prayer. But when dream texts were passed from king to king and country to country, dreaming achieved a new level of royal legitimation that would have been impossible, because imprudent and unnecessary, before Louis. In this case, then, we witness the formation, however shallow and short-lived, of a royal textual community that communicated in written dreams. Aethelwulf personally shifted onto royal shoulders, as the dreamers were always wont to do, singular responsibility for saving a sinful people. But we should note one great difference, for the priest's dream did not criticize kings for causing the sins of their people. A true *via regia* of dreams, one promoted by kings themselves, might have been shaped in this way, telling stories of saddened fathers trying to rescue their sinning peoples from sure perdition.

We are entitled, for a moment, I think, to contemplate Louis the Pious as a reader of this text. Not only was he supposed to have received the letter from Aethelwulf in which the text was described, but he may also have been a reader of the *Annals of Saint-Bertin*, where the letter was reproduced. At the time, Prudentius was a palace clerk with access to inside information on Louis's activities. It must have been in the archives themselves that Prudentius saw and was able to make a copy of the priest's dream. Moreover, Janet Nelson has speculated that Prudentius probably thought that Louis might read the annals since, in the entry of 838, he suppressed the rumor of a conspiracy against the emperor.[81] If Louis read the letter from Aethelwulf and revisited it in the annals, he would have encountered an Anglo-Saxon dream text filled with familiar oneiric symbols. For the text, with obvious debts to Bede, would have transported him to a literate otherworld with small books of good deeds and huge books of misdeeds. Louis would have known from the Bible that the book of life was a tally sheet in which the judgment of all nations was supposed to be recorded and read by God at the end of time.[82] Moreover, the image of the book would have reminded him that the actions of humans were not to be forgotten, but were stored away by God for Judgment Day. It should have been a familiar refrain, even if it had not always reached his ears. The poor woman of Laon and Walahfrid had both been otherworldly readers in their dreams. This preoccupation with books, writing, and reading must reflect at some level the monastic character of these Carolingian dream texts, for the world that they came from knew memorial books with their lists of the worthy dead, and it also knew scribal drudgery. Thus the writing seen in the dreams of Louis's theater was a richly associative symbol, for, in a world where nothing seemed solid or sure, it represented fixed and absolute truth. How much of this Louis put any stock in is difficult to say, but he must have read or had read to him the English dream text; otherwise, I suspect, Prudentius would not have dared to insert it in the court annals he was writing.

But whatever kings meant by sending and receiving oneiric messages, Prudentius probably meant something else. He was interested in dreams or, at least, one of his correspondents assumed that he was. While he was at court, a young poet sent Prudentius an account of a girl who had had fallen asleep and seen many people suffering and some prospering in the otherworld.[83] In the case of the annal entry, what we need to notice is that an anxious Prudentius, with some skill, had strung together a series of worrisome events for the year 839: the continuing discord between Louis and his sons, the shocking conversion of the court chaplain to Judaism, flooding along the coast of Frisia, the alarming dream of an Anglo-Saxon priest, pirates and rebels, and comets in the night sky.[84] In this way, he made his entry another exercise in the ordering of disorder, an attempt from the inside to draw Louis's attention to the troubled state of his empire. But the dream text was the most richly colored piece of his montage, allowing a foreign king to legitimize and a distant dreamer to say what needed to be said. If the sinning did not stop, then certain disaster awaited, for the Northmen would surely come and crops would surely fail.

Louis's return to power in the later 830s did not bring an end to the rebellion of his sons. Instead he found that he had merely divided their once-united opposition to his rule. For the last six years of his life, Louis strove constantly to return his sons to proper filial submission. Fulk, the first annalist of the *Annals of Saint-Bertin,* had been content to portray Louis as some oppressed father in a dreary domestic tragedy. In the eyes of the Astronomer, Louis was a latter-day David, suffering the outrages of his sons but loving them still.[85] For a long time, in fact, Louis had sought the almost impossible: to insert a new son into the already established division of an inheritable kingdom. He sought to secure young Charles's position by granting him extensive properties and vainly hoped to obtain for him the protection of one of his half-brothers. Pepin, however, died in late 838 and, since Louis the German was still rebellious, the emperor divided the kingdom between Lothar and Charles, leaving only Bavaria to his son Louis. Of the crumbling relations between the two Louises, Prudentius remarked that "it was sad to see, here the dutiful father, there the undutiful son, falling apart from each other."[86]

Early in 840, Louis the German marched his army into Alemannia; the emperor responded by driving his son back to Bavaria after Easter. On his way home from the campaign, he fell seriously ill with stomach and chest pains and, on an island in the Rhine River near Mainz, Louis the Pious realized that he was going to die. His illegitimate half-brother Drogo, the archbishop of Metz, was at his side and listened to his deathbed worries and final commands.[87] As Louis lingered, he refused to be reconciled with his recalcitrant son Louis, but finally forgave him with the parting reproach that he should not forget that it was he who had led his gray-haired father to a sorrowful death. As death closed in on him, Louis turned his head to the left and angrily shouted, "Hutz, Hutz! [Away, Away!]" To all present it seemed that in his final moments Louis had seen an evil spirit, who may have come to lead him off to hell (see Fig. 25). His eyes, said the Astronomer, lifted first towards heaven and then back again towards the enemy, until it appeared that this man who never smiled was finally laughing uncontrollably. In this paroxysm, the final battle between the emperor and the Devil who had dogged his days, Louis the Pious died.[88]

His body was laid inside a late antique sarcophagus in the cathedral of Saint-Arnulf in Metz (Fig. 16). On its sides this marble tomb depicts Pharaoh and his heavily armed soldiers chasing Moses and the Israelites across the divided waters of the Red Sea, but the waters have already begun to rejoin and the pursuers can be seen collapsing in a jumble of shields, careening chariots, and drowning horses.[89] For Drogo, who must have selected the tomb, and for Walahfrid earlier, Louis's life had seemed a Mosaic search for salvation. The Pharaonic pursuers, they must have thought, were those sins of greed, pride, and impiety that had filled the rebel breast; Louis himself had reached the far shore, there to stand with the saints raised above the churning waters of the world below. Louis's own metaphorical understanding of his life is lost to us, of course, but it must have resembled the one we see dimly on his now-shattered sarcophagus.

If other sick men in the land had had dreams of revelation, we should not deny Louis his own salvific vision. But we also need to recognize that Louis himself had permitted the construction of his theater of illusions. First he had promoted criticism of his father, and then he had not only allowed criticism of himself but had publicly confessed to his own sins, not just once but twice. He sincerely wanted to do what was right, but he could not discover what that was. And so he had opened the door to advice, and reforming, literate, and collectively righteous churchmen—monks and bishops all—were only too happy to step inside. Louis had been less in control of what could be said about him and to him, in part because he was a different sort of patron. Latin culture in his time, following a model of monastic diffusion, was moved outside his house. Ironically, learned culture was now also richer, at least in terms of the number of scholars at work. Thegan, like the Old Oligarch of Athens, would complain that Louis had been wrong to let lowly men learn too much.[90] Learned monks like Heito, however, and monastic dreamers like Wetti and Rotcharius all seem in their dream texts to be standing outside, looking in at a distant king they did not know. When scholars alienated from court began with their newfound distance to see kingship apart from living kings, and when they thought they saw order slipping from their small world, they turned to the criticism of their kings. Charlemagne had been too close and too awesome to be criticized by the scholars carefully assembled at his court; Louis was not.

Think of the dreams alone. Within his lifetime, Louis was said to have received the vision of the poor woman of Laon, the written account of Aubrey's meeting with the archangel Gabriel, and the account of the English priest's vision sent to him by a foreign king. We can only imagine what he thought of these dream texts, but my guess is that he received them with genuine concern. He may not have carried out their commands or he may have thought that he already had, but he could not but listen to their grating voices. The penance that they urged upon him he had already performed. For Louis must have shared with Jonas of Orléans the conviction that every man is a pilgrim in this tor-

mented world, and that all would soon be citizens and natives of the otherworld.[91] In the dark glass of the dreamers, kings were supposed to look upon
that land beyond; it was there, amidst the belching flames of hellfire and the reassuring presence of angelic guides, that Louis must have seen a beast mangling
his father's genitals, his breathless wife pulled down by punishing rocks, and
lists of sins dripping with blood in the book of life. With Louis's death, his theater of illusions may have shut down, but the show was about to go on the road.

CHAPTER FIVE

Civil Wars and Worse

audiet ciuis acuisse ferrum,
quo graues Persae melius perirent,
audiet pugnas uitio parentum
    rara iuuentus.

quem uocet diuum populus ruentis
imperii rebus? Prece qua fatigent
uirgines sanctae minus audientem
    carmina Vestam?

cui dabit scelus expiandi
Iuppiter? . . .

[Romans will learn that we once sharpened our swords,
Swords on which wicked Persians should have died,
And our young men, diminished by the sins of their fathers,
    Will learn that we waged war against each other.

What god should the people summon to forestall
A falling empire? By what prayer should the
Vestal virgins appeal to Vesta,
    Who has ceased listening to their chants?

To what god will Jupiter assign the task of atoning for
Our crimes? . . .][1]

For Horace, the gloom that shaded Augustan Rome was the guilt of civil war. What had been so meanly squandered at Pharsalus and Philippi was salubrious intercourse with the gods, for the lines of communication that had stood open since the death of Remus were violently severed by this new spilling of brother blood. No god would now listen to even heartfelt prayer, nor was anyone sure what sort of god to entreat for the mitigation of so horrible a crime.

Of all wars, it must be civil war that produces the greatest degree of self-reflection among its participants. Religious peoples frequently begin to speculate about the changed relations between humans and gods, since they quickly come to conclude that it must be their disrupted commerce with the divine that has caused them to go to war with an enemy who is no enemy.

Between 830 and 850 Carolingian intellectuals came to grapple with this uncivil dilemma. As they watched their own internal wars unfold, some men and women began to question the nature of the society they lived in, its assumptions, and its destiny. Most of all, they wondered what God was trying to tell them. If after the Battle of Fontenoy, they were bathed in guilt and profound perplexity about God's meaning, by 850 a prophet had appeared who would try to punch a revelatory hole through the hard wall of their confusion and miscommunication.

While Louis the Pious had lived, unity, peace, and tranquillity had everywhere been the ideals of Carolingian thinkers,[2] but violence, injustice, and civil strife had seemed more real. Disorder had come, as it always does, to define order. But it was in the period following Louis's death that writers turned to contemplate the fact of political division and territorial fragmentation, and the words *diuisio* and *discidium* came to occupy a prominent place in their language.

Let us stop for a moment to consider the fault lines that ran below the Carolingian world, tugging its territorial map into marvelous and unexpected shapes. By its very nature, of course, the Frankish kingdom had always been deeply divided; it was unity that had been the miracle of three generations of kings. At its base, Carolingian society was formed of a myriad of peoples joined together by brute force and the accidents of geographical abutment. In a famous, if often misunderstood, Pauline observation, Agobard of Lyons complained that should five individuals sit down together during his time they would find that none of them shared any law in common in the external world, though all were bound internally by the law of Christ. Looking out over his already fragmented world, the bishop saw servants and lords, poor people and rich, unlearned and learned, weak and strong, Gentiles and Jews, circumcised and uncircumcised, barbarians and Scythians, Aquitanians and Lombards, Burgundians and Alemannians, slaves and the free.[3] Conscious of the diametric differences that coursed through the Carolingian circle and of those social polarities that would forever obstruct the biblical hope *ut omnes unum sint* [that all might be one], Agobard had looked to Louis to set straight the diversity and confusion of laws in the land, and, in the name of Christian unity and dominance, had himself unpardonably attacked the Jews. In 839 when Bodo, the trusted royal chaplain of Louis, converted to Judaism, it was further proof to shocked contemporaries that Christian unity was crumbling.[4]

In fact, religious, linguistic, and legal pluralisms had long been the norm in early medieval society; government was, of necessity, laid on top what was already in place. In this traditionally divided realm, the bottom line for Frankish churchmen was the acceptance of minimum standards of religious observance and for kings a demonstration of simple loyalty. Centripetal forces were few in the Carolingian world, the church, court, and king being the most important. Under Pepin the Short's sure hand, the church had become an organ—however limited in range—of centralization in Francia through its extensive missionary work and its steady supply of able administrators. At the Carolingian court a practical synthesis of Germanic, Roman, and Christian cultures was achieved, but only for the handful of men and women collected sporadically in the shifting and reassembling household of the king. As agents of centralization, however, both church and court depended on the royal house, which, often as not, proved to be a fragmenting force in the kingdom. For though the Carolingian royal family was the greatest centralizing force of the early Middle Ages, it could not escape its own politics of familial fragmentation.

Even the concept of imperial unity had had an almost accidental birth, and this despite the labored Augustinian interpretations that surrounded Charlemagne's imperial coronation.[5] Charlemagne himself may well have conceived of the imperial title as largely personal, an individual honor paid to him personally, as Ganshof claimed, but his *Division of Kingdoms* of 806 anticipated Louis's *Ordinatio imperii* of 817. For while Charlemagne followed the Germanic custom of dividing his lands among his three living legitimate sons, just as he and his brother Carloman had received the divided kingdom of Pepin, he bestowed upon his son Charles the Frankish territory proper and left his younger sons with the outlying territories of Italy and Aquitaine. Still, no mention was made in this constitutional document of the inheritability of the imperial title. It was chance alone that left Charlemagne with but one successor, for his son Pepin died in 810 and young Charles in 811, leaving Louis as the sole surviving legitimate son. In these changed circumstances, Charlemagne heeded the imperial party at court that was probably spearheaded by Einhard. The imperial rhetoric that had preceded Charlemagne's elevation in 800 had taken hold in the minds of these men, despite the fact that Charlemagne himself later seems to have drawn back from its full implications and to have expressed second thoughts about the coronation in the company of his biographer. Nevertheless, in 813, Charlemagne summoned Louis to Aachen, and in the presence of an assembly personally crowned him and permitted him to share the title of emperor.[6] For his own part, Charlemagne may have believed that just as his father Pepin in his time and he in his own had emerged as lone kings, so Louis, by an unfathomable but certain twist of divine judgment, had been left alone among his sons. But if the inheritability of the imperial title was contingent upon chance survival, at least in the succession of a single son the conflicting notions of Germanic and imperial inheritance could coexist.

Under Louis, however, the idea of imperial unity or, at least, the concept of the indivisibility of the empire had been strongly, if briefly, asserted. By the *Ordinatio imperii* of 817, Louis's two younger sons were made kings and given lands, but Lothar was associated with his father as emperor, just as Louis had been in 813. Lothar was given primacy over his two younger brothers who thus were rendered subordinate rulers in the empire. The notion of imperial unity fostered by the *Ordinatio* quickly found a number of interested adherents. It was no coincidence that it was during these years that Agobard of Lyons first began his reform of local superstitions, legal heterogeneity, and Jewish pervasiveness, for, as questionable as these reforms may seem to us, to Agobard they represented a drive towards uniformity and unity. But the birth of Charles the Bald in 823 was to prove divisive, as Louis attempted, with some success and constant energy, to provide for his young son by changing the terms of his own earlier constitutional arrangement. It would be a mistake, however, to think that his opponents in the two revolts had had a common cause and that their concern was with high constitutional principles. Carolingian politics was always more complex than that, always more segmented and factional.

Yet constitutional illusions of imperial unity had cast a spell over some intellectuals and their perception of the nature of the Carolingian kingdom. The process of division, despite what they thought, was normal and would continue throughout the ninth century. The irony of the concept of unity—indeed, it is the supreme irony of ninth-century thought—is that it had been an illusion from the beginning. Empire and the concomitant notion of unity were aberrations in the larger design of Frankish history. The Merovingians had rarely achieved a consolidated kingdom under one ruler and then only by the bloody removal of rivals with brutal dagger thrusts and draughts of poison. The intellectuals of the ninth century seem to have forgotten, because of the impression made upon them by the towering singularity of Charlemagne and the early commitment of Louis to imperial unity, that the kingdom had been ruled for a good part of the eighth century by multiple rulers. The bastard son of Pepin of Heristal, Charles Martel, had had to overcome the supporters of his father's grandsons. His two sons Carloman and Pepin the Short had ruled jointly for five years until Carloman withdrew to a monastery in 747. Charlemagne and Carloman, the two sons of Pepin, who died in 768, ruled their respective parts of Francia in acrimony until the death of Carloman in 771. Partition would have occurred once more on Charlemagne's death had not two of his three sons preceded him to the grave. In Frankish history from the time of Clovis forward, therefore, partition was typical and only occasionally subverted by the happenstance of premature death and the survival of a single son. Thus, nature ofttimes cleaned up what the Merovingians and Carolingians never could. Charlemagne was hesitant to turn his back on ancestral tradition, and Louis the Pious answered to the same atavistic urge after 823 when he sought to provide for the most recent issue of his royal loins. Like his father, Lothar permitted his son Louis to share the imperial title in 850, but he also divided his territories among all his sons.

The principle of Germanic partition became a constitutional curse for the Carolingians only when the concepts of empire and unity were laid on top of it. With its untraditional and implicit principle of primogeniture and its traditional recognition of the right of partition, Louis's *Ordinatio* was an awkward solution to the perplexing problem of an ancestral Frankish kingdom that existed inside a new and unitary empire. In the case of the *Ordinatio,* Louis was burned twice: first by Bernard for his apparent abandonment of Charlemagne's agreements, then by his own sons when they perceived that their father was changing his own proper partition of the kingdom. Just as Louis was haunted after 830 by the notion of unity he had earlier promoted, the idea itself held fast for a generation of thinkers and was registered in their acute disappointment over an increase in the number of kings and, later, kinglets. In the 840s Carolingian thinkers were faced with the old reality of partition once again, and it struck hard at their illusions about the specialness of their Christian society.

When Louis died in 840, he left behind three sons: Lothar, who could claim the imperial title; the rebellious Louis the German; and young Charles the Bald. Almost immediately, like three puppies fighting over a bone (to borrow Marcus Aurelius's metaphorical dismissal of the Quadi seven centuries earlier), the brothers broke into open conflict. In part, their contest arose from the unsettled arrangements for succession left by Louis. Each son felt free to claim territories on the basis of whichever one of Louis's chief documents of division most favored him. Since Lothar appeared to be the strongest of the three, his two brothers soon formed a less-than-holy alliance against him. On 25 June 841, at Fontenoy-en-Puisaye near Auxerre, the brothers met in a battle that shocked contemporaries for its severity and for what they took to be its moral significance.

At dawn on the day of the battle, Louis and Charles climbed a peak near Lothar's camp and waited for the opening of hostilities. The battle was waged on a number of fronts, by both infantry and cavalry, but Lothar's forces finally withdrew, their enemies in faint pursuit.[7] The three major annals of the period all stressed the huge number of dead and dying produced by the battle. Later Regino of Prüm was to say that in this battle "the strength of the Franks and their famous valor was so weakened that after that they could neither expand the limits of the kingdom nor even protect its present boundaries."[8] For some Carolingians and many later historians, the battle marked a turning point in Carolingian fortunes, a singular event that spelled the violent end of Carolingian hegemony.[9] In truth, the Battle of Fontenoy was far from decisive in military terms. Lothar, despite his flight, claimed victory, and Louis and Charles failed to press home their advantage with the result that this Carolingian civil war dragged on desultorily until 843.

Yet the battle was far more important in another regard, for it created the unnerving conviction among contemporaries that there, on the bloodied fields of Fontenoy, they had broken the bonds that had bound them together as a Christian society. We can best descend into the deep pit of their disappointment through a heartrending poem by one of Fontenoy's warriors, Engelbert.[10] He had fought for Lothar that day and had watched his king scattering the enemy far and wide. But Engelbert was as divided in attitude as the Franks were in war. He celebrated the bravery and majesty of his hero in no uncertain terms, never acknowledging his retreat. Through his eyes we see, from the summit of some ridge, Lothar relentlessly driving his enemies across a stream. Yet the poet knew of his lord's defeat, for he said that this victor would have achieved his victory had his warriors fought as bravely as Lothar himself, but his dukes had deserted him just as Judas had once betrayed Christ.

But the tug and pull of two different tensions were at work in Engelbert's thoughts, for as much as he wished to sing for and comfort his hero, he also needed to damn civil war. Only an impious demon could enjoy this rupturing of fraternal concord. For the poet, Christian law had been shattered and Christian society wounded when Frankish blood flowed onto the fields of Fontenoy. Thus, Engelbert worked to undercut the idea put forth by the two triumphant brothers that the battle of Fontenoy had been a trial by ordeal in which God had chosen the righteous side. For the poet, Fontenoy was not God's doing but the Devil's.

What civil war chiefly meant for Engelbert was the fracturing of family: we find ourselves not in the middle of some constitutional squabble or on a vast field of battle with monumental armies on the march, but in the intimate confines of a desperate contest between kinsmen:

> Bella clamat, hinc et inde pugna grauis oritur,
> Frater fratri mortem parat, nepoti auunculus;
> Filius nec patri suo exhibet quod meruit.

> [War screams aloud. Everywhere ugly fights break out.
> A brother sets to kill his brother, an uncle his sister's son;
> No son gives to his father what he deserved.][11]

Images of death and dying, of slaughter and utter destruction, wrap round us like a death shroud as we read Engelbert's poem. The very marshes and fields shook with horror as Frankish warriors fell thudding to the ground. After the battle, Engelbert saw the fields of Fontenoy covered with fallen warriors wrapped in their winding sheets. He thought the fields looked as white with this dressing of death as they would in the fall when covered with immense flocks of birds. But now he saw the dead lying in the wet grass utterly alone in death, their carcasses carrion for scavengers. The very best of Frankish manhood, those wisest in battle, had fallen on the fields of Fontenoy that day.

The poet would not have us celebrate this battle, for there had been no glory in it, only ill chance and folly. Like a latter-day Job, Engelbert wanted this sad day to be stricken forever from the memory of men and the fields of Fontenoy to be forever covered by unending twilight.[12] Forgetfulness may seem at first a facile antidote for memories too horrifying to recall, but it was also utterly artificial, for the would-be forgetter wrote an unforgettable poem, whose haunting rhythm was soon set to music and sung.

What Engelbert wanted was not to forget but to execrate, to make impossible the creation of a glorious reputation for Fontenoy. The poem ends with images of death and darkness, its melancholy mood unrelieved as the poet left each Frank to master his own grief. We need to recognize the specialness of this

poem, for Engelbert was a man caught in a spasm of contradiction and unre-
solved conflict; he was at once the celebratory supporter of Lothar and the mo-
rose critic of a war that his king had, in part, caused. Horace would have recognized the sentiment if not the style of Engelbert's poem, for its subject is
essentially the self-reflective guilt engendered by civil war. Alongside the
dying soldiers of Fontenoy, the idea of Christian unity, however illusory it had
been, continued to collapse. The question asked by Engelbert's poem was one
that Charlemagne himself had asked towards the end of his life. Surveying a
corrupt kingdom and covetous church, he had wondered "utrum uere Christiani
sumus" ["whether we are truly Christians"].[13]

Finally at Verdun in 843 the famous treaty between the three brothers was
struck. Lothar obtained that oddly contorted kingdom stretching from the North
Sea to the Mediterranean that contained both Aachen and Rome. It could not
endure, of course, but it was a monument, however nugatory, to Lothar's imperial pretensions and to the cleverness of the treaty's framers. Louis the German
held eastern Francia, the Germanic territories that he had held since his father's
time. Charles, the most vulnerable of the three brothers, took western Francia,
where the practice of vassalage was already quickening the pace of devolution-
ary change. Like some strange amoeba splitting into three new cellular bodies,
the kingdom of the Franks was partitioned. In the backwash of this strange separation, arbitrary borderlines were produced that split families and parishes and
everywhere divided loyalties.

If the division of a royally constituted empire was the general problem that
Carolingian intellectuals were forced to reflect upon, tripartition was the special shape division had taken. Men like Gerward must have wondered what God
meant by so dividing Francia. In his case, we may have a running record of his
reactions, since Heinz Löwe has argued that the entries in the so-called *Annals
of Xanten* until 860 were likely the work of Gerward, though the last entries
were later revised by an annalist in Cologne. In his early annals, Gerward was
already preoccupied with the theme of threeness: he returned again and again,
using the same language, to the somber scene of three kings going their three
separate ways between 833 and 843.[14] Even in division, however, Gerward's
thoughts turned to images of unity. In 841, he tersely took notice of the recent
slaughter of Christians at Fontenoy, but immediately observed that a month
later three rainbowlike rings had formed in the sky and had encircled each other.
Behind the smallest of the rings, which was the richest in color, the sun shone
brilliantly. Hanging in the western sky was the largest ring, part of it seeming to
touch the sun. To the north lay a middling ring, which was linked to the bands of

the other circles. Still, Gerward said, the two larger rings appeared less significant than the smallest. Finally, small clouds that looked like little rings floated in from the northeast and clung to the larger rings in the morning sky. After midday, all the rings vanished.[15]

What Gerward probably saw were shimmering sun dogs created by frozen particles of water suspended high in the midsummer sky. But what he perceived were the symbols of a celestial commentary on Carolingian history that more than made up for its lack of specificity in the vibrant simplicity of its images. Gerward, that former resident of the court of Louis the Pious, had long been exposed to the strategies of ordering disorder, and in his annals he, too, collected striking patterns of natural calamities: flashing lights, strange stars, whirlwinds, earthquakes, and eclipses.[16] Like his friend Einhard earlier, Gerward saw in the stars and in a chaotic natural world the suggestive patterns of an unfolding history. He must have meant his readers to understand the three celestial rings as symbols of the three brothers: Charles the Bald to the west, who was thought to hold the largest of the three kingdoms; Louis the German to the north, with his middling-sized kingdom; and Lothar in the center with the smallest realm. As a partisan of Lothar by the early 840s and an inhabitant of his kingdom, Gerward believed that it was Lothar who bound together what remained of a once-united empire, both by his title and by the centrality of his small but resplendent kingdom. Hence Gerward imagined in the three linked rings an image of fraternal concord, a vision of future unity in the dark days of division following Fontenoy. His heavenly rings anticipated Verdun, and the clinging clouds, noble support.

If Gerward looked forward, Florus of Lyons looked back. The nostalgic memory of the lost empire of Charlemagne coursed through his thoughts in the early 840s. For once

Floruit egregium claro diademate regnum,
　　Princeps unus erat, populus quoque subditus unus.

[Under a bright diadem, a marvelous kingdom flourished;
　　There was one prince and also one subject people.][17]

In every town there had been a judge and law, and peace and virtue had abounded. Priests had ministered to the people, young people had studied Scripture, and even conquered peoples had taken up religion. The reputation of the Franks had, indeed, spread to the farthest ends of the world and the ambassadors of the Greeks, Romans, and barbarians had sought them out. The prince of this blessed kingdom, by the grace of the pope and with Christ's blessing, had deservedly been crowned in Rome, but this pinnacle of achievement had been squandered and the empire lost.

> Perdidit imperii pariter nomenque decusque,
>> Et regnum unitum concidit sorte triformi,
>> Induperator ibi prorsus iam nemo putatur,
>> Pro rege est regulus, pro regno fragmina regni.

> [The kingdom lost both the name and glory of empire,
>> And a united kingdom fell in threefold lot;
>> In fact, no one is now thought to be emperor there:
>> For king there is kinglet, for kingdom the fragments of a kingdom.][18]

Everywhere he looked, Florus saw a fallen empire, covered in soot, the victim of obduracy and grasping hatred. Even the elements had turned against the Franks, as God whipped them with deluge and disaster. The church had been abandoned, ecclesiastical law spurned, and pillage, violence, and adultery were sweeping across the land. Florus wondered aloud what the peoples of the lower Danube, Rhine, Rhône, Loire, and Po rivers would do now, a little while ago bound in harmony, now divided by a broken pact. The court was deaf to all legates and synods, and assemblies failed to meet in the divided kingdom. The general good was now shaken as each man pursued his own selfish interests and forgot entirely about God.[19]

Florus related this disastrous sequence of events to such celestial signs as the eclipse that had preceded the Battle of Fontenoy, where Christians had sharpened their swords against Christians, and to the appearance of Halley's comet in 837, which had signaled the death of Louis, the devastation of whole regions, the madness of war, and the splitting of the kingdom. Thus had the anger of God been visited upon a kingdom that proclaimed that it was at peace but lacked the decency of real peace. The Frankish kingdom was a wall threatening to collapse in great and sudden ruin. Long ago it had stood solidly, but now it leaned to one side, was cracked and faltering, and full of yawning holes. Florus imagined that Christ was a mason who had thrown down his plumb line and mortar in disgust and walked away from a crumbling kingdom. Thus, the Carolingian fate was the fulfillment of God's prophecy that he would chastise with a strong stick peoples who had obdurately abandoned their faith. Florus ended his poem with a prayer, beseeching God to let his people see in their minds these many evils, ruins, and dangers, for God lifts up the downcast but crushes the proud.[20]

With this variation on Virgil's motto of Rome's dutiful destiny, Florus re-
stated his profound longing for imperial integrity.[21] He was part primitivist in
his unswerving and uncritical love of a golden age just forty years before;
everything since had been a falling away from former glory. Like Louis's
critics, Florus had no doubt that present calamity was a consequence and reflection of sin. Nature in riot was the surest sign of God's continuing displeasure
with the uproarious lives of a once-faithful flock. Paradoxically, he thought of
kinglets and fragments of a kingdom both as products of God's wrath and as yet
another Carolingian sin provoking that wrath. Though his poem ends with a
homiletic call for reform, its language is suffused with the finality of damnation, for punishment was already at hand. It saddened him to see that people not
only misunderstood the magnitude of the changes they were witnessing or what
they had lost, but welcomed the savage wounds inflicted upon the weary kingdom.[22] In his plaintive summons for the Carolingians to mourn, Florus, in effect, had written a funeral eulogy for a fallen empire. Upon his shoulders fell
the duty, he thought, of telling others that their empire had been lost and that
this present kingdom divided in three was a degraded thing.

Florus was not alone, as many churchmen turned to ruminate over a process
of fragmentation that was beyond their power to halt. Paschasius Radbertus remembered the advent of Bernard of Septimania at the court of Louis as an event
that had opened a still unclosed and suppurating wound of social relations.

O that day, which very nearly brought everlasting darkness and crisis to
this world, which split into pieces and bit by bit divided a peaceful and
united empire, which broke apart brotherhoods, which separated relatives, which everywhere spawned hostilities, which scattered citizens,
which wiped out good faith, which destroyed charity, which violated
churches, and which corrupted everything! Whence daily civil wars and
worse, if I might put it so, arise.[23]

The last line was a paraphrase of the famous first line of Lucan's poem on the
Roman civil war, an allusion made by many in the 840s and beyond. It was in
the harsh glare of their own civil war that Lucan became one of the most popular
ancient authors of the ninth century.[24] Even to have conceived of their conflict
as a civil war rather than an inevitable dynastic dispute reveals how attached
Carolingian intellectuals had become to the idea of a unitary state based on a set
of shared assumptions. Some searched Lucan's poem for an understanding of
the formal meaning of civil war, though in the end they must have become
somewhat lost in the confusing maze of the poem's passionate retroflection.

Still, they would have met on its pages, as we do today, the true horror felt by a people who once knew a community of purpose but now pondered a future full of division.

In thinking about a fragmented kingdom, Carolingian intellectuals looked as often to the Bible as they did to Roman history. They recalled repeatedly that Christ, after expelling an evil spirit from a poor wretch, had been charged with being in league with Beelzebub, the prince of devils. He had pointed out to his accusers that Satan could not oust Satan, for "every kingdom divided against itself is brought to desolation; and every city or house divided against itself shall not stand."[25] The thinkers of the 840s were less interested in the context of Christ's comment than they were in its homespun political wisdom, which they freely applied to their own recent history. Both Gerward and Lupus of Ferrières were convinced, for instance, that the Northmen had fallen on their land because, as Christ had taught them, no kingdom could endure protracted division. Paschasius's hero Wala had worked, he said, to prevent "this glorious and most Christian kingdom from dividing into parts, since, according to Christ, 'every kingdom divided against itself will be desolated.'"[26]

Looking back from later in the century, Carolingian thinkers could not help but feel that unity had, in fact, passed with Louis the Pious. Hincmar would note that henceforth the kingdom was to be agitated and to lack internal solidity, while outside it was to be surrounded everywhere by pagans.[27] Thus, even the walls that protected their cities and the marches that stood at fractious frontiers gave the Carolingians little sense of security, since they believed that the process of fragmentation had come upon them from within, not from without. Unlike some modern historians, the Carolingians refused to blame the invaders for their troubles. Instead, like Polybius and Gibbon, they believed that imperial rot begins inside and, like the purulent core of a boil, must work its way to the surface.

Political oneirocriticism, which had been significantly absent during the civil war, found a new voice, the prophetic, towards the end of the 840s and early 850s. Prophecy has often been the companion of times that know "rebellion, discontent, and violent change."[28] Before historians have ventured very far out onto the murky pond of prophecy, they soon discover that political prophecy has more of animadversion than prevision to it. But it would be wrong for historians, knowing this, to condemn political prophets for what they are not.

Agnellus of Ravenna, living in a city that had fallen firmly within the orbit of Carolingian affairs after 774, inserted the prophetic revelations of Archbishop

Gratiosus into his history of the archbishops of Ravenna. He began with a curious story, for it was remembered at Ravenna that Charlemagne had once visited the city and dined with the archbishop. In the middle of the meal, Gratiosus
had begun to address the emperor in what seemed to be an inappropriate manner: "Father, O my lord king, father." Charlemagne immediately interrupted
him, wanting to know why a priest would call him father. When it was explained to him that this was a term of respect and not an insult, he was won over
and announced, as Jesus had to Nathanael, that Gratiosus was "an Israelite indeed, in whom there is no guile." Agnellus reported that not long after this incident, when Charlemagne took full control of Lombardy, frightening signs appeared, for men mounted on horses were seen fighting each other in a battle in
the evening sky and an earthquake followed.[29]

Without any warning or explanation at this point in his history, Agnellus
plunges the reader headlong into apocalyptic prophecy. By way of explanation,
some annotator added in the margin of the manuscript, "Gratiosus, the Archbishop of Ravenna, prophesied this, not the author of this work."[30] The archbishop protested that he was not a prophet, but that as a Christian he had as
much right as the pagans Nebuchadnezzar, Virgil, and the Sibyl to hear the inner voice of prophecy. Full of fury, he predicted coming calamity: wars, invasions, depredations of churches, famine, disease, and flood. The very sun and
moon would revolt, casting the earth in shadow. Men would turn against the
church and even Ravenna would be violated. The present empire of the Romans
would be desolated and many kings would sit on the imperial throne. Men of the
church would begin to rob the church, Christian would kill Christian, and the
Saracens would devastate lands far and wide. Rapacious kings at that time
would suppress their subjects and, sitting on the imperial throne, would destroy
the empire of the Romans and the Franks. According to this prophecy, utter desolation and destruction awaited the Western world.

But whatever Gratiosus actually foretold, if anything, it is through the prac-
ticed disdain of Agnellus that we witness its fulfillment. For it was the ecclesiastical historian who was convinced that his world was approaching cata-
clysm, especially during the controversial pontificate of Archbishop George,
who died in 844. According to Agnellus, Louis the Pious had indeed died under
the threatening sign of a comet that had surpassed even the brilliance of the sun,
and he had divided his empire among his three sons. These sons, however, had
begun to fight before finally achieving an unstable peace. Archbishop George,
seeking to enter into the affair and to sway the kings with money, had stolen
many of Ravenna's ancient treasures and had carried them to Lothar at Fon-

tenoy. There he found the army of the new emperor so huge that no animal could pass by it, nor could any small bird fly over it. In staccato style, Agnellus described the unfolding battle: the sound of arms, the wave of shields, and the widespread fear as bodies fell on iron swords. Lothar waded into the middle of the fight and everywhere saw his defeated troops fleeing, but the sound of swords lopping off limbs continued. Lothar had the strength of ten men when surrounded by the enemy, because he fought for an undivided empire and against puny kings. But victory belonged to Charles aided by his brother Louis. Agnellus glumly noted, with grim exaggeration, that more than forty thousand of Lothar's troops had died at Fontenoy.[31]

George, however, survived to be captured and humiliated by his conquerors. They forced him off his horse and, removing his raingear, made him walk at spearpoint into the camp of his enemies. After hearing of his crimes, Charles and his half-brother Louis wanted to send the archbishop into exile, but, because of the intercession of the Empress Judith, they agreed to allow him to return to his see. The young king lectured the warlike George before dismissing him. Agnellus, ever entranced by the aesthetic surface of his world, its golden artifacts and coruscating mosaics, could not resist describing Charles's sumptuous royal dress. But of the many objects stolen from Ravenna, only a few were returned in debased condition. Raging against the excesses of George and bringing to carefully ordered fulfillment on parchment the vaticination of Gratiosus, Agnellus's work breaks off abruptly. The final pages of his precious book thus cast a harsh and lurid light on the events of Agnellus's own lifetime: Ravenna had been despoiled; a thieving archbishop had squandered the dignity of a great see; to the north Christians had slaughtered Christians; the empire had been divided; and petty kings now sat upon the imperial throne. Whether Agnellus lived in the shadow of the dread expectations of Gratiosus or conjured up the darkness himself does not really matter, for prophecy always performs best on parchment and paper where it achieves its most satisfying denouement.

Despite the example of Agnellus, ninth-century intellectuals did not often succumb to apocalyptic thought, at least not in its more extreme forms. They might know the eighth-century commentaries on Revelation by Ambrosius Autpertus and Beatus of Liébana in Spain and might gaze upon the often garishly colored paintings of John's visions made in their own scriptoria,[32] but they do not seem to have been overly afraid that the end of time was rapidly rushing towards them.

But in 847, according to the *Annals of Fulda,* a certain prophetess by the name of Thiota began to excite the parish of Constance with her prophecies.[33]

Many things only known to God had been revealed to her from heaven, she proclaimed. Another source claimed that Thiota believed that an angel of the Lord had appeared to her.[34] What she learned from her divine messenger was that Judgment Day lay close at hand in 847, a message that soon excited the common people. Both men and women flocked to her, bringing gifts and clinging to her speeches. Even some men in holy orders abandoned church doctrines in order to follow this "teacher appointed by heaven." Thiota traveled to Mainz that year, perhaps driven out of Constance by her hostile bishop, the newly installed Salomon. There her popular apocalyptic message had the same effect and soon brought her to the attention of church authorities. At a synod of bishops held at the monastery of Saint-Alban in October, Thiota was examined by the new archbishop of Mainz, Hrabanus Maurus. The prophetess admitted that a certain unnamed priest had suggested those teachings to her and that she had related them to others for the sake of financial gain.

> And therefore, according to the sentence of the synod, the woman, who received a public whipping, gave up in disgrace the office of preaching that she had unreasonably taken up and dared to lay claim to against ecclesiastical custom. Finally in a state of confusion, she put an end to her prophecies.[35]

We have been forced to see the story of Thiota through the prism of this summary and unforgiving judgment, for no other views have been granted us. But, shaped by the conciliar condemnation, the hostile annalist was never an uninvolved reporter. He labeled Thiota a pseudoprophetess and rabble-rouser from the outset. Her prophetic capacity, in his opinion, had never been genuine but had been orchestrated by a priest, and her motives were not heavenly but mercenary. Here he must have remembered the biblical dismissal of people "teaching things which they ought not, for filthy lucre's sake."[36]

But the systematic discrediting of this herald of apocalypse must also suggest a degree of official worry. Behind such an incident must lie issues and events that we can scarcely reconstruct today; others, however, are obvious. For example, the Carolingian church, especially in the dioceses of two newly ordained and vigorous bishops, was not prepared to tolerate lay preaching, especially by a woman. Nor could it sanction, at a popular level, continuing revelation. The less-obvious issues raise certain questions. Did Thiota have clerical managers who facilitated her inspirational tour, just as Lucrecia would centuries later in Spain? Why did the lower classes and even parish priests respond with such fervor to her orations? They were struck, the annalist said, by terror.

But had they been unsettled by civil war, the division of the empire, the distant devastations of the Northmen and Moors, or were they simply convinced that Thiota had the ear of God? They were not, we need to remember, simply frightened by Thiota into fatalistic collapse, there to await the cataclysmic end of the world. Talk of the fulminating fires of hell racing across the earth was in the air, for that strange and controversial Old German poem, the *Muspilli,* was contemporary with Thiota, and its damnation of sin and of grasping nobles belongs to her intellectual world.[37] Thiota herself must have been a product of the general anxieties that were at work in her society. If people gave her gifts and if priests surrendered their holy orders to follow her, it must have been because they were convinced that she could intercede with God to soften the coming collapse. She had not, in other words, convinced them that the world was about to end, but that she could help them negotiate with God their place in its dissolution. In an age in which Mary had become, as Anskar knew, a prayerful pipeline to heaven, perhaps some people were willing to grant a special intercessory role to a woman like Thiota. But the church also knew how to deal with a woman who had no powerful patrons and no chance of securing saintly sanction. Neither Gottschalk nor Audradus was to prove as easy to manage.

But then Audradus Modicus's mission was not apocalyptic; it was prophetic. In some ways, he is the most neglected and misunderstood of all Carolingian writers, and for the remainder of the chapter we shall need to look closely at his uprooted career and his prosaic visions. Audradus was the only Carolingian thinker to compile a book of his visions, and while this should not induce us to rank him with a dream diarist of the stature of Aelius Aristides, we need to appreciate the specialness of his prophetic and dreamy voice.

Audradus had been a monk and priest of Saint-Martin of Tours since the time of Abbot Fridugis. His rather unusual Germanic name, derived from some form of Otrad, is found among a list of 219 brothers of Tours compiled before 834. We also see it inscribed in tiny rustic capital letters inside the triangular and curved spaces of the interlaced border on the incipit page of a now destroyed Turonian lectionary. André Wilmart suspected that Audradus was the book's copyist, though he was more likely the architect of the volume, its director rather than its scribe.[38] In 847, as Audradus himself tells us, he was summoned to Sens by Archbishop Wenilo, who was holding a synod in the city. There, after an election, Audradus was consecrated the *chorepiscopus* or suffragan bishop of Sens by Wenilo.[39]

But to be a suffragan bishop in the late 840s was to be a controversial officer in a controversial church.[40] A decade earlier Hrabanus Maurus had heard the grumbling of proud bishops who resented their suffragans. Yet even the apostles, he pointed out to them, had had helpers. So long as suffragan bishops were properly consecrated by their bishops, they could, he argued, accomplish much that was good for the church.[41] Wenilo must have concurred: his neighbors, Hincmar and the priests of Rheims, never did.[42] The archbishop of Rheims sent a letter to Pope Leo IV in which he sought information on the status of men who had been rashly ordained by suffragan bishops. When bishops died, he pointed out, their suffragans often exceeded their authority, turning over the goods and resources of the church to laymen. This had happened twice to his own church, he noted.[43] Hincmar may have been thinking of Rigbold, the suffragan bishop of Rheims, who had, without the knowledge of the bishop of Soissons, ordained Gottschalk a priest.[44]

Unlike Hrabanus, Hincmar never held the chorepiscopate in high regard. So suspicious of the office was he that, during his pontificate, he preferred to replace suffragan bishops in the diocese of Rheims with deacons, officers whose place in the church hierarchy was more surely subordinate and less problematic in the passing of episcopal power. Once, in order to humble his upstart nephew Hincmar, the bishop of Laon, he had condescendingly reminded him "that he was not much more than a deputy bishop, one whom the Greeks call a suffragan bishop."[45] In the undulation of ecclesiastical power in the ninth century, Hincmar surely possessed the most resolute of wills; he was always ready to assert his metropolitan authority against all comers. To collect, promote, and preserve his power, Hincmar was forever prepared to engage in controversies, and the struggle over the chorepiscopate is a good example. In order to knock aside one more prop holding up Gottschalk, he may have engineered a move to discredit and render invalid the actions of that rash suffragan bishop who had improperly ordained him.

Thus, in 849 the problems presented by Gottschalk and the chorespiscopate may have come together in Hincmar's thoughts. His letter to the pope must have been sent to Rome in that unquiet summer. Wenilo and his suffragan bishop discerned at least part of Hincmar's complex strategy, and they responded as best they could. In a vision—unfortunately undescribed—Saint Peter commanded Audradus to proceed to Rome, and his archbishop permitted him to go.[46] The suffragan bishop characterized this mission as an effort to intercede on behalf of the welfare of his brothers. On 29 June 849, Audradus, "the least of all the servants of God," (hence *modicus*), presented Pope Leo IV with a volume of his collected works. But, as Ludwig Traube long ago suspected, Audradus's trip to Rome must have been a rescue mission, an attempt, however late and however desperate, to put a stop to the continuing ecclesiastical war being waged against the position of Audradus and his fellow suffragans. In an introductory poem to the volume, he described himself as "suffragan bishop by the will of the people of Sens." Later, in his *Book of Revelations,* he again would lay special stress, as we have seen, upon the fact that he had been elected to his office and had been properly consecrated by his archbishop.[47] Thus, the pope was being reminded, none too subtly, that everything about Audradus's office was consistent with canonical practice.

One wonders what else Audradus gave to Pope Leo that June day, since the purpose of his composition was more to influence and petition than it was to buy favor. Late in 849, Lupus of Ferrières was also setting out for Rome in order to discuss church business. He begged his friend Marcward, the abbot of Prüm, to supply him with two blue mantles and two linen garments, which the pope was known to adore. "In accomplishing my mission I shall need to come to the attention of the pope," said Lupus, "but that cannot be easily achieved without offering gifts."[48] Why the abbot went to Rome is not known, but it has always been hard to believe that it was not connected with the case of Gottschalk, the friend of Lupus's youth. Earlier that year, Gottschalk's writings had been burned at Quierzy under the eyes of Charles the Bald, and the predestinarian monk himself had first been beaten and then imprisoned at Hautvillers in the diocese of Rheims. But Lupus, like Audradus, was not subject to Hincmar, Gottschalk's unbending enemy, but to Wenilo. Perhaps the archbishop of Sens had sent his suffragan and his well-connected, letter-writing abbot to Rome to make an end run round the interests of a neighboring metropolitan bishop.[49]

All was in vain. When Audradus returned home, he was summoned to Paris in November to a general synod held "for the benefit of the holy church of God." There, as he tells us, "not only he himself, but all the other suffragan bishops of Francia were deposed at the same council."[50] Hincmar and Pardulus of Laon seem to have been present, though the whereabouts of Wenilo are not known. King Charles was on the road to Bourges and still preoccupied by the problem of predestination, for it was there that he asked Lupus for his opinion.[51] At the Parisian council, Prudentius of Troyes may have attempted to present a more favorable interpretation of Gottschalk's teachings. But amidst the rain that fell that autumn and the gnawing worry that the doctrine of predestination threatened to undermine the pastoral church, no one seems to have stopped long to listen.

In 849, the predestination crisis and the attack on the chorepiscopate twist around each other like the separated and spiraling strands of a double helix. Whatever led Hincmar to work towards the overthrow of the chorepiscopate in

849, his fellow bishops may have supported him in Paris because of their general uneasiness over Gottschalk. They must have thought, in the gloom of Hincmar's harangues about predestination, that they were losing control of the church when a single rebellious monk could resist their authority.[52] Gottschalk, in effect, forced them to concentrate their power and to reassert episcopal authority. The chorepiscopate surely seemed to threaten the diffusion of that power and to complicate proper chains of command in a time of ecclesiastical emergency.

But the only suffragan bishop certainly deposed in 849 was Audradus himself. Rigbold somehow retained his office.[53] Was it the case that all were deposed, but some like Rigbold were returned to office newly recognized by their archbishops? Why, indeed, was Audradus not reconfirmed in his position? In his poem *On the Fountain of Life,* Audradus had spoken of Hincmar as his friend and spiritual guide, but it was this former friend who had played a key role in his deposition. Did Audradus emphasize that not only *he* but *all* suffragans had been deposed, because at some level he suspected that he was the real target? What might have stood against Audradus personally was that by 849 he had already assumed his oracular voice, one that he had recently revealed to the pope. As Thiota might have informed him, 848–49 was not the best time to be testing prophetic waters, at least not if your pond fronted the dry land of a strong and unsympathetic metropolitan bishop.

Both Hrabanus and Hincmar had turned with remarkable vehemence upon Gottschalk, not for some abstract doctrinal reason, but because his teaching seemed to be another revelation of division, the ecclesiastical equivalent of civil war. Not only was it schismatic, threatening to divide the church along doctrinal grounds into free-willers and predestinarians, but it taught that God had already divided Christians into the elect and the damned. Thus, at the levels of both philosophy and eschatology, Gottschalk seemed a divider of opinions and souls. Neither Hincmar nor Hrabanus could abide the thought of ecclesiastical moieties, here or in the hereafter. Their power flowed from their universal and metropolitan claim to shepherd the entire flock. And what would become of the sacramental function of the church over which they presided if people abandoned thoughts of good works and faithful adherence to the church and its rituals?

Hincmar went even further. He portrayed Gottschalk as a false prophet who had come to destroy church unity. At about the time of the Paris synod of 849, he wrote a letter to the cloistered and simple sons of his diocese to warn them against the rise of pseudo-Christs and false prophets. At the outset of his letter he assembled a string of scriptural condemnations of false prophets who would teach damnable heresies and lead the people into pernicious and evil ways. He warned them that it was "out of such circumstances, that Gottschalk, a certain man in our diocese known to you by name, appearance, and association, rose up."[54] Hincmar knew this false prophet: his reputation stank, his preaching was perverse, and in speech he was the most unyielding and obstinate of men. But, at Quierzy in early 849, the archbishop thought that he had found an antidote: the villified monk would be set so far inside his prison at Hautvillers that he would no longer be able to pollute the outer, ecclesiastical world with damnable division.

It was in the shadow of Quierzy and the continuing campaign against Gottschalk that Audradus arrived in Rome. When he appeared before the pope, the demonstration of his orthodoxy must have been foremost on his mind. As he handed over his book, he said: "I present to the Holy Trinity, through your hands, holy Pope Leo, the testimony of my publications [and] the titles of my books."[55] With some pride, Audradus would remember that the pope in the company of bishops and wise Roman priests had welcomed his work. After examining it and finding it pure, Leo remarked that it should be read by the faithful and decreed that, for the honor of his throne, it should be stored in the archives of the church of Rome. What Audradus wanted in Rome was the pope's imprimatur, but he also may have hoped to separate the issues of the besieged chorepiscopate and Gottschalk, which had been Hincmar's sticky web of complicitous association all along.

The work that Audradus gave to Pope Leo may have been a collection of thirteen books, but many of the fragments that survive belong to a later redaction, one inscribed after his return from Rome. The prose preface, for instance, is a record of that trip and can hardly have been part of the papal package of books. Moreover, the work as it exists today is introduced by a set of *tituli* and a proem in verse, both of which function as tables of contents. Probably only one of them was in the collection of books presented to the pope. But with these two tables and the surviving portions of the work, the design of Audradus's complex composition can be reconstructed. The first three books sang the praises of God: a doxological poem on the Trinity (book 1); a poetic account of the power of God, the Fall of Man, and his redemption (book 2); and a set of verses on the Incarnation of Christ and on the Holy Spirit (book 3). Another poem, now entirely lost, treated the appearance of the Word and the birth of Christ (book 4). The fifth book was a curious poem, *On the Fountain of Life,* which survives intact. Saint Peter was the subject of the next poem (book 6), the pontificate of

Saint Martin of Tours followed (book 7), and the martyrdom of Saint Julian and his comrades comprises the next four books (books 8–11). The twelfth book, the only one written in prose, was his *Book of Revelations*. The last book, now no longer extant, seems to have consisted of a psalm (book 13).

What Audradus called books were really the chapters of a connected composition that began with the Trinity and finished with his personal visions and a psalm such as 67 (68) or 54 (55) that promised "death to the reprobate and joy to the just."[56] Thus, we read downward from the Trinity, the kingdom of heaven, and the great works of Christ until we bottom out in the battles of beleaguered saints in this world. This structure of descent may have hinged on the lost fourth book, which treated Christ's human birth, for with it Audradus would have turned earthward to consider what it meant for God to enter this world, what it meant for divinity to be grounded. Book 5, with its complex allegory of the fountain of life, explored the sacramental meaning of Christ's death and of Easter. The poem on Saint Peter certainly suited a gift to Pope Leo, but it also celebrated Christ's creation of the church and his continuing authority in this world. Moreover, in 847, the very year that Audradus had become suffragan bishop, Wenilo had discovered the relics of two martyrs who had been sent into Gaul by Saint Peter. Their remains were solemnly translated to the famous monastery of The Living Saint Peter in Sens. In the rhythmic plummet of his poems, Audradus was searching for the equivalent, for that place of intersection where heaven touched the earth, that miraculous contact point between the worlds where a monk might receive his own electric vision of the divine. All the while, as we drop down, we come closer and closer to Audradus's home and to his native concerns.

Though not nearly as majestic as the descent of the divine imagined by Eriugena in the *Periphyseon,* Audradus's scheme nevertheless seems more personal and emotionally intimate. For we turn from the apostolic church in the sixth poem to Audradus's once and future church in the seventh. And there we meet Saint Martin:

Nam uir apostolicus, nulli bonitate secundus,
Vt sol in caelo, Martinus fulget in axe.

[For Martin, that apostolic man, second to none in goodness,
Glimmers in the heavens, as the sun shines in the sky.][57]

It was to catch such a star that the fortunate people of Tours had attached themselves to Martin, for the Turonian poet knew that at the saint's death the archangel Michael and all the saints had snatched up his soul and God had brought Martin home to heaven. The central conviction of Audradus's spiritual life was the belief that Tours, and hence western Francia, possessed an unconquered friend, a great patron, who hovered over them eternally in heaven.

The poems on Saint Julian, which immediately precede the *Book of Revelations,* transport us to the bloody battlefield of the martyrs. As his title announced:

Quattuor hinc pugnas fidei testantur et, omnem
Perfidiam extinctam, uires regnumque piorum.

[After this, four books describe the battles of the faithful and—
All treachery having been destroyed—the power and kingdom of the pious.][58]

The reader of the *Book of Revelations* cannot but recognize in this bald *titulus* the fundamental design of Audradus's own self-conscious calling: in his book, he, too, would be one of the final battlers against treachery, an intimate companion of those other mighty fighters, the saints.

For Audradus, the saints were already triumphant, their kingdom secure and their power manifest. When the cruel governor Martian finally decided that Julian and his fellow Christians must die by the sword, the saint could not resist one last, resounding rebuke. He informed the tyrant that while he and his friends would soon stand with Christ in glory, the governor would forever be buried in the shades of hell, there to suffer eternal torment, hellfire, worms, beasts, and grasping teeth. As the martyrs fell to the ground, the entire world trembled, and the air was shattered by thunder and lightning.[59] With the example of Julian's frightening prophecy for the Roman governor, Audradus left his readers at the end of book II with the sound of the unquavering voice of a holy man who had remained unshakable in a world punctured by malignancy and malevolence. The stage had been set for readers to turn to Audradus's own ongoing battle with the unholy and politically perverse.

The whole of Audradus's complex composition, and indeed of his career, led to the *Book of Revelations.* The language of prophecy suffused the parts of the larger package. The word that I took earlier to refer to his publications, *praedicatio,* was just the kind of word he liked to use, since it had another meaning, also hinting at powers of prophecy. Indeed, his preface began with talk of an *oraculum diuinum,* by which he meant the divine mandate given to him by Saint Peter in a vision. It was this certain conviction in his own prophetic capacity that drove Audradus to Rome and that governed his larger work.[60] In the proem perhaps seen by the pope, the suffragan bishop had not hidden his claim to be a prophet:

De grege Martini magni ecclesiae Turonensis
Praesulis ex uoto Senonum chorespiscopus idem
Praecipiente deo post hos scripsit duodenum,
Quo docet inducias mortalibus esse decennis
Temporis indultas et plurima dicta monentis,
Plenius ut libri textus haec ipsa retentat.

[From the flock of the great Abbot Martin of the church of Tours,
Audradus, suffragan bishop by the will of the people of Sens,
Wrote, after the prior books, and on the command of God, a twelfth,
In which he teaches that a truce of ten years' time has been granted
To mankind and he supplies many words of God's advice.
The content of the book preserves these very words more fully.][61]

The preceding titular preface is shorter but even more to the point.

Hostes prosaicus duodenus iudicat acre
Ecclesiaeque pios reparare prophetat honorem.

[A twelfth book in prose judges enemies severely
And prophesies that the pious will restore honor to the church.][62]

Audradus's world was dichotomous, an Augustinian division into sinful and faithful camps, but he was no Gottschalk, for he thought that his prophetic warnings would, if heeded, bind up a broken peace and restore a ruined church.

But modern scholars have been somewhat suspicious of Audradus the prophet and so of Audradus the poet. Walter Mohr argued that the surviving revelations had been contaminated by a later revisor. The visions themselves Peter Dinzelbacher simply classed as "möglicherweise unecht." And David Ganz wondered whether Audradus's central vision might not be understood as the bitter result of frustrated self-interest, since the monk had been "baulked of a bishopric."[63]

We need to keep in mind, however, that the *Book of Revelations* exists today not in the form in which it was presented to Pope Leo, but in a recension made after Audradus had returned to Francia and before his death sometime after 853. The work has also descended to us in fragmentary form. Alberich of Trois-Fontaines, in his thirteenth-century chronicle, reported some of Audradus's visions, but he edited, excerpted, and certainly skipped materials.[64] André Duchesne copied still other and seemingly more complete texts of the later revelations from a manuscript once owned by Jacques Sirmond, which is now lost.[65] The complicated textual history of the *Book of Revelations* has not reassured readers of Audradus, but has left them even more uncertain and wary.

Yet if the glass through which we must look at Audradus is smoke blackened and cracked, we should not, nevertheless, doubt the basic image that we see there, for it was Audradus's creation, and he had come to believe that he was a divinely inspired prophet. Like all true prophets, he claimed not to have set out to become one; rather, he had submitted to the divine will and to the collective good of "his brothers." God had picked him out of a sinful generation to speak to his people. In the first of the revelations, Audradus was visited by Christ, who shut down the lights of the world and spoke to him in the descending darkness.

> O you, man of sorrow, because you set your heart upon sacrificing yourself before me for the salvation of your endangered brothers, lo and behold I have today appointed you to be my faithful servant in all the things that I shall reveal to you.[66]

The Lord explained that he had blotted out the sun as a symbol to his foolish children. He hoped to spare them, if only they would return to maternal grace. Thus, Audradus had received his commission and Christ had conscripted a monastic herald.

This first revelation was not, however, a vision of God; it was a hearing. Later Audradus would undergo a full range of the physical sensations often associated with ecstatic experience. He would speak of being "seized" by the spirit of the Lord and of being in a state of rapture.[67] Often, he said, these seizures had come upon him while he was deep in purposeful prayer.[68] Some were certainly induced by lack of food and drink as the prophet fasted and prayed. On one occasion, in language like that of the Vulgate, he said that, one day while praying for the safety of the church, "cecidit super me mentis excessus" ["a trance overcame me"]. In this state, in which his mind left his body, Audradus was visited by an angel of the Lord, who transported his spirit to heaven.[69] Sometimes he would be transported, sometimes visited by divine forces.

Unlike other ninth-century visions, there is little action and no landscape in Audradus's otherworld: he does not seem to have done anything more than watch and listen. Nor would he walk about in some awesome purgatorial space, his only journey being the undescribed transport of his spirit to one of the lower celestial spheres. Hence, his role was almost purely passive. Only once did he speak to anyone, to an angel who wanted to know if he desired to hear more. In four of his ten ecstatic experiences he was simply a listener as Christ, unnamed angels, a doctor, and God the Father all either spoke to him or allowed him to overhear the stuff of their celestial conversation.[70] In other fragments, however, he was a watcher in the heavens, where he observed angels of the Lord, Christ, saints, and Carolingian kings.[71] No scene of punishment or purgation was ever enacted before his eyes, no rivers of fire, no boiling cauldrons, no screams of fornicators, no valleys of deformed light, no physical pain at all. Punishments were foretold, but they would be carried out on earth in the historical present. Audradus's prophetic revelations might have been heavenly in their setting, but they were entirely earthly in their import.

Now it is not impossible that Audradus's experiences were oneiric in nature. He avoided almost entirely the language of dreams and visions, because his revelations belonged to the more direct communication of prophecy. But around 846, as reported in Alberich's reading of the *Book of Revelations*, "an angel of the Lord weakened the left thigh of Audradus, removed his nocturnal illusions, and cured him of the pain in his liver."[72] The image evokes memories of Jacob wrestling with an angel who touched his thigh and so shriveled it. But Audradus may also have recalled that in the Song of Solomon, sixty brave men of Israel had collected around the bed on which Solomon wrestled with his worries. Each warrior gripped his sword tight to his thigh "because of fears in the night."[73] Audradus must have thought that his physical encounter with an angel was a special sign of divine approval, just as it had been for Jacob. It was these *timores nocturni* that had once worried Alcuin's poetical sleep.[74] What could these disturbances have been in Audradus's case but disturbing dreams, perhaps of a sexual or political sort? What he wanted in their place was direct angelic enlightenment. In a curious exchange in the verses *On the Fountain of Life*, Hincmar, who is an interlocutor in the poem and addressed as a dear friend, told Audradus that it was fortunate that he was abandoning dreams. Audradus responded that the dreams had, nevertheless, left him healthy. What exactly was meant by this curious exchange may now be beyond our grasp, but it may be that in his monastery Audradus was once famous for his divine dreaming. Even today the poem *On the Fountain of Life* strikes the reader as dreamlike, as though it were a walk through some strange and symbolic dreamscape. Late in the *Book of Revelations* an invisible being, perhaps Christ himself, and an unseen doctor of the church would compliment Audradus on his beautiful poetry.[75] Were these the whisperings of vainglory that the poet had heard before in his dreams?

By the time he came to write down his revelations, however, Audradus thought of himself not as a dreamer but as a prophet cut from Old Testament cloth. It is at this point that modern historians have jumped ship, refusing to accept Audradus's calling. Like Lord Byron, historians are wont to suspect that the best prophet is the past; that Audradus quite simply prophesied what had already transpired.[76] But unsympathetic dismissal of this sort does not help us to understand Audradus. Surely his revelations, like those of the Old Testament, demand a degree of internal examination and respect. The whiff of charlatanry and outright chicanery that has clung persistently to Audradus cannot easily be washed away, but it is the malodor that has always hung heavily about the person of the prophet.

In studying the seers of ancient Israel, Johannes Lindblom naturally worried about the possibility for fraud in prediction, but he soon came to change the terms of reference for us, inviting us to recognize that the "*pro* in the Greek term *prophetes* does not mean 'before' but 'forth'. Thus the Greek term indicates that the prophet is a preacher, a *forth*teller rather than a *fore*teller."[77] Hence, the prophet's place was not to foretell the future but to comment on the present: to insist on the need for reform and renewal. Where the apocalyptic visionaries of the Old Testament passively proclaimed the approaching end of time because they believed that nothing could be altered and all things terrestrial were doomed, the prophets, who lived in chaotic historical times, actively worked to summon a people back to God. Like Jeremiah, the prophet was an intercessor, a go-between, receiving messages from God and passing his insistent warnings on to a sinful people. Prophecy "is a scream in the night. While the world is at ease and asleep, the prophet feels the blast from heaven."[78] So overpowering is the call that the prophet cannot keep quiet. He must, for his sake and his people's, bellow God's message to a world mired in blind intransigence. On God's behalf, the prophets of Israel railed "against the king and his advisors; against dishonest rulers, wicked priests, cheating businessmen; against the apostasy of a nation."[79]

That the importunate agenda of the Old Testament prophets resounds in Audradus's visions should remind us that his prophetic expectations and his prophetic mode were shaped as much from outside as from within. Even the language in which he cast his revelations belonged to ancient Israel. The *Book of Revelations,* as he weightily reminds us in the *tituli,* was written in prose, unlike the rest of his volume. In terms of divine inspiration and personal passivity, there is, as Lindblom has observed, a kinship between prophets and poets. Both are vessels waiting to be filled with the divine word, but "the prophet himself is not a poet."[80] Hence, when Audradus the poet broke into prose in his twelfth book, he did so in order to keep company with the visionaries of the Old Testament, the insistent idiom of their prosaic language still ringing in his ears.

At Tours during Audradus's long residency there, the four major prophets—Isaiah, Jeremiah, Ezekiel, and Daniel—had come to occupy an important place in illuminations of the *Majestas Domini*. In a miniature in the famous Bible of Count Vivian, produced in 845–46 while Audradus was still resident at Tours, the prophets occupy medallions that fuse with the rhomboid field framing Christ (Fig. 15). Herbert Kessler speculated that the four prophets probably figured so prominently in the Turonian devolpment of a distinctive *Majestas Domini* iconography because they were all thought to have alluded to the fountain of life and, thus, had truly anticipated the coming of Christ.[81] Audradus, as the foremost Turonian commentator on the fountain, must have been keenly interested in the pictorial imagery of Christ as an overflowing center of divine connections. Moreover, as the foremost poet of Tours in 845, it is not impossible that Audradus was the author of the verses that adorn the Bible of Count Vivian.

That he had prophetic predecessors was central to Audradus's mission, though he did not insist that his readers notice. Traube, in his edition of the *Book of Revelations*, identified no biblical citations, but dozens of examples can be found. Ezekiel and Jeremiah in particular seem to have shaped Audradus's conception of the place and purpose of the prophet in troubled times. When he called himself a "legatus ecclesiarum" and referred to his mission as a "legatio," Audradus was not only alluding to Jeremiah, who, in full prophetic flight, had been appointed by God to be the "legatus ad gentes," but also to the proverb that had declared that "a faithful ambassador is health."[82]

What connected Audradus most firmly to Ezekiel was his annalistic style. The Lord had appointed Ezekiel to lay siege to Jerusalem and to cause her "to know her abominations," but God had measured out these sins in units of time, laying upon Ezekiel "the years of their iniquity." When the Lord spoke to Ezekiel, the prophet was careful to record the year, the month, and the day.[83] The rhythm of the entries in the *Book of Revelations* is also annalistic, possessing a measured adagio that was to attract the chronicler Alberich four centuries later. Indeed, some of the fragments that survive were further reduced to annalistic proportions by the chronicler.[84] But Audradus knew the genre, one in which he combined the form of the Carolingian monastic annal with the tempo of Ezekiel's abrupt encounters with his demanding God.

Audradus insisted that it was the Lord Christ himself who had invented the timepiece of a decennial truce by which the years of Carolingian repentance were to be weighed out. In March 845 an angel informed Audradus: "You should know that the Northmen will come to Paris and will turn back from there, and that ten years is granted to this people to repent.''[85] Thus Audradus started counting the ten-year truce (*induciae*) from early 845. He understood Christ's gift to be a breathing space in which God would hold back the Northmen and in which Christians, for their part, must repent their wicked ways. When, in 851, the Northmen again invaded Gaul, Audradus prayed for three days and nights, without taking food or drink, that God might have mercy on his people and not subtract any time from the period of the truce.[86] In the surviving fragments of the *Book of Revelations*, the years of the ten-year truce are counted off, at least until the ninth year beginning in March 853.

But, in fact, Audradus presented several revelations before the truce was announced. The first of these, the one in which he received his commission from the Lord, was signaled by a darkened sun. Audradus certainly knew that God had forewarned Joel and Ezekiel that his calling cards would be sunless stars and pillars of smoke. He would, he said, show wonders in the heavens, signs of an age in which ''your sons and your daughters shall prophesy, your old men shall dream dreams and your young men shall see visions.''[87] This was just the prophetic package of events that so impressed Audradus: dreams and visions worked by the Lord's spirit, the sun stopped, and the deliverance of those who would pray and hearken to the Lord.

If his first revelation had simply been the sanctioning of a prophet, the second was a judgment scene. Audradus was carried before Christ enthroned in the heavens. To the Lord's right and left were the Virgin Mary with all the bishops and the holy martyrs, all arranged in meticulous hierarchy. As Audradus watched, two demons approached and began to accuse humanity of its many crimes. When Christ the judge paid them no heed, the demons turned to the martyrs, as if to an unmoved jury, and reminded them of those men who had murdered them. At this point, Saint Martin strode forth from the crowd of bishops and argued against the demons. Mary so supported Martin's defense of mankind that, in reward, she bestowed a cowl upon him. As he put the hood on, angels swept down to carry away the demons. With the accusers gone, great joy broke out in heaven and the Lord ascended.[88]

The elements of judgment and intercession here are evident, but the sin cited was an old one: the slaughter of the martyrs. In turning from the earthly fate of Julian and his companions in the preceding books to this contemporary judgment scene, Audradus transports his readers to a heavenly setting raised above the battlefield below, but not by much. Saint Martin, cowled in victory, may have been the defender of humanity as a whole, but underlying the visionary scene as its proper referent was Carolingian chaos. It was in the light of this revelation that Audradus watched in horror as the evil of civil war spread throughout the kingdom and people remained unrepentant. But it fell to Saint Martin to save the skins of these sinners:

> Three brothers, jointly the kings of the Franks, with their Christian armies, crippled each other in a most horrible civil war and worse in the region of Auxerre near a place called Fontenoy. There father killed son, son killed father, brother killed brother, and blood relatives killed their kin. For the sake of crimes committed against churches and for the violation of fraternal charity, the mutual slaughter continued. Had a prayer of Saint Martin not intervened, not one of those kings would have escaped death.[89]

Yet the prophet was no foreteller here. He did not claim to have predicted the Battle of Fontenoy, only that he was able to read its meaning in the clarifying light of his revelation, for he now knew that such disasters were the divine payoff for the continuing sins of an unrepentant society. But these same sinful parties had continued to persecute the church. Thus, for Audradus, a circle of righteous suffering continued to connect Julian and the martyrs to current events and living sufferers. In his literary allusions, Audradus shared a defined intellectual space and a common set of symbols with the other thinkers of the 840s. He, too, connected Roman civil war to his own, for he was another to invoke Lucan's famous inaugural line. Like Engelbert and the others, he had also reduced a complex sequence of events and actors to the plain image of the family as a closed circle of Christian slaughter. By his time, this had become the literary signature of Fontenoy.

But Audradus's reflection on the Battle of Fontenoy has something distant and resigned to it. His images were borrowed ones, Fontenoy was past, and Audradus in the *Book of Revelations* had moved ever so slightly beyond the thematic centrality of civil war. For him, the continuing assault upon the integrity of the church was the greater crime, for that was the certain sign of a wayward people.

Despite the manifest meaning of Fontenoy and God's continuing condemnation, the obdurate survivors had continued to plunder churches and the poor. Audradus watched as they seized long established churches, confiscating them and their profits for their own use. "Then the entire ecclesiastical order began to be tossed about, and God was unhappy about this. He said that he would lash them [the survivors] with nine blows."[90] Thus did Pharaoh and the obdurate

Egyptians, who had received ten mighty blows from God, spring to the prophet's mind.[91] For Audradus, it was the angry God of Moses who had risen to rebuke the Carolingians, and he had brought new weapons of reproach to bear on them.

At dawn on the first day of March in 845, Audradus was praying for the salvation of the church and for a merciful God to open up human hearts when an angel transported him to the heavens. There he was informed that the Northmen were about to descend on the city of Paris and that Christians would be given that truce of ten years in order to repent. Thus, the first of the divine blows to strike Francia would come in the shape of men from the north. On 28 March 845, 120 Norse ships did sail up the Seine River to Paris. Audradus learned that King Charles with an army of cavalry and foot soldiers had come upon the Northmen, but could not stop them from entering the city, just as the Lord had predicted. On the evening before Easter Sunday, while Charles the Bald remained behind at the monastery of Saint-Denis, the enemy entered Paris. Finally the king and his nobles, with a great deal of money, bought off the Northmen, who then set sail for home. In the final fragment of the *Book of Revelations*, God the Father, when lecturing his Son, would recall this incident.[92]

In west Francia this attack on Paris was infamous, the shock of it rippling through the realm. At the church council held in Meaux-Paris beginning in June 845, Wenilo, Hincmar, and Rudolf of Bourges and their bishops openly lamented the attack, and their reasoning was very like that of Audradus's angel and also full of prophetic inspiration. The church, they said, was everywhere harassed and dragged down by troubles, everywhere the people were in need of correction. Four councils had previously attempted to deal with these fundamental problems, but somehow the jealousy and malice of the Devil and his agents had prevented the king and his people from learning of them. Because divine commands had been frustrated, they noted, the Lord had sent those cruel persecutors of Christians, the Northmen, to Paris. They remembered that the prophet Jeremiah had prophesied that from the north would come an evil that would spread out over the land and its inhabitants.[93] In 845–46, Lupus could only conclude that "the present age is infamous and God is certainly provoked to take vengeance."[94] Thus, Carolingian churchmen, almost down to the last moralizing man, had concluded that the Northmen were the agents of castigation sent by God against a sinful people, never that Carolingian defensive strategies were haphazard or insufficient.[95]

Audradus was no different, nor was he a historian. His account of the seizure of Paris in 845 is probative rather than descriptive. He knew nothing special about the event, nor was he willing to acknowledge that Charles the Bald had responded as best he could. The young king had decided early on that his only option was to defend the wealthy abbey of Saint-Denis, a strategy that ultimately worked.[96] Even more monastic tears would have flowed had Saint-Denis been sacked, but the distant prophet of Tours was interested in the symbol of plundered Paris, not in the venal trade-offs that a vulnerable sovereign necessarily had to make. What details about the attack Audradus does supply are correct, but there are few of them.

But if both the angel's announcement and the story of the assault were simply sketched, we nonetheless see in this fragment the essential structure of the pieces that make up the *Book of Revelations,* its prophetic pattern: fulfillment will follow upon revelation; history will bear out even vague prophetic previsions; and the Northmen will perform as if they were toy soldiers moved by some unseen hand. With Audradus we fall from heaven again and again, landing with a thump on the hard earth of historical updating.

If one were to judge from the extant *Book of Revelations,* during the first five years of Christ's unilateral truce, the kingdom seems to have been at relative peace and the prophet free of frightening visions, for he reported no startling revelations. But in the sixth year, not long after he had been deposed as suffragan bishop, Audradus fell into a trance in which he saw a vast and panoramic scene of judgment. He watched as the Lord and his saints, descending from heaven, settled on the celestial borderline between ether and air.[97] For three days and three nights the sun and moon were dark. When all the chiefs of the church, in an assembly of adoration, had gathered before Christ, he demanded to know who had squandered the inheritance that his Father had bought with his blood.

"Whose fault is it?" Christ asked. He was told without hesitation: "Culpa regum est." ["It is the fault of kings."][98] The folk of the ninth century, we need to remember, were never slow to assign blame, since they believed that they lived in a determined universe, one causally connected and free of the purely accidental and blameless. Every disaster had its corresponding cause, and in this case the saints rushed in to point holy fingers at Carolingian kings. But Christ claimed not to know these kings whom he had neither recognized nor established. Thus, at a stroke in Audradus's revelation, the constitutional world of the Carolingians began anew. Since Christ was widely thought to dispose and sanction all kings, his ignorance of them and downright denial of any role in their appointment left them utterly bereft of authority.

The saints identified Louis (the Pious) as the father of these blameworthy kings, whereupon he was led into the Lord's presence. Why, Louis was asked, had he sown this discord among his sons which now disturbed all the faithful? Louis, with a hint of apology, tried to explain to Christ why his complex constitutional maneuvers had come undone. Since Lothar had seemed prepared to obey the Lord and to respect his church, he had been established to rule the Lord's people in Louis's place. However, when he had become proud and disrespectful of the church, he had been removed. Seeing that little Charles was humble and obedient, Louis had set him up in Lothar's place to serve Christ and the church. The Lord immediately recognized the truthfulness of Louis's testimony and called the other parties before him in order to sanction Louis's actions.

> Let Lothar, because he said "ego sum," be overthrown. Let Charles, on
> account of his humility and obedience, be firmly fixed in his place. But
> what of the third?[99]

For though Christ earlier had feigned not to know these kings, he now seemed to know that there was a third son. Some of the saints informed the Lord that Louis (the German) had taken up arms against his father, but others argued that there was some good in Louis, for though he, too, had damaged the church by removing men who were employed in the church's service, he had assiduously sought out men from foreign lands to replace them. Thus, the Lord also confirmed Louis the German in his royal office. In Audradus's visions, a good word said in one's defense before the divine judge was to be sufficient for some measure of indulgence. This, as we have seen, was the central importance of having saintly intercessors in heaven: one wanted a friend like Martin standing forever by Christ's side, whispering in his ear as Carolingian courtiers did in their king's.

Along with Charles the Bald and his half-brother Louis the German, Lothar's son Louis (called the king of the Italians) was led before Christ in this scene being played out before Audradus's eyes on the edge of ether and air. The Lord said that he would enter into a treaty (*foedus* and *pactum*) with them, which it would be unlawful to break. Each of the three kings was confronted with a set of conditions on which their contract with Christ was to rest. They were not to be proud, but to restore churches to their proper state, to appoint suitable men to head up religious orders, to establish fitting rules for these orders, to prevent all people under their charge from violating churches, and to give justice to every person. If they agreed to these terms with sincere hearts, Christ said that he would bestow upon them the scepters and crowns of their kingdoms. But the chief condition, the one left until last, was that these kings ought to observe a perpetual peace. The kingdom as divided at the time of the Lord's overthrow of Lothar was to be fixed between the three of them, with no encroachment upon another's land.

The Lord was not finished arranging things yet, however. To each king he gave a saintly companion, a patron and protector devoted to the interests of a portion of the divided kingdom. Charles was to have the help of that mighty commander Martin, who would help him free Spain from infidels and unite his kingdom. Scythians, false brothers, and rebellions would vanish like smoke in a strong wind. Christ promised that Charles's heirs, if they observed the treaty, would one day stand before him and succeed to his kingdom. Saint Paul was appointed the guardian and protector of Louis the German and his kingdom. Finally Saint Peter was designated the helper of Louis, the king of the Italians. As each saint was named, Christ bestowed on them the scepters and crowns of their respective kingdoms. He assured each king that if he obeyed and preserved the treaty struck between them, he would be able to resist invaders and increase the size of his kingdom.

> For these three saintly princes, whom I have provided to you as commanders and helpers with the armies in their company, have, with their invaluable prayers, rescued the world from imminent condemnation.[100]

If the kings maintained their contracts, then the saints, these *duces optatissimi et inuicti protectores* [most desired leaders and unconquered defenders] standing in heaven at the Lord's side, would promote the interests of the king and his kingdom, both in times of peace and in times of war.

For Charles, however, the Lord had a special message. Since he had not hesitated to injure the interests of churches, exactly a year later he would suffer a terrible military defeat in Brittany, barely escaping with his own life. The treacherous and impious Vivian, who boasted of being abbot of Saint-Martin's, would die a foul death in Brittany and beasts of the forest would devour his flesh. Christ finished by warning King Charles that he ought to restore churches to their proper state and leave those alone that stood as he had established them.

Before ascending into heaven to sit at the right hand of the Father, Christ blessed the world. He explained that the earth had seemed damned by the elements because of the evils committed by men, but he commanded it to be bountiful during the next year. The three sunless days and moonless nights, he said, were a sign to all that he had visited his church and examined its condition in the world. Hence, Christ's cosmic visitation mimicked the earthly ones that the suffragan bishop must have carried out shortly before in the parish churches of Sens.

Audradus confirmed that, just as the Lord had predicted, Charles had marched to disaster in Brittany, Vivian was slaughtered, and churches were violated in that war. But, as the ambassador of churches, Audradus had sought to prevent his king's humiliation by showing the full text of his revelation to Charles's chamberlain, Rothbern. It seems likely that this chamberlain was, in fact, Ruadbern, the man celebrated by Walahfrid Strabo for his daring winter rescue of the Empress Judith in 834.[101] If so, Audradus's construction of Charles's court in his revelations rings true. Ruadbern must have been assigned to protect the interests of Judith and her son from the beginning. Audradus, text in hand, needed to go through just such an intermediary in order to reach the king, just as Aubrey had twenty years earlier.

But, according to the prophet, Charles neglected to heed the warning. Instead he returned ingloriously from Brittany and did not restore churches. In consequence God led the Northmen once more into Gaul, where they laid waste far and wide. God's anger at the immense evil he surveyed began everywhere to boil over upon those kings and their kingdoms, said the prophet. For three days and three nights, without food or drink, Audradus prayed for God's mercy and for the perpetuation of the God-granted but human-broken truce.

Nothing in what survives of Audradus's earlier visions could have prepared the Carolingian world for this elaborate and extended revelation. Nor could Pope Leo have seen a written account of this vision, since it concerned events of 850–51. The main thrust of the vision reveals an Audradus who had remained the protector of Tours, since what certainly underlay and shaped the sequence was a set of Turonian anxieties. The diocese of Saint-Martin included Brittany, but Nominoë, the governor of Brittany, at the time was attempting to dislodge eight bishops under the control of Saint-Martin's and to annex the Breton church. In the summer of 850, Lupus apparently wrote a letter to Nominoë on behalf of Wenilo, Hincmar, and the other high churchmen of west Francia. In it he charged the Breton chief with fomenting great disorder in his territory and damaging the diocese of Saint-Martin.[102] Christ's chief complaint in the vision was one shared by the monks of Saint-Martin: their churches had been alienated and their king bore the responsiblity for restoring them.

Before undertaking the campaign, which Lupus was to survive and to call sarcastically those "most magnificent celebrations" in Brittany, Charles the Bald held an assembly at Tours in February 851.[103] This assembly was probably called at the urging of the brothers of Saint-Martin's because it was their property in Brittany that was threatened. Tours was, therefore, to be the springboard to Breton war. Two men likely to have been present at the assembly were Count Vivian, the lay abbot of Saint-Martin, and Audradus.

In the famous presentation miniature of the Count Vivian Bible, painted six years earlier, we may well see both Vivian and Audradus (Fig. 17). The time was apparently Christmas 845. Charles the Bald had come to Tours and had renewed the ancient privileges of Saint-Martin's, a fact noted in the Bible's *tituli* and in one of Charles's charters.[104] Count Vivian stands to our right, the untonsured layman, nobly dressed and presenting the manuscript, and perhaps his monks, to the king (Fig. 18, no. 6, and Fig. 19). Wilhelm Köhler, whose interpretation of the miniature has become standard, thought that the three monks to the left (Fig. 18, nos. 7, 8, 9) were carrying the manuscript in their draped hands while the whole composition depicted a semicircle of monks and their lay abbot before the king.[105] But, upon close examination, one sees that the third monk does not hold the book, but has his hands, one holding a maniple, outstretched in a demonstrative gesture, as do the three monks in front of him (Fig. 18, no. 9, the outline being slightly exaggerated here for effect). Thus two monks bear the book (Fig. 18, nos. 7–8), while four monks dressed in chasubles, with maniples in hand, move in procession towards the center of the illumination (Fig. 18, nos. 9–12). This same group of four monks can be seen collected together below Vivian on the right side (Fig. 18, nos. 14–17). Their costumes are identical in decoration and color, despite some slight discoloration in two of the gowns today. Moreover, the facial appearances of the individuals and their costumes once again match (Fig. 18, no. 12 with no. 17; no. 11 with no. 15; no. 10 with no. 16; and no. 9 with no. 14). The central monastic figure presiding over the ceremony may be, as Karl Morrison has suggested, the choregus leading the monks in song and *laudes regiae,* or he may be some prominent individual such as the archbishop of Tours, Ursmar, from whom Lupus once requested a book in the library of Saint-Martin's (Fig. 18, no. 13). The scene in the painting, therefore, possesses four cardinal points: Charles the Bald (no. 1), Vivian (no. 6), the celebrant (no. 13), and the book (held by nos. 7–8).[106]

If this new interpretation is correct, then in the presentation miniature we do not see a semicircle of monks gathered in front of Charles the Bald, but the stages of a presentation ceremony. To our left, we see a line of six monks either being led by or moving towards the celebrant, who faces Charles the Bald directly. On our right, the four main monks have been gathered together in a group that stands behind Vivian, who is closer to the king. Although the double depiction of the four monks may seem odd, the painters of the manuscript had earlier employed a similar technique in depicting Saint Jerome twice in the same panel on folio 3v, once departing Rome and again paying his Hebrew teacher. In addition, the painter of the Genesis scenes in the Grandval Bible depicted different stages in the story of Adam and Eve by repeating the same figures in a single panel.[107] Thus the artist of the presentation miniature probably meant to indicate different moments in the processional ceremony leading up to the gift of the book to King Charles. The first to the left was the procession into the presence of the king, the second to the right was the actual presentation of the precious manuscript. The poet wished to draw our attention in particular to the active nature of this presentation scene:

> Haec etiam pictura recludit, qualiter heros
> Offert Vivianus cum grege nunc hoc opus.

> [This painting also depicts how the noble warrior
> Vivian with his flock now presents this book.][108]

He named the important monks who stand behind Vivian as Tesmund, Siguald, and Aregarius. He himself, he said, was the fourth. On the basis of the order of the monks described by the poet, Kessler has suggested that the poet is the gray-haired and bearded monk with the handsome dark chasuble (Fig. 18, no. 17, and Fig. 20). If this were true, then the portrait might be meant to depict Audradus himself, for he is the most likely poet of the *tituli* of the Bible. The *tituli* bear striking correspondence with Audradus's verse, not only in their emphasis upon themes like the *fons uitae*, but also in their language, phrasing, and poetic technique. There is, moreover, as Kessler has suggested, criticism of Vivian even in the *tituli* of his Bible, which would also fit with Audradus's attitude towards the lay abbot.[109]

The real villain of Audradus's long vision was this abbot (Fig. 18, no. 6), just the sort of evil man who had roused the ire of the Lord. Christ denounced Vivian for his pride and his boast that he held Saint-Martin and other churches. Vivian's true offense was that he was a lay abbot, a feature of monastic government regularly condemned by monks and bishops and recently criticized at the Council of Meaux-Paris.[110] Like Count Bego in the *Vision of the Poor Woman of Laon*, Vivian was, through the symbolism of the beasts devouring his corpse, typed in the prophet's vision as a grasping, greedy man. As Charlemagne was in the *Vision of Wetti*, so Vivian here was to be eaten by his animal nature, to be consumed by his very sin. Greed was the principal charge leveled by monks against their lay abbots. There may have been something to the charge in Vivian's case. Lupus once worked on behalf of a relative to insure the repayment of a pound of gold as insisted upon by Vivian.[111] Lay abbots naturally desired the revenues of the monasteries they held, but the nagging problem that ruined the days of their abbacies was that they could never belong to the elevated and exigent world of monastic virtue. Even in the dedication picture of his Bible, Vivian stands separate from his monks; he is not a part of their circle of values or experiences. But then Audradus may also have held some personal grudge against his abbot, or at least the Lord of his dreams did.

But, at another, less petty, level, the Lord of the long revelation was a kingmaker and peacemaker. The disasters of division that had befallen the kingdom since Fontenoy were the fault of unsanctioned kings. The Christ of Audradus's revelation was, however, wedded, just as Gerward had been, to the notion that the kingdom of the Franks must now be tripartite. With the overthrow of Lothar, who actually died in 855, his son, Louis II, king of the Italians, was to assume his place. Some have thought that Audradus's vision must have been contaminated or touched up around 855 in order to accommodate this sequence, but the vision never claimed that Lothar had died, just that he had been overthrown. The proper point of reference for this deposition was not recent history but the events of the 830s, when Louis the Pious had effectively undercut his son's imperial status. Moreover, Louis II had, in fact, been crowned emperor in 850 by Pope Leo, an event reported by Prudentius of Troyes in the *Annals of Saint-Bertin* and therefore well known to the diocese of Sens and its archbishop, to whom Prudentius was subordinate. Thus, the envisioned Christ of Audradus's revelation invented nothing. In May 851, the brothers Lothar, Louis the German, and Charles had met at Meersen to confirm previous measures. Prudentius thought their decrees important enough to reprint in his annals.[112] But the celestial pact struck in the vision did not correspond to any actual treaty, though it did reflect the contractual spirit of an age of division that had produced the Oaths of Strasbourg and the Treaty of Verdun. The Lord was not particularly interested in borderlines, for he treated these as fixed and tripartite. Moreover, he assumed that any territorial expansion should be at the expense of external enemies. In conceiving of Martin as the saint who would protect Charles's Spanish interests, we may even see the stirrings of that west Frankish religious zeal for the conquest of Spain. But Audradus does not take us very much beyond the royal expectations of his age, for in imagining a never achieved and perhaps never desired bond between these three kings, Audradus held fast to the model of the recent past: that the kingdom should continue to have three lines descending from the house of Louis the Pious.

Moreover, the old bitterness of the west Franks towards Lothar was slow to subside. Though it was a decade after Fontenoy, Audradus could not forgive Lothar for his presumption on that day. In the *Vision of Rotcharius* Charlemagne may have been bold enough to say "I am Charles," but he already stood among the saints. Here Lothar's "ego sum" was the proud boast that must bring him down. What had brought about the civil war was Lothar's vaunting boast that he was superior: "I am" the emperor had always been his claim. But Audradus's prophetic calling led him to make, I think, yet another association. For the Lord had once come to Ezekiel to tell him that because the king of Tyre had said "Deus ego sum" ["I am God"], he had decided to destroy him, to cast him into a pit, there to die like a drowning sailor swept into the middle of the sea.[113] Thus, the prophet may have come to predict the proud man's collapse not long after his son had taken up the imperial title.

If the revelation was written down as early as 851 or 852, it moved the constitutional arrangement of the Carolingians beyond a point that it had reached in fact. Tripartition achieved a new level of acceptance and legitimacy, with even the saints taking up regional assignments.[114] We have moved in this rare vision beyond the despair of Florus as he contemplated the division of the Frankish kingdom to a new world resigned to partition and seeking a Christian peace within a new order freshly sanctioned by God. Indeed, Audradus's Lord had no interest at all in the idea of empire; he was a royalist, not an imperialist.

What Charles the Bald was supposed to have ignored in 850, he chose to reject again in 853. In the third month of the ninth year of the truce proclaimed by Christ, "King Charles again called me to him," said Audradus.[115] This is another indication of the fragmentary character of the *Book of Revelations,* since nowhere else in the surviving work had the monk reported that he previously had an audience with the king. On this occasion, he was called to the famous council that met at the monastery of Saint-Médard of Soissons on 22 April 853.[116] In the presence of the princes of the church—the archbishops Wenilo, Hincmar of Rheims, Pardulus of Laon, and Amalric of Tours—and Queen Ermintrude, Audradus was grilled:[117]

> King Charles began to question me and to inquire about all those things to see if I might be caught in any lie. But once again I repeated in detail to him all those things contained in the speech of the Lord, as they were written down.[118]

Thus, the action of the previous vision flowed into the text of the next revelation, for there was still the matter of its unfinished business. Charles may have returned from Brittany with his tail between his legs, but he had not yet restored any churches. After Audradus's defense at Soissons, however, the king promised him repeatedly that within two months he would restore the church of Saint-Martin and others to their proper condition. Audradus observed, however, that he had done no such thing.

Instead, to anger God, he had summoned a certain deacon from Lothar's kingdom to take up the bishopric of Chartres. It was as if, said Audradus, he thought that no suitable cleric could be found in his own kingdom. So sharp is the criticism here that it must reflect the sting of Audradus's own deposition three years earlier. The king ordered Wenilo to ordain this Burchard bishop, but the archbishop called Audradus aside and expressed some doubts. He knew that some evil stories were spreading about this appointment and that Charles had acted this way in order to infuriate God. Nonetheless, Wenilo wondered whether God would be terribly angered by the ordination of Burchard, since these were troubled times and Burchard was, in any event, one of his own kinsmen, whose advancement he himself wished. Thus, Wenilo asked Audradus to pray to God for guidance and, if anything was revealed to him, not to hide it from his archbishop.

As odd as this may seem to us, Audradus was, in effect, commissioned by the archbishop to induce a vision.

> When I was praying as usual for the salvation of my brothers and on behalf of the business mentioned above, behold the Lord deigned to hear me and, descending from heaven, completely bathed me in his radiance where I was praying. And he said, "The day that Burchard becomes a bishop will be a cursed one."[119]

The Lord returned immediately to heaven, but an angel stayed behind to explaii to Audradus what the Lord meant. So long as Burchard was a bishop, said th angel, the fury of God would rain down upon his churches and ruin them. Th Almighty would prohibit the ordination by excommunicating anyone wh would ordain Burchard, so that he would be unable to lift his hand in episcop: blessing. Audradus reported the revelation to the archbishop, who soon sent copy of the written oracle to King Charles.

At Soissons, Burchard had been brought forward as the acting, but un dained, bishop of Chartres. It was Wenilo, according to the acts of the counc who had recommended his promotion. Various bishops, including Hincm were instructed by the council to urge Burchard to take up the bishopric no and witnesses to his good character were produced. There was some conc(

that the candidate might refuse out of fear of God. But he firmly asserted that if anyone accused him of some criminal charge, he was prepared to purge himself of the accusation. When no one came forward, the synod elected Burchard bishop of Chartres.[120]

The issues Wenilo raised with Audradus seem to have been behind Burchard's bravado at Soissons; the candidate had decided to stare down his accusers. All the parties had heard the rumors, and Audradus was as plugged into the current of gossip as his archbishop. But Chartres stood in need of a strong bishop, said Wenilo, and Burchard was just the vigorous sort Charles the Bald wanted. In 854, when Northmen were sailing up the Loire River towards Orléans, the new bishop helped to raise soldiers and ships to protect the city, and he succeeded in turning the invaders back. Indeed, Charles the Bald showed some skill as a recruiter of good men from his brothers' kingdoms, since he knew the value of human capital in an age in which real power flowed from the size and quality of service. Moreover, there was a matter of prerogative, since Charles had always claimed the right to promote his candidates to important bishoprics.[121] Burchard was his choice, Wenilo merely the front man.

But Burchard was not, in fact, ordained at Soissons, and Audradus seems at that time not yet to have had his vision. A month later, his oracular condemnation of Burchard must have been circulating in cloisters and at court, since Wenilo responded by convoking a council of bishops at Sens between May and July 853. There Audradus repeated his vision at Wenilo's request. At first, according to the monk, the officials at the council had not wanted to ordain Burchard, since they feared to go against so manifest a divine oracle. But in the end the power of the king had prevailed, and his bishops had relented, though they cannot have earned the respect of Audradus. In June of 853, in the ninth year of the divine truce, Burchard was finally ordained.[122]

Upon his ordination, said the monk, the anger of God spilled over onto the world. A burning wind leveled vines, storms and thunder followed, and the Northmen sailed up the Loire River. They put the monastery of Saint-Martin and its famous basilica to the torch. The monks fled to the monastery of Cormery, carrying in their arms the precious bones of their blessed Martin. Paradoxically, then, Burchard became the bishop of Chartres, but Tours paid the price.

Audradus could only surmise that God once again had sent the Northmen as agents of divine punishment. He blamed the three kings who must have broken the treaty forged with Christ. Instead of correcting their behavior, they had insisted on provoking the Almighty. Once the peace was broken, said Audradus, every evil poured down upon the church like the storm-tossed waves of an awful sea. *Après moi le déluge*, the prophet must have thought: "Thus, the greatest part of my legation was rendered fruitless and widespread confusion and curse began to overwhelm us."[123]

Audradus's last surviving vision continues in the same spirit of resignation. Yet it served as a fitting summary to the *Book of Revelations* as a whole, since in it God the Father reviewed for Christ what had transpired during the decennial truce. The Father reminded Christ that, after his Resurrection, he had been put in charge of the people on earth. But look, he said, how this society has deserted you and turned tyrannical arms against you. Nor could the Father forget how, at the request of his Son and the saints, he had granted a truce so that these people might repent and draw back from evil. Instead of repenting, these people, forever full of pride, had multiplied their evil doings. So angered was he that he drew his sword and would have killed them. Then the Northmen fell on Paris and there was some unhappiness, but still they stubbornly persisted in their crimes. Again he would have destroyed them all, but for his Son's intercession on their behalf.[124]

Thus, at the end of the *Book of Revelations,* readers find themselves gazing at an extraordinary scene, a shockingly intimate portrait of a family reviewing a recent crisis, with a furious father scolding his son for having hung out, as it were, with the wrong crowd. Christ had put his trust in untrustworthy people and had been too lenient in his dealings with an unrepentant people. For Audradus, then, heaven itself was rent by the competing impulses of divine anger and divine intercession. On the one side stood the God of Moses with his just drive to condemn a fallen and still sinning mankind; on the other, the forces of sweet intercession represented by Christ, Mary, and the saints. The idea that heaven was as unquiet as earth and that the Father and Son were as unable as the Carolingians to enforce a lasting peace must have unnerved Audradus in his last days.

In prophecy, Audradus had discovered a vehicle that could transport him not only to the heavens, but also to the proximate edge of current events and to the outermost circles of the royal court. By 850 he must have been an old man, perhaps in his late sixties, when he found himself bypassed for high office and by events. The dislocation of moving to Sens after a lifetime at Tours must have been unsettling, and the war waged against the chorepiscopate must have alienated him even further. But, if we may trust his account, he had already been visited by revelations before any of these things had occurred. His earliest visions, the ones he must have revealed to the pope, had been relatively bald, unspecific, and inoffensive. They were a Rorschach test, the only pattern in the spreading black ink being the one imposed by the interpreter himself. The last visions were just the opposite: they were controversial, contemporary in their concerns, and politically pointed.

Prophets demand to be heard, but their mission finally must be defined by the nature of the audience they choose to address. Audradus's early visions seem to have been public: he shared them with Wenilo, probably with his brothers, and with Pope Leo and his curia. The later visions were private or, at least, they had a more private purpose, since they spoke chiefly to the king and his royal court. Hence, Audradus passed written versions of his two longer visions to the king. One was slipped to Charles's chamberlain; another went via Wenilo. Both surfaced, and twice he appeared at councils to explain: at Soissons he was grilled by the king himself, and at Sens his vision was an agenda item. It is not, in fact, unlikely that Charles the Bald questioned Audradus. Indeed, everything factual that the monk tells us about the Council of Soissons fits with what we know from its surviving acta. Moreover, he supplied a piece of information that we might not otherwise know: that Queen Ermintrude herself was also in attendance. The identification of Ruadbern as the chamberlain of Charles is another touch of impressive realism in the revelations, one hard to dismiss as mere fancy.

Audradus's contemporaries may, indeed, have taken him more seriously than we generally have. Not only was he extremely learned, as his imaginative poetry suggests, but he had the respect of other clerics or he would not have been summoned to Sens to assume the office of suffragan bishop. Audradus had truly been one of the *primi* of Saint-Martin's, as the *tituli* had described him and the other monks who gathered before the king in 845. Nor, I think, can one doubt Wenilo's respectful interest in Audradus's prophetic capacity. Long before the controversy over Burchard, the archbishop had allowed Audradus to travel to Rome at the behest of a divine oracle from Saint Peter himself. What Audradus had to say about Wenilo's actions at Soissons also rings true. The archbishop confessed his personal interest in the advancement of his kinsman, but he wanted some assurance that God approved. This was the very issue on the mind of Burchard and the other bishops who gathered at Soissons and Sens.

Thus, Audradus seems to have had some credibility as a prophet in his own time. He may have been stripped of his ecclesiastical office in 849, but as a prophet he was never officially censured and never silenced as Gottschalk had been. Yet, in the end, he had failed to sway the people who mattered most. Charles the Bald twice rejected his visions, and even Wenilo must have been happy to have had the Council of Sens override Audradus's vision and ordain

Burchard. Slowly Audradus came to realize that, because he was unable to change the actions of king and court, his prophetic mission had failed.

One of the reasons why he could never have succeeded was, of course, that he was hardly disinterested. His visions concerned the things that mattered most to him personally: the Norse attacks on his part of the kingdom, his king, his former monastery, the restoration of churches to ecclesiastical control, an unjust lay abbot under whom he had served at Saint-Martin's, and the outrageous appointment of a foreign cleric to the bishopric of Chartres. The last of these concerns revealed his regional self-interest. In the long vision some saints had praised Louis the German for importing high clerics from other realms, but Audradus could not abide the same practice when applied to his own kingdom. He imagined patronage as a river of promotion that ran locally and in only one direction. At court and church councils, Audradus must have seemed in the end to have been but one of many competing parties, each seeking to prevail with whatever tools of persuasion they had at hand. His prophetic voice might have gained him an audience or two, but it could not lift him above the tumultuous din of the royal court.

Yet the dates of his visions are interesting. One cannot help but notice that Charles the Bald did not question Audradus until 853 about the specifics of his vision of 850–51. For this vision to have been discussed so long after the events had taken place must suggest that Charles the Bald was not concerned with the predictive character of Audradus's prophecies but with their narrative quality, for they furnished certain circles within his kingdom with an alternative history, with a different and damning interpretation of recent events. Audradus truly was, in this sense, a forthteller rather than a foreteller. How could the revelations ever have pretended to be anything else, since the fulfillment sequences tacked on at the end of each required a knowledge of the predicted events. What emerged from his revelations, therefore, was not a helpful road map to the future but an oneiric commentary on contemporary calamity.

When the saints in heaven cried out, "It is the fault of kings," they gave collective voice to the working hypothesis of the disgruntled of the day. The dominant idea of the age was that only royalty could change things, only kings could stop the slide towards disaster. But like most Carolingian thinkers, Audradus laid too much stress on the ability of kings to repair a kingdom that seemed out of control. Hence, by 850, he had narrowed his audience to include just Charles the Bald and a few people close to him. Dreams and visions were arrows aimed directly at the royal heart, hence their intense and hurrying place in the thought of the age.

By narrowing his audience to the powerful, Audradus may have avoided the fate of Thiota, but he would also possess none of her popular charisma. If she had had apolitical and apocalyptic visions, Audradus dreamed almost entirely of things political and personal. He may have aspired to be like Saint Paul as imagined by Thegan, who thought that the apostle had been carried up to the third heaven by God so that he might learn from the angels how men were to be ruled.[125] Yet, in truth, Audradus was another of those Carolingian thinkers, heirs to the searching spirit of Louis the Pious's reign, who wanted an inside look at the reasons for the drift of their times and who were prepared to pay the price to obtain it.

But what remains most interesting about Audradus's revelations is what he had come to accept with hardly a whimper: that regnal division was here to stay. In his conception of an artificial and untrue division of the kingdom, we can measure the distance that Carolingian intellectuals had traveled since Fontenoy towards accepting tripartition as the divine design of the Frankish kingdom. The Christ of the long vision reflected the contractual spirit of an age that had come to realize that division was now a permanent feature of their world, and that it was best secured by oaths and agreements. Since these were human devices and not to be relied upon, Audradus's Christ had supplied patron saints to protect and promote the interests of the separated kingdoms. To divide up holiness in this way may have merely replicated the local patronage structures of the Carolingian church, but it was also another sign of the slide towards entrenched division. Christ had become as aware of partisan royal interests as Audradus was. Something of the universal pretension of the older Carolingian order of Charlemagne had died by Audradus's day. Empire was by then a distant and degraded notion for many Carolingian intellectuals, though not for all. What mattered now was the protection of the church and the health of the divided realm. But if something had been lost, something had been gained, for, unlike Engelbert and Florus, Audradus had stepped into the future with his acceptance of divinely sanctioned division. A new pragmatism had begun to sweep through Europe by 850, for seven short years after Verdun it was apparent to Audradus and his kind that even Christ was not going to put this imperial Humpty-Dumpty back together again. For the Carolingians, the "worse" in Lucan's oft-quoted characterization of civil war was surely the torment of intellectual adjustment that their own civil war had forced upon an unwilling generation of thinkers.

CHAPTER SIX

The Property of Dreams

To dream of enlarging one's property and possessing an estate that is more valuable, indeed, even splendid—one that is costlier and somewhat better than one's present estate—is good.

To dream of robbing a temple or stealing the votive offerings of the gods indicates bad luck for everyone. It is only auspicious for priests and prophets.[1]

Thus, according to Artemidorus, men and women in the ancient world might innocently and without unnatural design dream dreams of property and prosperity. Neither he nor his clients seem to have worried much that they must have been coveting at night and in dream the lands of neighbors that were forever denied them in the bright light of day. To dream of stealing the movable property of a shrine, the golden statues and exquisite instruments of supplication, may have foreboded ill fortune, but no one seems to have dreamed that one could actually steal the land on which a temple stood. To dream of stealing religious property remained the safe prerogative of priests, for only they could handle the things given by the gods without danger. Had Hincmar of Rheims known the *Oneirocritica,* he might have smiled at the thought.

But we moderns, who believe in the outright ownership of land and in the immaterial and evanescent quality of dreams, cannot easily appreciate the propertied dimension of the ninth-century dream. We must work our way back towards it by examining that intense contest for property that colored Carolingian social relations. Our starting point should be F. W. Maitland's observation that medieval society was concerned not with ownership of land but with possession: "it is possession that has to be defended or recovered, and to possess without dispute, or by judicial award after a dispute real or feigned, is the only sure foundation of title and end of strife."[2] On this point turned a thousand acrimonious property disputes in the ninth century, and the only arbiter of worth was the king. Thus, royalty found itself once again the special target of appellants and petitioners, both those who thought that they already held possessory rights and those who wanted to hold more and better lands.

While one side of this petitionary history of ninth-century property was being worked out on the field of vassalage, with its oral agreements and brutally necessary deals, which are only occasionally reflected in surviving oaths, the other belonged to the church, and it was well and often too fully written down. From these latter, ample records Emile Lesne was able to compile a vast and minutely detailed history of ecclesiastical property in the Middle Ages. But we would do well to remember Maitland's warning against "overrating both the trustworthiness of written documents and the importance of the matters they deal with as compared with other things for which the direct authority of documents is wanting."[3] If we must now turn to the heavy end of an untrustworthy and lopsided record, it is because there we shall find more examples of oneiric artifice working to annex and implicate Carolingian kings.

By the middle of the ninth century, the status of church property had become the leading edge of ecclesiastical complaint. This was, in part, the unexpected harvest of Charlemagne's educational reforms. As the number of competent clerical readers and writers peaked in the 840s and 850s, more claims about ecclesiastical properties could be and were recorded.[4] Moreover, the higher clergy of the realm, after nearly a century of generous support and protection by the Carolingian royal house, was prepared to defend its real and imaginary estate against all encroachment. It has been estimated that the amount of land held by the church tripled in the first seventy-five years of Carolingian rule. The medieval church would never hold more property than it did by the end of the ninth century.[5] In the 880s, when Notker the Stammerer wrote of bishops' palaces adorned with many-colored carpets, soft cushions, and sumptuous tapestries, of the episcopal high table outfitted with silver service plates and jewel-encrusted goblets, and of prelates wrapped in silken gowns dyed purple, his was a monastic and imperial protest against the luxury, excess, and avarice of a fat episcopate at the end of this period of church growth.[6] But J. W. Thompson and J. Dhondt's discovery of the actual dissolution of the Carolingian royal fisc has tended to obscure the fact that by 850 it was the higher clergy that thought that its estate was dissolving.[7] For the division of the kingdom after Louis the Pious's death and the shifting borderlines that followed for the rest of the century introduced a principle of uncertainty into property rights that shook the church and forced it to fortify.

In late 840, with Louis laid out in his sarcophagus and his sons jockeying for advantageous position round the royal post, Odo, the abbot of Ferrières, remained uncertain which way the royal winds were blowing: "Placed in the middle and full of uncertainty we are drifting about, since we are unable to determine who is in the best position to claim our region for himself."[8] He guessed wrongly and sided with Lothar; when Ferrières fell within Charles the Bald's territory, he was deposed. Nearly thirty years later, Hincmar of Rheims could be found complaining that not only his diocese but even his parish stood divided between two kings and two kingdoms. He wondered what his church could accomplish if its lands lay asunder.[9] Because actual possession was the stronger and the right to own the weaker concept, political disruption worked in the middle of the ninth century as it had in the middle of the eighth century to dislodge and shift lands. But there were forms of compensation. In the case of the church, some lands that fell within the disposition of the king were subject *ad nonas et decimas*—an annual rent, as it were, paid to the church and assessed at two-tenths of what the land produced.[10]

Churchmen made so many and such different claims about property in the ninth century that the reader of the surviving documents is left reeling under their considerable weight. Some lands were held outright while others belonged to the church in name only. The former needed protection, the latter repossession. Pious people might donate their lands to a church or monastery, but these lands passed under different conditions: some were given outright while the revenues of others might be given *ad nonas et decimas*. Other new lands were accepted as benefices from royal hands. Carolingian bishops and abbots frequently became vassals of the king and performed military duties. Hincmar of Rheims, however, resisted the practice, for he denied that bishops should commend themselves into vassalage or take oaths. Moreover, he said:

> The churches entrusted to us by God are not so many benefices and properties of the king of the sort that he can, as he sees fit, give them or take them away inconsiderately, since all the things which are of the church are consecrated to God.[11]

The Le Mans forger, as Walter Goffart has characterized him, went even further. By the early 860s, this unnamed cleric in the employ of Robert, the bishop of Le Mans, had assembled a set of real and false documents to assert the church's claim to the monastery of Saint-Calais. As he fashioned his spurious materials, the cleric came to hold a rather radical conception of church property: that his church probably *owned* all the land in the province of Maine. Those tenants holding the land at the moment needed only to pay a regular tribute to the cathedral. The effect of this would have been to cut out the king as the middleman between the church and its putative property.[12] Charles the Bald may never have seen the package of false documents, but at the Synod of Verberie in 863 he dismissed as groundless the aggressive property claims of the church of Le Mans that were based upon them.[13]

The failure of forgery of this sort may help to explain why property dreams turned in the direction they did. For no matter how clever they were, they could not claim to be legally binding documents. Instead, they offered themselves as small windows through which readers might gaze upon a more authentic landscape, where dreamers witnessed the true history of the divine disposition of land. It did not matter that supporting documents were absent, for the dream redactors of the ninth century were prepared to write their own oneiric history of property. Most often, their dreams were warnings to those who dared to tamper with the things of the church. Behind these dreams lay the cry of Audradus Modicus and others: that in the wake of civil war the church was once again being despoiled, its properties were being alienated, and laymen had been improperly placed in control of monasteries. If kings were not to blame—though it had been revealed to Audradus that they were—at the very least they were responsible for the proper restoration of the pristine church. The disappointments and desires of literate and confident clerics like Audradus must be the background noise that forever reverberated round the walls of the Carolingian court. To deprive a churchman of his office or a cathedral or monastery of a piece of property was sure to lead to loud, long, and literate complaint.

Against the general din of this learned discontent, we need to prick up our ears to listen to Lupus of Ferrières's ready whine. He may have been the finest humanist of the ninth century, but he, too, was a pleader for property.

Late in Louis the Pious's life, Lupus was to be found loitering at court, where he had managed to attract the attention of his fellow Bavarian, the Empress Judith. In the full flush of ambition, he wrote to a friend, who may have been his own brother, that the queen had summoned him in September 837 to appear at the palace: "she is very influential and many believe that some worthy position is about to be bestowed upon me."[14] If so, he said that he would at once retrieve

Figure 1. The stilling of the storm at sea. The Hitda Codex, Hessische Landesbibliothek, Darmstadt MS 1640, fol. 117v. Reprinted by permission.

Figure 2. Psalm 3:6 (3:5): King David, assisted by an angel, rises from his bed to greet Christ *(center)*. The Utrecht Psalter, Bibliotheek der Rijksuniversiteit, Utrecht, cod. 32, fol. 2v. Reprinted by permission.

Figure 3. Psalm 3:6–7 (3:5–6): Christ sleeps in place of David, who was surrounded by his enemies *(left)*. The Stuttgart Psalter, Württembergische Landesbibliothek, Cod. bibl. 23, fol. 4r. Reprinted by permission.

Figure 4. Psalm 6:5–7 (6:4–6): While David lies on his bed, Christ floats in the clouds above him and sinners are punished in a pit below the king *(left half)*. The Utrecht Psalter, Bibliotheek der Rijksuniversiteit, Utrecht, cod. 32, fol. 3v. Reprinted by permission.

Figure 5. Psalm 60 (61): King David lies uneasily upon his bed of worry. The Stuttgart Psalter, Württembergische Landesbibliothek, Cod. bibl. 23, fol. 72v. Reprinted with permission.

Figure 6. Psalm 40:4 (41:3): The Lord has overturned the sickbed of King David. The Stuttgart Psalter, Württembergische Landesbibliothek, Cod. bibl. 23, fol. 52v. Reprinted by permission.

Figure 7. Psalm 75:6–7 (76:5–6): Proud horsemen are cast into a dead sleep by demons *(bottom center)* while other demons whisper to the foolish in their sleep of riches and vanities *(bottom right)*. The Utrecht Psalter, Bibliotheek der Rijksuniversiteit, Utrecht, cod. 32, fol. 43v. Reprinted by permission.

Figure 8. Psalm 75:6–7 (76:5–6): A rider has been cast into a dead sleep while a demon whispers to a sleeper of riches and vanities. The Stuttgart Psalter, Württembergische Landesbibliothek, Cod. bibl. 23, fol. 88v. Reprinted by permission.

Figure 9. Psalm 72:14–20 (73:14–20): Dreamers on their beds, which are perched precariously between the saints above and the damned below *(left side)*. The Utrecht Psalter, Bibliotheek der Rijksuniversiteit, Utrecht, cod. 32, fol. 41v. Reprinted by permission.

Figure 10. The Elders of Apocalypse rise from their thrones to greet Christ in Majesty. A drawing of the mosaic of the cupola of the chapel of Aachen as seen by Ciampini in the late seventeenth century; repr. from P. Clemen, *Die romanische Monumentmalerei in den Rheinlanden* (Düsseldorf, 1916), p. 23, fig. 5.

Figure 11. Charles the Bald gazes upward from his throne upon a scene of the twenty-four Elders of the Apocalypse rising from their thrones to present crowns to the Lamb of God (ca. 870). The *Codex Aureus* of Saint-Emmeram, Munich, Bayerische Staatsbibliothek, Clm. 14000, fol. 5v–6r. Reprinted by permission.

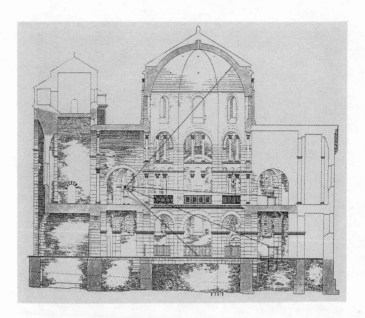

Figure 12. Charlemagne's sight lines from the stone throne in the arcade of his chapel at Aachen: upwards towards the mosaic of Christ in Majesty, across to altars that stand on two levels, and down towards the central space where the congregation gathered. From Clemen, *Die romanische Monumentmalerei in den Rheinlanden*, p. 9, fig. 2.

Figure 13. Psalm 34:15 (35:15): David being lashed by his enemies. The Stuttgart Psalter, Württembergische Landesbibliothek, Cod. bibl. 23, fol. 43v. Reprinted by permission.

Figure 14. Psalm 7:2–3 (7:1–2): David has prayed to the Lord lest his soul be seized by a raging lion. The Stuttgart Psalter, Württembergische Landesbibliothek, Cod. bibl. 23, fol. 7r. Reprinted by permission.

Figure 15. Christ in Majesty (*Majestas Domini*) encircled by the four gospelists (Matthew [*top right*], Luke [*bottom right*], Mark [*bottom left*], John [*top left*]) and four prophets (Isaiah [*top roundel*], Daniel [*right*], Jeremiah [*bottom*], Ezekiel [*left*]). The Count Vivian Bible (sometimes called the First Bible of Charles the Bald), Paris, Bibliothèque Nationale, MS lat. 1, fol. 329v. Reprinted by permission.

Figure 16. The existing fragments of the sarcophagus of Louis the Pious set against a drawing of the lost pieces. Cliché *La Cour D'Or,* Musées de Metz. Reprinted by permission.

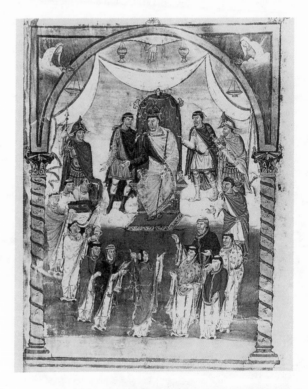

Figure 17. The presentation of the Count Vivian Bible to Charles the Bald in late 845. The Count Vivian Bible, Paris, Bibliothèque Nationale, MS lat. 1, fol. 423r.

Figure 18. An outline drawing of the figures in the presentation miniature of the Count Vivian Bible, fol. 423r. For an identification of the numbered individuals, see pp. 147–48.

Figure 19. Count Vivian, a detail. The Count Vivian Bible, Paris, Bibliothèque Nationale, MS lat. 1, fol. 423r. Reprinted by permission.

Figure 20. Possible representation of Audradus Modicus *(center)*. The Count Vivian Bible, Paris, Bibliothèque Nationale, MS lat. 1, fol. 423r. Reprinted by permission.

Figure 21. A drawing of the relief sculpture of Hincmar of Rheims's tomb. *Left to right:* Saint Denis, Saint Remigius, Archbishop Hincmar, the Virgin, Christ as a child, Saint Nicasius (?), Tilpin (?), King Clovis being baptized by Saint Remigius. From Bernard de Montfaucon, *Les monuments de la monarchie française . . .* (Paris, 1729), vol. 1, pl. 28.

Figure 22. Psalm 30:18 (31:18): A demon leads a naked sinner to a fiery cauldron filled with upside-down sinners while the psalmist looks on. The Stuttgart Psalter, Württembergische Landesbibliothek, Cod. bibl. 23, fol. 38r. Reprinted by permission.

Figure 23. Psalm 43:8 (44:7): A bicameral world with the saints above and sinners below. Demons stoke the fires of punishment. The Stuttgart Psalter, Württembergische Landesbibliothek, Cod. bibl. 23, fol. 56r. Reprinted by permission.

Figure 24. Psalm 1: Demons torment sinners with tridents and cast others into the pit with hooks *(bottom right);* David as king *(above right);* David as psalmist *(above left).* The Utrecht Psalter, Bibliotheek der Rijksuniversiteit, Utrecht, cod. 32, fol. 1v. Reprinted by permission.

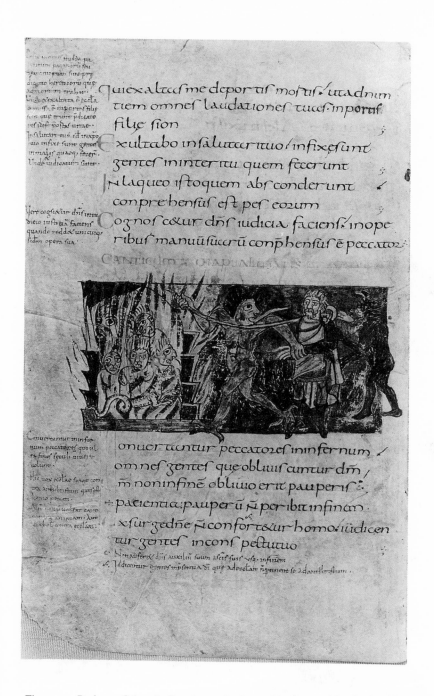

Figure 25. Psalm 9:18 (9:17): One demon leads a noble sinner with a hook while another pushes him towards the fireplace of hell, which is crammed with sinners and has a dragon as doorkeeper. The Stuttgart Psalter, Württembergische Landesbibliothek, Cod. bibl. 23, fol. 10v. Reprinted by permission.

Figure 26. Bronze equestrian statue of a Carolingian king (possibly Charles the Bald). Musée du Louvre, Paris. Reprinted by permission.

his friend, that they might wile away their time poring over books, perhaps in search of unseen works of Cicero or puzzling over the prosody of Virgil.

But instead of a great bishopric and a library crowded with ancient books, Lupus received the modest monastery of Ferrières, and that not for three more years. After Odo's deposition in 840, Charles the Bald approved his election as abbot. Lupus swore his undying faith to the young king, but he was almost as insecure as Odo had once been. After informing Charles that Odo had left his former monastery, the new abbot arrived at Ferrières only to find that the old one was still in place. Concerned that he would appear to have lied to the king, he quickly dashed off a letter to Jonas of Orléans at the palace in order to give his version of events.[15] He had some reason to worry, for he, too, was climbing up that rickety and crowded ladder of clerical competition that stood at the center of the Carolingian court. The delicate outline of his own footprint was surely to be found traced upon Odo's back.

Later in his career, Lupus still had enemies. While on campaign for Charles, he had had the misfortune to be captured. After his release, his enemies at court seem to have argued that he had secured his freedom by betraying the interests of his king, and an attempt was made to replace him as abbot.[16] Once again Lupus secured the support of his friends and was allowed to retain his monastery.

But Lupus was hardly a free man. He owed almost everything to his young king and paid constantly with his service. He was a petitioner for royal causes, a royal inspector of monasteries with Prudentius of Troyes, and sometime secretary to the king and queen, and to synods and archbishops.[17] In his rich correspondence, we see the abbot preoccupied with Charles's schedule, for Lupus revolved around the king like a small moon circling Jupiter. He needed to know at all times when and where he was next to attend the king, but he found it an expensive proposition both to travel to court and to stay there for a month or more.[18] While he does not seem to have been a close political advisor of Charles, Lupus did counsel Charles about the nature of good kingship and, when called upon, about the problem of predestination.[19] No doubt Lupus would have preferred a more exclusive role—to have become something like Charles the Bald's secretary of higher education—but instead he was called upon throughout the 840s to go to war.

Soon after becoming abbot, Lupus was complaining to Jonas about the campaigns that his monastery was forced to support during these dangerous times. In 844, he himself was on campaign with Charles in Aquitaine when he was captured. Later he recounted to a friend the huge disaster he had endured on behalf of his king, for he had suffered the loss of all his supplies. On another campaign, he lost ten horses, a considerable fortune in the ninth century.[20] Five years later, Lupus was asking the bishop of Laon to intercede with the king on his behalf, so that he would not be sent into battle again. His argument was one that Alcuin had used a half-century before: that he was utterly useless on the field of battle. Like Claudius of Turin earlier, Lupus lamented that war took him away from his books. He longed to be allowed to perform duties consistent with his learning. None of this seems to have swayed the king, for in 851 Lupus was present at that disastrous campaign in Brittany on which Count Vivian lost his life.[21] Near the end of his own life, the abbot warned a young contemporary, Odo, the abbot of Corbie, to be more careful in battle and to be content with administrative duties rather than the excitements of war.[22] That was certainly the approach to service that Lupus had always tried to take.

These, then, were some of the duties that Lupus carried out, often grudgingly, for Charles the Bald. In return he received both his position and his place. But Lupus felt he deserved more: not more preferments, which he turned down, but what was owed to his monastery.[23] The cell of Saint-Josse in the Pas-de-Calais, the cell that once had been given to Alcuin, had belonged to Ferrières since the time of Louis the Pious. Under the abbacy of Odo, however, the cell had been given to a retainer of Lothar. When a short while later Charles the Bald took control of the region, he in turn handed the cell over to one of his own vassals, Count Odulf.[24] For the next decade, the abbot's letters were to be peppered with references to the lost cell and the consequent deprivation of the monks of Ferrières.

Lupus called upon his contacts at court—Louis, the abbot of Saint-Denis, and Hincmar—to press his case with the king.[25] He also kept Marcward, the abbot of Prüm, informed about the status of the controversy. He must have turned to Marcward because he knew of the special friendship that had grown up between that abbot and the king in 833 when Charles had been imprisoned at Prüm.[26] But it must have also seemed advantageous to Lupus to search outside the church for support. In one letter, he confessed that a certain Lady Rh. had been financing his campaign for the restoration of Saint-Josse.[27] But Count Adalhard, the noble warrior of Fontenoy and the uncle of Queen Ermintrude, was his most important lay contact. After Lupus approached the great man, he thought that Adalhard himself might restore the cell to Ferrières or that in him he had, at least, secured a powerful ally at court. At one point, Lupus learned that Charles had made promises to Marcward and Adalhard about the restoration of his property, but nothing came of it.[28] Part of the politics of lobbying in the Carolingian world consisted of the lobbied forever promising importunate lobbyists that they would speak to someone above, would press their case, and demand redress. Many times this must have been a disingenuous ploy to postpone complicated suits for which there could be no easy or quick resolution. Lupus himself must have employed this political strategy with his own suitors as often as Adalhard and Charles did with theirs.

But Lupus was not to be stopped. He wrote directly to Charles himself, rehearsing the promises about Saint-Josse made by the king and his mother.[29] He laid it on thickly, bemoaning the lot of his starving monks, who depended upon the income of this cell. His persistent complaint was that his monastery had lost the place from which "we regularly received our food and clothing." When Lupus wrote up the articles of the Synod of Ver in 844, the last and most important of these reflected this personal theme: that the spoliation of church property led "many servants of God to suffer a lack of food, drink, and clothes."[30] We may never be in a position to measure the actual poverty of the monks of Ferrières, but we cannot afford to ignore the rhetorically accomplished quality of Lupus's griping.

He pleaded with Charles, in the matter of Saint-Josse, not to jeopardize his own salvation. Lupus hoped, for the king's sake, that God would not hold him responsible for the deprivation that had befallen the monastery of Ferrières and other poor people. He also encouraged the abbot of Saint-Denis to warn the king about the danger to his soul, for it was widely held that Charles not only risked a horrible final punishment but that he would continue to squander his happiness in this present life until he reunited the church he had divided. Charles was reminded that there was no time like the present to repair this wrong, since even a young man might die. Lupus was so fond of this argument that he repeated it inappropriately when warning the much reviled and much older Nominoë about the dangers of despoiling the Breton church.[31]

Charles the Bald, once the student of Walahfrid Strabo, surely understood the literary dimensions of this discourse. For over a decade, he fended off the rhetorical pressure of the abbot and his agents. He had strategies of his own, even more effective than those of Lupus. When the matter seemed to be coming to a head in 847, the king claimed that he could resolve the case only in the presence of the parties concerned, but Odulf was ill and could not come to court. To his friend Marcward, Lupus quipped that Odulf was apparently too ill to come but not sick enough to die, "which on account of his absolutely sure damnation we should regret."[32] Thus Lupus, a better reader of Martial than this would suggest, retreated from his explosion of epigrammatic honesty into a formal expression of piety.

For Lupus, Saint-Josse was an affair about property rights and personal services. He claimed that the cell properly belonged to Ferrières by the irrevocable donation of Judith and Louis, a fact that he hammered home at every opportunity. Moreover, church property, he asserted, ought not to be handed over to secular hands by kings, a principle that he had helped to reiterate at the Synod of Ver.[33] Lupus believed, furthermore, that he was a deserving servant of the king, whose monastery had also suffered "on account of our constant service to him—which was not earlier exacted from my predecessors—and on account of the loss of our cell." He had, he said, served the king with all his strength, indeed with more than he had to give. Thus, the two things—the right to possess the cell and his own fidelity—were the fissured rocks on which he tried to build his unconvincing case. In a letter to Hincmar, he compared his own service to Count Odulf's. He asked what that layman had done for the king: had he, in fact, subdued a foreign nation or united the divided kingdom?[34]

Saint-Josse was finally returned, twelve years after it had been calved off Ferrières.[35] Lupus had never held any sophisticated theory of church property; he simply knew that the right to possess the cell belonged once and for all to his monastery. His general complaint was that the laymen who had taken over monasteries had looked upon them as revenue-producing lands and not as houses of God.[36] He termed this pillage. Only once did he seem on the verge of breaking through to a higher realm of reflection on property, but then he was basking in the warm glow of the restored Saint-Josse:

> The sweetness of the life to come would be more sluggishly sought, if it were not for the bitter taste of this present life that we more often experience. Many people are delighted with this life, such as it is, but surely even more would be delighted if unending good fortune followed upon their every wish.[37]

Between the honeyed and the fetid, a world of unending delight and this one with its foul disappointments, stood the reflective abbot of Ferrières. He had fought for over a decade to recover a plot of land, but he now imagined heaven as a volitional Cockaigne wherein all might have all. One who went through this life without sorrow was bound to be stupid, he thought, unless he reminded himself that both he and the emperor had received goods in this world and that both might die in the twinkling of an eye.

If weighed down by illness, if assaulted by extreme want, if struck by a
decrease or loss of property, how could one not be moved to give thanks
to that blessed parent whose concern takes for granted that the one suffering is worthy of correction? This is a privilege that God himself established.[38]

If uninvited poverty and the loss of property were the monastic way upward to
God, Lupus should have thanked the king and Odulf for his decade of diffi-
culties. He never did. He too longed for a sweet garden of material delights, but
he must have hoped that it would be free of that constant competition of grasping and avaricious wills which he had seen too much of in his time.

While Lupus ceased complaining about the case after his cell was returned,
he never showed any deep awareness of Charles's dilemma. In the first decade
of his reign, the young king had been desperate to find loyal fighting men, but
he had lacked an abundance of lands and revenues with which to pay these soldiers.[39] Charles must have thought that since Saint-Josse had been cut off from
Ferrières by his brother Lothar—although briefly returned by himself—he
could use it to a more practical end. According to Nithard, Count Odulf had
urged men to break their oaths of fealty to Charles in August 840, when the king
was most vulnerable and everyone in the west was uncertain whether Lothar
would succeed in dominating his brothers.[40] Nobles like Odulf were prepared to
jump to the camp of a rival king if the price was right. Saint-Josse was simply
the payment for the count's loyalty, and the move apparently succeeded.

Yet Charles must also have realized that Lupus, armed with the notion of the
inalienability of church property, his own faithful service, and the power of the
pen, would never let the matter rest. An absolutely supportive subject might
have acceded to the king's needs as Adalhard himself may have done in giving
up the lay abbacy of Saint-Martin of Tours so that Charles could appoint Vivian,
the greater power and more useful warrior in the region.[41] But just as Adalhard
probably expected benefits to flow from his self-sacrifice, so Lupus sought a
benefit for his monastery now.

Lupus may not have been much of a warrior, but his campaign for the restoration of the cell had been an active political and rhetorical exercise from the beginning. He had played both the inside and the outside.

To recover our property, I might even now have imitated the ancients in
their cunning art of high learning, had I not come to realize from my own
experience how useless it is. If even Virgil were to come back to life and

attempt with all the power of his three poems to stir the hearts of some people, he would not be given the chance to read to us today.[42]

Yet even here Lupus was spinning a rhetorical web sticky enough to catch many of his contemporaries, if not the king himself. Later still, when asking the bishop of Troyes for material support, Lupus admitted that he had never condemned the art of rhetoric, "which teaches us to ask for the greater amount in the hope of obtaining the lesser."[43] But all the rhetorical tricks of the clerical courtier had seemed useless in 845. What good was his learning, he asked with considerable confidence in his skill, if no one would listen? Saint-Josse still lay in Odulf's possession. If Lupus was Virgil, then Charles was Augustus, and the *pax Carolina* was, like his heavenly Cockaigne, achievable. But these things were not so, and the realization of constraint and limitation courses through the correspondence of Lupus of Ferrières.

Yet, for all his learned despair, Lupus won the day and won ours. Carolingian kings have always been at a distinct disadvantage in the written record of ecclesiastical property.[44] Charles the Bald may have left behind a good-sized body of charters, but they do not speak to us as directly or as humanly as Lupus does. They do not explain; they record. And even on this front, the dry record of land transactions was invaded by the likes of the Le Mans forger with false documents and pseudohistories. It may even be that the forger's thoughts about the meaning of property were more advanced than those of a busy king. But, in his own time, Charles had held the upper hand in disposing of property: he dismissed the claims of Le Mans and finally restored Saint-Josse to Ferrières. But in the written records of disputes in which one side speaks with craft and cunning and the other hardly speaks at all, we need to proceed carefully. But the complainers demand to be heard, and their dreams keep bubbling to the surface awaiting an audience.

Lupus knew the art. When he was in his early thirties and not yet abbot, he had, at the request of Waldo, the abbot of Saint-Maximin of Trier, composed a work on the life of Saint Maximin. One has to wonder, however, whether Lupus had first conceived of the project in 838 when Count Adalhard already had a strong connection with the monastery over which he was to become lay abbot.[45] The controversy over Saint-Josse lay in the future, but when it broke Lupus quickly turned to a powerful man whose acquaintance he had begun to cultivate years earlier.

It was in the *Life of Saint Maximin* that Lupus broke into what M. L. W. Laistner once characterized as his "Ciceronian thunder" against the degeneracy of the day: *Sed o nostri temporis mores degeneres!* People now loved money more than justice, their own interests more than the common good. He doubted whether any of his contemporaries would dare, as Maximin had, to protect a man like Athanasius hunted by the emperor.[46] For Lupus, the lessons of Maximin's life bore a special message for the ninth century, and Maximin continued as the powerful guardian of the royal house and even of his humble biographer.

To make the connection, Lupus carried over into his composition a chapter from an older account of the saint's life.[47] Once Charles Martel had become so ill from fever and lack of food and drink that his life had been in danger. While he slept, Saint Maximin appeared to the prince and indicated that Charles should follow him to the site of his tomb. When the startled dreamer awoke, he asked the attendant who stood at his bedside whether he had seen the saint who had just spoken. The guard had not and so the prince described how the saint had gone outside, commanding that he who wanted his health restored should come along to his burial place. While the sleeping Charles was borne on a litter towards the sepulcher, Maximin again appeared to the prince. He had already, he said, beseeched the clemency of God on the prince's behalf. But the saint warned him not to give in to vice. As soon as Charles awoke, he made a vow and then withdrew into a chapel where he called for food, and over the next thirty days slowly recuperated.

> Not unmindful of this kindness (*beneficium*) he enriched the monastery of Saint Maximin with estates, of which one was called Petriasala, another the church of Witmar, and a third Clémency. To Saint Peter he presented the villa Andadana.[48]

Thus, in Lupus's reworking of this episode, one benefaction led directly to another in a reciprocal relationship built on an exchange of favors; saintly protection flowed one way, property the other. Though in Lupus's time it must have been the monks of Trier who wished to cherish this memory of an ancient link forged between their saint and the royal family, it is worth noting that Charlemagne himself, when granting certain immunities to the church in Trier in 772, would refer to Saint Maximin as "our special protector." In the *Life of Saint Maximin,* Lupus finishes with stories that show the saint as the great protector of King Pepin, his son, and his men, for he had vowed to save them from disease and bouts of madness.[49]

Merovingian saints and Carolingian nobles continued to confront each other in dreams, but most often these encounters were angry and violent disputes over

property and its right use and proper ownership. If there was an occasional oneiric encouragement to give estates to the church, more often, like the dreaming
cleric in Notker's *Deeds of Charlemagne,* people dreamt of thieves being
hauled off to hell. They were visited by visions of magnificent thief-catchers,
like the giant Polyphemus, who could touch the stars and cross the Ionian Sea
without wetting his thighs.[50] His hugeness was a none-too-subtle comment on
the puniness of the robber and the ineluctability of divine punishment. Most
churches and monasteries had saintly protectors who rose up like giants to suppress thievery and who were in the end as tough and brutish as the thieves they
punished.

In one case, a local noble named Centulf was supposed to have persuaded
King Dagobert that the monks of Vertou near Nantes had more than enough
property and should give up some of it to support the king's soldiers. The monks
prayed for help to Saint Martin, a former abbot of their monastery. That night,
while the invader lay sodden with food and drink, dreaming on his beautiful
bed, John the Baptist and Saint Martin materialized before his eyes. Their
gowns were radiant, their gazes menacing. Centulf wanted to know who they
were and why they had dared to disturb him. They had hardly identified themselves and expressed their outrage at this insult to their properties when John began kicking the thief in the stomach. As Centulf vomited, Saint Martin began to
beat him on the head with a stick. After the assault, Centulf, "that man who was
then invading the properties of Saint Martin and who was attempting to harass
the monks of that place, died."[51]

When another noble encroached upon the lands of the same monastery, the
saints Peter, Martin, and John the Baptist appeared at the end of the sleeping
man's bed one night. They wanted to know why he had dared "to invade the estates of the saints and of God." Peter judged that the thief should receive a lash-
ing. Each of the saints then whipped him, one stroke apiece, with a braided lash
not unlike the one used to pummel the psalmist in the Stuttgart Psalter (see Fig.
13). The man at once "not only returned what he had stolen, but even handed
over to them what he legally possessed."[52] Holy extortion had its proper place
in dreams, the flip side, as it were, of what must have happened all too often in
daily life as predacious nobles and their private armies bullied churchmen into
forfeiting rich estates. But it left the ninth century with saints who were every
bit as violent and materialistic as the noble ruffians who could be found in every
town of northern Europe. The shadow of the saint that fell across Europe in the
ninth century, to use David Herlihy's phrase, was deadly dark, and it hid in its
enveloping shade the saint's single-minded pursuit of property.[53]

The toughest saint of them all, at least as construed by Hincmar, was Saint Remigius of Rheims. When some people on one of his estates once fell to drinking and decided that they would rather burn their wheat than hand it over to the saint, he cursed them and their offspring. The men were marked to receive hernias and the women goiters. For the next three centuries, the residents of this accursed place suffered from disfigurement and agony. Finally, by Charlemagne's command, these people, because of their continuing rebellion, were slaughtered or sent into exile.[54]

Hincmar established himself as the manager of Remigius's reputation; he wrote the digressive and fascinating *Life of Remigius, Bishop of Rheims*, translated the saint's relics, and wrote the inscription that stood above the saint's tomb. In the twelfth century, Hincmar would still be remembered at Rheims as the close associate of Remigius. Hincmar's tomb, which is now destroyed, contained a set of relief sculptures that depicted Hincmar in the act of kneeling before the Virgin; behind him stood Bishop Remigius, as always backing up his episcopal heir (Fig. 21).[55] There is a homiletic quality to much of Hincmar's *Life of Remigius*, as huge bits of it were designed to be read out to the people of Rheims. But what we always need to remember is that in this work, which was written by 878, we gaze at the saint through the gauze of Hincmar's own preoccupations, and the most persistent of these was with the continuing property interests of Rheims. The penultimate item of the *Life of Remigius* is the magnificent and probably genuine last will and testament of Saint Remigius. It consists almost entirely of a lengthy inventory of the properties left by the saint and the circumstances under which he had received many of them. An even longer version of the will was recorded by Flodoard in his *History of the Church of Rheims*.[56] Remigius called on his successors and heirs to protect his properties against all alienation, against invaders, and against thieves. Indeed, a number of the estates that Hincmar fought to reclaim throughout his episcopate had been mentioned in Remigius's will. In a world as dominated by clerical competition and material concerns as the mid-ninth century was, Hincmar saw in the figure of Remigius the episcopal defender of property par excellence: "most often," the archbishop said, "he appeared as a punisher to those who would devastate and take advantage."[57]

If in his own time the saint had crushed those who would tamper with the things of his church, now, from his sepulchral locus of power in Rheims, Remigius was all the readier to punish *raptores, alienatores,* and *peruasores,* that crowd of malefactors who dared to handle his goods. In the time of Louis the Pious, for example, two brothers who were acting as foresters for the emperor were supposed to have decided that a portion of woods that Remigius had always claimed as his own should properly belong to the imperial fisc. To make their point, one of the brothers put his pigs to pasture in the woods. When he spotted a wolf among the swine, the man leapt up onto his horse and promptly rode into a tree. With his brains oozing out upon the ground, the invader died. The other brother, in another part of the woods, came to a large rock and proclaimed that all the forest up to that point belonged to the emperor. As he demonstratively struck the rock with a pickax, particles flew straight into his eyes and blinded him. "And so both received proper payment for their audacity and mendacity," wrote Hincmar.[58] In his own time, a certain Blitgar was supposed to have bought a manse and to have begun violently ejecting the servants of Saint Remigius. When they cried out for help from the saint, Blitgar laughed at them: "Now you will see how much Saint Remigius helps you."[59] Even as he derided them, however, he began to swell up with hatred and anger and died on the spot.

Hincmar knew that it fell to him to superintend the saint's property. Not only was he the heir of Remigius's foundation and the present protector of his lands, but property was the legitimate concern of bishops: "Indeed, it is by the command of the Holy Spirit that the properties and resources of the church are entrusted to the power of the bishop."[60] But if he was the keeper of these lands, it was the king who was charged with forcibly defending them: "Because just as the properties and resources of the church are entrusted to the bishop to dispose of and to manage, so they are entrusted to royal power to defend and guard."[61] These lines remind one of that bifurcation of functional roles that had existed at an ideological level in the west since the times of Stilicho and Cassiodorus, when barbarian peoples supposedly became the designated defenders of Rome and Italian nobles the brains behind them. The archbishop was forever trying to educate his king and the royal family about their proper role as the defenders and restorers of ecclesiastical property. Among both the surviving and lost letters that he sent to Carolingian kings, there was constant talk about the divine origins of ecclesiastical property. He sent at least eight letters to Louis the German about church property and two to Lothar II. To the noble Erluin, he suggested that he might work towards the redemption of King Louis's soul by urging him to restore things stolen from Rheims.[62] If Hincmar wanted his account of Remigius's life to warn his parishioners about the dangers of tampering with the property of Rheims, he also may have thought his lessons suitable for the eyes of the heirs of Charles the Bald. Hincmar imagined that Remigius and his fellow saints had the power to mellow an angry God. Since these Carolingian kings, as both Audradus and Hincmar believed, had always found ways to infuriate God, their only chance of salvation lay with the saints, and what saints like Remigius wanted was their property back.

But neither Remigius nor Hincmar was of a particularly forgiving nature. Hincmar could never quite forget old injuries. In 878 he still remembered bitterly how, after the death of Louis the Pious and the division of the kingdom among his three sons, Charles had divided up the diocese of Rheims among his men. He had, for instance, given the villa of Leuilly as a benefice to Richuin. But Remigius was so unhappy that he soon appeared to Bertha, the noble's wife, while she lay asleep at the villa. He told her that she was in the wrong place, since this property belonged to others. "Get up as quickly as you can and get out!" he commanded her. To Bertha this seemed merely an idle vision, which she casually ignored. Remigius appeared before the woman a second time and ordered her to depart. On a third visit, finding her still there, he announced that now she would certainly depart, because others would carry her out. With that, he struck her with a stick, leaving an immense welt on her body. A few days later she died. Flodoard tried to soften the story slightly, since he emphasized that the saint had refrained from beating the woman on the first and second visits as an example of his great patience.[63] Nevertheless, Bertha did die. No one should think, said Hincmar, that "Saint Remigius does not now take vengeance upon those who invade his property and oppress his church, as he did in earlier times."[64] In other words, Remigius had not gone soft in his heavenly retirement; he was as formidable a foe as ever.

Nor did a troubled time require anything less, thought Hincmar. For in August 858 Louis the German invaded the kingdom of Charles the Bald, seizing the cities and palaces of Ponthion, Sens, Orléans, and Attigny. It was a time of great and memorable betrayal. Audradus Modicus, who was probably dead by then, would have been dismayed, but perhaps not surprised. His revelatory Christ had so emphatically insisted upon a lasting peace between the brothers because he knew how frangible fraternal concord always was in the Carolingian world. Thus, the punishments for failure were laid down, waiting for the oathbreakers. But what would have shocked Audradus was his archbishop's treachery. For Wenilo not only went over to Louis the German; he may have encouraged him to invade. His treachery was so infamous that the memory of it may have survived in song, as Wenilo (Guenilo) became Ganelon in the *Song of Roland* and Audradus may have been transformed (however unfairly) into his sidekick Hardré in later epic stories.[65]

By the late summer of 858 Louis the German was seeking legitimacy. He may even have hoped to be crowned king of west Francia at Rheims, but Hincmar, not about to change horses now, stood in the way. He sent a letter to Louis, now lost, "about the invasion of his brother's kingdom, advising him against this course of action with appropriate and useful chastisements, lest this invasion lead to his damnation."[66] Slowly Hincmar began to rally the western Frankish church behind Charles. Louis's journey to Rheims seemed to him ill advised, and he sought to postpone it.[67] At Quierzy in November 858, a synod of prelates from the dioceses of Rheims and Rouen was convoked to consider Louis's requests and the general problem of the invasion. The letter that was sent from the synod to Louis was, according to Flodoard, written by Hincmar and was "full of episcopal restraint."[68]

The golden promise that Louis had laid out in his own letter to these prelates was that he would restore the church and its properties in western Francia if they recognized him. He had heard the grumbling of his brother's churchmen about Charles's treatment of them and their property before he invaded, but he probably heard it again from the unhappy Wenilo as he passed through Sens in September. These complaints would have echoed Audradus's earlier list of outrages. But Hincmar and his fellow bishops found Louis's offer less than sincere. They knew that an invader could be no respecter of property and that one who knowingly sinned would descend alive into hell.[69] The central argument made at great length in the letter from Quierzy was that Louis was placing his very salvation in jeopardy. Hincmar invited the king to examine his soul to see if he could justify his invasion. Louis was encouraged to conjure up in his mind's eye that day when he would leave this life, when the whole world, all power, and all wealth would disappear, and when he would stand all alone without his wife and children, and without the whispering words of his counselors and vassals.[70] On that death day, a sinner would see all his sins. Devils would rise up to bind and menace him, punishing him for the vices and foul deeds he had refused to repent in this world. Such a man, now naked and powerless, would be dragged by a demon to a cauldron filled with other upside-down men (see Fig. 22).

But Louis's badness had not begun in 858, for Hincmar reminded him that he had once overthrown his own father.

> We beg you, Lord, to hold up before your mind's eye that day when with
> all human beings your soul will take back its own body and you will come
> before the face of the eternal judge in the sight of the angels and mankind.[71]

Around this invader of his brother's property Hincmar constructed an image of hell, trying to outline its reasons and its isolations so that Louis would be unable to avoid the logic of its horrific inevitability. There could be no escape, and the people who now gave him bad advice would be of no help when he was being swallowed up by hellfire.

The bishops were unsparing in their reproach. As Louis marched through his brother's kingdom, he had brought a little piece of hell to earth. Cruelties and abominations were committed in the parishes he passed through. Families were once again divided, Christians set against each other, and Christian king against Christian king; these were calamities worse than even the Northmen had wrought.[72] Did people now deserve to flee from the marauding Northmen into a maelstrom of royal violence? Louis was told to read the Book of Kings where he could see how he should respect his brother ruler. The keepers of the church would not in any way support his attempt to increase his earthly realm because this would dishonor heaven. He was urged, instead, to examine his own conscience, for his own royal house had become sacrilegious. How could he restore the house of God when he himself had, like Judas, stolen the things of Christ, overthrown the rights of religious communities, and been irreverent towards the very bishops who consecrate reigning kings? Moreover, if Louis had come to restore the condition of the church, he had best begin by respecting its properties. The immunities, gifts, and grants made by Charlemagne, Louis the Pious, and Charles the Bald ought to be honored.[73]

The heart of Hincmar's letter to Louis, then, was a discourse on the properties and condition of the church. He had few arguments at all to make on good kingship, on the moral problems raised by invasion, or on the worthiness of Charles the Bald. Rather, Louis was called upon to set right property disputes with Rheims, to choose officials who would not lay waste to the harvests, wine, and meadows of the church, and to appoint judges and *missi* who would respect the property of the church and its people. For it was one of the chief duties of the Christian king to defend and stoutly protect the *res et facultates ecclesiasticas*.[74]

But, as he composed the letter to Louis, Hincmar must have still thought that it lacked an exemplary proof, an example that, by its familiarity and relevance, would shock the king into radical reform. He said that a king ought to shine with good works like the lights upon a twinkling candelabrum.

> But if you destroy by a bad example those who ought to be raised up to good through you and your people, it will without doubt be necessary for you to be tortured in punishment in the next world.[75]

He found the desired example of the dangers of the royal misappropriation of property in Charles Martel, who stands at the dead center of the letter as the fitting and consanguineous companion of a hellbound king.

Since Prince Charles, the father of King Pepin, was the first of all the kings and princes of the Franks to separate off and divide up church properties, he was for this reason and this reason alone utterly and eternally ruined. For Saint Eucher, the bishop of Orléans, who was in retreat at the monastery of Saint-Trond, was, while praying, transported to another world and, among the other things that the Lord revealed to him, he saw Charles tormented in the lower infernal regions.[76]

When he asked why, he was informed by his angelic guide that Charles was being punished according to the judgment of the saints who would sit in future judgment with the Lord. For this prince had stolen and divided their properties and must surely receive sempiternal punishment for his sins. He must also pay for the sins of all those who had given properties and resources to the Lord and to his saints in the hope of redeeming their souls. Thus, in breaking a contractual relationship between saints and sinners based on an exchange of land, Charles Martel had stretched the envelope of his personal culpability.

When Eucher returned from his state of rapture, he called for Saint Boniface and Fulrad, the abbot of Saint-Denis and chief chaplain of King Pepin. After relating what he had experienced, Eucher supplied them with a test of the story's validity. If they went to the tomb of Charles and found that his body was missing, they would know that what he had told them was true. Upon opening Charles's tomb at Saint-Denis, the two holy men saw a dragon fly out and noticed that the inside of the tomb was blackened as if burnt.

Hincmar claimed that eyewitnesses to these events had lived until his own time and that they had repeated all to him "truthfully by word of mouth." Since the vision was supposed to have taken place before the Synod of Les Estinnes in 743, and Hincmar had begun his monastic studies at Saint-Denis around 814, it might almost have been possible for the seven-year-old Hincmar to have heard monks in their eighties narrate the tale of Charles Martel's infernal misfortune. But everything suggests the contrary: that the vision of Charles in torment was essentially shaped by the rich and persistent mind of Hincmar himself. The eighth-century version of the *Life of Eucher* contained no mention of the episode, but in several later manuscripts an account dependent on the letter of 858 was inserted. The *Life of Rigobert,* written late in the ninth century at Rheims, repeated the ninth-century form of the legend exactly as received from Hincmar's letter. The author admitted that he had included it to show the damnation that falls upon those who steal ecclesiastical goods.[77] Adrevald of Fleury and others attempted to use the story to explain why King Pepin's brother Carloman had given up the terrific burden of temporal power.[78] At Rheims itself, Flodoard repeated the expanded story.[79] After the ninth century, the legend continued to appear in histories, for its message was, in medieval terms, always a relevant one.[80]

But, in the end, the threads of this exemplary vision return us to Hincmar and to his preoccupation with church property and the events of 858.[81] Twenty years later when writing the *Life of Remigius,* and still centrally concerned with church property, he would repeat the story of Charles Martel, noting there that Pepin had restored to Rheims and to other churches some of the stolen properties.[82] In the *Life of Remigius,* Eucher's vision functions as the turning point in the fortunes of modern Rheims. In the episcopal letter as well, after the story about Charles, Hincmar had attempted to focus Louis's attention on the positive consequences. King Pepin had called together a synod at which he undertook to restore the ecclesiastical lands stolen by his father. Since some of these lands now lay in unfriendly hands and could not be returned, he granted a portion of the revenues from those lands, the *nona et decima,* until such time as they could be properly restored to the church. The Emperor Charlemagne had decreed that neither his son nor his successors should tamper with or overturn these restorations. Hincmar claimed to have in hand a copy of the relevant capitulary, and he had heard Louis the Pious personally affirm its measures. A falling away from these standards could only fulfill the promise of the psalm that God would grind into stubble, burn like firewood, and sweep away in a mighty storm those who dared to possess the sanctuaries of God.[83]

Hincmar did not compose the vision of Charles Martel's damnation in a vacuum. In fact, it reflected some of the dream literature that the Carolingians had already created. As we have seen, Charles Martel had already figured in the *Life of Saint Maximin,* though to an entirely different effect: there as the donor of lands, here as their despoiler. There the tomb of Saint Maximin had been the magnet attracting a feverish prince; here Charles was to be removed from the company of the saints resting peacefully in their tombs at Saint-Denis. What Charles Martel lacked was staying power; he was not to be allowed to sleep quietly in his sepulcher in the dusty corner of a magnificent church as though he had done nothing wrong, nothing offensive to God and his high churchmen. He was instead a thievish prince who had been snatched out of his tomb by some combustible demon, their mighty struggle blackening the crypt. The dark dragon that had taken up residence in the prince's tomb may have been on guard to prevent his forbidden return (see Fig. 25).

What has generally been overlooked is that Hincmar here lifted a complete line from Heito's *Vision of Wetti,* from precisely that point where the shocked Wetti had asked his guiding angel why the unnamed Charlemagne was suffering so horribly.[84] Here, however, the archbishop left the passage in an even more suggestive form. So famous was Wetti's story and its Charlemagne sequence that Hincmar might have reasonably expected his audience, or at least Louis the German, to be able to recreate in his mind the unfolding scene with Eucher and his angel. The bishop of Orléans needed only to express his bewilderment for the angel to answer an unasked question: why was this particular king suffering in this way? The scene had become a type.

Hincmar may also have learned from Heito of the advantages of the suggestive over the explicit when imagining royal dreams. His sinner and the specific sin he had committed were named here, but not the punishment. Indeed, in much of Hincmar's dream work there would be an unfinished and abrupt quality. He was, after all, a powerful and busy man, and his few dream texts betray a certain impatience. If his dream texts were direct and pointed, they were so in an almost polemical and certainly political way, but the price paid for this was in the realm of literature, for a dream text such as Eucher's lacks that richness of images of the otherworld that Carolingian readers knew from Wetti and the rest.

Moreover, the archbishop of Rheims had no reason to make a balanced historical assessment of Charles Martel, who was never the larcenous bogeyman of Carolingian history that Hincmar made him out to be.[85] Yet Hincmar and the bishops gathered at Quierzy in November 858 felt called upon to alert Louis the German to the danger in which he had placed his everlasting soul. In fairness to King Louis, we need to recognize that these same bishops had been preoccupied by the issue of the possession and despoliation of property before the invader had come, and they still would be worried about it once he had gone. But late that year, as Louis hoped to travel to Rheims for his coronation, Hincmar could only recall the damage done to the church and its lands in previous periods of civil disturbance. Rheims had suffered terribly, he thought, during the early 840s and was still trying to recover its alienated lands. This new invasion threatened more of the same confusion and opportunism.

Not everyone in the west took the line that Hincmar did. Lupus, in the diocese of the collaborator Wenilo, was silent for once. But, by early January 859, Charles the Bald had gathered his forces together and had driven Louis back to Germany. Eriugena, acting as the royal poet he occasionally was, broke forth in celebratory song:

Nunc reditum Karoli celebramus carmine grato;
    Post multos gemitus gaudia nostra nitent.
Qui laeti fuerant quaerentes extera regna,
    Alas arripiunt, quas dedit ipsa fuga.
Atque pauor ualidus titubantia pectora turbans
    Compellit Karolo territa dorsa dare.

[With a welcoming song, we celebrate the return of Charles.
    After much moaning, our joy bursts forth.
Those who were happy when trying to gain foreign kingdoms
    Now put on the wings of fearful flight.
The overwhelming fright that gripped their trembling hearts,
    Forced them to turn their craven backs to Charles.][86]

Unlike Hincmar, the philosopher was here largely unconcerned with church property. Instead he expressed his outrage that Louis the German had dared to overthrow Christ's own king and to upset the divine disposition of kingdoms. The inscription on Charles's coins in the 860s read simply, GRATIA DEI REX, thus making the same fundamental assertion: only God could make a king. Eriugena prefaced his discussion of Louis's brazen invasion with a marvelous dialectic that set the true history of Christ against the fictions of Homeric heroes and Virgilian fantasies of dead Romans.[87] Heiric of Auxerre, who was probably a student of Eriugena around the time of the invasion, wrote his own short lament on the rabid assault of Louis upon his pacific and Davidic brother Charles.[88]

Yet when the archbishop, who deserved considerable credit for fending off the invader, wrote to his king in February 859, it was not to celebrate his return to power but to scold him. He urged Charles to think about the rapine and poverty that continued in his kingdom, for which he was partly to blame. The king's own men had welcomed the confusion of the previous months as an opportunity to seize church lands. Hincmar admonished Charles to send these men home and to command all his men to behave properly.

> And do not neglect that letter which the Synod of Quierzy sent last year, by the authority of Wenilo [of Rouen] and Erchenrad [of Chalons], to your brother Louis at the palace of Attigny. I gave a copy to my nephew Hincmar [of Laon] to give to you when he was with you in Burgundy. Re-

read the chapters of that letter carefully, because—believe me—they were composed more for you than for your brother.[89]

Thus, Hincmar invited his reborn king to reread the letter that he first had seen while hiding out in Burgundy in the dark fall of 858. It was, as we have seen, a letter that chiefly contained articles about how rulers ought to preserve and protect church property, and the awful penalty they would pay if they did not. For there Charles the Bald would once again have encountered Charles Martel and the hellish future that awaited all avaricious kings.

Even Prudentius, in the *Annals of Saint-Bertin,* had to admit that in 859 Charles had engaged in distributing to laymen monasteries that previously had been held by clerics.[90] Hincmar was more pointed. He had three specific complaints to bring to Charles's attention in his letter of early 859. It was widely reported that the king had said that he would do nothing about the depredations, for each person ought to protect his own properties as best he could. This did not, of course, square with Hincmar's view of royal responsibilities. He had also heard that those with complaints of this kind had received cold comfort from the king at court, being discharged from his presence with no hope. Finally, and Hincmar had to admit that he believed this, however unwillingly, thieves were still able to force churches into compromising deals, which they then violated.

Hincmar's various campaigns to recover alienated church properties were not without their successes. Indeed Flodoard compiled an entire chapter of the *History of the Church of Rheims* on Charles's restorations.[91] The king was forthright in explaining that out of great necessity he had been compelled, however reluctantly, to give lands from the bishopric of Rheims to his faithful men, "whence they might gain some worldly benefit while in my service."[92] Lupus was familiar with this kind of argument, but it took him longer than Rheims to reclaim his piece of land. In 845 Charles had admitted that out of necessity, as a sort of stopgap measure, he had alienated lands of the church of Rheims. But he entirely restored them, and he was not alone, for other kings in the last half of the ninth century also restored church lands.[93] Some of Hincmar's victories were relatively quick. The villa of Vandières was supposed to have been given to Saint Remigius, but Angilram, one of Charles's company, asked the king to grant it to him and the king agreed. When Hincmar got wind of this, he went rooting in his archives and found a charter that described the donation of the villa to Rheims, which he at once sent to King Charles. He warned him not to go against canon law by usurping church property. Persuaded by the charter, the king withdrew from his intrusion into the villa and restored it to church use.[94]

Some victories in property disputes took much longer. When Flodoard said that Hincmar had labored to rejoin the villa of Neuillay-Saint-Front to the church of Rheims, he surely understated the complexity and duration of the case, for Hincmar had doggedly pursued the issue for thirty-five years. Towards the end of his life, he composed a brief and remarkably restrained history of this piece of property.[95] Neuillay had been given to the church of Saint Mary of Rheims in 771 by Carloman, and his brother Charlemagne at first had confirmed the donation. But in 794, Charlemagne had given the villa as a benefice to one of his nobles, while revenues *ad nonas et decimas* were paid to the church of Rheims. Louis the Pious, in his turn, gave the land to Donatus, who, with the intercession of Count Bego, was able to obtain certain estates from the villa as a direct possession. But Donatus had sided with Lothar in the revolt of 833, and so Louis the Pious had turned the land over to another of his supporters, a former official of Charlemagne. About 843, Charles the Bald returned the benefice to Donatus, who later commended his son to the king, and this son was given the villa as a benefice. When Louis the German invaded in 858, however, Landrada, Donatus's wife, and her sons supported the invader. Upon his return to power, Charles granted the villa to the monastery of Orbais. When the king came to Rheims in 871, Hincmar showed him the tomb of his great-uncle Carloman in the church of Saint Remigius. He seems to have taken this opportunity to talk about the villa and to show him the charters in the archives of Rheims. Charles was also reminded again that those who delayed returning church lands risked damnation. So the king restored the villa, which another noble now held as a benefice, to the church of Rheims. When the family of Donatus began to complain that some portion of this land and its properties belonged to them, the king sent *missi* to investigate. Again the villa was entirely returned to the church. In 875, however, with Charles the Bald on his way to Rome, the descendants of Donatus and Landrada took their claims to Queen Richildis and Louis the Stammerer and for a time recovered the land. When Charles returned from Rome and came to Rheims in July 877, he firmly returned the villa to Hincmar and his church.

Thus, in his short memorandum, Hincmar takes us on a roller-coaster ride from which we dizzy watchers can see how fractious, how slippery, and how unstable property and the right to possess it were in the ninth century. Of one thing Hincmar was steadfastly certain: the villa of Neuillay rightfully belonged to his church. Moreover, he had the documents to support this rightful possession, and they attested, at various points, to royal sanction. But at the end one is left wondering whether the ride was really over. Donatus's family had roots that ran almost as deeply into the history of this villa as had the church of Rheims. Talk of damnation and of Charles Martel snatched by demons may adorn Hincmar's pages, but possession of property, blood ties, and noble families must have mattered as much, though it is a side of the controversial history of Carolingian property that we too seldom see. Charles the Bald, however, could not afford to ignore it.

When Louis the German died in 876, Charles the Bald, now emperor, marched into his brother's former kingdom in the false hope, one must suppose, of taking another step towards the restoration of his grandfather's empire. At Andernach, he suffered a disastrous defeat at the hands of his nephew Louis the Younger. In the *Annals of Saint-Bertin,* Hincmar was less than sympathetic. He portrayed the invading army of Charles as a band of plunderers who were not very different from the Northmen, who at that very moment were sailing up the Seine. In one of his more evocative descriptions, Hincmar imagined the fleeing troops at Andernach rushing back over a crowded and narrow path, trampling upon each other, overrunning the baggage train and the traders trailing the emperor's army.

> And so was fulfilled the prophetic proclamation: "Woe to thee that spoilest; shall thee not also be spoiled?" Everything that those plunderers with the emperor possessed was now plundered and so were they. Those who could escape on horseback had now only their lives as the spoils of war. The others, who were not killed, however, were so robbed by the local people that they were forced to conceal their genitals with hay and straw as they fled naked from the field. Thus it happened that a mighty blow fell upon a plundering people.[96]

Only a mind as quick and confident as Hincmar's could have conceived of this utterly deflating image of noble imperial warriors preyed upon by peasants and fleeing naked from the battle. He was careful not to call the emperor himself a plunderer, but in 876 he must have recalled the arguments that he had made to Louis the German and Charles in 858. In both years it was God who had sent the thieves home with their tails between their legs.

With Charles the Bald dead the next year, Hincmar did not give up his pursuit of property claims. If anything, he became even more determined. He conducted a campaign of letters against Bernard, the count of Toulouse, who had alienated properties of Rheims in Aquitaine. The same old chestnuts were still smoldering in the fire: that these lands had been given to the church of Rheims and were recorded in the will of the saint, that Bernard had placed his soul in everlasting peril by unjustly holding ecclesiastical properties, and that he risked ecclesiastical censure in this life and damnation in the future one.[97]

Moreover, in 878 Pope John VIII was fighting what Hincmar called a fierce battle against two counts who had dared to plunder his properties. At a synod held in Troyes, the pope described why he had excommunicated these men and sought the approval of the bishops. They asked for the privilege of writing a response, which Hincmar himself apparently composed and read out. Not only did he approve of excommunication for this crime, but he welcomed the papal prosecution of those who plundered and ravaged churches. The synod produced, in fact, a formula for excommunicating those who had stolen the ecclesiastical property of the pope, but it was sufficiently general to be applied to other cases.[98]

In 878, as he wrote the *Life of Remigius,* Hincmar still had church property first and foremost on his mind, and he had another generation of kings to train. There he not only repeated the story of Charles Martel's fate but supplied another oneiric example. Once, he said, King Pepin, the father of Charlemagne, hit upon the idea of obtaining the rent from the villa of Anizy-le-Chateau near Laon, as he had taken others. So he visited the villa, but while he slept there one night, Saint Remigius appeared and demanded to know why he was there. "Why have you forced your way into this villa, which a person more pious than you gave to me and which I presented to the church of my lady, the blessed mother of God?" The "more pious one," according to Flodoard's version of the will of Remigius, was Clovis, who had given Anizy to the saint.[99] After his question, the saint began to whip the king so stoutly that much later he still had bruises on his body. After Remigius had gone, Pepin arose from his unsettling sleep, his body on fire with fever, and withdrew from the villa as quickly as he could. For days, bruised and febrile, the king rested and tried to recover from the saint's fury.

> Thereafter no prince of the kingdom stayed in that villa until recent times—and the same went for Coucy and Leuilly—except for Louis, the king of Germany. When he invaded the kingdom of his brother Charles, he stayed at Leuilly, but fled from there shamefully the next morning before the advancing forces of his brother. He barely escaped.[100]

Thus Hincmar continued to associate Louis's abortive invasion of 858 with other examples of the theft of church property by kings. He may even have meant to suggest here that Remigius had visited Louis the German in his sleep as he had once visited Pepin, thus providing the real reason for Louis's hasty withdrawal from west Francia. Charles the Bald owed everything to the great saint of Rheims and to the man who managed the saint's spectacular show.

The point of Hincmar's dream sequences was never to damn the remembered wrongdoings of Charles Martel or Pepin the Short, but to warn living kings about the dangers of tampering with ecclesiastical property. In Hincmar's reading of history, God would surely punish plunderers and thieves with disgrace and defeat. The greatest example of this truth in his own lifetime had been the fate of Louis the German in 858–59. Twenty years later, it still flitted in and out of his thoughts.[101] That Louis's reversal had very little to do with the problem of church property, and that it had even less to do with Charles Martel and Pepin, mattered not at all to Hincmar, who with dogged persistence had interwoven the issues of royal success and ecclesiastical prosperity for most of his career.

But if "human dreams do not easily forget old grudges," as Vladimir Nabokov once wrote, then the archbishop of Rheims was surely one of the ninth century's most human dreamers, for he seemed unable to finish with Charles the Bald.[102]

The emperor had died in October 877 as he retreated from Italy. Hincmar had never shared Charles's dreams of empire, and the description of Charles's death he recorded in the *Annals of Saint-Bertin* is mocking and cold. The archbishop thought that the already feverish emperor had been poisoned by his Jewish physician and had finally succumbed in a shepherd's cottage in the Alps. His companions had removed his innards and filled the cavity with wine and spices. They then set out on the long journey back to Saint-Denis, where the emperor wanted to be buried. Soon, however, the corpse became so fetid that the porters could not continue. The body of Charles the Bald was placed inside a barrel that was covered with tar and wrapped in leather. Even this failed to inhibit the smell, and so Charles the Bald was buried in his stinking barrel at Nantua.[103]

Even if everything Hincmar recounted were true—and a similar story is echoed by other annals—the archbishop here had gone out of his way once again to demonstrate the final folly of Charles's imperial aspirations. It was God who had stopped short both the emperor and his nephew, who had been rushing to Italy to prevent his uncle's entry. Neither Hincmar nor his God had ever had much sympathy for adventurers, not in 858, not in 876, and not now. Moreover, in making Charles seem all too human, the annalist outdid himself. The king's body in death did not smell of roses and lilies, the sweet perfume of the saint, nor was there any spark of power left in his corpse—no potent relics that might have moved his bearers to complete their long journey, no spiritual presence to enforce his now dissipated royal will. Instead, the emperor had died as ignobly as any peasant, his abandoned corpse smelling like the rotting flesh of every-man, and his skeleton squeezed into a barrel, not into the majestic tomb that awaited him at Saint-Denis.

But Hincmar was not finished with Charles yet. In the *Life of Remigius* the archbishop had already retold and interpreted the incredible story of the girl from Toulouse who had been brought back to life by the saint after she had experienced the prison of the infernal regions.[104] He drew out some lessons for his flock:

> Some people, on account of their good works, are preordained to join the company of the elect. But, on account of some bad deeds, for which reason they die defiled, after their deaths they are destined to be punished harshly in the flames of the purgatorial fire. Some will remain in this condition until the final day of judgment, being cleansed of the squalor of their vices by this lengthy examination. Others, however, because of the prayers of their faithful friends, alms-giving, fasting, tears, and masses, are released from their punishment and will come to enjoy the reposeful place of the saints.[105]

Since Charles and other powerful people had ended their days polluted by the sins of ambition and avarice, they required just this kind of release from the purgatorial fires that consumed them even as Hincmar wrote the *Life of Remigius*.

Towards the end of his own life, Hincmar turned to the contemplation of this realm of purgation, wherein old debts were being settled. At some point, probably in late 877, he sent a letter to his beloved brothers and religious men because he thought that they should know what had happened recently in his parish. A man by the name of Bernold, who was known to the archbishop, had fallen sick.[106] He had already received the rites of the dying and hovered on the edge of death. For four days he took neither food nor drink and could only communicate by gestures when he needed water. Finally he lapsed into unconsciousness and seemed already dead, except that some small movement could be detected in his breathing and his face remained ruddy. In the middle of the night, the sick man opened his eyes and asked his wife to bring a confessor quickly because he could not last long. When the priest arrived and had attended to his office, he was invited to take up a chair beside Bernold. The priest was then told by Bernold that he must listen carefully to what he was about to tell him. If Bernold was unable to repeat the things he had been ordered to pass along, then the priest must fulfill his mission.

With tears and much wailing, Bernold began. He said that he had been transported from this world to another. There he came to a place where he saw forty-one bishops, among whom were Ebbo, Pardulus, and Aeneas. They were ragged and filthy, and they looked as if they had been burned by fire. All of them alternated between a state of utter cold, in which they wept and their teeth chattered, and one of burning heat. Bishop Ebbo called to Bernold by name, begging him to help them, since he still had the freedom to return to his body. When Bernold asked how he could assist, he was told to seek out the people of these bishops, both clerical and lay. "Tell them that they should give alms and prayers on our behalf, and that they should see that holy offerings are made on our behalf."[107] But Bernold wondered how he was to find these people. The bishop immediately provided him with a guide, who led him to a great palace where a gathering of their people even then stood about discussing these bishops. The visionary relayed his message to them. At once, the guide led Bernold back to a place where he found the bishops again, but now they were joyful. They were clean-shaven, washed, and clothed in white vestments, long robes, and sandals, though they still lacked chasubles. Ebbo thanked the visitor for the success of his mission, because previously he and his companions had suffered from a harsh form of imprisonment and a hard jailer, but now their confinement was lighter and their keeper was gentle Ambrose.

In the opening scene of the vision, Bernold takes us deep into Hincmar's agonistic world of competitive and compromised bishops. These sinners stood ready to receive their release by the very means the archbishop had prescribed in the *Life of Remigius*: alms-giving, prayers, and the arrangement of masses by the faithful. But where Bernold met these parishioners is not immediately clear. Ebbo had chosen him as ambassador because he could return to his body, but he and his otherworldly guide crossed no frontiers and returned to no familiar place in the world. Indeed Bernold seems never to have awoken in order to deliver his message. The dreamer instead carried out his entire mission in the dream, as though he were slipping unaccountably in sleep between the parties. No waking interrupted the flow, no awkward moment intervened as the dying man had to lift himself off his sickbed to seek out the parishioners of this crowd of bishops.

Instead Bernold found, without any obvious direction from his silent guide, a great dream palace and in it a throng of clerics and laypeople already deep in discussion about the fate of their prelates. But why a palace, when bishops were surely best remembered in their own churches by a prayerful congregation? The dream redactor has taken us instead straight to the source of the sin of these bishops. These were men who had been too worldly, too concerned with the business of the palace and not enough with their flocks. Those people, both clerical and lay, whom they had helped, were not to be found in a church, but like the bishops themselves in the employ of the king. The palace was a metaphor for secular power in the *Vision of Bernold,* and the proper home of the three bishops who had strayed from their assigned duties. Wetti had been warned in his dream of the dangers of the palace, and a later dream text from Rheims would repeat the opinion that Ebbo had jeopardized his soul by lingering too long at the palace.[108]

No reader of Hincmar's letter would have been suprised to find Ebbo suffering in the infernal regions, his ragged garments blackened by the "flames of the purgatorial fire." Hincmar had always striven to discount and discredit his predecessor and his men. Indeed, he once wrote to Pope Nicholas I to ask whether he needed to bother putting Ebbo's name on the list of the bishops of Rheims displayed at the entrance to his church.[109] The reader of Bernold's vision might, however, have been surprised to see Ebbo receive any form of absolution in a text circulated by Hincmar, but even there Ebbo was not fully restored to office. Indeed, none of the defiled bishops regained the right to wear chasubles and, therefore, were unable to celebrate the Eucharist. Moreover, Ebbo was no longer the archbishop of Rheims; he waited like all men for the final judgment.

Ebbo's companions were also men who had lingered too long at the palace. Though Pardulus, the bishop of Laon, was apparently the good friend and ally of Hincmar, he was also a propertied courtier of the king. In fact, Pardulus came from a rich family that held some lands of the church of Rheims. Under Pardulus, these lands were controlled by the church of Laon and the bishop's family.[110] While Hincmar seems not to have complained while Pardulus lived, he later may have had cause to do so when looking back at the loss to Rheims. One piece of property in particular had become a problem by 869. The villa and chapel of Follembray became one of the bones of contention between the churches of Laon and Rheims. Aeneas, who had been a secretary and strong supporter of Charles the Bald, was lifted up to the episcopal see of Paris in 858. Though the episcopal careers of Pardulus and Aeneas never overlapped, they were connected by the problem of Laon. For Aeneas was a good friend and ally of the archbishop's rebellious nephew Hincmar, the bishop of Laon. At the palace of Attigny in June 870, the two Hincmars disputed before a synod about metropolitan authority, and about Follembray. At the end of one heated session, after Charles had left the building, Hincmar of Rheims stood by a window talking to a friend. As night began to fall, Aeneas and Bishop Frotarius, the friends of the younger Hincmar, approached the archbishop to seek a reconciliation.[111] Again we shall likely never know what grudge the church of Rheims bore towards the bishop of Paris, but his place in the lower regions in Bernold's vision and the presence of his people in that great dream palace must mean that he, too, had been typed with Ebbo and Pardulus as a worldly bishop, one too taken with the corridors of power and property.

But the compromised bishops were just the first scene in the dying man's dream. Bernold came next to a dark and gloomy spot that stood not far from a place bathed in brilliant light and redolent of sweet flowers.

> And I saw lying there in the bloody mire of that festering place our lord, King Charles. Worms were gnawing at his body and had already eaten so much of his flesh that nothing remained of his body except sinew and bone.[112]

Charles called out to Bernold by name, wondering why he would not help. The traveler wanted to know how he could assist, whereupon Charles asked to have a rock set under his head as a pillow.

> Then he said: "Make your way to Bishop Hincmar and tell him this: Because I did not listen to the good advice that he and other faithful men gave me, for my faults I now suffer the punishment you see. And tell him, because I always had confidence in him, to help me now, that I might be freed from this punishment. Let him demand that all those who stood on my side and who were faithful help me now, because if they struggle on my behalf I shall soon be freed from this punishment."[113]

Bernold inquired about the illumined and fragrant place he noticed in the distance. It was, the king announced, the *requies sanctorum*, the reposeful place of the saints.

The visionary at once traveled there and saw so much clarity, sweetness, and beauty that it exceeded his capacity to express. There he saw a joyful crowd of men of different orders dressed in white robes. Beautiful chairs on which no one had yet sat were waiting to be filled. He also saw a church, and when he entered it, he discovered Bishop Hincmar himself and some clerics fittingly dressed and ready to sing the mass. Hincmar was given the message from Lord Charles, and Bernold at once returned to the place where the king had been. But he now found Charles changed: his body was again whole and clothed in royal raiment.

The very gloom had lifted from the place. Charles congratulated Bernold on the success of his mission.

The Charles the Bald whom we first meet in Bernold's vision was the one who had been buried in the barrel in Nantua, a rotting corpse now being reduced to sinew and bone. In that state of putrid confinement, divested of all authority and royal regalia, he at last had come to a great realization, almost a cry: "If only I had listened to Hincmar and to my other loyal advisors." This, of course, had become Hincmar's own late complaint. After reaching his peak of power and prestige in the early 860s, he had slowly been frozen out of the king's inner circle in his last years. Before the king departed for Italy on his last fateful voyage in 877, Hincmar had been called upon only to take charge of a portion of the king's library.[114] Yet overnight Charles's death had given Hincmar the opportunity to move up the ladder again, for he could advise young and vulnerable kings: first Louis the Stammerer and then his two sons, Louis III and Carloman, for whom he composed the work *On the Governance of the Palace.* As in the *Life of Remigius,* the vision was a warning against the damnation of souls that faced those who neglected the prudent counsel of saintly bishops. The greatest of men might fall into a putrid pit, but the prayers, alms, and oblations of the faithful could still free even the greatest sinner.

Bernold did not find Hincmar in the real world, however, but in a church set in a saintly place in the otherworld. Thus, with Bernold we have moved from a great palace of worldly allies to a blessed church filled with pure prelates performing mass. Though this might seem odd to us, Hincmar's ideas about the otherworld were typically Carolingian. Both saints and sinners were thought to exist on the same horizontal and purgatorial plain, though they lived in different houses and experienced different sensations. But it was, as Hincmar would explain, a special way of understanding the future that would allow him to imagine himself as already saved in this dream. A decision had already been made about his goodness, but, like Charles, even he awaited the final judgment. He surely thought that one of those unoccupied chairs had already been reserved for him.

Thus, the living Hincmar saw in the *Vision of Bernold* not only a demonstration of his blessedness but also of his immense intercessory power. Few people could claim to have a foot in each world, but, like the saints, Hincmar maintained that he could improve the lot of those living and dead, if only they would listen to him. Flodoard said of Bernold's vision that Hincmar "labored piously and faithfully through his own efforts and those of men faithful to the king and subject to himself to obtain the release and repose of the soul of Charles."[115]

Thus, Hincmar had become not only the dream's publicist but the active intercessor for his dead king at the end of 877.

Yet here too he refused to bring about a full restoration to office. Although
Carolingian writers played willy-nilly with the labels *rex* and *imperator,* Hincmar's failure to grant the imperial title to Charles was purposeful. For him,
Charles's pursuit of the title had always bordered on the irresponsible and gran-
diose. But it would not do for us to follow Hincmar in this neglect, since we can
understand little about Charles the Bald if we do not take account of his imperial
hopes, hopes that connected him to his grandfather and to the promise of the
past. As practical and ruthless as Charles the Bald could be, he was also a ro-
mantic, and we must not deny that side of his character if we wish to understand
some small measure of his motivation. The one important thing the dreamer did
restore to Charles was his fine dress. Sumptuous clothes had always meant a
great deal to Charles, as Agnellus and the annalists had noted.[116] But even here,
where vestimentary distinctions mattered, Hincmar was careful to refit Charles
into "royal raiment" and not the magnificent, Grecized imperial garments he
would have preferred.

After leaving Charles, now properly repaired, Bernold next encountered two
nobles. The first, a man named Jesse, he found buried in a great rock up to his
armpits. Bernold was told to seek out his friends and beg for help. Just beyond
the rock, Bernold saw a deep valley and dark pit filled with black, pitchlike water. When the dreamer asked what the pit was, Jesse told him to look more
closely. Suddenly an explosion of flame and smoke rose from the pit and shot
high into the sky. Bernold watched as four demons drove a crowd of souls like
animals down to the black and freezing water. If only they had people who had
cared about them, said Jesse, they would not now suffer so. After Bernold
found a few of Jesse's friends, who even then were talking about him, he returned to find Jesse freed from his boulder and dressed in white garments, sitting upon a decent seat.

After the accustomed thanksgiving, Bernold walked on until he encountered
Count Othar, unshaven, ragged, and black. The noble tried to hide himself from
Bernold, not daring, as T. S. Eliot said of his hollow men, to meet a stranger's
eyes "in death's dream kingdom." When the dreamer asked why he was hiding, Othar said that the guardian who had urged him in his life to do bad things
had told him not to reveal himself to Bernold. But Othar begged the traveler to
seek out his wife, his people, and his friends, and to tell them to give alms and to
pray on his behalf. In particular, there was one person to whom he had entrusted
his gold and silver who had not as yet donated a single denarius to the church on

his behalf. At once Bernold found himself near Voncq, and he encountered people to whom he delivered his message. When he returned to Othar, he found the count now shaven, washed, and dressed in white garments. His guard had also been changed. Othar congratulated him on his successful mission.[117]

Voncq was a villa near Attigny in which the church of Rheims had long held property rights. Not only was it mentioned in the will of Remigius recorded by Hincmar, but Charles the Bald had given the archbishop permission to construct a cell there, perhaps not long before he died.[118] Though Jesse remains unidentified, a Count Other was mentioned in one of Charles the Bald's last great charters, the one in which he founded his royal chapel at Compiègne on 5 May 877. That day he turned over for the maintenance of his chapel certain lands which "Count Other once held."[119] How Othar had run afoul of the property interests of Hincmar and the church of Rheims is not now known, but he had come to figure in the thoughts of both Charles the Bald and Hincmar in the later 870s.

Last, Bernold witnessed a curious debate in the otherworld between a noble (*honestus homo*) and a peasant (*rusticus homo*). They were arguing over Bernold's fate, almost as if the dreamer were not there and this were the tug and pull of forces representing better and baser things. The noble, always more generous, claimed that Bernold would soon return to his body, and that if he charitably continued his good works, he would one day return to a good house in this other world. But, with a wild look in his eyes, the peasant asserted that Bernold could not leave. According to the noble, Bernold had fourteen more years yet to live; according to the peasant, he had only fourteen days. The noble insisted that he was right and called on the peasant to look up and see the approach of Bernold's confessor. With this connection we return to the start of the story, to that point when the priest had entered Bernold's room and had celebrated mass. The bread and wine of communion finally revived Bernold, bringing him back to life. This was another demonstration of a Hincmarian truth: that the Eucharist had a medicinal and therapeutic quality for the sick.[120]

On this note Bernold's vision concluded, but Hincmar, now assuming his own voice, began to interpret and explain it. He had heard some people talking about Bernold's experience, but the *redivivus* had not yet been able to visit him. Hence, Hincmar summoned that priest of good character who had listened to Bernold and ordered him to narrate the story as it had been told to him. Hincmar admitted that he was inclined to believe that the account was true, since he had read again and again of such things happening in Gregory's *Dialogues*, in Bede's ecclesiastical history, in the writings of Saint Boniface, and in the *Vision of Wetti*, which had happened in his own time while the Emperor Louis had reigned. Rereading these things, said Hincmar, we are always terrified and unsure. While we live in our bodies we cannot imagine what awaits us once we have cast off our bodies. But we must not neglect the remedies that God has given to us in this life to insure that we take up our abodes in heaven. Though we constantly fear death, when it comes it can be conquered.

> For the sake of our lord, formerly King Charles, let us also pray most zealously that the Lord confer eternal goods upon that one through whose power the Lord bestowed temporal goods upon us.[121]

Thus, when reflecting on Charles the Bald, the archbishop could not help in the end but think of royal salvation as a trade-off, with properties and possessory rights flowing to the church in this life and release from purgatorial fire to the king in the next. Even here, however, he resolutely maintained that all these lands were the gifts of God; all along, the king had been merely a middleman passing them along to their rightful possessors.

Hincmar was convinced that the reason why the reposeful place of the saints had been set so close to Charles was that it would trouble his conscience and force him to aspire to a better place. But Bernold's vision also taught, according to the archbishop, that release from punishment was obtainable through a good will and good works. Moreover:

> For the sake of clarity, we often read in the Bible of future events as if they had already occurred in the past. We recognize that the visions of the prophets and other holy ones were revealed through different appearances.[122]

This, he must have thought, would account for his own appearance in the dream. He and his good clerics were already shown celebrating mass in the beyond, because their future was certain to be full of blessedness. Throughout the *Vision of Bernold,* a peculiar species of time had been encountered, one that blurred both the lines between past, present, and future and the boundaries that separated the worlds. Bernold seemed to travel effortlessly between the realms in an oneiric continuum. The point of the political dream had always been to breach the borders between the worlds, so that in their imaginations the powerful might be able to tie together present and future, this world and the next, and find their proper place in the in-between world of purgatory. Nowhere was the efficacy or immediacy of episcopal intercession to be better demonstrated than in Bernold's dream.

There can be little doubt, despite Jean Devisse's equivocation, that Hincmar was the main author of Bernold's vision.[123] Even if a man by the name of Bernold once lived and had a similar story to tell, his dream, according to the manuscripts and Flodoard, was written down and shaped by the archbishop. But Bernold's dream thoughts so closely repeated Hincmar's wide-awake ones that it is almost impossible to believe that Hincmar was not the author of the dream text. The dream is both thematically and stylistically consistent with the visions of Eucher and Pepin the Short. Moreover, the man who had stooped to borrow a line from the *Vision of Wetti* for Eucher's vision and who had had Saint Remigius put exactly the same question to both Pepin and the noblewoman Bertha was not above creating dream texts. Indeed, at the end of Bernold's vision, Hincmar had the boldness to cite his own textual inspirations. The *Vision of Wetti,* in particular, supplied the basic elements of the plot: a sick man on the edge of death transported to the terrestrial terrain of the otherworld in which, in the company of a guide, he saw people ranked in different abodes according to their merits (as in the *Vision of Rotcharius*). In that vision Charlemagne had been gnawed at by a beast; in the *Vision of Bernold* Charles the Bald was being worried by worms. Even Jesse imbedded in his rock reminds us of Queen Ermengard pinned down by grasping boulders in the *Vision of the Poor Woman of Laon.* That the desired destination of all the people in the otherworld was the *requies sanctorum* returns us to the identical language and images from the story of the reawakened Toulousan girl in the *Life of Remigius.* With that basic account of a dead person returned from the otherworld to life, Hincmar must have conceived of Bernold as another *redivivus,* one privileged to watch and report back to his own time on the fate of famous people trapped in purgatorial flames.

Yet Bernold's dream was not all that gruesome. There is an unimaginative sameness to Hincmar's three royal dreams, or at least a lack of rich and engaging imagery. Souls released from torment always wear white, just as good cowboys in movies always do. The blackened walls of Charles Martel's tomb, the singed garments of the bishops, and the charred condition of the count were the charcoal remains of purgatorial punishments the reader never has the opportunity to see. For the most part, purgation in Hincmar's dream texts takes place offstage, beyond the prying eyes of an inquisitive audience. Only once do we see more. But the pit into which nameless sinners were mercilessly being driven by demons reminds one of some of the standard imagery in the Utrecht Psalter, another product of Rheims (see Figs. 4 and 9). Although the *Vision of Bernold* was the richest of Hincmar's dream texts, it is also the most awkward. The reader is often left wondering where Bernold is at various stages in his dream, what world he occupies. The guide introduced by Ebbo never speaks and soon disappears from view entirely: we never learn whether he was an angel or simply another member of Ebbo's circle. Bernold never encounters the jailers about whom the sinners complain. Nor do we learn why Ambrose, who was a favorite author of Hincmar, was considered a gentler keeper than the rest.[124]

Where the dream of Bernold achieves its most interesting effect is in its bumpy procession through the blackened estates. Bernold first encountered the episcopate, then suffering royalty, and finally the nobility. For Hincmar, this would have constituted something like the full social register of the politically important, or, to put it another way, these were the only players with property. At the end of the dream, almost as if it were an appendix, we meet an angry peasant and a kind noble, but the rustic found himself outmatched by his better at every point. He was the advocate of false and misleading information meant to torment the dying Bernold with doubt and confusion. In the end, Hincmar was unable to rise to the level of a true estates satire, because he stood too far inside the social system he surveyed to satirize it. What he wanted was not so much to reform these groups as to demonstrate his own centrality to the system, for he stood at the center of Bernold's dream, waiting for his king to beg forgiveness.

Yet, if he lacked the originality of Heito or the heartfelt passion of Audradus, Hincmar was still the architect of a dream tradition at Rheims. Later in the century, his example led to the creation of the richest dream of them all, the *Vision of Charles the Fat*. In the tenth century, as collected in the pages of Flodoard, Rheims continued its dream work, but without the same political thrust.[125] Hincmar had been the oneiric politicizer par excellence at Rheims and also its chief and most successful disseminator of dream texts. His dreams were primarily didactic rather than descriptive, their point being to teach the powerful through letters and hagiography how to avoid perdition.

Not long after Charles the Bald's death, Hincmar addressed a letter of instruction to the new king, Louis the Stammerer, that touched on a number of Bernold's lessons. First he offered Louis his services.

> For we read [in ancient histories] that good kings, newly constituted, summoned good advisors to them and that the people of those kingdoms received many good things through these good kings and those good advisors. But the peoples of those kingdoms with poor kings and poor advisors received much that was awful.[126]

Hincmar was suggesting here the very thing that Bernold had seen in his dream: Hincmar's preeminent place as the political and religious advisor to west Frankish kings. If Flodoard's report is to be trusted, then Louis the Stammerer should have been one of those, perhaps the first and most important, to have received a copy of Bernold's vision with its request for people to pray for Charles. After all Bernold's message was more suited to Louis's eyes than any other's, as Hincmar actively drummed up prayers and alms for the rescue of his beleaguered progenitor. If this is so, then Hincmar must have used Bernold to wear down Louis's resistance, to convince him of the deadly seriousness of this business of being a king, and of the necessity of collecting at his side the best of all advisors.

Other moments in the letter suggest that Hincmar thought that Louis had already read or heard about Bernold. He warned him that the Lord loved those who were humble and penitent, but damned those who loved vain pomp and voluptuous flesh. If Louis heaped up piles of silver and gold and covered himself with precious clothes, he should remember that this merely flattered the flesh, which would eventually court rottenness, worms, dust, and ashes.[127] One can almost hear Hincmar-cum-Bernold breathing down the neck of the new king. The good advisor, Hincmar told Louis, was to urge "each person, but especially the king, to walk with his God. For if he is bad he will suffer as great a punishment in the other world as he inflicted in this one."[128] As he wrote these lines, images of Charles Martel and Charles the Bald in their imagined hells must have swum before the eyes of the old Hincmar. By the 870s the history of royal dreams was rich enough in example and texture for Hincmar to have expected that a new king would grasp the interplay of its images, and that to threaten him with hellfire in a letter would conjure up in his royal mind recent illustrations of the same.

Aside from promoting his own political position, Hincmar had been most keen to warn kings about tampering with church property. He understood that in the troubled ninth century property was power. Nobles may have thought the church was too rich, and the king may have needed lands to support his government, but Hincmar and his clerical contemporaries held fast to their right to possess lands granted long ago to their saints. These saints, as they imagined them, had responded to the times, paying ruffians back with rough treatment and thieves with sudden death. Church synods conveniently neglected the degree to which, by their own machinations, churchmen themselves had unhinged property from other churches. Crowding in around the king, churchmen at court trampled upon each other as they made their cases. Sometimes their claims were legitimate, sometimes not, but the effect of the whole complex movement for property redress and restoration was to leave behind a highly rhetorical record, a loud and plaintive cry to the king. The worst thing to befall the complainer at court, said Hincmar, was to be sent away unheard and hopeless. But the king had no way to silence for long the petitions of Lupus about Saint-Josse or those of Hincmar about Neuillay.

Property dreams never became a central element in property disputes; instead they were designed to illustrate the consequences of theft. The saints and the saved both waited in dreams for their opportunity to complain. In the rhetorically charged literature about property, they occasionally had their chance. Despite their complaining, or perhaps because of it, the church seems to have succeeded in holding onto and increasing its property for most of the ninth century. By the end of the century, another emperor wanted nothing more than to have a monk tell him how his great-grandfather had ruled an avaricious episcopate with an iron fist. But perhaps that rebuke, too, was richly deserved, a fitting response to the dreamers and to the terrible beating that kings like Charles Martel had received in imagined oneiric hells.

CHAPTER SEVEN

In This Modern Age

Tempora mutantur, nos et mutamur in illis.
[The times are changing and so are we.]

This was the motto that Matthias Borbonius assigned to the Emperor Lothar. I
wish that the attribution were true, that we could for a moment imagine Lothar,
that hopeful grandson of Charlemagne, thinking about what he had seen in his
lifetime, not just about the hoary fields of Fontenoy and the imperial splendors
of ruined Rome but about the historical transformation of his age and the muta-
bility of its human parts. But the line is too perfect and too literary, too self-conscious in reflection and too resigned in thought ever to have sprung from Lothar's active mind.[1]

Carolingian kings doubtless did think about history and their place in it, but
they never recorded their thoughts. Instead, those who search for the ideas of
Carolingian kings soon find themselves lost inside the forest of symbols planted
around these kings by their intellectuals and artists. Percy Ernst Schramm came
closer than any other scholar to reassembling this symbolic universe piece by
precious piece, but even he was unable to reconstruct the royal understanding of
history itself.[2] What royal symbols meant to men like Lothar—those crowns
and cups, starry mantles and sceptered fists, horn blasts and ceremonious ven-
eries—must lie forever beyond our reach, both the subtle texture of their immediate meaning and the richly associative quality of the combined symbols having vanished as the players parted from palace and church. If we could collect in

our minds images of the survivng artifacts of Charles the Bald—the *cathedra Petri, Codex Aureus* of Saint-Emmeram (see Fig. 11), the Sacramentary of Metz, the *Ciborium* of Arnulf—and add to them the ancient objets d'art in his possession—the so-called Cup of the Ptolemies, Roman coins, and imperial cameos—and then set them down in the midst of the court gathered together in some magnificent, but now destroyed, chapel such as Compiègne or the monastic church at Saint-Denis, we would still have brought together only a small and inadequate portion of the world of sights and sounds, peoples and places that must have crowded in upon Charles's thoughts. As a room changes when one moves furniture about, adding a couch here, removing a mirror there, so the Carolingian king's symbolic universe was unfixed, always being subtly made and remade anew each time he moved. The fullness of its momentary meanings must forever be lost to us.

Yet it would be wrong to think that kings lacked an imaginative response to their world or that historians can neglect the few fascinating glimpses we have of their thoughts about history. Einhard, for instance, claimed that Charlemagne liked to be entertained while he ate his main meal each day:

> While eating he listened to some music or to a reader. Histories and accounts of the deeds of the ancients were read out to him. He was fond of the books of Saint Augustine, especially the one called the *City of God*.[3]

Though Einhard's account of Charlemagne's dinner entertainment comes to us in refracted form, perceptibly bent by Suetonius's sketch of Augustus's own dinnertime amusements, we can see in it the rough outlines of the emperor's taste in literature. Of all the books of Augustine, the one that most interested him was also the most historical, the *City of God* with its special reading of Roman history. But what Charlemagne liked even more was to listen to ancient Germanic poems that celebrated the deeds and wars of barbarian kings. So stirring did he apparently find them that he had them written down so that they might be preserved.[4]

Yet, as fascinating as this information is, where does it take us? That Charlemagne would have been enthralled by Germanic poems that sang of mighty warriors is understandable. It was another expression of his abiding interest in Germanic culture. Not only did he have the poems and tribal law codes written down, but he began, according to Einhard, a grammar of his native tongue and named the months and winds in German. But what did he see in the *City of God?* Was it, perhaps, that he understood, as Augustine had, the sack of Rome as the triumph of Germans who had converted to Christianity over a people still

compromised by paganism? When Charlemagne set up the monumental equestrian statue of Theoderic in the courtyard of his palace at Aachen, he may have
been making a similar sort of statement about Germanic accomplishment.[5]

Or perhaps not, for the problem we face here is that we encounter Charlemagne's musings on history, such as they are, indirectly and in almost iconic
form. His court poets, gathered together from England, Ireland, Italy, and
Spain, do not seem to have encouraged his interest in Germanic culture. Moreover, Carolingian intellectuals did not share all of his interests and must have
resisted some of them. Theoderic was to be vilified, as we have seen, during
Louis the Pious's reign by Walahfrid Strabo, and Einhard prudently chose not to
mention the statue at all.

One wonders, too, what Louis the Pious must have thought as he gazed upon
the great Ostrogoth in his courtyard. Did he prefer the paintings of his ancestors
and of great generals such as Alexander and Hannibal that decorated the palace
walls at Ingelheim?[6] He must have pondered what picture would be painted of
him, what signal act would represent his own greatest achievement. But that
again may be to overreach.

What we find almost impossible to do—to reconstruct the intellectual history of royal thought—Carolingian thinkers were also reluctant to engage in,
except in the context of dreams and dream interpretation. There they could
imagine kings thinking about their times and about their place in history.

The last dreams of the Carolingian empire are of final things: the end of the
Carolingian line, the loss of empire, and the deaths of kings. These royal
dreams are as rich in historical associations and in political focus as those that
had preceded them, but the tone has changed. For now a certain melancholy
dream thought runs through these texts: was it too late for kings to make a difference? Too many deeds had been written in Walahfrid's dream book of Frankish
history for them to be undone. The older rallying cry, "culpa regum est," had
been polemical and pointed, but it had contained a belief in the efficacy of criticism: a corrected king could lead the people out of the morass into which sin had
delivered them. Audradus and his contemporaries had thought that God's judgment on the land was manifest, for they had daily witnessed his awesome anger.
Yet, just as Audradus had come to grips in his revelations with division and political pluralism, the final dreams of the ninth century confronted a world without familiar and legitimate kings. The question in the end was not whether they
could find a good king, but whether they could find a Carolingian king at all,
one who would be a stable point in a shifting world, one in whom the old world
order could continue.

The realization that the kingdom would remain divided reflected sober reality, but it did not cease to hurt. As the Carolingians sadly realized, tripartition had been but a beginning of the process of fragmentation. Contemporaries believed they would eventually live in a kingdom with countless kings. The last annalist of the *Annals of Xanten,* who carried on Gerward's annals at Cologne, said of the year 868: "As the Prophet said, 'For the transgression of a land many are the princes thereof' and at that time four kings ruled in the kingdom that once was Charlemagne's."[7] Louis the German held the east: Bavaria, Alemannia, Saxony, and Thuringia. The eastern annalist thought of his king as wiser and more just than the others. Charles the Bald, Louis's brother, ruled Gaul and Aquitaine, but the annalist could not resist observing that his kingdom was frequently invaded by pagans. Moreover, Charles had been forced to buy off the invaders with monies raised by taxation, since he was never able to defeat them in battle. Louis II, the elder son of Lothar, held (northern) Italy and Benevento, but constantly harassed Pope Nicholas and had not yet been able to expel the Moors. The annalist, reflecting the new royal order of things, neglected to identify Louis as emperor, even of Italy. Last, he saw that Lothar II, whom he judged a lightweight, held Burgundy and Provence, but had illegally tried to divorce his wife.[8] Thus, this cleric, living in Cologne towards the end of the third quarter of the ninth century, laid down his conceptual map of the changing Carolingian world. Its dimensions were familiar ones, but the geographer's unease is palpable.

If his predecessor Gerward had been somewhat pessimistic around 841, this annalist has turned up the heat a notch or two. So great were the calamaties assaulting his times, he wrote, that many despaired of their very lives. His last entries were the gloomiest of all. "Spare thy people, O Lord, lest the heathen rule over them," he prayed quoting Joel. But the invaders still came: the Northmen to ravage Ireland and Gaul, and the Moors to seize Benevento. "Everywhere the Catholic church is surrounded by a troublesome throng of pagans; everywhere it sighs anxiously, thinking that the times of the Antichrist approach."[9]

It was not the Antichrist who came, however, but the Northmen and swarms of locusts. While priests prayed for deliverance in 873, the annalist could not but recall Egypt's fate, for he believed that God was repaying "their transgression with the rod, and their iniquity with stripes."[10] For men like the last annalist of the *Annals of Xanten,* it was simply too late; God's wrath was too apparent for the kingdom to correct itself. Audradus would have warmed to the annalist's view of later Carolingian history as a story of unfulfilled penance and squandered peace, but he might have been surprised by the tone of historical resignation.

Anchoring the pessimism of some intellectuals in the later ninth century was a sense of finality. They turned back to survey what they thought of as the turbulent sea of recent history, but all they could see were the royal promontories behind them that had jutted far out into the water and that had withstood, as Eriugena said of Charles the Bald, the crashing waves of adversity that had battered their granite faces.[11]

After 830 and the collapse of Louis the Pious's effective authority, the rock that overhung the Carolingian seashore, casting an ever-lengthening shadow over the rest, was Charlemagne. Nithard began his history of the civil war of the 840s with a short account of Charlemagne's reign for the same reason that Gibbon began his *History of the Decline and Fall* with the prosperous and peaceful Age of the Antonines: to move from higher to lower, from better to worse. Nithard finished his history as he had begun, with his eye on Charlemagne:

> For in the times of Charlemagne of good memory, who died almost thirty years ago now, peace and concord existed everywhere, since the people marched along the same straight road, that being God's own common road. Now, on the contrary, since each person marches along any path he wishes, conflict and strife rise up everywhere. Then there was abundance and happiness everywhere; now there is penury and sadness.[12]

But, in between, Nithard had moved from a publicly held nostalgia for bygone days to a more private pessimism about a realm riven by the sins of selfishness and self-interest.[13]

If Einhard's biography had fed an image of Charlemagne as the perfect prince to the disillusioned intellectuals of the late 820s, by the end of the century Notker had no one left to convince. He simply began with God's golden boy:

> When the all-powerful arranger of things and orderer of kingdoms and times had smashed to bits the iron and clay feet of that wonderful statue set down among the Romans, he erected among the Franks the golden head of another statue, no less wonderful, in the form of the illustrious Charles.[14]

But this was another king's dream into which Notker, another dream interpreter had dared to slip.

Notker took the Roman empire to be the fourth kingdom represented on that quadripartite statue seen by the king of Babylon. That statue, however, had been destroyed, and an entirely new one had come to take its place. Thus, in the totem pole–like parallelism at work here, Notker as another Daniel would make of Charlemagne another Nebuchadnezzar, another king of kings, whose golden head the Frankish king had come to replace.[15] For Notker, then, Charlemagne marked the beginning of a new phase in the divinely sponsored passage of power. But he was only its first part, the golden pinnacle of a statue that should continue with breast of silver, belly of brass, and legs of iron. In the reduced expectations of the later ninth century, the scale of Notker's statue had surely shrunk. Charlemagne does not symbolize the Carolingian royal dynasty as a whole, nor the first of four world empires; he represents himself. The new statue, like Gulliver laid out among the Lilliputians, lay completely within the confines of the ninth century, contained within four generations of kings. The feet of iron and clay were the kings of his own diminished and fragmenting age, the grandsons and great-grandsons of Charlemagne.

Writing in the 880s, Notker was the recipient of a half-century of speculation on the measured descent of those generations of kings whom Gibbon wrongly ridiculed as "the dregs of the Carlovingian race."[16] Charlemagne remained everyone's royal measuring stick, even for those who wrote down dreams. Someone seems to have remembered Einhard's report that the emperor, in his determined effort to learn how to write, "was in the habit of carrying around writing tablets and notebooks, which he stored under the pillows on his bed, so that, when he had the time, he might practice making letters."[17] The monastery of Saint-Gall later claimed, in fact, that it was in possession of the very wax tablets that Charlemagne had kept at his bedside.[18] These were the tangible relics of that most private of all worlds, wherein a great king had once slept and dreamt.

Just as the story of Paul's vision of paradise and of the third heaven once led someone to imagine the *Vision of Saint Paul,* so Einhard's comment on Charlemagne's bedroom writing exercises gave a cleric, around the year 870, the opening he needed to set down a *Vision of Charlemagne.*

> Wherever he stayed at night, either at home or on campaign, Charles, once the emperor of the Franks and other peoples, was accustomed to having lamps and writing tablets set nearby, and whatever he saw in his dreams worthy of being remembered, he took the trouble to set down in writing, that he might not forget it.[19]

Thus Charlemagne was supposed to have believed, as J. W. Dunne once recommended, that the best dodge for remembering dreams is a notebook and pencil under one's pillow.[20]

It was said that one night when the emperor had fallen asleep, he saw an individual approaching who held a naked sword in his hand. When the apprehensive Charlemagne asked the figure who he was and where he had come from, he was invited instead to accept the sword as a gift sent to him by God. He was commanded to read what was written on the sword and to remember it exactly, since at appointed times its predictions would come true. Charlemagne took up the sword and began to inspect it carefully. He discovered that it bore inscriptions in four places. Near the handle, at the swordedge, he read the word RAHT; further down, RADOLEIBA; on a third spot, NASG; and finally near the point, ENTI. Waking, he ordered the lamp and writing tablets to be brought to him, and he at once wrote down the scattered words that he had read in his dream.

In the morning, after prayers, Charlemagne described his experience to his advisors and asked them to provide him with an explanation of the dream's meaning. All were silent save one, Einhard, who, being wiser than the rest, responded that the one who had given the sword to the emperor would also reveal its meaning. With the matter thrown back into his own lap, Charlemagne set forth what seemed to him to be the significance of the dream.

He believed that the sword itself represented the power that had been legitimately given to him by God. He recognized that it was by means of arms and violence that he had been able to subject many enemies to his power. Moreover, in his own time even more than in the time of his parents, the enemies of the Franks had been subdued and there was widespread prosperity. Thus, he reasoned that the first word, RAHT, must refer to the present and signified an abundance of all things. The second word, RADOLEIBA, he took to refer to the time of his sons, after he had passed from this world. Then there would be no bountiful crops and peoples who were now subdued would revolt. RADOLEIBA, therefore, indicated that failure in all things was fast approaching. After his sons had died and their sons had begun to rule, NASG would obtain. For the sake of filthy lucre, these kings would increase tolls, and they would use their might to oppress travelers and pilgrims. With great recklessness and dishonor, they would shamelessly collect up riches for themselves. Even the properties of the church which he and his ancestors had bestowed upon clerics and monks would be shamelessly handed over as benefices to royal supporters. Thus, NASG signified greed. The word that he had read at the tip of the sword, ENTI, could, he thought, be understood in two ways, for it must signify either the end of the world or the end of his royal line.

"The dreamer himself interpreted these things just so," claimed the writer of the vision. He explained that the abbot Einhard had told the monk Hrabanus about the dream. Later, when Hrabanus was an archbishop, he used to relate this event to many people, one of whom was the writer himself. Some of these predictions had been fulfilled in recent times, but some were coming true right now, in these "modern times." For after the death of Charlemagne, during the reign of his son, the Emperor Louis, the Bretons and many of the Slavs had revolted, and the kingdom had been beset by a great want of things. After Louis's death, his sons, Lothar, Pepin, and Louis, had begun to spread N A S G throughout the kingdom. Indeed, Pepin had despoiled the monasteries in Aquitaine. The number of church properties and movable goods that he had handed over to his royal supporters was so great that the writer felt it was too long to list. He observed that Lothar had acted similarly in Italy. A relevant letter existed in the archives of Saint-Martin's of Mainz, which had been written during the time of Lothar's son. It had been sent by the bishops of the Roman church to Louis the German, who had been seeking to learn, through Bishop Witgar, what sort of peace the church should have. From the letter the bishops sent in answer to Louis, the cleric excerpted a single gloomy line with which he concluded the *Vision of Charlemagne:* "The holy Roman church, with its protector and people, is now everywhere being wounded, plundered, ripped apart, degraded, and utterly ruined."[21]

The *Vision of Charlemagne* was written by someone located at Mainz in the 860s or early 870s. This individual could not have seen a document that called Witgar the bishop (of Augsburg) much before that. The writer claimed, moreover, to have been in the company of Hrabanus Maurus when he was the archbishop of Mainz, which was between 847 and 856. If we take as precise the remark that the letter of the bishops was written to Louis the German at a time when only one son of Lothar was still living, then that would suggest the period between late 869 and 875.

Just as Hincmar's explanation of how he had personally learned about Eucher's vision had been barely plausible, so was this writer's explanation of his source. Einhard and Hrabanus had known each other for a long time—at Charlemagne's court in their salad days, and certainly afterwards when they were abbots in the same part of Louis the Pious's empire. But later generations, long removed from the hierarchical divisions of Charlemagne's court, had a tendency to overestimate how important these two men were in earlier times. The Mainz writer, moreover, began the *Vision of Charlemagne* not with some new and novel incident but with a detail lifted from Einhard's biography, for he was striving to secure immediate credibility. He counted on his learned readers recalling at once that unforgettable, if somewhat childish scene of the studious *pater Europae* tracing letters by lamplight.

The author must also have belonged to the circle of Liutbert, who was the archbishop of Mainz between 863 and 889. Liutbert was to east Francia almost what Hincmar was to the west, the central advisor to a lateral line of Carolingian kings, except that, unlike the archbishop of Rheims, he was also a warrior of some fame. He would also be remembered at Mainz as an especially learned and lettered man.[22] The author of the *Vision* was not only familiar with the archives of the church of Mainz, but he seems to have known the background to a sequence of letters involving his king and the episcopate. This may place him very close to the archbishop himself.

More tantalizing still are those intriguing words in Old High German that Charlemagne read on his dream sword, for their presence suggests that the *Vision* was specifically designed for the eyes of Louis the German. Other remarkable Old High German compositions can be associated with Louis. That strange apocalyptic poem, the *Muspilli,* was written in the margins and empty folios of a manuscript of one of Augustine's sermons, a codex that had been presented to Louis the German before 837 by the bishop of Salzburg. The Old High German translation of Tatian's *Diatessaron* or Gospel harmony, may not have been made for Louis the German, but it survives in a manuscript copied at Mainz during Louis's reign. The same can be said of the *Heliand,* the Saxon epic on the life of Christ, which was copied at Mainz and survives in a fragment at the Vatican.[23] Indeed, Archbishop Liutbert was one of those who encouraged his king's interest in and identification with things Alemannic. When Otfrid of Weissenburg had completed his great rhyming *Evangelienbuch* with its seven thousand lines of German, he may have dedicated the book to King Louis and to three others, but he first sent it to Liutbert for approval. In that letter, Otfrid also reminded Liutbert that he had once studied under Hrabanus Maurus, also a former archbishop of Mainz, as though in east Francia and in royal circles a connection with Hrabanus was a badge of respectablility. Works by Hrabanus apparently outnumbered all others in Louis the German's personal library.[24] The author of the *Vision* also employed the strategy of invoking Hrabanus.

Thus, the snatches of German inscribed on the sword played directly to Louis's several fascinations, for a text that combined Charlemagne, a symbolic sword, and fragments of Old High German was baited with just the right lures to attract and hold his attention. Later, for the benefit of Charles the Fat, Notker would remember Louis in similar terms. As a boy, Louis had caught the attention of Charlemagne, who predicted his greatness. Notker's purpose in recalling the meeting of Charlemagne and Louis the German was to demonstrate the line of legitimacy that led directly from Charlemagne to Louis the German's own son, Charles the Fat. Notker also related how Louis had scorned the proffered gold of the Northmen but had shown great interest in the quality of their swords. He had weighed them in his hands and bent them, testing Viking metal and so Viking manhood for its strength. Thus, the iron king, who always "loved the hardness of iron more than the glitter of gold," had an expert's interest in swords and a king's skill in taking the measure of men.[25] Few individuals in Liutbert's time can have known as well as the archbishop did just the right cords to pull when tugging at Louis's complex and reminiscent heart.

Yet the dream sequence as set out in the *Vision* does not require us to engage in what Patrick Geary has called the discipline of textual archaeology, as though lying behind the *Vision* was a prehistorical text struggling to get out, but buried so deep that even the recorder of the dream misunderstood it. To Liutbert's circle, the *Vision* would have made complete sense. Indeed, to read the four German words as though they once made up a sentence such as "Radoleiba brandished Savior" is to misunderstand the emblematic and categorical quality that the author assigned to the separated words.[26]

It is also to neglect the biblical referent, for the scene in the *Vision* bears striking resemblance to the sequence of events in the fifth chapter of Daniel. At a great feast, King Belshazzar saw, in a moment of great strangeness, a disembodied hand write four words on a palace wall, but none of his wise men were able to interpret them. Then Daniel was brought forward. He proclaimed that these words contained a prophecy of the coming ruin of Belshazzar's kingdom, for God had numbered its days. Put this together with the symbolism of the crumbling statue in Nebuchadnezzar's dream with its four ever weaker royal segments and the basic ingredients of the *Vision* are in place.

These biblical associations are no doubt more difficult for us to make than they were for Louis the German to understand. Notker once reminded Charles the Fat that his father had been especially devoted to studying Scripture, a statement that seems to be supported by the contents of Louis's library, which was filled with works of biblical commentary, and also by a revealing incident. In 865, while at a conference with his brother at Douzy, Louis asked Altfrid, the bishop of Hildesheim, the meaning of certain difficult passages in the Bible, in particular that curious line in Psalm 103 (104):17: "The highest of them is the house of the heron." Hincmar, that great gadfly, happened to overhear the conversation and went home and promptly wrote a short treatise on the passage for

Louis.[27] Hrabanus Maurus himself wrote an entire commentary on Daniel for Louis. The second book, he told the king,

> begins at the time when King Belshazzar held a banquet for his nobles (*optimates*) and saw the fingers of a hand writing on the wall. He heard the prophet interpret this to mean that the kingdom would be taken from him and given to the Medes and Persians.[28]

Hrabanus said that he would also discuss the prophetic visions of Daniel. Thus Louis the German had been instructed in the meaning of Daniel by his own favorite author. The hermeneutical ground had been prepared for him to read the *Vision of Charlemagne* in a particular way, as someone at Mainz with good connections may have known.

Still, the words that Charlemagne read were not written on some palace wall but on a sword that the dreamer understood as a symbol of his divine legitimation and of his power of coercion. By the 860s this perception of Charlemagne's success had become common. Said the poet to Louis the Pious:

> Belliger ipse pater cum regna adquireret armis,
>   Intentus bellis assiduusque foret.

> [Your warrior father himself obtained kingdoms by arms,
>   For he was committed to and persistent in war.][29]

Though Ermold meant to criticize Charlemagne here for excessive interest in war, later writers could only look back with admiration at his military success. Carolingian kings, including Louis the Pious, saw themselves first and foremost as warriors. At his palace at Ingelheim, Louis looked upon those walls adorned with paintings celebrating the military might of his ancestors: Charles Martel was depicted conquering the Frisians, Pepin the Short the Aquitanians, and Charlemagne the Saxons.[30]

Although people of the later ninth century knew that they once had dominated other peoples by the force of arms, they now worried that their own swords were rusting away from weakness and cowardice.[31] The sword itself was a symbol of central importance to Germanic society, though the Carolingians and their thinkers had worked to Christianize it. Charlemagne himself revealed something of this preoccupation when he asked Alcuin to explain Christ's various references to swords. Charlemagne, this Davidic king, was also reminded that David himself, elected and loved by God, had subdued many peoples with his conquering sword.[32]

But by the later ninth century such reflections may not have been comforting. The successes of the Northmen and other invaders may not have been great in material terms, but at a symbolic level, whether Christian or Germanic, they suggested that Frankish manhood was failing. The annalist meant to equate swords and success when he said of 852 that in that year "the iron of the pagans [that is, the Northmen] glowed white hot."[33] On the other side, all was frigid. We need to remember how precious and how closely connected with the rites of manhood was the sword of the Frankish warrior. At puberty he was invested, in a rite of initiation, with a sword, shield, and horse by his father or lord.[34] Thus, in the *Vision,* Charlemagne held the very symbol of Carolingian power, that symbolic sword given to him by his divine father. In his pages, Notker would contrast the strength of the emperor's mighty sword with the swords of his heirs, which were, he thought, either broken or rusting. These were not the tools to subdue hostile peoples. To deprive a king of his sword was to deprive him of symbolic power. Thus, when Louis the Pious was deposed in 833, his enemies ritually removed the sword from his thigh.[35] The *Vision of Charlemagne* conjured up for its audience around 870 an image of a swordless future full of military setbacks. Other literature that celebrated successes would be created, but it, too, would be addressing the same theme of imagined impotence, though from the other side. But the *Ludwigslied,* that roistering song about a magnificent King Louis hammering the Northmen, would stand alone and its focus would be singular: upon a single battle and single warrior.[36] Roland was in the wings awaiting the birth of this new heroic ethic, but Charlemagne, we need to recall, had not been, in Einhard's terms, a great field warrior; rather, he was a general who meticulously planned wars and who preferred to watch his enemies flee without a fight.

The *Vision of Charlemagne* did not set out to praise Louis the German; it wanted his attention. He, too, was guilty of N A S G, though not as pointedly condemned as Pepin and Lothar. What the *Vision* conjured up before his eyes was the sword of divine legitimacy, the sword of his ancestors, the one that spoke to him in German. What it called for was reform.

Between 863 and 870, Liutbert wrote to Louis the German about the need for the king and his brother, Charles the Bald, to restore peace to the church. Some of the language and imagery of the letter reminds one of the *Vision*. The church, he said, was mightily wounded and might require amputation to save the rest of its body. He called on Louis, who had already sent letters and legates to his brother, to work with him to repair the church. Indeed it was in September 870 in Cologne that Liutbert, together with other metropolitans, presided over a synod on the well-being of the church, but, said the eastern annalist, there were ominous sounds in the night, the voices of evil spirits that hung over and unnerved this gathering.[37]

The *Vision* completely ignored Charles the Bald, claiming mistakenly that Louis the Pious had been survived by three sons, Lothar, Pepin, and Louis. In fact, Pepin predeceased his father and the three succeeding sons had been Lothar, Louis, and Charles. The early death of Pepin was a detail of royal chronology that might have been more easily forgotten around 870 than it would have been by Hrabanus and his circle before 856. Yet the writer did know that Pepin of Aquitaine had been accused of tampering with church properties, a fact that Pepin himself may have acknowledged. This should have been common knowledge at Mainz, since, as part of his Aquitanian policy, Louis the German had made Pepin's son Charles the archbishop of Mainz in 856.[38]

If the sequence of Pepin's demise was a mistake, the neglect of Charles the Bald in the *Vision* may have been deliberate. In 869, upon the death of Lothar II, Charles had marched into Lotharingia and was crowned at Metz. In the east, Louis the German and his advisors maintained that Charles's act was presumptive and that Lothar's lands ought to be divided fairly between Louis and Charles. The point of leaving Charles out of the *Vision* would be the same as Audradus's prophetic overthrow of Lothar: to deny the legitimacy of a divine place in the sun to a usurpative king. He simply did not exist in God's greater scheme. This was a message that Louis the German would have welcomed in late 869 and early 870, just as he had in 858. Moreover, in the *Annals of Fulda,* which was written at Mainz, Charles was frequently called a *tyrannus* rather than *rex,* thus being denied legitimacy and title with the stroke of a Moguntine pen.

The *Vision of Charlemagne* is full of dream devices and debts. Its structure is the already familiar one of an introductory episode, the dream with its predictions, and a conclusion that verifies and updates. Moreover, as in Aubrey's dream in Einhard's church, there was an archival imperative: the dreamer was commanded to hold fast in his memory what he was about to learn. He rushed to write down the words, because, as so often before in political dreams, they were the solid and legible artifacts of divine truth. The genius of the author of the *Vision* was to have imagined a more suitable setting for a king's dream; no otherworldly journeys or bishops were to disturb its royal dignity.

Even the unidentified messenger of God came to Charlemagne as Carolingian court etiquette demanded, not to drag him off to another world but to hold conference with him where he was. Though the emperor at first had sought to learn who this messenger was and where he had come from, he soon left off this line of questioning. As Aubrey had not worried overmuch when he failed to recognize an archangel and Bernold blindly followed his unknown guide, so Charlemagne simply accepted the messenger for what he was. Though in this Belshazzarlike vision Einhard may have been cast as Daniel, Charlemagne had no need of an interpreter; he was royally sufficient. Still, if the *Vision of Charlemagne* cast the king as both dreamer and dream interpreter, made him both Nebuchadnezzar and Daniel, it elevated the role of the dream's disseminators, that curving line of speakers that slipped sinuously from Einhard through Hrabanus to the writer at Mainz.

What this writer so brilliantly captured was that late ninth-century conviction that time was running out, that the end of a particular royal history was within sight. This view of final things as seen from inside Charlemagne's head was surely a product of the final phase of Carolingian historical thought. The *Vision* measured the whole of Carolingian history in just four generations of kings. This royal descent may have been mapped on a graph of Babylonian design, but Charlemagne represented a new order in the world. Yet, in its periodicity and finality, the dream offered no escape from the downward thrust of time; not even royal penance seemed able to prevent the final disaster of extinction. We need to notice that as the dreamer read the inscriptions on the sword from handle down to tip, he described a descent in both chronological and moral time from better to worse. The dreamer saw the kingdom slipping ineluctably from times of peace and prosperity to times of revolt and widespread want. With this grim and unpromising language, the author must have hoped to shock Louis the German into restoring peace to a disturbed church and into recovering church property from greedy nobles. But, as Louis the German would have done in the 870s, we need to turn the sword around, to look at it from tip to handle. When we do so, we find Charlemagne and his golden past looming over us like Theoderic's equestrian statue standing in the courtyard at Aachen, vigorously static and monumentally imposing.

We should not forget that, by the 830s, to talk about Charlemagne was to talk about modernity itself. The preface to Einhard's biography of Charlemagne was to set the standard for this discourse on modern times. Einhard confessed that he did not wish to offend with his new book those who scorned even old histories, but he knew that there must be many people who believed that the state of the present age ought not to be neglected or allowed to pass into oblivion and silence. He judged it better to preserve this record of recent history rather than to allow the most illustrious life of this most excellent king, the greatest of all men of his age, and his deeds, scarcely imitable by the men of this modern time, to be destroyed by the shadows of forgetfulness.[39]

It was, as we have seen, as a critic of the mid-820s that Einhard had found new meaning in the example of Charlemagne, for he seemed to suggest to his worried contemporaries that it was by neglecting his model of good government that the Franks had lost their royal way. But to talk of the forgotten Charlemagne and of the spreading shades of oblivion was both a literary strategy designed to enhance the dramatic importance of the biography and a heartfelt admission by Einhard that he felt himself to be a thoroughly modern man with all the negative connotations that might call forth.

Einhard's early readers implicitly understood his negative sense of modernity, for they shared his belief that things had gone disastrously wrong since Charlemagne's death. Lupus of Ferrières read the biography in this way, as did Walahfrid Strabo. In his reedition of the biography, Walahfrid picked up on Einhard's theme:

Charlemagne supplied the dark and, as I might put it, the almost blind condition of the kingdom committed to him by God with a new illumination of all knowledge, and, with God lighting the way, he returned light and vision—for the most part unknown before—to this rude land. But now, with learning disappearing again, the light of wisdom, which is less loved, grows rarer among most people.[40]

With this metaphorical play of shadows and sunlight, ignorance and learning, Walahfrid joined Lupus in longing for the enlightened age described in Einhard's biography. He could not but marvel that Einhard's reputation had not only survived but had grown during the jarring upheavals of Louis the Pious's reign.[41] In counterposing the times of Charlemagne and those of Louis, Walahfrid was ready to acknowledge that his own negative sense of modernity sprang from an awareness of recent troubles.

Indeed the very word *modernus,* which had been relatively rare before, achieved some currency in the mid-ninth century.[42] Although Carolingian writers often employed the term to distinguish between what we would call the early Middle Ages and antiquity,[43] Einhard and his contemporaries came to use the adjective to describe their own historical time, the period of the present generation or of the present king.[44]

Modernus was a word that figured prominently in some royal dreams. In their respective versions of the *Vision of Wetti,* Heito and Walahfrid had referred to the specialness of Charlemagne "in this modern age." Hincmar said that after Pepin the Short's frightening dream, no prince had dared to inhabit the invaded villa of Anizy "until modern times," by which he meant 858.[45] Finally, in the *Vision of Charlemagne,* the writer observed that some of Charlemagne's prophecies had come true in earlier times, some "in modern times." Thus, by his reckoning, even Charlemagne was no longer a modern man; he belonged to a now receding age. With Einhard and Walahfrid, the writer shared a sense of modernity that had been activated by an awareness of present calamity and that defined itself against the superior age of Charlemagne.

This sense of modernity percolates through most royal dreams because political oneirocriticism was in the business of dealing with present history gone wrong and the need for immediate reform. Whether stated expressly or not, the image of Charlemagne and his golden time always seemed to stand behind the later dream authors, beckoning them back. In some quarters, the old emperor's name evoked a nostalgia that was, of course, a condemnation of the present rather than a genuine longing for the glories of a lost age. By its very nature, nostalgia is a species of comparative reflection with a dark underlining to its golden hue. The phrase *modernum tempus,* as employed by Carolingian thinkers, was often negative in connotation. With regret they realized that what distinguished them from the people of the past, what made them modern, was their experience in an age of failing light.

Yet, in the basic patterning of power in the ninth century, little seems to have changed. The sons of Louis the Pious were haunted by the constitutional curse with which they had haunted their father. A king in the ninth century was fated to a life of misery if he had either no son or too many sons. The former fate awaited both Lothar II and Charles the Fat, who both complained of barren wives and vainly sought legal divorces; the latter was the fate of Louis the Pious and Louis the German. Only Charlemagne, as befitted his charmed life, was left with only one son to succeed him. Ironically, Louis the German, the son who had discomfited his father's last years with open rebellion, was himself plagued by three rebellious sons: Carloman, Louis the Younger, and Charles the Fat. In 863, Carloman was accused of crimes against his father and was deprived of all public honors. By 866, however, Louis had forgiven this son and given him lands taken from his brother Louis, who responded with revolt. In 871, Louis and Charles were upset that a part of their inheritance had been given to Carloman, so they attacked their father. In the midst of these filial rebellions, Pope Nicholas sent a letter, no longer extant, to the sons of Louis the German about the necessity of honoring parents. If Louis ever stopped to consider the nature of his troubles with his sons, it must have occurred to him that he had come full circle; he had begun as a son insulting his father, but he had ended as a father insulted by his sons. It was a constitutional curse from which the Carolingians could never escape.[46]

The major annals for 873 provide parallel accounts of a fascinating example of this tug-of-war between fathers and sons. What we are privileged to see— and this one time in some depth and from different perspectives—is how the competing interpretations of the parties were played out in public spectacles. For the contest for power that seemed to drive fathers and sons apart in fact joined them together in shared assumptions about the divine disposition of power. That was the great lesson of Louis the German's life; he became his father or, at least, relived his paternal problems, though with more finesse. What mattered in these familial contests was success, for from it flowed the right to label events, the power to command the descriptive and interpretive language of historical triumph. The interpretation of paternal oppression and filial revolt was, therefore, at the end of the day and in the words of the annalists, a syntax of success.

On 26 January 873, Louis the German convoked an assembly of his bishops and counts at Frankfurt to consider the condition of his kingdom. "There the Lord marvelously revealed his goodness and exposed the badness of certain men waiting to ambush Louis," said the *Annals of Fulda* in its introduction to the incident. In the presence of the assembled *optimates* and Louis, an evil spirit entered Louis's youngest son, Charles the Fat, and tormented him so severely that six strong men could barely restrain him. This annalist, who was located at Mainz, characterized the event narrowly, in the unequivocal terms of the triumphant and of the hindsighted:

> For he who wished to ensnare a king selected and ordained by God was himself ensnared. He who was insidiously advised to set traps for his father fell himself into the traps of the Devil, so that, from the diabolical trembling he experienced, he might learn that no plan can succeed against God.[47]

The annalist either saw or imagined the king and his men crying as they watched the sad scene play out before their eyes.

The troubled prince, now bellowing, now muttering, was led into the church where the bishops might properly pray for him. It seemed as if Charles, in his frantic struggle, was threatening to bite his guards. As Louis the German looked upon his writhing son, he turned to his middle son, Louis the Younger, and said:

> Do you not see, my son, into whose power you and your brother deliver yourselves when you think to conspire against me? Can you comprehend now, if you would not before, that, by the judgment of Scripture, "there is nothing covered that shall not be revealed"? Therefore, confess your sins, do penance, and humbly beseech God to forgive you. To the extent that I am able, I, too, forgive you.[48]

After Charles's demonic possession had passed, according to the annalist, the prince orally confessed to those listening that by entering into a conspiracy against his father he had surrendered himself to that hostile enemy, the Devil.

The Cologne continuator of the *Annals of Xanten* accepted this interpretation, but he supplied an extra layer of information:

> King Louis's two sons, Louis [the Younger] and Charles, came to Frankfurt "full of wicked thoughts": to establish a tyrannical rule, to put off their oaths of the previous year, to deprive their father of his kingdom, and to send him into custody. But "God, the just and patient judge," revealed a great wonder to all gathered there, for with all watching an evil spirit entered Charles and horribly filled him up with many different sounds. But on the same day, with the help of prayers and the incantations of different priests, the evil spirit was driven out. The older brother, when he had seen this frightening spectacle, fell down at the feet of his father and confessed that he was guilty of this heinous crime. He begged forgiveness. The pious father with sure control handled everything wisely.[49]

Rimbert, the archbishop of Bremen, attended the assembly and watched as Charles the Fat commenced his clamoring. Many bishops might have prayed for Charles's release from the demon, but only Rimbert's words, said his hagiographer, had been effective in driving the demon out.[50]

From these eastern sources we can reconstruct the basic outlines of the event. The resentment of the two sons towards their father had been building since 870, because they believed that their ailing father had unfairly enhanced the royal prospects of their brother Carloman. In 871, the two unhappy sons attempted to involve Charles the Bald on their side. Near Maastricht in August, Louis the German and Charles the Bald met to discuss their respective problems with their sons, but no solution was found. By 872, Louis the German thought that he had finally "pacified" his sons, but he misjudged them as royal fathers were so often wont to do in the ninth century.[51] His sons appeared in Frankfurt in 873 with conspiracy on their minds. If the *Annals of Fulda* was somewhat vague about the purpose of the plot, the *Annals of Xanten* was not. Louis and Charles intended to overthrow their father, imprison him (as Louis the Pious had twice been kept in custody), and impose their own illegitimate rule.

But what happened to Charles the Fat at Frankfurt? The sources all agree that, in the presence of the assembly, he began to make a great racket. He spoke, according to the *Annals of Xanten,* in a babble of tongues, now shouting, now whispering, now muttering. He was dragged into the church, into the true society of all things holy, where God would hold the upper hand. All the while, Charles squirmed and resisted his guards. In the cathedral, bishops like Rimbert must have attempted to exorcize the disturbed man. As all of this unfolded, Louis the German turned to Louis the Younger to lecture him on the dangers of conspiracy. Either before or after this lecture, the younger Louis begged the forgiveness of his father and received it. When Charles himself came around, he confessed that to conspire against his father, as he had done more than once, was to turn himself over to the Devil.

Thus, for both eastern annalists, the conflict was resolved when the rebellious sons accepted their father's reading of events, his vocabulary and typology of paternal power. This spectacle of demonic rebellion and injured fatherhood was played out as much for the assembled crowd of the powerful as it was for the rebellious sons. From the entry in the *Annals of Fulda,* one senses that Charles had noble supporters at Frankfurt who were urging him to fight for his fair share of the kingdom. Thus, the dramatic quality of the incident may have been heightened by the message it sent to the background actors about right relationships between fathers and sons, and between superiors and inferiors.

But we cannot afford to lose sight of the self-serving logic of the king: to work against established royal power became, by definition, an act of the Devil. For ruling Carolingians, all power was bicameral: above stood the higher assembly of Christ, his saints, and his duly-selected king presiding over the faithful; below stood the Devil and his agents grilling the wicked. It is this essential division of powers that we see sketched again and again in the Stuttgart and Utrecht Psalters (see Figs. 23 and 24). Charles the Fat's fit was, as Janet Nelson so aptly put it, an intrusion of "wild power into the ordered structures of the kingdom."[52] From the perspective of the father-king, a son's rebellion was necessarily demonic because it was disruptive. The Devil has often been deemed a central figure in the social equation of the Christian family, for he is the Archrebel without equal, his revolt against paternal authority being the model of all filial revolt. In the civil disturbances of the 830s, the Devil was regularly cited as the cause of dissension between a father and his sons, but before Charles the Fat's outburst the demonic possession of a son had never been demonstrated.[53]

Yet this interpretation of the event depended on the paternal perspective adopted by the *Annals of Fulda* and *Annals of Xanten,* for those annalists saw the son's possession through the father's eyes. Hincmar of Rheims described a more intriguing set of circumstances in the *Annals of Saint-Bertin*.

> While King Louis of Germany delayed there [at Frankfurt], the Devil, transforming himself into an angel of light, appeared to Charles. The Devil told him that his father, who was seeking to destroy him for the sake of his brother Carloman, had offended God and would in a short time lose his kingdom. Moreover, the Devil said that God had set aside that kingdom for Charles himself and that he would obtain it before too long.[54]

According to Hincmar, Charles was struck with fear, since the Devil inhabited the house in which he was staying. He tried to escape into a church, but the Devil followed and asked Charles what he was afraid of: "For, if I had not come from God to announce what will happen in the near future, I could not have followed you into this house of the Lord."[55] With cunning persuasion, he convinced Charles to receive communion from his hand and, after the prince had consumed a tiny portion of the host, the Devil entered into him.

Next Charles and his brother Louis attended the assembly at Frankfurt along with the bishops and laymen of the kingdom. All at once, Charles, having been possessed, stood up in their midst and announced that he had decided to withdraw from the world and that he would not have sexual intercourse with his wife. He unbuckled his sword and let it fall to the ground, but as he tried to undo his belt and cloak, he began to tremble. While Louis the German and the gathered lords looked on in shock, bishops and other men rushed forward to restrain Charles. The prince was led into a church where Archbishop Liutbert, now dressed in priestly garb, began to say mass. As the celebrant read the Gospel, Charles started to shout out "Woe, Woe!" in German and continued to do so until the service was finished. His father ordered the bishops and other faithful men to take his son to the sites of the holy martyrs so that he might, from their worthiness and prayers, be freed from the demon and returned to sound mind.

Last, Charles was ordered to go to Rome, but, as Hincmar noted, he put off that journey for a variety of reasons.

For Hincmar, Charles the Fat was less a political conspirator than he was one who had been utterly deceived by the Devil. The distinction is an important one, for the eastern annalists believed that to conspire against the king, even to think conspiratorial thoughts, was to call forth the Devil. Hincmar, on the other hand, put the Devil in charge from the start, for he had come to Charles before the assembly, haunted his house, spoken dark thoughts to him about his father and eldest brother, and followed him into a church. Satan often disguised himself as an angel of light, but Charles proved unable to penetrate his splendid mask.[56] Still, he had his doubts. He fled into a church where he imagined the Devil could not follow, and he accepted the host from his satanic hands. Hincmar held, of course, that the sacraments depended upon the disposition of the receiver, so that even a morsel of the host might spiritually and physically revive one man, like Bernold, but destroy another, like Charles the Fat.[57] The prince had forgotten, as Hincmar surely had not, that after Christ himself had given Judas a morsel of bread Satan had entered into that traitor.[58]

Hincmar moves us as readers between the chaotic world of secular princes with their demonic temptations and the ordered world of the church. The Devil's false mass was to be offset by Archbishop Liutbert's true and corrective mass. In Hincmar's account, Louis the German has faded almost entirely into the background, because Hincmar wished to downplay, in this case, the father's role in the son's madness. Charles's problem was not with his father but with a satanic rejection of the established order of this world. If the poles of the *Fulda* account were the positive and negative charges of father and son, they had been transformed in the *Annals of Saint-Bertin* into the right order represented by the church and the disturbed order represented by this world with its devilish temptations and its smoldering jealousies.

Hincmar had on his mind another example of the dangers of rebellion, one that interested him even more, for Charles the Bald's son Carloman had also been persistently rebellious. But in 873 he finally fell. Three years earlier, Carloman had been deprived of his monasteries and had been kept under close watch by his father. However,

> one night, Carloman escaped from his father and fled to the Belgian province. Many accomplices and sons of Belial came to him. He committed so many cruelties and such great devastation in keeping with the work-

ings of Satan that it can scarcely be believed, except by those who witnessed and suffered that savagery.[59]

Hincmar himself had tried to remind Carloman and his supporters of "the sweetness of the heavenly kingdom and of the horror of eternal torment," but to no avail.[60] These sons of the Devil were always the agents of rebellion and resistance in the Bible and were so typed in Hincmar's demonization of Carloman. Hincmar set the story of Carloman's final fall in 873, immediately prior to the account of Charles the Fat's fit. Unlike Charles, however, Carloman had made, he thought, a direct assault "on the holy Church of God and on the other kingdoms falling under his father's control."[61] There was no innocence in him, no attempt to elude the Devil, only perversity and the inversion of the orderly hierarchy of power. If Nelson is right, Charles the Bald may have set his rebellious son up for a cruel fall.[62] At Senlis, he arranged for Carloman to be stripped of all his ecclesiastical orders, effectively making him a layman again. The Devil, according to the annalist, at once encouraged Carloman's supporters to think that the way was now clear for Carloman to become a king, whereupon Charles felt it necessary for the charge of treason to be reentered against his son. When he was found guilty and sentenced to death, the sentence could be commuted to one of blinding, and Carloman realistically removed as a threat to his father's throne.

If Charles the Bald did, in fact, arrange the blinding of his son with malice aforethought, then we should rethink the world of politics adumbrated for us by the clerics of the ninth century. We then must set Charles not in a warmer world of high morals and wise rulers but in the colder strictures of a familial *Realpolitik*. The annalists also play with us and our understanding of events, for *Fulda* and *Saint-Bertin* are inverse images of the two cases of filial revolt. As Hincmar treated Charles the Fat sympathetically but damned the closer Carloman, so the Mainz author of the *Annals of Fulda* condemned Charles the Fat but regarded the western Carloman as the victim of a cruel father: "That tyrant Charles of Gaul, having put aside his fatherly compassion, ordered his son Carloman, who had been set aside in the office of deacon, to be blinded."[63] One could afford to sympathize with the troublesome sons of foreign kings, because, as everyone knew, this was one way of undermining a rival power; it was the proper politics of family.

But beyond the moral relativism of the annalists, who clung to their regional and royal interests, there was a bottom line beyond which kings were unprepared to go, or so Hincmar hoped. The archbishop reported that in 873 Carloman fled to his uncle's kingdom.

> Louis turned the blind Carloman over to Archbishop Liutbert to be kept in
> the monastery of Saint-Alban at Mainz, thus proving by this abundantly
> clear sign that he disapproved of the wicked things that Carloman had in-
> flicted on the holy church of God, on a Christian people, and on his fa-
> ther, whenever and wherever he had had the opportunity.[64]

It would be naive, however, to think that Louis, in the end, had discovered a set of shared paternal values that overrode his own political interests. For Carloman, blinded, was useless to Louis: he was a piece of errant driftwood, not a treasure, cast up on familial shores in the east. In the west, the escape from custody of his sightless son hardly raised a ripple of concern from Charles the Bald.

But one has to wonder about the case of Charles the Fat. We should at least search for a more sympathetic understanding of his outburst at Frankfurt, this time not from the father's standpoint but the son's. Did Louis the German appreciate, one has to wonder, the revealing social drama that was played out before his eyes? For his son was a victim of the same almost irresistible urges that had driven him to be a rebellious son himself in the 830s. In hindsight, the problem seems to have been a simple one, though it was no less intractable for being simple. Kings can theoretically control everything except the timing and success of reproduction and succession. Charles the Fat, like his father before him, was stuck behind a long-reigning sovereign, and his pursuit of power, therefore, was necessarily perverted into secondary channels. In a world that demanded social dependency but scorned it as well, a subordinate son could but dream of independence from his father. Filial restlessness was the penalty paid by royal fathers for long and successful careers. Under Louis the German and Charles the Bald, the tension had reached a razor sharpness, because these kings had learned a crucial lesson. "Do not grant power to your sons in your lifetime, it is better for them to beg from you than you from them," Lupus advised Charles.[65] Notker would say of Louis the German that with his penetrating eyes he was extraordinarily quick to spot plots and disperse evil.[66] The way in which Charles the Bald kept the ambitious Carloman forever off balance and the horror of his final blinding may suggest the alacrity and brutality of a newer paternal understanding of the demands of this politics of the royal family. It was the lesson that Charles the Bald and Louis the German had learned from their own father and his manifest mismanagement of his sons. They kept their eyes open for the least sign of filial revolt, and Charles the Fat's fit was treated as an immense rupture in the fabric of normal filial behavior. "Madness in great ones must not unwatch'd go," another king one day would say of another wayward son.[67] Yet, despite the dangers of facing these ever vigilant fathers, the promise of power continually whispered in the ears of princes, telling them that the kingdom would soon be rightfully theirs and that they might, therefore, with reason, hasten the inevitable.

But Charles the Fat tried not to listen to his mumbling Devil. If Hincmar supplies us with a reliable report of Charles's actions—and perhaps he could since his king was in communication with the sons of Louis—then we can attempt another explanation. Charles the Fat was apparently fed up with dynastic politics. He was prepared to do what Carolingian kings had done before; he would withdraw from the world as Pepin the Short's brother Carloman had done over a century before. Many Carolingian rulers, including Louis the Pious and Lothar, had also longed to retreat to monasteries, either early on when their prospects for advancement were poor or later, in their final days, when it was difficult to continue living the exacting life of a peripatetic and beleaguered ruler. Even Charlemagne had not ruled out the possibility of monastic retirement.[68]

When Charles the Fat began to strip off his clothes in the presence of the assembled magnates of the realm, his was a public gesture expressing his symbolic rejection of the world. First he threw off his sword, the very symbol of his secular manhood and of his status as soldier. So, too, when he claimed that he would no longer touch his wife, the prince aspired to the sexual abstinence of the monk. There was in Charles's public display a very real criticism of his father; everything that he had been destined for he now publicly rejected—both arms and marriage. A decade later, the monk of Saint-Gall still felt it necessary to remind Charles that "life in this world cannot be carried on without marriage and the employment of arms."[69] Hincmar and Notker may have admired monasticism as the highest form of human life, but they wanted their kings to remain kings and not to cast off the tools of their trade. Yet, in 873, Charles was determined to retreat from the world of limited possibilities and paternal pressures that he thought his father had made for him.

But this father won the right to label his son's vision demonic. If Charles had succeeded, we might have had a very different account of the vision: a story of an angel of light either delivering a king unto his rightful kingship or into monastic retreat. He had, after all, been a very strange Devil, more angelic and luminiferous than the official sources would admit. For this spirit did not advocate the overthrow of a king or the commission of some indescribable horror; he merely whispered prophetic truths to Charles. Within three short years, Charles the Fat would, indeed, be a king in his own right, just as the spirit had foretold.

Three months after the incident at Frankfurt, the two rebellious sons were back doing princely chores, hearing judicial disputes on behalf of their father, the king. The hands of those six strong men may no longer have held Charles fast, but he still must have felt the hands of Louis the German's paternal power grasping his shoulders, pushing him to do his filial duty. Within a year, however, another disturbance rippled across the domestic surface of east Francia, casting up another royal dreamer.

Early in 874, Louis the Younger met secretly with some of his father's advisors at Seligenstadt in the presence of the relics of Marcellinus and Peter. When Louis the German heard about this furtive gathering, he immediately rushed back from Bavaria. In February the king came to his palace at Frankfurt, where he consulted with his faithful supporters "on the harmony and state of the kingdom," said the *Annals of Fulda*.

> During the Lenten season [which began on 24 February 874], with his worldly business out of the way, Louis devoted himself to prayer. One night he saw in his dreams his father, the Emperor Louis, placed in dire straits. That one spoke to him in Latin: "I beg you, through our Lord Jesus Christ and the Holy Trinity, to rescue me from these torments in which I am now held, that at last I might be able to gain eternal life."[70]

When Louis the German awoke, he was extremely frightened, according to the annalist, and sent letters to all the monasteries of his kingdom. He asked the monks to pray to the Lord on behalf of the suffering soul of his father.

Hincmar was one of those churchmen who received a request from Louis that he and his clerics pray on behalf of his father, who had "appeared to him in a vision, imploring that he rescue him from the punishment in which he was being held."[71] The language of Louis the Pious's importunate request here is so similar to the *Fulda* report as to suggest that Louis the German was indeed the common source of both. The archbishop sent a letter to Louis, full of citations, on the measure and quality of prayer. In addition, he sent copies of Louis's letter and his response to Charles the Bald.[72] Everything suggests that Louis did have an oneiric experience that he took very seriously. For him to have written to the archbishop of Rheims as well as to all the monasteries of his own kingdom was no idle whim, but a deliberate and expensive operation. Moreover, he seems not to have merely delegated the job of praying for his father's soul to monks and priests, but also took it up himself. At Easter he traveled to the monastery of Fulda "for the sake of prayer," said the annalist.

The Mainz author of the account in the *Annals of Fulda* followed with an interpretation of the dream:

> From this, we should understand that although the Emperor Louis [the Pious] had done many things praiseworthy and pleasing to God, nevertheless he allowed many things contrary to the law of God to be done in his kingdom. For, not to mention other things, if he had forcefully resisted the heresy of the Nicolaitans and had taken care to heed the warnings of the archangel Gabriel, which were contained in those twelve chapters that the Abbot Einhard brought for him to read and act upon, perhaps he would not be suffering so. But because God, as it is written, allows no sin to go unpunished and because, according to the Apostle, "not only those who do these things, but those who consent to those doing them are worthy of death," he was justly ordered to undergo this punishment. For while he was advised to and had the power to correct the errors of those under his control, he was unwilling.[73]

Thus, the *Fulda* account of Louis the German's dream can be broken into two parts: the dream as the king reported it and the *Fulda* annalist's interpretation. The first is supported by Flodoard's register of Hincmar's letters, though the facts are relatively sparse. At Frankfurt Louis the German had a dream of his father suffering in torment and pleading for his son to rescue him. But Louis the Pious's language is evocative, recalling, in particular, the *Vision of the Poor Woman of Laon*. In both, a suffering father stuck *in tormentis* seeks the *uita aeterna*. That dream, the product of Heito and Reichenau, had circulated widely in eastern Francia and must have been seen at some point by Louis the German himself. Its imagery of Charlemagne's torment and of his plea to Louis the Pious for rescue had become for another son a formula for the release of his own father.

But that must mean, then, that Louis the German himself was a reader of selected dream texts and that memories of them had worked to shape his understanding of his own uneasy experience. It may be some indication of the influence of those dream texts that Louis specified that his father had spoken to him in Latin, just as those works would have done. Moreover, it was the *Vision of the Poor Woman of Laon* that had criticized Louis the Pious so sharply. When Louis the German had himself been a rebellious son, he must have found this critique of his father's errors comforting. But a half-century later the dream must have been unsettling, since his own dream came to complete it, placing his father in that state of suffering predicted by the Reichenau vision. The bottom line in both dreams was the demand for a son-king to accept responsibility for the release of a tormented father. Only kings, the sequence seemed to suggest, could make amends of the proper sort, only they could orchestrate that symphony of prayer that would burst through to the Lord, only they could personally pray for a compromised king because only they understood what it was to be compromised by the possession of power.

But if Louis the German's dream was softly shaped by one dream text, the *Fulda* annalist's interpretation was deliberately based on two others. The annalist assumed the role and words of Wetti's angel, informing his audience that although the emperor had done many praiseworthy things that pleased God, nevertheless. . . . [74] This had become for both *Fulda* and Hincmar a blank to be filled in according to the nature of the king being criticized. But if Charlemagne had been punished for his sexual sins, Louis the Pious was to be condemned for not having run a tight enough ship. His great failure, and this had become a commonplace of Carolingian historiography, was a lack of firm command, not a personal sin.

But the *Annals of Fulda* moves us to yet another dream text and to an even more intriguing set of associations. The annalist dragged up as proof of the emperor's neglectful nature Aubrey's vision from the *History of the Translation of the Blessed Martyrs, Marcellinus and Peter*. He knew that the archangel Gabriel had dictated a book of twelve chapters that was given to Louis the Pious. He also knew from Einhard that the emperor had not enacted its suggested reforms. The somewhat ambiguous Latin of the annal does not, however, make it absolutely clear whether the sin of clerical concubinage (Nicolaitanism), which had been a worry of Wetti, was part of Reichenau's wish list of reforms or of Gabriel's. If it came from Einhard's lost work, then the annalist located at Mainz knew things about the twelve-chaptered book that were not contained in the *History of the Translation* itself. At places like Mainz, with its Fulda connections, Einhard's book had certainly been influential. [75]

Moreover, the association of Louis the German's dream with Aubrey's vision takes us back to the events that surrounded the king's experience and back to Einhard's church at Seligenstadt. Louis the Younger, who had been scolded for plotting a conspiracy against his father just months earlier, met there secretly with some of his father's advisors "in the presence of the Saints Marcellinus and Peter." To King Louis in Bavaria, it immediately seemed that his son must be conspiring against him again, and so he rushed back to Frankfurt.

But, behind what happened next, there were doubtless events that have disappeared entirely from view. Did Louis the Younger learn at Seligenstadt of Aubrey's vision and Louis the Pious's failure to reform? Did he perchance send some word of these things to Louis the German, in order to remind his own wrongful father-king of the pressing need to correct his own abuses and injustices? If so, Louis the Pious was partially responsible, since he had been the first Carolingian king to play at this dangerous politics of penance as he scratched away at his father's reputation.

But Louis the German was unable to resist the dream that the image of his son at Seligenstadt suggested to him. We find him already deep in prayer at Frankfurt before the dream, but for what if not for divine assistance in dealing with some problem already raised by his son? He, too, must have known of the archangel Gabriel's message to his father, since the man who had first received it from Gabriel, Ratleig, had been his own chancellor twenty years earlier.[76] The *Vision of the Poor Woman of Laon* would have already suggested to many Carolingian readers that Louis the Pious must undergo a purgatorial experience, and there his son finally found him, pleading for prayers.

Louis the German's fervent request for prayers on behalf of his father in 874 suggests just how personally worried he was by this dream. His visit to Fulda led the monks to begin a new *Book of the Dead* the following year. The manuscript itself survives in the Vatican Library. Below the title NOMINA DEFVNCTORVM REGVM runs a list of Carolingian kings starting with Pepin the Short and ending with Lothar II, who had died in 869. Smack in the middle is *Hludouichus imperator* with his death date. This column of the royal dead was a direct response to Louis's visit to Fulda and his request for the monks to pray for his father and, perhaps, for all royal relatives. At the top of the next column, a different scribe in 876 entered the name of Louis the German himself.[77]

But it remains far too coincidental that, within a month of the young Louis's visit to Einhard's saints, the old Louis should have been dreaming of his own father, another Louis, in torment. The *Vision of the Poor Woman of Laon* and Louis the German's own dream had always been more about sons than fathers, for though Louis may have worried about his father's everlasting soul, it was his own fate of which he was reminded in 874. He was now sixty-eight years old and often in ill health. He must have wondered what sins would follow him into the grave and who would pray for him as he now prayed for his own father. Thus, he urged the monks of Fulda to regularize, indeed to institutionalize, prayer for dead kings so that he himself, when he died, would not slip through some forgetful crack in penitential time but would be remembered richly by the holiest of monks.

As Reichenau had been a textual dream community during Louis the Pious's reign, so Mainz became one under Louis the German. All of the dream texts discussed in this chapter had a primary connection with Mainz. Not only did the author of the *Vision of Charlemagne* reveal his special knowledge of Mainz, but the *Annals of Fulda* was written at Mainz throughout the period of these dreams and visions. Liutbert may not have been the author of the *Annals of Fulda*, as Hincmar was the author of the *Annals of Saint-Bertin*, but he must have been the dominant and supervisory presence. In addition, he had an insider's knowledge of Louis the German's doings, his letters to bishops, and the public spectacles of the royal family. Though the books and documents of Mainz have not survived in any great number, the ones that do suggest the nature of Liutbert's scriptorium.[78] Texts like the *Heliand,* the *Vision of Charlemagne,* and the *Annals of Fulda* were all either written or copied at Mainz. The sure sign that the *Vision of Charlemagne* was meant for Louis the German is the presence of those four Old High German words on Charlemagne's sword. They suggest the deliberate nature of Liutbert's circle and its literary interests.

Dream texts like the *Vision of Charlemagne* may still have been peripheral documents, calling from the edges of public discourse for royal action and reform, but in Louis the German they apparently found a receptive audience. What he experienced in some cold bedroom in Frankfurt on that February evening in 874 is irrecoverable, but as he described his dream to Liutbert, to his abbots, and to Hincmar of Rheims, he did so in words and images reminiscent of those written by Heito and Einhard a half-century earlier. His dream takes us inside other dream texts or, rather, into a dream loaded with literary dream thoughts. There is no way, I think, to avoid the conclusion here that Louis the German's dream was the product of that *via regia* of dreams that Carolingian clerics had spent a century constructing. Charles the Bald may have dismissed the revelations of Audradus, and Louis the Pious those of Einhard's blind man, but this king finally dreamed within the oneiric contours of his age. Carolingian kings had probably been listening to the dreamers all along. The triumph of the tradition was the formulaic nature of Louis the German's dream; even the Mainz dream interpreter could not now step outside the measured confines of its oneiric dimensions. He, too, was explaining one dream text in terms of another; he, too, could not escape the dream discourse of Wetti and his angel.

The times were changing, as the author of the *Vision of Charlemagne* reminded his king, but Louis the German may have been changing almost faster than they were. The world of ideas into which he woke in Frankfurt in 874 was more connected than his grandfather's had ever been, as churchmen like Liutbert fed his fascination with things biblical and German. Still, it was difficult to go too far forward when ancestral dreams kept dragging him back, reminding him of Charlemagne and of unhappy sons, of the glimmering gold of memory and of the rust of discontentment, the two poles of royal reflection in this modern age.

CHAPTER EIGHT

Charles the Fat's
Constitutional Dreams

Hunc circa passim uarias imitantia formas
Somnia uana iacent . . .

[Around him lie empty dreams, scattered here and there,
Imitating unstable shapes . . .]
> Ovid, *Metamorphoses*

To turn to the last dreams of the Carolingian empire is to return to Rheims and to the stubborn contours of Hincmar's constitutional claims. It is also to attempt to weave together the separated and gossamer-fine strands of a single scene in the tapestry of later Carolingian history, the one in which the power of empire could be seen slipping through the hands of Charles the Fat.

By the early 880s, the character of royal power was changing as the cast of royal players changed. Leaving the stage were Charles the Bald, his sons, and all but one of his grandsons; gone were all the direct heirs of the Emperor Lothar; departing, too, were all the sons of Louis the German, save one. If we follow the lines of Louis the Pious's genealogical tree downwards, by 882 our fingers run up against a scattering of boys and bastards or stop suddenly at dead ends. It is no wonder, then, that the later ninth century wrestled with the problem of legitimacy, the great questions being who could claim to be king and on what grounds?

Royal blood remained important, but so was effective power. Throughout Frankish history the pendulum of dominance had always swung back and forth between royal and noble interests in an arc that took generations to traverse. In the 880s and 890s, many ambitious noble families cannot have been displeased as they saw an opportunity either to assume power and titles or to secure advantage by propping up weak and rivalrous kings. Even to seal off the dead ends of royal lines, as Louis the Pious had once done by removing Bernard of Italy, was never to shut them down. Bernard's heirs, the so-called House of Vermandois, clung to the edges of royal power, remembering their unjust displacement and waiting for their rightful return to power. In the end, it was not that the genetic line of Charlemagne failed, but that a stricter definition of the royal family worked to remove royal rivals. The house of Charles Martel would not remain sufficiently open to the illegitimate and the energetic, which was a great irony, since Charles himself had been a bastard and his grandson, Charlemagne, had been born to a father and mother who had not yet formally wed. Caught in squabbles over succession, the Carolingian royal dynasty in the end came to experience what it had once visited upon the Merovingians, the enervation of practical power and a growing reliance upon the residues of symbolism and tradition that still clung to the royal house. In the flux of the late ninth century, this inverse relationship of dwindling royal power and clinging conservatism was most keenly felt at Rheims, where Hincmar and his successor labored to prop up the remnants of the Carolingian royal house.

Symbolism already meant more than it should have in 877. With his Italian campaign in disarray and death closing in upon him, Charles the Bald made two richly symbolic gestures. First he sent Pope John VIII hurrying back to Rome with a gift for Saint Peter: a gold and jeweled sculpture of the savior nailed to the cross. Then he handed over to his queen "the broadsword called the sword of Saint Peter with which she was to invest [his son, Louis the Stammerer] again with the kingdom."[1] Charles, therefore, confirmed that Louis was to succeed him, and he entrusted Richildis with the symbols of his power—his crown, royal robes, and golden scepter—which she was commanded to convey to Louis. Thus, on his deathbed, Charles the Bald's thoughts were on Rome and religion, salvation and empire, separate preoccupations that he could combine comfortably in the person of Saint Peter. With the sword of the apostle, he could transmit the symbol of empire to his son, but not the reality. Yet the idea of western Francia's proper place in the empire was to be Charles the Bald's final legacy to Francia.

But Louis the Stammerer's problem in late 877 was simply to hold onto royal power amidst the competing noble factions in his kingdom. With Charles on his way to finding a place in Bernold's dream, Hincmar stepped forward once again to manage a vulnerable king. On 8 December the archbishop was at Compiègne, where, after long negotiations between the royal and ecclesiastical parties, he consecrated and crowned Louis. Within sixteen months, Louis the Stammerer was dead at the age of thirty-three. Around Louis's oldest two sons, nobles now began to scheme. Louis III won a marvelous victory over the Northmen at Saucourt in 881, but the next year he suffered a fatal accident. He chased after a girl, who prudently fled into her father's house, but the young king, in hot pursuit, had forgotten that he was on horseback and rode straight into the lintel of the doorway. He died within days. Now the other son, Carloman, stood alone as king of west Francia, and Hincmar became his principal advisor, even composing the work *On the Governance of the Palace* for him. The image of Hincmar as the wisest of advisors stood, as we have seen, at the center of the *Vision of Bernold*. But Carloman was as unlucky as his brother. On a hunting trip in late 884, he was accidentally stabbed to death by one of his companions.[2]

Lothar's direct male line had ended in 875 with the death of the Emperor Louis II. Of Louis the German's male line, only Charles the Fat, the high-strung son encountered in the pages of the annals, was still alive in 882; thus, the empire fell to him more or less by default. Regino later would say that everything seemed to have come easily to Charles. What his ancestors had acquired with great violence and much work fell into Charles's hands without conflict or tension.[3] Gone by 900 were the memories of Charles the Fat's fit and that mix of frustrated ambitions that had chased his middle age. Pope John VIII, the man who had crowned Charles the Bald emperor, also crowned Charles the Fat in 881. Charles proved to be the last Carolingian emperor who could trace his ancestry back to Charlemagne in a direct and legitimate male line. He became the nominal emperor of most of the territory that once had been held by Charlemagne. When his brother Louis died in 882, Charles also became king of all eastern Francia and, when his nephew Carloman died in 884, his sphere of influence extended to western Francia, over which he also became king. Thus in the ninth century, titles, if not power, continued to accrue to those who managed to outlive their relatives, so long as right and royal blood flowed through their veins.

But by Charles's time the Carolingian empire was driven by a different set of political realities from those his great-grandfather had known. Its politics of entrenched powerful families and vested regional interests would never allow him to exercise effective control. People may have looked to him for protection, but they soon learned what he could deliver.

When a large Danish force besieged Paris in November 885, the defenders of the city turned to him for help.[4] Abbo of Saint-Germain-des-Prés, whose contemporary poem captures the desperate mood of the city, described with what optimism and surpassing hope the residents awaited the arrival of the emperor, who rode into the city with great pomp, looking for all the world like the resplendent heavens. He promptly sold the farm: the Northmen were given the right to winter in Burgundy, free passage along the Seine, and the promise of silver.[5] The very next year they returned to Paris to resume their siege. From the dark hole of this humiliation, Abbo turned to celebrate noble heroes like Odo of Paris, who had remained at the barriers and who had refused to abandon Paris to its fate. Charles, he said, had gone home to die; Odo stayed put and became king:

> Interea Karolus, regno uita quoque nudus,
> Viscera opis diuae conplectitur abdita tristis.
> Laetus Odo regis nomen regni quoque numen
> Francorum populo gratante fauenteque multo
> Ilicet, atque manus sceptrum, diademque uertex.

> [Meanwhile Charles, having lost his kingdom and his life,
> Sadly embraced the earthen insides of the created world.
> At once, to the cheers and support of many Franks,
> Odo joyfully received the name and power of king,
> A scepter in his hand, and a crown upon his head.][6]

The medieval landscape is littered with these partings of the ways, one man rising starlike to kingship, another sinking into the sodden soil. Yet no period, I think, witnessed a more dramatic swing of fortunes than occurred in those few fluid years between the two Charleses. Of 888, the Regensburg continuator of the *Annals of Fulda* would say:

> Many kinglets rose up in Europe in the kingdom of [Arnulf's] cousin [Charles the Fat]. For Berengar, the son of Eberhard, was making himself king in Italy. Rudolf, the son of Conrad, resolved to hold onto the upper part of Burgundy in the fashion of a king. Louis, the son of Boso, and Guy, the son of Landbert, therefore proposed to hold as kings the Belgian parts of Gaul and Provence. Odo, the son of Robert, usurped for his use the land up to the Loire River and the province of Aquitaine. Afterwards Ramnulf set himself up as king.[7]

Charles the Bald may once have mocked the nobles' pretentious boast that "we can all be kings," but in 888 Frankish nobles, with their own royal claims founded on the almost incestuous politics of royal marriage, mocked back.[8] The annalist, in protesting against this crowd of petty and usurpative kings, revealed his own sore spot, for some of his contemporaries would surely have charged that even his king, Arnulf of Carinthia, belonged to this gathering of the illegitimate. The annalist of Saint-Vaast called these men self-made kings, a sure form of derision and denial since only Christ could make a true king.[9] Looking back from early in the next century, Regino of Prüm would with more measure write:

> After [Charles the Fat's] death, the kingdoms over which he had power, as if left in the lurch without a legitimate heir, broke away in sections from his empire and did not wait for a lord of hereditary descent, but each set out to create a king for itself from its own innards.[10]

For a society that cared as much about the authority of royal blood as the Carolingians did, this break in the natural descent of its kings led in some quarters to the exaggerated assertion of old claims and the invention of new oneiric strategies.

At Rheims, Hincmar and his successor Fulk were at once the most creative and conservative of constitutional players. Odo may have been the natural choice for king of western Francia in 888, acclaimed by many and the hero of the ruined ramparts of Paris, but the church of Rheims stoutly defended its right to constitute kings. This was, of course, the obstinate legacy of Hincmar himself. Not only had he been the one to orchestrate the crowning and consecration of Charles the Bald at Metz in 869, but it had fallen upon his shoulders alone to consecrate and crown Louis the Stammerer. In the *Annals of Saint-Bertin,* Hincmar revisited the profound significance of coronation rites and his own role in shaping these moments of high and ceremonious statement.

Fulk was never to forget. When Odo was crowned king in February 888 at Compiègne by Walter, the archbishop of Sens, Rheims viewed the consecration as presumptuous and irregular. Fulk had his own rival candidates, first one of his relatives, Guy of Spoleto, and then, Arnulf of Carinthia. Odo realized, said the *Annals of Fulda,* that without the support of Arnulf, he would have no peace, and so in August he commended himself to the king of east Francia at Worms. Later that year he received a crown from Arnulf's representatives and agreed to be consecrated and crowned by Archbishop Fulk at Rheims in November.

We need to remember that as adroit as Odo was in the pursuit of the necessary and multiple proofs of legitimacy, so was Rheims in its search for recognition of its right to constitute kings. The church of Sens may have claimed a similar privilege, but Odo's recoronation by Fulk was meant to outweigh it. Thus, in November 888 there was in Rheims an uneasy reconciliation of Odo's claim to be king and Rheims's claim that it alone could consecrate one.

Wedged between Flodoard's accounts of the depositions of Louis the Pious and then Archbishop Ebbo is a dream text called the *Vision of Raduin*, which may throw some light on the constitutional claims of Rheims.[11] Raduin was a Lombard monk, who had, according to Flodoard, once been the abbot of the monastery of Berceto south of Parma, which had been dedicated to the memory of Saint Remigius by Archbishop Moderamnus of Rouen. On the day of the Assumption of the Virgin Mary, after the celebration of the morning mass, Raduin remained behind in the choir of the monastery of Saint-Remigius to pray. There, fatigued from saying psalms and prayers, he fell asleep and soon saw Mary, the mother of God, all aglow and striding forth from the tomb of Saint Remigius. Walking beside her were the saint himself and John the Evangelist. The Virgin gently laid a hand on the monk's sleeping head and asked him what he was doing there and where Archbishop Ebbo was. Raduin answered that Ebbo was, by command of the king, away looking after the business of the palace. Mary wondered out loud why the archbishop would so diligently frequent the gates of the palace when it added nothing to holiness. The time would very quickly come, she predicted, when he would not benefit from such things. Raduin was afraid to say anything in response.

Mary next asked the monk what royal disputes were then stirring up the people. The monk thought that Mary must surely know more about this than he did, but he answered that their kings were now seduced by greed and were plundering with vain audacity. "For that was the period when the Emperor Louis was suffering from the insults of his sons," Flodoard explained parenthetically. Reaching out for the hand of Saint Remigius, Mary reassured Raduin:

> Look to this one! Authority over the empire of the Franks was permanently handed over to him by Christ. For just as he was able to convert this people from infidelity with his teaching, so, too, he possesses for all time the unbreakable right to constitute a king or an emperor over them.[12]

After receiving this message from Mary, Raduin suddenly awoke.

Although there has been a good deal of disagreement about the date of the *Vision of Raduin,* it was probably composed late in the ninth century.[13] The all-important place of Mary and Remigius in the dream text is a sure indication that the piece was produced at and for the benefit of Rheims. Flodoard was one of the very few to have known the text, probably because he had seen it in the archives of the cathedral. He inserted it where he did in his history of the church of Rheims because of its mention of Ebbo, but it is of a piece with his other dream stories. Earlier in his work, he had supplied a story about Moderamnus that involved Saint Remigius and visions.[14] That account was placed immediately before his retelling of the tale of Pepin the Short dreaming of Saint Remigius while he slept at the villa of Anizy. Thus, with the *Vision of Raduin* we find ourselves once again gazing at the dream quilt of Rheims patched together with conspicuous stitches by Flodoard.

But no matter where the church historian placed Raduin's patch in his assemblage, there is much to suggest that the *Vision of Raduin* was written well after the 840s, most likely in the wake of the death of one of the two Charleses. If it had been written much earlier, one would expect a more informed and bitter review of Ebbo's controversial career. Before the late 870s, Hincmar and the church of Rheims were always more nervous about Ebbo and his continued support than Raduin's dream ever is. But the case against Ebbo here is neither damning nor devastating; it is incidental, almost a bit of background detail. Mary merely alluded to Ebbo's future problems as though, if he had avoided politics, he might have survived.

The Virgin herself had become a figure of great and intercessory significance to the church of Rheims by the later ninth century. Not only was the cathedral of Rheims rededicated to her in 862, but Hincmar offered precious objects and wrote poems in her honor.[15] Hincmar regularly linked the names of Remigius and Mary, especially when it was a matter of protecting church property.[16] In the twelfth century, Hincmar's dedication to the Virgin was still remembered; his tomb showed him kneeling before the Virgin and her Son (see Fig. 21). Indeed Flodoard himself also collected a number of miracle stories about Mary, many of which also featured Remigius and had their setting in dreams.[17]

But what pushes the *Vision of Raduin* forward to the period between 877 and 888, I think, is Mary's final statement, with its crystalline assertion of the right of the church of Rheims to constitute kings and emperors. It was, in fact, the point of the vision, the single line towards which everything else led. That Saint Remigius had baptized Clovis and, hence, converted the Franks to Catholicism was central to the identity of the church of Rheims and to Hincmar's claims to constitutive power. Indeed, at the far right of the relief sculpture on Hincmar's tomb stood Clovis, with fleur-de-lis scepter in hand, being baptized by the saint (see Fig. 21). On 9 September 869 at Metz, as Charles the Bald waited to be crowned king of Lotharingia, Hincmar had read a statement into the record:

> [Your] father of holy memory, Lord Louis, the pious and august emperor, came from the line of that famous Clovis, king of the Franks, who was converted with all his people and with three thousand Franks—not counting women and children—by the orthodox preaching of Saint Remigius, the apostle of the Franks. He was baptized along with them on the vigil of holy Easter in the metropolitan church of Rheims. He was anointed with chrism provided by heaven, of which we still have a portion, and he was crowned king. Pious and august Louis came from the line of Saint Arnulf, from whose flesh he traced the origins of his own. And he was crowned emperor at Rheims by Stephen, the pope of Rome.[18]

Thus, Hincmar surrounded the issue of Charles's coronation with Rheimsian connections, with wordplay (Louis and Clovis being the same name and Stephen meaning *coronatus*), and with extravagant claims. For Clovis had already been king before his conversion and had not needed Remigius's constitutional touch. Hincmar imagined Clovis undergoing a very Carolingian crowning and anointing. His purpose was to sketch the inaugural line that led from Clovis to Charles the Bald, which was at the disposal of Remigius's heirs. Most striking of all, Hincmar may have meant the example of Louis the Pious to suggest that the most fitting place for the coronation of a Frankish emperor was in front of the altar of the Virgin in Saint-Mary's of Rheims.

As the sword of Saint Peter was being carried northward in late 877, Hincmar may have wondered what opportunities now lay ahead for Louis the Stammerer and the church of Rheims. But he evidently was untroubled by the rivalry with the church of Sens, which would erupt amidst the constitutional confusion of 888. As Antioch, Alexandria, and Rome had once wrestled over their respective claims to apostolic primacy over the Catholic church, so in 888 the churches of Sens and Rheims wrangled over which archbishop had the right to crown Frankish kings. If the *Vision of Raduin* is associated with this dispute, then its pointed language begins to make more sense, for in it Remigius was said to hold a gift or right to constitute (*donum constituendi*) kings and emperors that was unbreakable (*inuiolabile*) and permanent (*semper*). These words were carefully chosen to challenge a new and unauthorized consecration, such as Odo's by the archbishop of Sens. The power of Saint Remigius was, of course, the power of the one who managed his reputation, cared for his relics, and kept his cult.

But it was one thing for the archbishop of Rheims to claim Remigius's right to consecrate a king, quite another to assert that the saint could establish an emperor. Yet, that is just what the *Vision of Raduin* boldly proclaimed. Before 875 such a declaration would have seemed almost ridiculous. But Charles the Bald had expanded the imperial horizons of west Francia. He had made realistic the Virgin's proclamation that *auctoritas* over the Frankish empire had been delivered to Remigius. Fulk may not have been a royal official in his early career as once was supposed, but he had certainly been exposed to the imperial pretensions of Charles the Bald's later court.[19] Only between 877 and 890 could Rheims have centrally concerned itself with the making of emperors, and the most pregnant of these moments surely fell in 888 with death of Charles the Fat. There was, of course, no case to be made in favor of Rheims's right to consecrate an emperor, but in the shifting patterns of power in 888, imagining such a right must have made it seem more real.

As for Hincmar, although he may have disapproved of the distracting quality of Charles's imperial hopes, he had constitutional designs of his own. He once wrote to Charles the Fat, praising him for respecting the interests of his cousins Louis III and Carloman. He also urged him to supply them with wise counselors who might teach them how to honor the servants of God, how to fulfill divine precepts, and how to govern their kingdoms. Flodoard said that he sent a copy of this letter to Hugh, the abbot of Saint-Martin.

And he urged [Hugh], if he were able, to prevail upon Charles [the Fat], because he had no son, to adopt as his son one of those two little kings and under the hand of his good and strong care to nurture him, so that he might establish him as his heir either in part or in whole.[20]

Can Hincmar really have thought that he might, in this way, spread west Frankish kings all over the Carolingian map? The idea doubtless appealed to Hincmar and the powerful Hugh less for imperial reasons than for royal ones, since both thought it much better for the western kingdom to be ruled by only one son of Louis the Stammerer.

But if in 882, shortly before his death, Hincmar was thinking about the prospect of imperial vacancies, so would Fulk and his church between 887 and 890. The *Vision of Charles the Fat* was to become one of the most popular of Carolingian dreams, spreading out in an independent manuscript tradition that reached through Hariulf of Saint-Riquier and William of Malmesbury to the popular press: Helinand of Trois-Fontaines and Vincent of Beauvais.[21] Indeed, Theodore Silverstein has argued that even Dante was touched by this Carolingian dream text.[22] But the *Vision of Charles the Fat* was composed at Rheims and soon afterwards copied by scribes at the monastery of Saint-Bertin (Sithiu) near Saint-Omer where Fulk had been abbot until he went to Rheims and over which he regained control after 892. The oldest manuscript of the dream surviving today is a tenth-century copy preserved at Saint-Omer.[23] From its Saint-Bertin beginnings, the *Vision of Charles the Fat* reached Belgian and Netherlandish readers such as Hariulf and Lambert.[24] The only curiosity in this reasonable reconstruction is Flodoard's failure to mention the dream, a problem to which we shall return.

The *Vision of Charles the Fat* expressed some of the same constitutional concerns as the *Vision of Raduin,* but with greater purpose and deeper design. The dream is presented in the form of a personal and verbatim statement by Charles himself.[25] He introduces himself as the king of the Germans, patrician of the Romans, and emperor of the Franks. One Sunday night after evening service he had gone to his bedroom, wishing, he said, to snatch some sleep. Suddenly a startling voice told him that his spirit would leave his body, that he would see the just judgments of God and some predictions meant for him, and that sometime later his spirit would be returned.

Straightaway Charles's spirit was seized and carried away by a brilliant white figure, who held in his hand a flaxen ball of thread that shot out powerful rays of light like a comet. Unraveling the ball, the white figure ordered the dreamer to take the thread and knot it firmly to the thumb of his right hand, for by it he was to be led through the labyrinthine punishments of the infernal regions. With the thread as the link to his guide, Charles was ushered into deep valleys filled with burning pits of pitch, sulphur, lead, wax, and fat. There he spotted the bishops of his father and his uncles. In a state of profound shock, he asked them why they were suffering such hideous punishment.

> We were the bishops of your father and uncles, but instead of admonishing and preaching to them and their people about peace and concord, we spread disorder and were the instigators of wickedness. For this reason we now burn in these infernal pits and with us there are other lovers of murder and rapine. Your bishops and the people of your attendants, who at present also love to act in this way, will join us here.[26]

The emperor trembled while he listened to this confession, but not for long, as black demons flew down and attempted to seize the thread he held in his hand with hooked iron tools. But they could not grasp the thread with its repelling rays. Next the demons ran behind his back, trying to hook him with their tools and so propel him into the sulphur pits. Similar scenes, probably influenced by Drythelm's experience, can be seen in the Utrecht and Stuttgart Psalters (see Figs. 4, 24, 25).[27] Charles's guide, however, threw a thread from the shining ball about his shoulders, doubled it, and pulled him forcefully up.

Then the Carolingian emperor and his guide began to ascend some fiery mountains, from which marshes and rivers, burning and bubbling with all kinds of metals, flowed. There he encountered the innumerable souls of the vassals and princes of his father and brothers immersed, some to the tops of their heads, some to their chins, and some to their waists. They, too, confessed to Charles that while they had lived, they had loved to engage in battle and to commit murder and theft for the sake of greed. But they had done so in the company of Charles himself, his father, his brothers, and his uncles. The result was that they now endured a whole range of excruciating torments in these seething rivers of metal. Thus metal was once again, as it had been for Wetti and the poor woman of Laon, a symbolic element in the punishment of those who had once pursued gold. As the emperor heard the confession of his nobles, a crowd of souls behind him cried out, "The mighty shall be mightily tormented."[28]

Looking back in their direction, Charles saw a horrible scene: the banks of the boiling river were covered with pitch and sulphurous ovens full of dragons, scorpions, and serpents. There he saw more of those nobles, who cried out to him:

Look at us, Charles! See how awful these torments are that we suffer because of our wickedness and pride, and because of the wicked advice we gave to you and to our kings; all for the sake of greed.[29]

While these suffering souls groaned in their agony, dragons with open mouths, spitting fire, sulphur, and pitch, attacked Charles and tried to swallow him. His guide now tripled the thread and once again powerfully pulled the emperor out of his dire straits.

Then the two travelers descended into a valley that was gloomy and dark but burning like a hot oven on one side, yet indescribably splendid and sweet on the other. Turning towards the dark side, which was belching flames, Charles saw some kings of his own line who were undergoing dreadful punishment. The emperor was so disturbed by the spectacle that he imagined that the jet-black giants who filled the valley with flame would cast him in there as well. In the depressing gloom, the incandescent thread lit Charles's way as he moved on. For a brief moment, he thought he saw one side of the blackened valley brighten. There two fountains flowed, one with boiling water, the other with clear cool water, and these spilled into two tubs to which his brilliant thread now led him.

There, standing in boiling water up to his thighs, was his father Louis [the German], writhing in unbearable pain and anguish. Louis spoke to his son:

> Have no fear, my Lord Charles, because I know that your spirit will return to its body. God let you come to this place so that you might see why—for what sins—we must endure this excruciating pain. For one day I stand in this tub of boiling water and the next I am conveyed into that other tub full of the most agreeably cool water. This reprieve was made possible by the prayers of Saint Peter and Saint Remigius, by whose protection our royal line has so far ruled. If you come quickly to my assistance and with my faithful bishops, abbots, and priests arrange for masses, offerings, the singing of psalms, vigils, and alms, I shall soon be freed from this tub of boiling water. For my brother Lothar and his son Louis were released from these punishments because of the prayers of Saint Peter and Saint Remigius and have already passed over to the joy of God's paradise.[30]

Louis the German then pointed out two tall tubs full of boiling water that stood to his left. He warned his son that these had been prepared for him unless he mended his ways and did penance for the foul crimes he had already committed.

As Charles stood shivering in horror, his guide said that he should follow him to the right-hand side of that lustrous valley of paradise. There Charles saw a gathering of glorious kings bathed in brilliant light, among whom he spotted his uncle Lothar crowned with a precious diadem and sitting upon a gorgeous topaz rock. Beside him sat his son Louis, who was similarly crowned. With a firm but friendly tone, Lothar addressed Charles as his successor in the empire of the Romans. He knew that Charles had passed through that place where his father was being punished, but he assured him that Louis would finally be released due to the mercy of God. Indeed he and his son had been freed from their punishments because of the prayers of Saint Peter and Saint Remigius,

> to whom God gave great apostolic office over the kings of the Franks and over the entire Frankish people. If Saint Remigius does not favor and support the remainder of our line, our family will soon cease to rule and govern. Therefore, you should know that the power of the empire will soon be taken from your hand and that you will live but a short time afterwards.[31]

Then Louis, the son of Lothar, turned to Charles and informed him that "Louis, the son of my daughter, ought to receive by hereditary right the empire of the Romans which you have held up until now."[32] It seemed to Charles that the little boy Louis instantly appeared before his eyes. His great-grandfather Lothar likened the lad to the child whom Christ had set up in the midst of the disciples as closest of all to God.[33] He then commanded Charles to hand over the power of the empire to little Louis through the thread of the ball that he held in his hand, and so Charles did.

> Untying the thread from the thumb of my right hand, I bestowed upon him, by means of that thread, complete monarchy over the empire. At once the blazing ball of thread shot into his hand as if it were a brilliant sunbeam. After this spectacular event, my spirit returned to my body, though I was left fatigued and frightened.[34]

The remainder of Charles's account is testamentary in nature. He wanted all to know, whether they liked to hear it or not, that God had decided that the entire Roman empire should pass into the hands of Louis. Charles realized that because of his approaching death he would be unable to act on Louis's behalf, yet he believed that God, who judges the living and the dead and whose eternal kingdom and sempiternal empire endure for all ages without end, would confirm and complete what his dream had foretold.

This remarkable political dream has the telltale marks of a Rheims composition.[35] As in the *Vision of Raduin,* Remigius's role as patron saint of the Franks was highlighted, for he in particular was said to have the power to constitute and protect their kings and emperors. The idea that Remigius was the special apostle to the Franks had earlier been maintained by Hincmar at Metz in 869. Fulk himself reminded Pope Formosus that Remigius had been established as the apostle to the Franks by the authority of Rome and the grace of God.[36] By introducing himself as the "emperor of the Franks" in the *Vision,* Charles reflected that Rheimsian belief in an "empire of the Franks," which was also expressed in the *Vision of Raduin.* When Fulk took office as archbishop in 883, he wanted everyone to know that he fully understood the apostolic foundations of the church of Rheims. His see, he asserted, was honored by the entire Gallican church because Saint Peter himself, the very first of the apostles, had appointed Saint Sixtus as bishop and had given him charge over the whole of Gaul, and Pope Hormisda, in his turn, had acknowledged Saint Remigius's special primacy in Gaul. Fulk vowed never to let his church suffer disgrace.[37] Thus, for Fulk as for Hincmar, Peter and Remigius were the solid links in a chain of power that bound the archbishops of Rheims to God and to Gaul. When these two fundamental saints appeared together in dreams as intercessory figures, they made up the most powerful of saintly tag teams.[38]

If Carolingian kings had been taught by their *Fürstenspiegel* to heed the advice of their counselors, the archbishops of Rheims had refined that dictum to read that the only advice worthy of heeding came from the representatives of Remigius. The text that most influenced the author of the dream in this regard was Hincmar's *Vision of Bernold*. Both dreams assumed the form of otherworldly voyages conducted by guides. The land where the king suffered in each was made up of two parts, one dark and the other light and sweet, and the dream traveler was assured by the people he met that he would return to his body. Bernold, too, had seen sinners driven by demons towards a pit filled with black and putrid water in a dark and deformed valley. In the *Vision of Bernold,* Charles the Bald had lamented that he had not listened to Hincmar's sound counsel; in the *Vision of Charles the Fat,* bad bishops lamented that they had failed to admonish their kings and negligent nobles confessed that they had filled their kings' ears with bad advice. In a relationship built upon the give-and-take of good advice, the worst thing of all, Hincmar once had said, was not to be heard. Thus the dream texts of Bernold and Charles the Fat shared a search for audiences of lay listeners on whom they could work the magic of their intercessory and advisory claims. To win that audience and to score points over rivals, dream texts were prepared to cast a harsh spotlight on bad bishops. The real Charles the Fat had not been alone in his disdain for a greedy and grasping episcopate. It was a fashionable hatred by the late ninth century. But Charles wanted his preoccupation documented, and so he had commissioned Notker to lampoon greedy prelates for him: to tell him stories of ridiculous bishops who thought they were kings or might be kings, who dressed in princely silks and imperial purple, and who drank exotic and fragrant drinks from jewel-encrusted cups in which flowers floated.[39] Out of group denunciations of this sort emerged the first flickerings of a genre of estates satire that would not achieve precision until the twelfth century, but Hincmar in the *Vision of Bernold* had been the pioneer and the author of the *Vision of Charles the Fat* his sophisticated imitator.

The political circumstances surrounding the references in the last sequence of the *Vision of Charles the Fat* hold the key to understanding the whole, for what we witness is essentially an adoption. The little Louis shown to Charles the Fat was Louis of Provence, sometimes called "Louis the Blind." His great-grandfather and grandfather on his mother's side were respectively Lothar I and Louis II, both emperors. His mother Ermengard was the daughter of Louis II and Empress Engelberga, and was almost as impressively ambitious as her mother. His father was Boso, the brother of Queen Richildis, whom Charles the Bald had married in early 870. In 876 Charles had established Boso as his representative in Italy and not long afterwards Boso had married Ermengard. Hincmar imagined that this had been a foul plot against the interests of Charles, but Regino described a public wedding that was magnificent and officially approved. According to Regino, too, it was Charles himself who gave Provence to Boso and who ordered him to be called king, "so that in the manner of the ancient emperors [Charles] might be seen to be the lord of kings."[40] If this were true, it might almost mean that Charles the Bald, like Napoleon nearly a thousand years later, had begun to play with the idea of establishing a familial network of petty and inferior kings whom a great emperor might bestride.

But there is no proof that he did, for in 879 Boso still lacked a kingdom; his crown had been a ducal and not royal one.[41] Then, according to scornful Hincmar, proud Ermengard made a speech to her husband that cannot but remind one of Theodora's magnificent challenge to her vacillating husband Justinian:

> [Ermengard] convinced Boso that, as the daughter of the emperor of Italy and former fiancée of the emperor of Greece, she did not wish to go on living if she could not make her husband a king. So Boso managed to convince the bishops of those parts to anoint and crown him king. They did so in part because they were worn down by his threats, in part because they were seduced by greed for the abbeys and villas that were promised to them and afterwards delivered.[42]

When Boso died in 887, Queen Ermengard attempted to promote her seven-year-old son both to the now-vacant kingship of Provence and, at a meeting with the dying Charles the Fat, to the position of emperor. She was a woman who shot high, her hopes as much imperial as royal. In 890 at Valence, Louis was crowned king of Provence. Ten years later, when Berengar of Friuli encountered difficulty with Hungarian invaders in Italy, Louis was crowned king of Italy. Pope Benedict IV went further, proclaiming him emperor in 901, but the honor was short-lived. The very next year, under military pressure from Berengar, Louis gave up the crown that his grandfather and great-grandfather had worn before him. In June 905, he once more managed to chase Berengar from Italy, only to have him return the favor and add to the ordeal the loss of his sight. Louis, now blind, retired to Provence where he lived on until 928.

If there is general agreement that the *Vision of Charles the Fat* was written at Rheims, there have been two schools of opinion about when it was composed, some holding that it was written in the few years after Charles the Fat fell sick and died, others that it was composed around 901 when Louis briefly became emperor.[43] The year 888 may prove to be the most likely date, for the dream has primary reference to the events that surrounded the passing of Charles the Fat.

The nagging shades that followed the dreamer as he walked towards the valley of the kings were familiar to all royal watchers by 888: the mortality of princes, the predominance of boy kings, and the lack of legitimate heirs. The author of the *Vision* realized that the age-old framework of the royal family had somehow come unhinged, for to promote the adoption of a boy of crooked ancestry was a desperate measure. Charles the Fat held the empire, but had no legitimate heir. Regino of Prüm was to lament in his *Chronicle* that after the death of Charlemagne all glorious things began to fail and fortune began to turn sour for the Carolingians: "their royal line was perishing and growing enfeebled, partly because of unripe age, partly because of the sterility of their wives."[44] Though this explanation ignored the tightening grip of a more restricted definition of family and did not square with the pure dynamism of later ninth-century royal actors, as I think even Regino knew, many must have believed that a fruitless and immature dynasty was God's own handiwork.[45] What Regino said of 880 was even truer of 885, when no direct male descendants of respectable age or proper birth remained alive except Charles the Fat. Regino would speak of Arnulf of Carinthia, the bastard son of Louis the German's son Carloman, as though he were the last of the Carolingians.[46] Charles the Fat himself had only one son, Bernard, but he, too, was illegitimate. Thinking of the two bastards, Arnulf and Bernard, Notker sadly contemplated the withering tree of the Carolingian line:

> Aside from that tiny splinter Bernard, only one small bough [Arnulf] now sprouts, under the solitary treetop of your protection, from that once most bountiful root of Louis [the German].[47]

Notker, like most of his contemporaries, realized how desperately Charles longed for a legitimate successor. The emperor and his supporters hoped to see little Bernard come of age, a sword girt to his side, or some as-yet-unborn little Louis or Charles nestled on his father's knee.[48] The very survival of his line was a matter that preoccupied Charles in the last years of his life. If the monk of Saint-Gall could evoke the despairing depths of Charles's heartache in a few short lines, the ache itself must have lain very close to the surface for all to see. Charles the Fat, as his fit had shown, had never been very good at hiding his emotions. Perhaps no Carolingian was.

In 885 at a synod in Frankfurt, however, Charles the Fat was to be entirely frustrated:

> For he wished, as the rumor has it, to depose unreasonably certain bishops and to constitute Bernard, his son from a concubine, as the heir to his kingdom. But because he doubted that he could do this on his own authority, he arranged to carry it out, as if with apostolic authority, by means of the pope of Rome.[49]

Charles must have hoped that the pope would not only erase his son's illegitimacy but also confer upon him the imperial title. Pope Hadrian III, however, died on the way to Frankfurt and the emperor, according to the annalist, was extremely sad. At the end of 885, Charles was still scrambling to find a new and supportive pope so that he might secure Bernard's lawful succession to the throne, but it was not to happen, and Charles must have hated all the more the bishops who had stood in his way.

He must also have begun to suspect by 886 that he would die without a legitimate heir, and that thought may have led him to contemplate an even more desperate adventure. Fourteen years earlier he had announced to his shocked nobles that he would no longer share his wife's bed. In 887 Liutward, the bishop of Vercelli and close confidant of the emperor, was accused of committing adultery with the Empress Richardis. At a council, Charles

> publicly protested that, while this marriage had been joined more than ten years before by the bonds of legitimate matrimony, he had never had sexual intercourse with her. Richardis, in response to her accuser, declared that she was free not only from intercourse with him, but with any man, and she was proud of her unspoiled virginity.[50]

As a devoutly religious woman, Richardis invited her husband to test her claim by single combat or some other ordeal. All of this makes Charles seem the accuser, his wife the defendant, and Liutward the co-respondent. Though the fall of Liutward has often been seen as an attack on Charles's power by Arnulf's supporters, it may at least be suspected that the charge against Richardis was brought by Charles himself in an effort to lay the grounds for a very special divorce. Lothar II had impugned his legitimate wife Theutberga in a similar fashion, claiming that she had had intercourse with her brother Hubert, so that he might divorce her and marry his mistress Waldrada. Perhaps Charles hoped that by divorcing his wife he could find another way to legitimize his bastard, but

Richardis put him in his place and no divorce was obtained; he remained without even the hope of legitimate offspring.[51]

The situation presented in the dream sequence, therefore, is not without some connection to the events at the end of Charles's life. In 887, separated from his wife Richardis, denied the legitimation of his bastard, disgraced by military setbacks, and beset by illness, Charles was losing what little control of the empire he still had.[52] He withdrew into Germany and traveled to Kirchen in order to meet Louis II's daughter Ermengard and her son Louis. The *Annals of Fulda,* with unwonted mystery, simply reported that there the emperor "joined Louis to himself as if he were an adopted son."[53] He also extended certain privileges and granted rights, "legali ordine et hereditario iure," to Ermengard and her son Louis.[54] It is this last phrase that rings a bell, for in the dream text Louis II had said the same thing to Charles: that the empire belonged to the boy Louis by hereditary right.

It is not impossible that, as Charles felt power slipping away in 887, he thought it worth one last desperate attempt to make a new family. If he could not have his own son Bernard legitimized, he might at least adopt a new one. At the same time, he may have hoped to find a way, however improbable, of undermining Arnulf, for no one would be more damaged than his bastard nephew by the adoption of Louis of Provence. It was a brilliant strategy, but conceived of too late. Moroever, Carolingian kings were not Roman emperors who lived in a society that had a long-standing familiarity with the advantages of adoption and its legal intricacies. Nor did the author of the *Vision* belong to that rich Roman tradition towards which his thinking was groping. In the end the dreamer admitted that he could do little to secure the succession of Louis. Yet in an age whose royal lines had become so messy, the language of adoption was in the air and the winds were blowing mostly out of Italy. Pope John VIII had written to Charles in 878 of his recent adoption of Boso, and Fulk had heard that Pope Stephen V had adopted his relative Guy. Spiritual fatherhood of this sort may not have meant much in practical terms, but families like Boso's must have seen it as an additional badge of legitimacy.[55]

With the quasi-adoption of Louis of Provence, the emperor was able to stir up trouble that would ripple across Europe for decades, but it cost him dearly, since, as Timothy Reuter has suggested, Arnulf may have finally deposed Charles because of the threat to his own position raised by this adoption.[56] Further south, the implications of Charles's unusual move were still being felt in 890 when Louis was crowned king of Provence. The acts of his election at Valence are laced with imperial mementos. The archbishops observed that when that most glorious Emperor Charles died, Provence had been left without a king and had suffered severely. But the church and nobles were in agreement that Louis, the grandson of the Emperor Louis II, should be constituted a king, for "no one was more suited to become king than that one from imperial stock who has now grown up to be a boy of good character." Moreover, they recognized that "the outstanding Emperor Charles had already granted royal dignity to him."[57]

But if in 887 Charles the Fat was a father in search of a son, Louis of Provence was a son in search of a missing imperial father. Boso, for all his *honores* and his self-secured crown, had never been unambiguously royal. He may have hinted at his elevated status with flamboyant lines like "Ego Boso dei gratia id quod sum," but all his posturing would not wash away the royal uncertainty that clung to his self-promoted person.[58] The most tantalizing aspect of the *Vision* is that it mirrored so many of the longings and imperial strategies of the circle of Ermengard and Louis. Even if it is unclear from the annal entry just what Charles was up to in 887, the motives of Ermengard and her mother are transparent: to secure Louis of Provence's royal and imperial legacies. Ermengard's speech to Boso in 879 might have been a creation of Hincmar, but it still expressed some small portion of her genuine imperial pride. She remembered that she was not only the daughter of an emperor but had also once been betrothed to the Greek emperor. Her mother, moreover, had been (and, in a limited sense, still was) empress. In the *Vision,* the Emperor Louis II laid special stress upon Ermengard and ignored Boso completely. Little Louis was "the son of my daughter," he said, because whatever imperial claims the boy had came via his mother and not his father.

The two women moved rapidly in 887 to secure Louis's position. Boso died on 11 January and by February Engelberga seems to have already made contact with the emperor and his archchaplain Liutward. It was probably at this time that the visit of Ermengard and her son was arranged. By May Ermengard and Louis had visited Charles in eastern Francia, and in August their representative, Count Wingis, sought out Charles at Lustenau near Saint-Gall, where charters were issued in favor of Ermengard and Engelberga.[59] One is forced to wonder if in May Charles conceived of marrying Ermengard, and hence in June devised the plan to rid himself of Richardis. Such a marriage would have given him an instant imperial family, one that obviated the legal uncertainties associated with the adoption of Louis. The sources, however, do not even whisper of such a scheme, though the sequence of meetings suggests that something was afoot. Moreover, the Bosonids had always known how to move very quickly when it came to arranging advantageous, indeed overly ambitious, marriages: Charles the Bald's first wife had hardly died before Boso set the king up with his sister, and Boso himself married the Emperor Louis II's daughter with some dispatch. In the spring of 887, with Boso still warm in his grave, Engelberga and Ermengard may have been no less ambitious in contemplating new marriages and they too moved with breathtaking Bosonid speed to explore their imperial prospects.

Thus the contacts between Ermengard's circle and the imperial party had been carefully established. Louis and his mother did not just appear on Charles's doorstep one day in May, and Charles did not adopt Louis on a whim. All had been scrupulously arranged in advance through deliberate negotiations and conferences. It would be wrong to think that either party acted without deeper designs, since though their plans were dangerous, the rewards were immense: for Ermengard, Engelberga, and Louis a return to the full flush of imperial power; for Charles a dynastic future of his own making. In a world of shrinking prospects and cresting limitation, neither could hope for more.

But why would Rheims, where the *Vision* was composed, have become involved in the promotion of Ermengard's son? Rheims certainly held properties in Provence, and Hincmar had had occasion to advise both Boso and Ermengard not to tamper with them.[60] But, more to the point, we need to recall how the events of 887–88 affected Rheims. Under Hincmar, the church had already begun to map out a strategy of adoption as a solution to Charles the Fat's problem, but Hincmar's Carolingian candidates had died prematurely. Like Hincmar, Fulk wanted nothing more than to see one of Charles the Bald's heirs ascend to the throne of west Francia, but in 888 Charles the Simple had seemed too young, as Fulk later admitted. In February, as Odo was being crowned in Compiègne, Fulk and his ally Rudolf, the abbot of Saint-Bertin and Saint-Vaast, were supporting Guy of Spoleto's bid for the kingship of west Francia. When that scheme failed, Fulk, Rudolf, and Count Baldwin II traveled to Germany to see if they might persuade Arnulf to come to west Francia as their king.[61] Arnulf may have been tempted by their siren pleas at first, but not for long. In late July, Odo, newly victorious in battle against the Danes, was at Worms, where he secured the support of Arnulf. Five years later, Fulk could still recall the sting of that defeat. Flodoard saw a letter sent to Arnulf in which

> [Fulk] recalled how, when the Emperor Charles, the uncle of Arnulf, died, he was moved to join the service of Arnulf, desiring to receive his lordship and rule, but that king had sent him away without any advice or comfort. Hence, since [Fulk] no longer placed any hope in [Arnulf], he

was forced to accept the domination of that man Odo who, not being a member of the royal family, has misused royal power like a tyrant and whose lordship [Fulk] has since then unwillingly endured.[62]

Thus, between June and October 888, Fulk was a disappointed and anxious man, lunging at solutions to his constitutional crisis. With Guy chased back to Italy and Charles the Simple not yet a reasonable candidate, Fulk was open to other offers. He would not capitulate to Odo until November.

If the *Vision of Raduin* asserted against Sens and Odo the absolute right of Rheims to crown a king and emperor, the *Vision of Charles the Fat* advanced a candidate. We need to remember that the text does not commit Rheims to anything very specific and had limited implications for western Francia. But in the summer of 888 Fulk had few respectable candidates for emperor or king. With the Danes still occupying parts of the kingdom, Fulk realized that no one would accept the boy Charles as king. But to advance another Carolingian boy, one more distant and with imperial credentials, as the heir to Charles the Fat might have seemed a prospect worth exploring in something as insubstantial as a dream text.

So close to the interests of Ermengard and Louis of Provence is the *Vision of Charles the Fat* that we are allowed to suspect, I think, that an understanding had been reached in that anxious summer of 888 between Fulk and Ermengard. What the archbishop would have wanted from Ermengard's circle was help in undermining Odo's claims. Since Provence, where Boso's family held sway, bordered Odo's kingdom, Ermengard and her brother-in-law Richard would have been valuable allies in the struggle against Odo. But Fulk, through his recognition of Louis's claims, probably also wanted recognition of his own right to consecrate Carolingian kings and emperors, for, in the end, that is what imagining the succession of Louis meant. As Charles the Fat had been both emperor and king of west Francia, so would Louis be. He was to receive, as the dream said, complete control over Charles the Fat's empire. Hence a false king like Odo was denied any legitimacy in this Rheimsian dream, which was surely its main point. Ermengard's people must have agreed, for their part, not to recognize the pretender. Perhaps they were also prepared to grant that the pope or Fulk would be given the opportunity to crown Louis emperor, as Louis the Pious had been crowned, before the altar of the Virgin in the church of Rheims.

To cast another hypothesis onto a tapestry already thick with unprovable reconstructions cannot hurt so long as the reader understands how tattered that tapestry is. Perhaps the *Vision of Charles the Fat,* with its intense and almost intimate connection to the events of 887, was a piece commissioned by Ermengard and her circle. Just as Lothar had once commissioned one of his brother's monasteries to make a magnificent book of Gospels, perhaps Ermengard and her party commissioned a dream text. The central place of Peter, the patron saint of Italy and emperors, and Remigius, patron saint of Rheims, may be a sign of that special partnership. But the *Vision* chiefly sought to explain why Charles the Fat had adopted Louis. In 888, Rheims must have thought that there was little danger in swimming in these imperial waters. Dream texts had always had more to do with exploration than with dangerous commitment; they remained to the end a strategy of indirection. But Fulk was determined to find a Carolingian king he could support rather than the pretender Odo. The genesis of the *Vision of Charles the Fat* is surely to be found, therefore, in some unrecorded wedding of the interests of Ermengard and Fulk.

Still, it must worry us that Flodoard, who seems to have known the minutiae of a half-millennium of ecclesiastical history, did not find the *Vision* in the archives of Rheims. If he had, he surely would have published it. But if it were a commissioned piece, its natural audience would have been Ermengard's circle in Provence. Indeed there are some points of similarity between the *Vision* and the acts of Louis's coronation at Valence in 890. But the surviving manuscripts can be traced back to a point of origin in Fulk's neighborhood, to Saint-Bertin, where he and his ally Rudolf had been in charge throughout those delicate years. It may only be accidental that no copy of the *Vision* survived at Rheims, but we should also recall how quickly things had changed. By 891 Fulk had begun to campaign for Charles the Simple's right to the west Frankish throne, and in 893, in fact, crowned him. In 891, his relative Guy of Spoleto was crowned emperor, so that Fulk would not likely have had any interest in advocating another imperial candidate after that date.[63] By the early 890s, then, Fulk himself would have had little interest in preserving in the archives of his church a dream text that no longer corresponded to the aspirations of his see. But the copy that must have been sent to Rudolf at Saint-Bertin survived and from it, as if from an urtext, the manuscripts spread.

It is not necessary for us to think that Fulk himself composed the *Vision,* for he had assembled a circle of scholars who were capable of writing it. Flodoard noted that Fulk had attracted learned men like Remigius of Auxerre and Hucbald of Saint-Amand into the orbit of his influence. Perhaps the most likely author of the *Vision* was the cleric who wrote the *Life of Rigobert* at Rheims around 890. He was a man with just the sort of background knowledge necessary to create the *Vision*. He had read something called the *Annals of Various*

Kings, which apparently no longer survives, and he had inserted into his *Life of Rigobert* Eucher's vision of Charles Martel.[64] The last textual community of dreams in the Carolingian empire, therefore, can be situated at Rheims. The senders were Fulk, an unnamed cleric, allies such as Rudolf, and Ermengard and her son Louis; the targeted audience was that wider ecclesiastical and noble world that now entertained kinglets and imperial hopefuls, men like Odo and Arnulf. For the dream called on that disturbed world to return to the dead certainties of Carolingian imperial rule as approved by Remigius.

But if, as I suspect, Ermengard and her circle commissioned the *Vision of Charles the Fat,* then once again we can see how far the politics of dreaming had penetrated the royal house itself. If the royal dream had begun as a clerical tool used to criticize and persuade kings, by the late ninth century it had become an instrument of political suasion that even would-be emperors might employ on occasion. The textual community of clerical writers and royal readers that earlier had been supposed by the dream texts themselves had grown richer by far when real kings began to dream royal dreams as Louis the German had, and when imperial hopefuls like Ermengard began to look upon the politics of dreaming as a reasonable strategy for the publication and promotion of their ambitious designs.

But in our search for the documentary locus of the *Vision of Charles the Fat,* we must not lose sight of its literary splendor. If Dante read the text and the Grimm brothers gathered it up among their German tales, it was not because they were interested in its precise historical origins; it was because of the *Vision*'s symbolic and structural elegance.[65]

Yet the beginnings of that brilliance were historical, for its author meant to answer those questions that lingered in the long summer after the emperor's death: why had Charles adopted Louis and how had he been received in the otherworld? Contemporaries were fascinated by the spectacle of Charles's death, for in it they hoped to see something of the momentous majesty that was supposed to surround a great man's death, that glimpse of heaven or hell that never accompanied the passing of the common man. Or was it that Charles the Fat's fall became the final Carolingian metaphor? In his sudden plummet from the very pinnacle of power, did they see in miniature a model of all Carolingian history, the path that led too quickly from Charles the Great to Charles the Fat? The reflectiveness of Regino has that thought lying behind it. Yet observers also longed to save the last emperor from hellfire. One annalist reported that as Charles was being buried at Reichenau, the heavens opened, by which everyone was to understand that even though he had been scorned by men and had been stripped of earthly possessions, he was still welcomed by God. Another said simply that he was *caelestem possessurus,* about to take possession of his place in heaven.[66] Regino's comment, as one might have expected, is the most interesting of all:

> Since towards the end of his life he was deprived of his offices and stripped of all his properties, there was, we believe, a struggle not only with regard to his purgation, but also, and this is more serious, with regard to a trial. Yet he bore all of this, they say, most patiently, giving prayers of thanks now in adverse times just as he had in prosperous ones. Thus he now receives or doubtless will receive the crown of life that God has pledged to those who love him.[67]

Thus, around the death of Charles the Fat people constructed a marvelous mise-en-scène against which his life was to be tested first by humans and then by God.

Many were convinced that Charles was about to occupy heaven, but when had he passed God's muster? The *Vision* had an answer. It caught Charles at a moment in 887, some months before his deposition, at a time very like that occasion in May when the real Charles had gone to meet Ermengard and Louis. The emperor was not far from death, but he still held all his offices and all his power. He did not yet realize how little time was left to him as he scrambled for radical solutions to his dynastic dilemma.

In his dream Charles took an abbreviated journey through his family history, but it was a journey that had been shaped by the previous dream travelers Bernold and Wetti. Though the valley he entered was crowded with kings, Charles was like our finger following one of the lines on a genealogical tree: he took a detour along the black line that led to Louis of Provence. Along that *via regia,* Charles may have met bad bishops and violent nobles, but they only existed in his dream because they had once obstructed royal action. We never meet named individuals; no Ebbo or Aeneas, no Bego or Jesse reminds us of personal grudges that needed settling in the hereafter. Charles's dream was not about a rotten episcopate or selfish nobles, but about dynastic continuity.

As Charles and his guide approached the valley of the kings, we as readers return to a familiar landscape, to a small world of connected and compact purgatorial spaces. Charles could cross from one side of the valley to the other, for he knew that ease of mobility so common to the undead traveler. The laws that govern the otherworld were suspended for this premature and unnatural visitor, just as they would be much later for Dante. Descending into the valley of the kings, Charles confronted a biform world, the left-hand side pitch black and oven hot, the right-hand side wonderfully bright and refreshingly cool. But the emperor had to begin on the left in the crushing and caliginous heat before he could enjoy the sight of a terrestrial paradise. Charles passed kings from his own family suffering horribly, but we never learn their names. For a Rheims writer, this gathering of royal sinners may have included Charles Martel, Pepin the Short, and Charles the Bald, a rogue's gallery of Hincmar's creation.

Confronting royal fathers may have become a common motif of Carolingian dream texts, but in the *Vision of Charles the Fat* Louis the German served as something more—a bridge connecting the worlds of past and future, punishment and paradise. His son's dream was not about him, but about moving beyond him to make a new family. Yet Charles needed to see his father first, for the fate assigned to Louis would be his own if he did not set things right. Indeed it fell to the father to point out to his son the two nearby tubs, both filled to the brim with boiling water, that had already been set up to receive him. There would be no reprieve for Charles the Fat as his entire body sank into these scalding waters. As he spoke to Charles, Louis the German stood in his own boiling tub up to his thighs. To be punished by being immersed according to the degree of one's demerit was an image popularized by the *Vision of Saint Paul* and by Wetti.[68] But Louis already had one foot pointed in the direction of paradise; he was an in-between man. The bubbling waters rose only as far as his thighs, and he received a reprieve of restorative refreshment every other day. These kind favors may have been due to the saints, but the language of hot pools and cold ones is that of the Roman bather, reminding us that this imagery had descended over the centuries from late antique and early Christian sources.[69] Louis's two tubs were like the biform valley, one side punishingly hot, the other sweet and cool. Like Charlemagne, Louis the Pious, and Charles the Bald before him, this king also pleaded for his son to arrange the religious offerings that would secure his release. The grammar of royal dreams, its vocabulary and syntax of images and settings, had by the end of the century become fixed.

But Louis's role in the dream was to point the way to paradise, to the other side of the valley where Charles would find his more blessed relatives and make a new family. In Louis's case, the prayers of Peter and Remigius had for some reason stopped short of freeing him from punishment. Was he left there to wait on his son and the fulfillment of imperial destinies, or were his sins much graver than those of his released relatives? Lothar assured Charles that Louis would ultimately be released because of the prayers of Peter and Remigius, but that reprieve also seemed to depend upon the actions of his undead son, for everything turned on the successful passing of imperial power.

As the emperor entered the blessed half of the valley, he saw other Carolingian kings bathed in the light of holiness and divine approval. Perhaps we should imagine that Charlemagne and Louis the Pious, now freed from their earlier torments, finally found in the *Vision of Charles the Fat* the uncompromising company of saintly kings so long denied them in the imaginings of the time. But they remain unnamed, for blessedness in royal dream texts also brought anonymity and oblivion. If Louis the German and his suffering royal kin had been forced to stand on the dark side, on the sweet side of the valley the emperors, sumptuously dressed and crowned, sat peacefully upon semiprecious stones as they had once sat upon jewel-encrusted thrones. Here Charles received an audience with the two emperors who mattered. Lothar was quick to come to the point: the Carolingian family line was running out, now being represented by only the *quisquiliae nostrae propaginis* ["the paltry remnants of our line."][70] Without the support of Remigius it would soon die out. The emperor announced that Charles would not live long, nor hold the empire much longer.

With this statement, the axial one in the *Vision,* Charles was informed that he should no longer expect to produce an heir of his own, but must make a new arrangement for succession. Immediately Louis II informed Charles that the empire rightfully belonged to his grandson, thus implying that Charles had merely been holding it in safekeeping for a member of Lothar's line. The little fellow at once materialized before Charles's eyes, waiting to be welcomed. Lothar invited Charles to take up the boy Louis as Christ had once called on the disciples to welcome another child as the greatest in the kingdom of heaven.

Of all the symbols in the *Vision of Charles the Fat,* the most fascinating is the thread of bouncing light that the guide had wrapped around the emperor's right thumb. Not only did it pull Charles out of desperate straits, but it repelled the black monsters who swept down upon the dream traveler. Thus, the magical string both lighted the way through the purgatorial pitch black and bound Charles to his reassuring guide. Though this string might seem at first to be some dim and universal memory of the thread with which Ariadne saved Theseus from the confusion of the labyrinth, it was even more richly symbolic, for it was the thread that tied both the dream story and the Carolingian line together. By following the thread Charles was led to his ancestors, as though at some level the thread represented the royal line itself. Lothar was explicit. It was "by means of the thread of the ball" that Charles was to pass the empire to Louis of

Provence. Thus, in joining the thread to the boy, Charles not only designated Louis as his heir but connected him to the continuing genetic and legal line of the Carolingian royal family. He was, in the context of the dream, adopting Louis as his son and making Lothar's family his own.

But we need to notice that the luminescent line had been unrolled from a brilliant ball of thread at the beginning of the dream and that at the end it rolled up cometlike into the hand of Louis. Thus what had begun as a visit to the otherworld ended as an investiture, for the golden ball was for the Carolingians a symbol of imperial power, the *Reichsapfel* that represented worldly dominion.[71] Angelomus of Luxeuil also once told the Emperor Lothar that Theodosius had been possessed of such excellence that he was able to obtain the "singularem totius orbis monarchiam."[72] In the dream of Charles the Fat, the lustrous orb stands for this "totam monarchiam imperii," the completeness and perfection of territorial and imperial power that Charles wished to transfer to Louis of Provence.

One of the most impressive pieces of ninth-century art is a tiny bronze equestrian statue, once washed in gold, that the visitor can with luck find today in another labyrinth, the Louvre. It is a statue of a mustachioed Carolingian king sitting solidly on a somewhat timorous horse. In his outstretched left hand, the king holds a golden globe; so firmly does he grasp it, so perfectly does it match the shape of his hand, that it must have seemed to some that he would never let it drop (Fig. 26).[73]

Neither would Charles the Fat, not even in sleep. If the orb passed from one imperial hand to another, the dream seemed to say, then there would be nothing for the likes of Odo ever to pick up.[74] When the shining sphere flashed across to Louis, the emperor awoke, for his dream work was done and power had passed to another generation and to an adopted son. The *Vision of Charles the Fat* may not have led us, as Dante would have, into the dim recesses of an infernal world crowded with infamous sinners, but its magic was the magic of that incandescent cord that pulled Charles—and the reader along with him—straight to one possible future; its wonder was the wonder of the thread that joined and bound imperial fathers and imperial sons in the hope of a new *translatio imperii*. The hope may have been groundless and the design stubbornly partisan, but the greatest marvel of all was that anyone might have imagined that such a text could make a difference, that Rheims was just a dream away from discovering the imperial champion who would breathe life into the dead ends of a once-vibrant dynasty. Dreams, as Fulk must have known in his summer of despair, die hard. But they do die.

Time to Wake

Why, you're only a sort of thing in his dream! If that there King was to
wake, you'd go out—bang!—just like a candle![1]

Alice knew better, of course. The Tweedle twins could spend all the time they
wished imagining what might be going on in the snoring head of the Red King;
she would not. "Nobody can guess that," she announced with solid common
sense. Moreover, if she were only a thing in his dream, then what were they?
"Ditto, ditto," they answered in mock duplicity. But they were also doubly
misleading, for Carroll's mischievous boys belong to that strange circle of
dream interpreters and dream imaginers who have always gathered beside the
king's sleeping form, explaining to others the contents of his dreaming head.

The royal house was so central to the explosion of literary activity in the
ninth century that we should not have been surprised to find Carolingian intellectuals imagining royal dreams and royal dreamers. Throughout history, the
via regia of dreams has always been the imaginative work of those interested in
the meaning and manipulation of power. But the Carolingian discovery of the
politics of dreaming may still surprise us, since it sprang up so suddenly and
with such delicate flowering after three centuries of oneiric aridity.

It would, however, be unwise to exaggerate the relative importance of these
dream texts, for, however fascinating they might be, we need to recognize that
they were but peripheral pieces of the substantial literary outpouring of the age.
Around them, at times shaping and absorbing them, swirled the deeper waters

of the annals, poems, letters, and princely mirrors. Whatever scholarly assessment one makes of their renaissance (once dismissed by Oswald Spengler as but a "ray of light from Baghdad"), we must, with some amazement, acknowledge the vibrant and profoundly exciting nature of the Carolingian rediscovery of the written word, "the preserver of history" as Alcuin had called it.[2] The men and women of the ninth century used these *litterae* to communicate, to record, to entertain, and to cudgel, but for some of them writing was a way of fixing what seemed unfixed and stabilizing what seemed unstable. That drive towards the permanent and enduring had also been at the core of Charlemagne's educational reform. The body of Carolingian writing was meant to be as lasting a monument to this desire to achieve the solid and spiritually uplifting as Charlemagne's palace chapel at Aachen with its heavy stone vaults and soaring dome.

But it would be wrong to dismiss the political dream texts of the Carolingian world as mere curiosities, for they were not the least part of a remarkable literary moment in history. Within a century, the Carolingians had recovered a part and reinvented other features of a tradition of political oneirocriticism that had lain largely dormant since late antiquity. But they shaped what they knew of that tradition according to their own needs, so that we end with many admonitory and few consolatory dreams, and though we encounter dreams of dynastic decline, there are none that prefigured the births of imperial stars. Still the Carolingian royal dream was a very special kind of text, one that perfectly met the expressive needs of groups of resolute writers. But the rise of a Carolingian tradition of royal dreams would not have been possible had a set of necessary conditions not developed in the second half of the eighth century at the court of Charlemagne. For without the attachment of circles of learned men and women to the courts of Carolingian kings, there would have been few literary dreams, fewer letters, and little poetry.

From this fusion of interests—writers wanting patronage and royal patrons wanting poetry and public service—a literature of political dreams was reborn. The danger in such a relationship, as it must always be in centralizing and courtly societies, was its capacity to create and sustain delusions. For the dream writers like their fellows were centripetal thinkers in a centrifugal age, doomed by position and patronage to invest ideas and emotions in a center that could not hold.

Yet their dreams were of a piece with the age, for the dreams of the ninth century were more reflective than formative, shining, as it were, with the reflected light of dominant political concerns. In moving from the problem of Charlemagne's lust to Louis the Pious's fractious family, from the division of a kingdom to its property disputes, and from worries about the end of a dynasty to hopes for dynastic continuity, Carolingian political dreams carry us along the most prominent ridge of clerical concern. Though they may not have entered into or have changed historical actions very often, these dream texts followed the shifting flash points of political anxiety. If we probe their politics, we find a tone of urgent alarm, for to compose an oneiric fiction was not an idle activity: it was the imperative strategem of the committed.

Most great abbeys and cathedrals refused to play at this oneiric game and no lay magnates seem to have been its patrons. But those monks and churchmen who did play established textual communities of readers and writers who reinforced common feelings of group identity and shared political commitments. Even the prophet Audradus had readers in his religious communities at Tours and Sens who were prepared to listen to his special message. Indeed, around many of the dream writers we can identify clerical patrons, readers, and copyists. At Charlemagne's court, at Reichenau, Saint-Gall, Liutbert's circle at Mainz, and, of course, at Rheims, these textual communities took shape as part of active scriptoria. There dream texts begat other dream texts: writers begat imitators, Heito begat Walahfrid, and Hincmar begat Fulk. Kings and queens were, in name if not always in fact, the targets and target audiences of this literature. When Louis the German reported that he had had a dream very like those of the poor woman and Wetti, the Carolingian *via regia* reached its climax, for what greater success could there be than for a real king to have dreamt as he had been taught to dream by successive clusters of clerics. The *via regia* of dreams had finally penetrated the rumpled head of the Red King himself.

The dream writers of the ninth century can have had few illusions about their work. Their texts were politically purposeful, with an audience to reach and messages to convey. Louis's unadorned experience suggests that the circle of dream writers and readers had always included the king, just as the texts had claimed, and that, beyond the artifice and rhetoric, dream texts occasionally reached their intended audience. The remarkable thing was not that Audradus was sent packing from the synod of Soissons, but that Charles the Bald had taken any notice at all of his prophecies. Louis the Pious may have been harassed by harsh dream texts, but he had been, in a limited sense, the patron of the dream assault upon his father's reputation, as Walahfrid must have known when he sent his version of the *Vision of Wetti* to court. Again we would do well to ask ourselves whether the dreams only reflected political thought or might, on occasion, have influenced it. The promise of the latter had driven Einhard to send his little books to Louis, though he later noted that they had done little good.

As I began to study these dream texts, I wondered how well the people who wrote them had understood their times. It was not an unfair question, I thought, since the dreams claimed to present a divine reading of the historical present, albeit one shaped by a sure knowledge of the future. They had, I now know, a surer understanding of their age than I had any right to expect, but dream texts were about remaking a world gone wrong, not about making an objective analysis of it. What rings truest of all in the dream work of the Carolingians was the surpassing hope that these texts might lead to reform and royal recovery.

In writing down dreams, these thinkers refused to resign themselves to defeat. Rather, they wanted to move their kings and so their world back onto the path that would lead to God's merciful favor. Einhard and Audradus may have complained that their kings had ignored their warnings, and the very composition and circulation of dream texts may have been the strategy of those desperate to convince the obdurate, but they nevertheless wrote because they must have thought that they and their dreams might make a difference. Einhard and the others showed, indeed, an encouraging degree of confidence in their royal society and its chances for improvement.

Unable to restructure a kingdom seemingly out of control, the men who resorted to dream texts first tried, through their sophisticated "ordering of disorder," to draw the king's attention to the calamitous condition of the kingdom. When this seemed to accomplish little, when partition, disunity, and civil war had visited them despite the pointed criticism, they fell back on Audradus's cry: "culpa regum est." It seemed to them that their kings had stubbornly refused to listen to good advice, a crime to which Charles the Bald later confessed while worms ate his face in Bernold's sanguinary dream. In imagining their calamitous history, in ordering its moments of disorder and focusing on its supposed disasters, the dream writers fashioned an alternative history of the ninth century, one that has shadowed and shaped both their own and our understanding of their times. Stephen's nightmare history was inside them and of their own making, since it was, in the end, the truest product of the particular perspective that had been granted to a family of kings and its clerical clients.

Dream texts tried, in their moments of greatest optimism, to reorder the hierarchy of the real world: to subordinate kings and nobles to Christ, to rock-hard saints, and to the church. But like the saints' relics that bishops carefully guarded in the magnificent crypts of their cathedrals, dream texts needed special tending by the powerful. The advantage to the church was that dreams, like relics, focused a beam of radiant light upon the efficacy of religious intercession, for the redemption of the souls of less-than-perfect princes rested with the prayers, alms, and masses of the faithful, all meticulously orchestrated by merciful bishops and anxious abbots. A truer compact between people and rulers was, thus, struck in the imagined heavens and hells of the dream texts, and its facilitator was the earthly churchman.

Carolingian dream literature was not, of course, the product of the humble or the unknown. In clothing these texts in the garb of humility and anonymity, with poor women and blind men as the main actors, dream texts betrayed their connections with power and the powerful. The texts came from the highest of clerics, from Heito, Liutbert, Hincmar, and Fulk, and from the vociferously committed, such as Einhard, Lupus, Audradus, and Walahfrid. These people were already deep inside the political structures of their day, with access to the king and friends in high places, but they wanted the divine edge that the dream voice gave them in pressing forward their views. It would be wrong, however, to dismiss their oneiric pleading as crassly self-serving, for everything suggests their sincerity, if not their complete honesty. Beyond the necessary dissimulation of the dream texts themselves stood intensely held beliefs that men like Heito and Hincmar wanted to send upwards to king and court. Part of the mystery play being acted out at the Carolingian court was that learned men like Einhard were playing Daniels to their imagined Nebuchadnezzars. By the time the *Vision of Charlemagne* was written down, this typology had become fixed and familiar.

But it would also be wrong to regard the Carolingian dream record as one entirely filled with fictions, for we cannot ignore, in a few cases, persuasive claims of truthfulness. I am thinking here not just of Louis the German's dream with its external and corroborating proofs, but of the *Vision of Wetti* with its several eyewitnesses. There is no avoiding, I think, the possibility that behind a few of the ninth century's political dreams were actual dream experiences. If we can catalogue as fictional something as blatantly political as the *Vision of the Poor Woman of Laon,* can we so easily and entirely dispose of Walahfrid Strabo's personal and bookish dream of consolation? To do so, I think, would be to deny Walahfrid some small portion of what he claimed as his human experience. The way around this problem is to deal with historical dreams as written records, to assess, as I have tried to do, their context, and to listen to their importunate voices.

The politicization of the ninth-century dream was a reflection, however sporadic and tenebrous, of the fervent commitment of Carolingian intellectuals to the survival of their kingdom. What these writers wanted most of all was to save their kings and so themselves from what they thought of as an approaching disaster, but "the disaster" itself kept changing shape as their own perception of the kingdom's primary problems changed: from sexual sin to territorial fragmentation, from the theft of property to bitter modernity, and from royal penance to royal extinction. It should be obvious to us that it was in the best interests of these thinkers to preserve a political world that they had done so much to realize and from whose creation they had specially benefited, but probably less obvious to us is the ease with which they could have abandoned it by transferring their allegiance to other noble houses. But the identities of both the royal family and the churchmen belonged together; it was why both suffered from the disease of reminiscence. The very survival of the Carolingian line depended, as Raduin and Charles the Fat had discovered in their dreams, on the constitutional power of Christ and his saints. But the magic of the Carolingian name and the ideals of good and royal governance held the dream redactors fast to the center of the Carolingian royal family.

The rich tradition of political oneirocriticism that they had fashioned with such purpose and deliberation in so short a space of time must testify to the cultural cohesion of their small world of court scholars and Carolingian kings tied together by bonds of patronage and property. Perhaps these thinkers were too close to the center of power to see crises objectively, but we need to remember that they were actors themselves, centrally involved in bringing about change. As long as the Carolingian monarchy held together, they could maintain a common cultural identity, but once it had passed, so did the intimate network of personal associations that had supported their ideas. Throughout the ninth century, as these thinkers had spoken to each other about the wider world, political oneirocriticism had kept pace, a witness itself to Carolingian cultural continuity. The myriad interconnections of the dream texts were part of the fabric of an ongoing cultural conversation. Thus, Einhard with his defense of Charlemagne as a family man had answered the dream critics of Charlemagne's lust, and Notker's comic assault upon fat and politically pretentious bishops expressed a truth shared by Bernold, Raduin, and the dreaming Charles the Fat. The dream literature of the ninth century possesses a certain topical reflexivity, as the dreamers turned again and again to the political issues and controversies that mattered most at the time. What governed this dream literature and set its pace was a chronology of central events and problems. Thus Audradus's *Book of Revelations,* which was, in a sense, his dream diary, imitated the design of the greater Carolingian *via regia* of dreams: it was a running, almost annalistic commentary on change as seen in moments of great crisis. Indeed, strung end to end, these Carolingian dreams read like oneiric annals.

But towards the end of the century, when the Carolingian house ceased to be an effective force for governing the kingdom, something snapped: annals ceased publication and the politics of dreaming died, not to be succeeded by anything comparable in the tenth century.[3] The conversational din of the Carolingian court, with its chattering monks and whispering courtiers, had sounded for over a century, but it now turned suddenly silent. An echo would be heard at Cluny, but faintly amidst the pervasive hush, for Cluny had no king and no court. When the Red King finally awoke, so did the dreamers who had gathered at his bedside.

No dream could halt the transformation of the Carolingian world or revive a failing dynasty. Despite the dreams and the steady and inspired rule of men like Louis the German and Charles the Bald, Francia was undergoing dramatic decentralization as a host of new kingdoms arose and with them a new breed of heroes: castellans, local lords, and self-made kings who had the singular virtue of being close and protective, even if they lacked the purity of royal blood and could not provide the same warm shelter for scholars. The cult of Charlemagne, which had been a barometer of changing Carolingian fortunes throughout the century, could now comfortably recede into the refracted light of legend, and his empire could become part of a past age rather than remain the haunting pinnacle of the present. Roland was already taking shape in the imaginations of a new world in which Charlemagne would dream again, but now in a symbolic language crowded with leopards, lions, and bears.[4] When metaphors change we should watch carefully, for an entire world of perception and ideas may have changed with them.

At the end of the ninth century, even the metaphor of royal sleep was being transformed. At Paris during the three-month siege by the Danes, Odo and his warriors found that they had no time for sleep; instead those dreamless defenders fletched arrows, readied boiling oil for Viking heads, and stood guard along ruined ramparts. Far to the south, the watchmen of Modena were warned not to sleep:

O tu, qui seruas   armis ista moenia,
Noli dormire,   moneo sed uigila!

[O you warriors who watch these walls,
Do not sleep, I warn you. Stay awake!][5]

The world that Charlemagne's poets had imagined for him was surely passing when noble men and not their kings were called upon to forgo sleep. And when the sons of the Carolingian dynasty stopped coming, so, too, did that remark-able river of royal dreams. This may be a more telling sign of change than the charred remains of Dorestad, for it suggests the collapse of that complex set of conditions that had sustained the learned conversation and political assump-tions of an age. At the end of the ninth century, Carolingian dreamers might well have said with Prudentius, *uigelemus, hic est ueritas;* time to shake off sleep and wake to the truth of the new Europe taking shape around them.[6] But they said nothing at all, perhaps because they were already awake and now knew that Carolingian history had never been some imaginable nightmare of descending darkness, but their own once bright and burning dream.

Notes

Classical authors have been cited according to the standard subdivisions of their works. Square brackets indicate the entire length of a citation. Line references, especially in poetry, follow a period in a page reference; hence p. 14.57 refers the reader to line 57 found on page 14. The following abbreviations are employed in the notes:

AB	*Annales Bertiniani,* ed. F. Grat, J. Vielliard, and S. Clémencet (Paris, 1964)
AF	*Annales Fuldenses siue Annales regni Francorum orientalis,* ed. F. Kurze, in MGH:SRGUS (Hanover, 1891)
ARF	*Annales regni Francorum inde ab a. 741. usque ad a. 829 qui dicuntur Annales Laurissenses maiores et Einhardi,* ed. F. Kurze, in MGH: SRGUS (Hanover, 1895)
AV	*Annales Vedastini,* ed. B. von Simson, in *Annales Xantenses et Annales Vedastini,* in MGH:SRGUS (Hanover, 1909)
AX	*Annales Xantenses,* ed. B. von Simson, in *Annales Xantenses et Annales Vedastini,* in MGH:SRGUS (Hanover, 1909)
CSEL	*Corpus Scriptorum Ecclesiasticorum Latinorum* (Vienna, 1866–)
FS	*Frühmittelalterliche Studien*
MGH	*Monumenta Germaniae Historica* (Hanover and Berlin, 1826–)
Cap.	*Capitularia regum Francorum*
Con.	*Concilia*
Ep.	*Epistolae*
PLAC	*Poetae Latini Aevi Carolini*
Schriften	*Schriften der Monumenta Germaniae Historica*
SRGUS	*Scriptores rerum germanicarum in usum scholarum*
SRM	*Scriptores rerum Merovingicarum*

SRG n.s.	*Scriptores rerum germanicarum. Nova series*
SS	*Scriptores*
PL	*Patrologia Latina,* gen. ed. J. P. Migne (Paris, 1841–64)
VKM	Einhard, *Vita Karoli Magni,* 6th ed., ed. O. Holder-Egger, in MGH: SRGUS (Hanover, 1965)

INTRODUCTION

1. R. E. Sullivan, "The Carolingian Age: Reflections on Its Place in the History of the Middle Ages," *Speculum* 64 (1989): 279 [267–306]. See also Leopold von Ranke, "Zur Kritik frankisch-deutscher Reichsannalisten," *Philologische und historische Abhandlungen der königlichen Akademie der Wissenschaften zu Berlin* (Berlin, 1854), 415–35; repr. in Ranke, *Sämmtliche Werke,* ed. A. Dove and T. Weidemann, 54 vols. (Leipzig, 1875–1900), 51:95–121.

2. E. H. Kantorowicz, "The Carolingian King in the Bible of San Paolo Fuori le Mura," *Selected Studies* (New York, 1966), p. 92 n. 45 [82–94].

3. R. L. Kagan, *Lucrecia's Dreams: Politics and Prophecy in Sixteenth-Century Spain* (Berkeley, Calif., 1990).

4. P. Dinzelbacher, *Vision und Visionliteratur im Mittelalter,* Monographien zur Geschichte des Mittelalters, 23 (Stuttgart, 1981); S. Kruger, *Dreaming in the Middle Ages* (Cambridge, 1992).

5. E. E. Evans-Pritchard, *Essays in Social Anthropology* (London, 1962), p. 58.

6. From William Allingham's diary entry of 7 February 1868; see *The Oxford Book of Dreams,* ed. Stephen Brook (Oxford, 1983), p. 3.

7. See T. S. Eliot, *The Wasteland,* in *The Complete Poems and Plays of T. S. Eliot* (London, 1969), p. 75.430.

CHAPTER ONE: THE SLEEP OF KINGS

1. Seneca, *Ad Polybium de consolatione* 7.2; Arrian, *Anabasis* 7.9; Plutarch, *Alexander* 23.1 and 8.2; Ammianus Marcellinus 16.5.4; Livy 21.4.

2. Pliny, *Naturalis Historia* 18, preface; Augustine, *Confessiones* 8.5 (12) and 10.30 (41); Epictetus, *Dissertationes ab Arriano digestae* 1.5.3; Seneca, *Epistolae* 122.1–3.

3. Suetonius, *Vitae Caesarum:* Claudius 33; Otho 11; Caligula 50.

4. Procopius, *Anecdota* 13.28, 15.11, 12.27, 13.30–32, 15.8–9. On Justinian, the lawgiver, as deprived of sleep, see Giulio Silano, "Of Sleep and Sleeplessness: The Papacy and Law, 1150–1300," in *The Religious Roles of the Papacy: Ideals and Realities, 1150–1300,* ed. C. Ryan, Papers in Mediaeval Studies, 8 (Toronto, 1989), pp. 348–49 [343–61].

5. I wish to thank Professor Martin Kitchen for the references to Stalin and Churchill.

6. Astronomer, *Vita Hludowici imperatoris* 58, ed. G. H. Pertz, MGH:SS 2 (Hanover, 1829), p. 643.

7. See Lupus of Ferrières's letter to Altuin, 8, ed. L. Levillain, in Loup de Ferrières,

Correspondance, 2 vols., Les classiques de l'histoire de France au Moyen Age, 10 and 16 (Paris, 1927 and 1935; repr. 1964), 1:68.

8. Einhard, *epistola* 40, ed. K. Hampe, MGH:Ep. 5 (Berlin, 1899), pp. 129–30. On this letter, see K. Hampe, "Zur Lebensgeschichte Einhards," *Neues Archiv* 21 (1896): 626 [599–631], and p. 82 above.

9. Astronomer, *Vita Hludowici* 58, MGH:SS 2:643. The Astronomer does, however, link astronomical phenomena with misfortunes in the empire in two other places: *Vita Hludowici* 59, MGH:SS 2:644, and 62, MGH:SS 2:646–47.

10. Ermold, *In honorem Hludowici* 3, ed. E. Faral, in Ermold le Noir, *Poème sur Louis le Pieux et épîtres au roi Pépin,* Les classiques de l'histoire de France au Moyen Age, 14 (Paris, 1932; repr. 1964), p. 112.1460–61; Poeta Saxo, *Annales de gestis Karoli Magni* 3, ed. Paul von Winterfeld, MGH:PLAC 4 (Berlin, 1899), p. 31.25–34.

11. Lucretius 5.974, and Virgil, *Aeneid* 2.265; Ermold, *In honorem Hludowici* 3, ed. Faral, p. 102.1308–9; Astronomer, *Vita Hludowici* 30, MGH:SS 2:623; Ermold, *In honorem Hludowici* 3, ed. Faral, pp. 130–32.1724–38. See also J. M. H. Smith, *Province and Empire: Brittany and the Carolingians* (Cambridge, 1992), pp. 65–66.

12. Nithard, *Historiarum libri IIII* 3.4, ed. P. Lauer, *Histoire des fils de Louis le Pieux,* Les classiques de l'histoire de France au Moyen Age, 7 (Paris, 1926; repr. 1964), p. 96. On this incident, see J. L. Nelson, *Politics and Ritual in Early Medieval Europe* (London, 1986), p. 214.

13. AB 876, pp. 208–9; AF 876, p. 88; Regino, *Chronicon* 860, ed. F. Kurze, MGH: SRGUS (Hanover, 1890), p. 79, and *Chronicon* 891, pp. 136–37; AV 885, p. 58. On the nature of warfare in the ninth century, see C. W. C. Oman, *A History of the Art of War in the Middle Ages,* 2 vols., 2d rev. ed. (London, 1924), 1:75–100, and J. France, "La guerre dans la France féodale à la fin du IXᵉ et au Xᵉ siècle," *Revue Belge d'histoire militaire* 23 (1979): 177–98.

14. Engelbert, *Versus de bella quae fuit acta Fontaneto,* stanza 13, ed. E. Dümmler, MGH:PLAC 2 (Berlin, 1884), p. 139. See also E. Faral, "Le poème d'Engelbert sur la Bataille de Fontenoy (841)," in *Mélanges de philologie offerts à Jean-Jacques Salverda de Grave* (Groningen, 1933), pp. 86–98. To avoid confusion with Angilbert of Saint-Riquier, I have employed Faral's spelling, Engelbert, for the poet of Fontenoy.

15. *De ratione temporum: de nocte,* ed. K. Strecker, MGH:PLAC 6.1 (Munich, 1978), p. 190.100–101; Lupus, *epistola* 70, ed. Levillain, *Correspondance* 2:6; Ps. 103 (104): 23, 20; Nithard, *Historiarum* 2.6, ed. Lauer, p. 58. P. K. Marshall, "The Learning of Servatus Lupus: Some Additions," *Mediaeval Studies* 41 (1979): 516–17 [514–23], has suggested that Lupus, in his remarks about the courier who could not sleep alone, was indulging in sexual innuendo and alluding to similar references by Jerome and Cicero. While this is possible, of course, even Marshall observed that this was out of character for Lupus. Modern readers may not be able, in such an instance, to go very much beyond Lupus's bald statement that the young man was afraid of the night.

16. Einhard, VKM 9, p. 12; Paschasius Radbertus, *Epitaphium Arsenii* 2.18, ed. E. Dümmler, in *Philologische und historische Abhandlungen der königlichen Akademie der Wissenschaften zu Berlin* 2 (Berlin, 1900), pp. 88–89 [1–98]; AB 864, pp. 113–14. A similar attempt on the life of Louis II was reported in AB 871, p. 183.

17. Pepin fled at night from his father Louis the Pious: A x 831, p. 8; Carloman fled at night from his father Charles the Bald: A B 870, p. 178; and Charles the Simple fled from the besieged city of Rheims: A v 894, p. 74.

18. On the notion of the palace as a *societas*, see K. Brunner, *Oppositionelle Gruppen im Karolingerreich*, Veröffentlichungen des Instituts für österreichische Geschichtsforschung, 25 (Vienna, 1979), pp. 26–27; J. Fleckenstein, *Die Hofkapelle der deutschen Könige*, vol. I, *Grundlegung: Die karolingische Hofkapelle*, M G H:Schriften 16. I (Stuttgart, 1959), pp. 44–112, 231–39.

19. Einhard, *Translatio et miracula sanctorum Marcellini et Petri* 2. I, ed. G. Waitz, M G H:SS 15. I (Hanover, 1887), p. 245. See also Hincmar, *De ordine palatii* 19–21, ed. T. Gross and R. Schieffer, M G H: *Fontes iuris Germanici antiqui* 3 (Hanover, 1980), pp. 68–72, who discusses the administrative officers employed to protect the king from petty concerns and unwelcome intrusions. For a translation of *On the Governance of the Palace*, see *Carolingian Civilization: A Reader*, ed. P. E. Dutton (Peterborough, Ont., 1993), pp. 485–99. On the workings of the Carolingian palace, see Fleckenstein, *Die Hofkapelle der deutschen Könige*, I:11–164.

20. Astronomer, *Vita Hludowici* 45, M G H:SS 2:633–34; Ermold, *In honorem Hludowici* 2, ed. Faral, p. 74.932–33.

21. Notker, *Gesta Karoli Magni* 1.5, ed. H. F. Haefele, M G H:SRG n.s. 12 (Berlin, 1959), p. 8, describes royal bedchambers as "caminata dormitoria." The royal houses described in the *Breuium exempla ad describendas res ecclesiasticas et fiscales*, ed. A. Boretius, M G H:Cap. I (Hanover, 1883), pp. 255.33–34 and 256.29, were provided with fireplaces. On the conditions for common subjects, see P. Riché, *Daily Life in the World of Charlemagne*, trans. J. McNamara (Philadelphia, 1978), pp. 159–60.

22. Walahfrid Strabo, *Metrum Saphicum* stanza 5, ed. Dümmler, M G H:PLAC 2:412.

23. *Carmina Scottorum* 7.3, ed. L. Traube, M G H:PLAC 3 (Berlin, 1896), p. 690, and see the new edition in P. E. Dutton, "Evidence that Dubthach's Priscian Codex Once Belonged to Eriugena," in *From Athens to Chartres: Neoplatonism and Medieval Thought: Studies in Honour of Edouard Jeauneau*, ed. H. J. Westra (Leiden, 1992), pp. 25–26 [15–45]; *Breuium exempla*, ed. Boretius, M G H:Cap. 1:254.10–11, 255.16–17, 256.16–17, 31–32; *Capitulare de uillis* 42, ed. Boretius, M G H:Cap. 1:87.1–2; S. Dufrenne, *Les illustrations du psautier d'Utrecht: Sources et apport Carolingien* (Paris, 1978), p. 85. On the Utrecht Psalter, see D. Tselos, *The Sources of the Utrecht Psalter Miniatures*, 2d ed. (Minneapolis, 1960); J. H. A. Engelbregt, *Het Utrechts Psalterium. Een eeuw wetenschappeljke bestudering (1860–1960)* (Utrecht, 1965); F. Wormald, *Collected Writings*, vol. I, *Studies in Medieval Art from the Sixth to the Twelfth Centuries*, ed. J. J. G. Alexander, J. J. Brown, and Joan Gibbs, (Oxford, 1984), pp. 36–46; F. Mütherich, "Die verschiedenen Bedeutungsschichten in der frühmittelalterlichen Psalterillustration," FS 6 (1972): 232–44.

24. Alcuin, *carmen* 42, ed. Dümmler, M G H:PLAC I (Berlin, 1881), pp. 253–54.1–4; Peter, *carmen* 41, ed. Dümmler, M G H:PLAC 1:75.42–44.

25. On the issue of Einhard's dependence on Suetonius, see Louis Halphen, "Einhard, historien de Charlemagne," *Etudes critiques sur l'histoire de Charlemagne* (Paris, 1921), pp. 60–103, and his introduction to Einhard, *Vie de Charlemagne*, ed.

Halphen, 4th ed. (1923; repr. Paris, 1967), pp. v–xiii; F. Ganshof, "Einhard, Biographer of Charlemagne" (1951), *The Carolingians and the Frankish Monarchy: Studies in Carolingian History*, trans. J. Sondheimer, (Ithaca, N.Y., 1971), pp. 1–16.

26. Suetonius, *Vitae Caesarum:* Augustus 78 and Vespasian 21; Einhard, v k m 24, p. 29. See also J. Fleckenstein, "Karl der Grossen und sein Hof," in *Karl der Grosse: Lebenswerk und Nachleben*, ed. W. Braunfels, 4 vols. (Düsseldorf, 1965), 1:47–50 [24–50].

27. Notker, *Gesta* 2.3, ed. Haefele, MGH:SRG n.s. 12:52; *Gesta* 2.12, MGH:SRG n.s. 12:72.

28. *Annales* 5, ed. Winterfeld, MGH:PLAC 4:64.381–88.

29. *Chronicon Laurshamense*, ed. K. A. F. Pertz, MGH:SS 21 (Hanover, 1869), pp. 357–59. On this tale and its textual complications, see R. Folz, *Le souvenir et la légende de Charlemagne dans l'empire germanique médiévale*, Publications de l'Université de Dijon, 7 (Paris, 1950), pp. 342–43. See also *The German Legends of the Brothers Grimm*, trans. and ed. D. Ward, 2 vols. (Philadelphia, 1981), 2:79–81, no. 457.

30. Marguerite Yourcenar, *Memoirs of Hadrian*, trans. G. Frick (1951: New York, 1984), p. 20.

31. *Pippini regalis et nobilissimi iuuenis disputatio cum Albino scholastico*, PL 101:976C1. See also L. W. Daly and W. Suchier, *Altercatio Hadriani Augusti et Epicteti philosophi* (Urbana, Ill., 1939), pp. 137–43. Paschasius Radbertus, *Epitaphium Arsenii* 1.5, ed. Dümmler, p. 27.

32. Freculf, *epistola*, in *Epistolae uariorum* 14, ed. Dümmler, MGH:Ep. 5:319.15–16. A variation of the same formula was employed by Freculf in the letter-preface to the first volume of his world history: see *Epistolae uariorum* 13, ed. Dümmler, MGH:Ep. 5:317.12–14.

33. *Annales Hildesheimenses*, ed. G. Waitz, MGH:SRGUS (Hanover,1878), p. 28. Also Thietmar, *Chronicon* 4.47, ed. R. Holtzmann, MGH:SRG n.s. 9 (Berlin, 1955), pp. 185–86, and Ademar of Chabannes, *Historia* 3.31, ed. Waitz, MGH:SS 4 (Hanover, 1841), p. 130. On this incident and the accounts of it, see Folz, *Le souvenir et la légende de Charlemagne*, pp. 87–93, and B. Stock, *The Implications of Literacy: Written Language and Models of Interpretation in the Eleventh and Twelfth Centuries* (Princeton, N.J., 1983), pp. 511–12.

34. *Chronicon Novaliciense* 3.32, ed. L. C. Bethmann, MGH:SS 7 (Hanover, 1846), p. 106.

35. For the story of Charlemagne's resurrection at the time of the First Crusade, see Ekkehard of Aura, *Chronicon uniuersale*, ed. Waitz, MGH:SS 6 (Hanover, 1844), p. 215. On the second coming of Charlemagne, see Folz, *Le souvenir et la légende de Charlemagne*, pp. 138–39, and M. Reeves, *The Influence of Prophecy in the Later Middle Ages: A Study in Joachimism* (Oxford, 1969), pp. 320–31. See also *The German Legends of the Brothers Grimm*, 1:34–35, nos. 26 and 28; F. Kampers, *Die deutsche Kaiseridee in Prophetie und Sage* (Munich, 1896; repr. Aalen, 1969), p. 58; K. Heisig, "Die Geschichtsmetaphysik des Rolandsliedes und ihre Vorgeschichte," *Zeitschrift für romanische Philologie* 55 (1935): 52–71 [1–87].

36. On the biblical theme of death as sleep, see Ps. 12:4 (13:3); John 11:11–14; and 1

Thess. 4:13–15. Astronomer, *Vita Hludowici* 26, ed. Pertz, MGH:SS 2:620, refers to the big sleep, the *dormitio* or death of Pope Leo III in 816. See also Paschasius Radbertus, *Epitaphium Arsenii* 1.5, ed. Dümmler, p. 27.

37. Matt. 8:24; Mark 4:38; Luke 8:23. For the Reichenau wall painting, see M. Backes and R. Dölling, *Art of the Dark Ages*, trans. F. Garvie (New York, 1969), p. 156. In the middle of the bottom register of an ivory book cover from the so-called School of Charlemagne, now in the Bodleian Library, Oxford, the stilling of the storm is also depicted: see Backes and Dölling, *Art of the Dark Ages*, p. 97. On the political implications of this imagery, see I. S. Robinson, "Church and Papacy," in *The Cambridge History of Medieval Political Thought, ca. 350–ca. 1450*, ed. J. H. Burns (Cambridge, 1988), pp. 255–56 [252–305].

38. Ps. 120 (121):4; P. E. Dutton and E. Jeauneau, "The Verses of the *Codex Aureus* of Saint-Emmeram," *Studi Medievali* 3d ser., 24.1 (1983): 94, 110, and pl. 4b [75–120]; also repr. in Jeauneau, *Etudes érigéniennes* (Paris, 1987), pp. 593–638.

39. Alcuin, *carmen* 96.1, ed. Dümmler, MGH:PLAC 1:321.1–5.

40. Prudentius, *Hymnus ad galli cantum*, ed. M. P. Cunningham, Corpus Christianorum: Series latina 126 (Turnhout, 1966), p. 3.3–6.

41. *Liber manualis* 2.3, ed. P. Riché, Sources chrétiennes, 225 (Paris, 1975), p. 128. See. Ps. 16 (17):8. See also Dhuoda, *Handbook for William: A Carolingian Woman's Counsel for her Son*, trans. Carol Neel (Lincoln, Nebr., 1991).

42. Prudentius, *Hymnus ante somnum*, ed. Cunningham, Corpus Christianorum 126, p. 33.134.

43. Ps. 6:6 (7). On the Stuttgart Psalter, see E. T. de Wald, *The Stuttgart Psalter. Biblia folio 23 Wurttembergische Landesbibliothek Stuttgart* (Princeton, N.J., 1930); B. Bischoff, "Die Handschrift, paläographische Untersuchung," in *Der Stuttgarter Bilderpsalter Bibl. fol. 23 Wurttembergische Landesbibliothek Stuttgart*, 2 vols. (Stuttgart, 1965), 2:15–30.

44. I Thess. 5:6; Alcuin, *epistolae* 304 and 304a, ed. Dümmler, MGH:Ep. 4:462–63. See also A. Wilmart, *Precum libelli quattuor aevi karolini nunc primum publici iuris facti cum aliorum indicibus* (Rome, 1940), pp. 33–35. Alcuin, *carmen* 45, MGH:PLAC 1:259.75–76; *Song of Roland*, ed. G. J. Brault, *The Song of Roland: An Analytical Edition*, 2 vols. (University Park, Pa., 1978), 2:172.2845–48.

45. Alcuin, *carmen* 100.2, ed. Dümmler, MGH:PLAC 1:328.3. See Boniface, *carmen* 7.2, ed. Dümmler, MGH:PLAC 1:21.1, and Wilmart, *Precum libelli*, p. 100.13.

46. Alcuin, *carmen* 122, ed. Dümmler, MGH:PLAC 1:350. W. Meyer, "Über das Gebetbuch Karl des Kahlen in der königlichen Schatzkammer in München," *Sitzungsberichte der philosophisch-philologischen und historischen Classe der königlichen bayerischen Akademie der Wissenschaften zu München* (Munich, 1883), pp. 424–36, and R. Deshman, "The Exalted Servant: The Ruler Theology of the Prayerbook of Charles the Bald," *Viator: Medieval and Renaissance Studies* 11 (1980): 385–417.

47. Alcuin, *carmen* 96.1, ed. Dümmler, MGH:PLAC 1:321.3; and see Ambrose, *Explanatio psalmi* 35.25, ed. M. Petschenig, CSEL 64 (Vienna, 1919), p. 67, and Apuleius, *Metamorphoses* 1.18. Theodulf of Orléans, *Versus contra iudices*, ed. Dümmler,

MGH:PLAC 1:504.413–14. See also Alcuin, *carmen* 61, ed. Dümmler, MGH:PLAC 1:274–75.19–22.

48. 1 Pet. 5:8; Alcuin, *carmen* 121 stanza 9, ed. Dümmler, MGH:PLAC 1:349.

49. Dufrenne, *Les illustrations du psautier d'Utrecht,* p. 85 and n. 109; Ps. 75:6–7 (76:5–6); Prudentius, *Hymnus ad galli cantum,* ed. Cunningham, p. 4.37–38.

50. See the entry on the *Te lucis ante terminum* in the *New Catholic Encyclopedia,* 18 vols. (Washington, D.C., 1967–89), 13:955–56. Variations of this prayer were known in the ninth century: see Wilmart, *Precum libelli,* pp. 99–100. On Carolingian private prayers, see also Wilmart, "Le manuel de prières de Saint Jean Gualbert," *Revue Bene-dictine* 48 (1936): 259–99, and P. Salmon, "Livrets de prières de l'époque carolingienne," *Revue Bénédictine* 86 (1976): 218–34. Dante, *Purgatorio* 8.10–18.

51. Fridugis, *De substantia nihili et tenebrarum,* ed. Dümmler, MGH:Ep. 4:553–55 [552–55]; also ed. C. Gennaro, *Fridugiso di Tours e il "De substantia nihili et tene-brarum,"* Publicazioni dell'Istituto universitario di Magistero di Catania, serie filoso-fica, saggi e monografie, 46 (Padua, 1963). See Exod. 10:21–22. On the philosophical controversy, see M. L. Colish, "Carolingian Debates over *Nihil* and *Tenebrae:* A Study in Theological Method," *Speculum* 59 (1984): 757–95. On Fridugis himself, see P. God-man, "Alcuin's Poetic Style and the Authenticity of *O mea cella,"* *Studi Medievali* 3d ser., 20 (1979): 555 [555–83]. Charlemagne, *epistola,* ed. Dümmler, MGH:Ep. 4:552.

52. 1 Thess. 5:5; Prudentius, *Hymnus matutinus,* ed. Cunningham, p. 7.1–2; Hra-banus Maurus, *De uniuerso siue de rerum naturis* 10.6, PL 111:291C9–10. On Hra-banus's sources, see E. Heyse, *Hrabanus Maurus' Enzyklopädie "De rerum naturis": Untersuchungen zu den Quellen und Zur Methode der Kompilation,* Münchener Be-iträge zur Mediävistik- und Renaissance-Forschung, 4 (Munich, 1969). Gottschalk, *Horarium* 3.2, ed. Strecker, MGH:PLAC 6.1:100.13–14.

53. L. Varga, *Das Schlagwort vom "Finsteren Mittelalter"* (Baden, 1932); F. C. Robinson, *"Medieval, the Middle Ages,"* *Speculum* 59 (1984): 750–51 [745–56].

54. Einhard, VKM, preface, p. 1; Walahfrid Strabo, VKM, prologue, pp. xxviii–xxix; see also pp. 208–9 above; Paschasius Radbertus, *Epitaphium Arsenii* 2.7, ed. Dümmler, p. 67.

55. G. Silagi, *"Karolus—cara lux,"* *Deutsches Archiv* 37 (1981): 786–91; Poeta Saxo, *Annales* 3, ed. Winterfeld, MGH:PLAC 4:34.125 and *Annales* 4, MGH:PLAC 4:54–55.361–370. Gottschalk, *Horarium* 2.3, ed. Strecker, MGH:PLAC 6.1:99.4–5.

56. "Eine Predigt des Lupus von Ferrières," ed. W. Levison, in Levison, *Aus rhei-nischer und fränkischer Frühzeit* (Düsseldorf, 1947), p. 563 [557–66].

CHAPTER TWO: THE *VIA REGIA* OF DREAMS

1. Edward Gibbon, *The History of the Decline and Fall of the Roman Empire,* ed. J. B. Bury, 7 vols. (London, 1909–14), 2:322, and see 2:317–27.

2. But see the illuminating works of E. R. Dodds, *The Greeks and the Irrational* (Berkeley, Calif., 1951), pp. 102–34; P. Brown, *The Making of Late Antiquity* (Cam-bridge, Mass., 1978); P. Burke, "L'histoire sociale des rêves," *Annales: E.S.C.* 28.2 (1973): 329–42.

3. C. G. Jung, *Symbols and the Interpretation of Dreams* (1961), trans. R. F. C. Hull, vol. 18 of the Collected Works of C. G. Jung (Princeton, N.J., 1950), pp. 213–15.

4. See Freud, *The Interpretation of Dreams* (1900), *The Standard Edition of the Complete Psychological Works of Sigmund Freud*, trans. and ed. J. Strachey, 24 vols. (London, 1953–74), 4:142, where Freud likens dream censorship to press censorship. See also the ninth of his *Introductory Lectures on Psycho-Analysis*, *Standard Edition*, 15:139. For an excellent brief introduction to the wide range of dream theories, see C. W. O'Nell, *Dreams, Culture, and the Individual* (San Francisco, 1976).

5. Jerome, *epistola* 22.30, ed. I. Hilberg, CSEL 54 (Vienna, 1910), pp. 189–91, and see P. Antin, "Autour de songe de saint Jérôme," *Revue des études latines* 41 (1963): 350–77. For Odo's dream, see John of Cluny, *Vita sancti Odonis* 1.12, PL 133:49A; for other oneiric rejections of the pagan poets at Cluny, see J. Evans, *Monastic Life at Cluny, 910–1157* (New York, 1931; repr. 1968), p. 102. Suetonius, *Vitae Caesarum: Tiberius* 14.

6. G. Sabba, *The Dream of Descartes*, ed. R. A. Watson (Carbondale, Ill., 1987), p. 2; Homer, *Odyssey* 19.560–67; Virgil, *Aeneid* 6.893–96. On the latter, see W. Everett, "Upon Vergil *Aeneid* VI.893–898," *Classical Review* 14 (1900): 153–54, and E. L. Highbarger, *The Gates of Dreams: An Archaeological Examination of Vergil, Aeneid VI, 893–99*, The Johns Hopkins University Studies in Archaeology, 30 (Baltimore, 1940). On the ancient distinction between true and false dreams, see G. Björck, "*Onar idein*. De la perception de rêve chez les anciens," *Eranos* 44 (1946): 307 [306–14].

7. See Burke, "L'histoire sociale des rêves," pp. 334–38; C. S. Hall, "What People Dream About," *Scientific American* 184.5 (1951): 60–63, and *The Meaning of Dreams*, 2d ed. (New York, 1966), p. 61; D. Eggan, "The Manifest Content of Dreams: A Challenge to Social Science," *American Anthropologist* 54 (1952): 469–85; O'Nell, *Dreams, Culture, and the Individual*, pp. 7–21.

8. Aelius Aristides, *Sacred Tales*, 2.1–4. On the composition of this work, see C. A. Behr, *Aelius Aristides and the Sacred Tales* (Amsterdam, 1968), pp. 116–30.

9. For this approach to medieval dream literature, see P. Dinzelbacher, *Vision und Visionliteratur im Mittelalter*, Monographien zur Geschichte des Mittelalters, 23 (Stuttgart, 1981); J. Le Goff, "The Learned and Popular Dimensions of Journeys in the Otherworld in the Middle Ages," in *Understanding Popular Culture: Europe from the Middle Ages to the Nineteenth Century*, ed. S. L. Kaplan, New Babylon Studies in the Social Sciences, 40 (Berlin, 1984), pp. 23–26 [19–37]; A. Morgan, *Dante and the Medieval Other World*, Cambridge Studies in Medieval Literature, 8 (Cambridge, 1990), esp. pp. 1–107. For the ancient world, see J. S. Hanson, "Dreams and Visions in the Graeco-Roman World and Early Christianity," *Aufstieg und Niedergang der römischen Welt. Principat* 23.2 (1980): 1395–427.

10. It is interesting to note that dream literature was not treated at the major international congress on fabrications and forgeries sponsored by the Monumenta Germaniae Historica. See *Fälschungen im Mittelalter. Internationaler Kongress der Monumenta Germaniae Historica, München, 16.–19. September 1986*, MGH:Schriften 33.1–5 (Hanover, 1988).

11. Freud, *The Interpretation of Dreams, Standard Edition*, 5:608. The statement

was an addition to the 1909 edition of the work, as Strachey notes, and is also to be found in the third of Freud's *Five Lectures on Psycho-Analysis, Standard Edition,* 11:33.

12. Freud, *The Interpretation of Dreams,* 5:353. See also the 1911 addition to Freud, *On Dreams, Standard Edition,* 5:683; the tenth lecture of *Introductory Lectures on Psycho-Analysis, Standard Edition,* 15:153 and the expanded statement in 15:159; *Moses and Monotheism, Standard Edition,* 23:12. In *The Interpretation of Dreams,* 5:409, Freud says that a man who dreamt of sitting across the table from the emperor was, in effect, placing himself in opposition to his father.

See also C. E. Schorske, "Politics and Patricide in Freud's *Interpretation of Dreams,*" *American Historical Review* 78 (1973): 328–47, and W. J. McGrath, "Freud as Hannibal: The Politics of the Brother Band," *Central European History* 7 (1974): 31–57. S. Rothman and P. Isenberg took the opposite position in "Sigmund Freud and the Politics of Marginality," *Central European History* 7 (1974): 58–78, which is followed by McGrath's response, pp. 79–83.

13. On Freud and history, see A. Besançon, "Vers une histoire psychanalytique: 1–2," *Annales: E.S.C.* 24 (1969): 594–616, 1011–33; P. Gay, *Freud for Historians* (New York, 1985), esp. pp. 30–31. On Freud's own view of the history of dreams, see the fifth lecture of *Introductory Lectures on Psycho-Analysis,* 15:85–86, and the letter to Maxime Leroy (1929), which survives only in Leroy's French translation, trans. A. Richards, *Standard Edition,* 21:203 [203–4].

14. See the anthologies: *The Understanding of Dreams or the Machinations of the Night,* ed. R. De Becker, trans. M. Heron (London, 1968); *The World of Dreams: An Anthology,* ed. R. L. Woods (New York, 1947); and *The New Word of Dreams,* ed. Woods and R. Greenhouse (New York, 1974).

15. Artemidorus of Daldis, *Oneirocritica* 1.2. See *The Interpretation of Dreams: Oneirocritica by Artemidorus,* trans. with a commentary by R. J. White (Park Ridge, N.J., 1975) and S. R. F. Price, "The Future of Dreams: From Freud to Artemidorus," *Past and Present* 113 (1986): 3–37. Dodds, *The Greeks and the Irrational,* p. 109; Cicero, *De diuinatione* 1.2:4 and 1.40:89; Francisco de Quevedo, *Dreams,* trans. and ed. R. K. Britton (Warminster, 1989), pp. 38–39.

16. H. Kenner, "Oneiros," *Paulys Realencyclopädie der classischen Altertumswissenschaft,* ed. G. Wissowa, W. Kroll, and K. Mittelhaus, vol. 18.1 (Stuttgart, 1941): 448–59; D. Del Corno, *Graecorum de re onirocritica scriptorum reliquiae,* Testi e documenti per lo studio dell'antichità, 26 (Milan, 1969); A. Brelich, "The Place of Dreams in the Religious World Concept of the Greeks," in *The Dream in Human Societies,* ed. G. E. von Grunebaum and R. Callois (Berkeley, Calif., 1966), pp. 293–301; C. A. Meier, "The Dream in Ancient Greece and Its Use in Temple Cures (Incubation)," in *The Dream in Human Societies,* pp. 303–19; Dodds, *The Greeks and the Irrational,* pp. 102–34; Peter Frisch, *Die Träume bei Herodot,* Beiträge zur klassischen Philologie, 27 (Meisenheim am Glan, 1968).

17. M. Dulaey, *Le rêve dans la vie et la pensée de Saint Augustin* (Paris, 1973), pp. 13–68; J. B. Stearns, *Studies of the Dream as a Technical Device in Latin Epic and Drama* (Lancaster, Pa., 1927); W. Schetter "Das Gedicht des Ausonius über die Träume," *Rheinisches Museum* 104 (1961): 366–78; J. Collart "La 'Scène du songe'

dans les comédies de Plaute (Remarques sur quelques procédés formels)," in *Hommages à Jean Bayet,* ed. M. Renard and R. Schilling, Collection Latomus, 70 (Brussels, 1964), pp. 154–60; P. Kragelund, *Dream and Prediction in the Aeneid: A Semiotic Interpretation of the Dreams of Aeneas and Turnus* (Copenhagen, 1976); and Brown, *The Making of Late Antiquity,* pp. 40–41, 66–67.

18. Dodds, *The Greeks and the Irrational,* pp. 104–5. See also W. S. Messer, *The Dream in Homer and Greek Tragedy* (New York, 1918); J. Hundt, *Der Traumglaube bei Homer,* Greifswalder Beiträge, 9 (Greifswald, 1935); and A. H. M. Kessels, *Studies on the Dream in Greek Literature* (Utrecht, 1978).

19. Petronius, Frag. 30.3. See also H. Musurillo, "Dream Symbolism in Petronius Frag. 30," *Classical Philology* 53 (1958): 108–10. See also Lucilius 15.527–28; Cicero, *De diuinatione* 2.58–61:119–27; Dulaey, *Le rêve,* pp. 18–20; R. J. Getty, "*Insomnia* in the Lexica," *American Journal of Philology* 54 (1933): 1–28; and on the Latin usage and its Romance derivatives, F. Schalk, *Exempla romanischer Wortgeschichte* (Frankfurt am Main, 1966), pp. 295–337.

20. Macrobius, *Commentarii in Somnium Scipionis* 1.3.2 and 1.3.8, ed. J. Willis (Leipzig, 1963), pp. 8, 10; Calcidius, *Commentarius* 256, ed. J. H. Waszink, *Timaeus a Calcidio Translatus Commentarioque Instructus,* 2d ed., Plato Latinus, 4 (London, 1975), p. 265, calls the god-sent dream an *admonitio.* Plato, *Republic* 10.614b–621d. On Greek philosophers and dreams, see I. Dambska, "Le problème des songes dans la philosophie des anciens Grecs," *Revue philosophique de la France et de l'Etranger* 151 (1961): 11–24; D. Gallop, "Dreaming and Waking in Plato," in *Essays in Ancient Greek Philosophy,* ed. J. P. Anton and G. L. Kustas (Albany, N.Y., 1971), pp. 187–201; H. Wijsenbeek-Wijler, *Aristotle's Concept of Soul, Sleep and Dreams* (Amsterdam, 1978).

21. See Dodds, *The Greeks and the Irrational,* p. 107, and his change of opinion in *Pagan and Christian in an Age of Anxiety: Some Aspects of Religious Experience from Marcus Aurelius to Constantine* (Cambridge, 1965), p. 39. See also Price, "The Future of Dreams," p. 4.

22. Virgil, *Aeneid* 3.147–78. See R. Humphries, "The Dreams of Aeneas," *Internationale Zeitschrift für Individualpsychologie* 5 (1927): 344–48; P. Defourny, "Songes et apparitions dans l'Enéide," *Nova et Vetera* 21 (1939): 187; R. Steiner, *Der Traum in der Aeneid,* Noctes romanae: Forschungen über die Kultur der Antike, 5 (Bern, 1952).

23. Brown, *The Making of Late Antiquity,* p. 36; Artemidorus, *Oneirocritica* 1.9 and 1.2.

24. Artemidorus, *Oneirocritica* 2.30 and 3.9.

25. Artemidorus, *Oneirocritica* 1.2, trans. White, *The Interpretation of Dreams,* p. 18.

26. Victor of Vita, *Historia persecutionis Africae prouinciae* 2.6, PL 58:206C–207B.

27. In a 1946 BBC broadcast, Jung told his listeners that since 1918 he had noticed peculiar and repeated incidents of violence in the dreams of his German patients. He claimed, in fact, to have anticipated from the interpretation of these dreams the myth of the blond beast promoted by the Nazis. See Jung, "The Fight with the Shadow," *Essays on Contemporary Events,* trans. Hull, vol. 10 of the Collected Works of C. G. Jung (New

York, 1964), pp. 218–26. On the historical implications of Jung's theory of dreams, see L. Aurigemma, "Carl Gustav Jung: esquisse d'une oeuvre," *Annales: E.S.C.* 28.2 (1973): 358–65 [343–67]. For another perspective, see the pre-1939 dreams collected by C. Beradt, *The Third Reich of Dreams,* trans. A. Gottwald (Chicago, 1968), and the concentration camp dreams related by J. Cayrol, *Lazare parmi nous,* Cahiers du Rhône, 82 (Neuchâtel, 1950), pp. 15–66.

28. Suetonius, *Vitae Caesarum*: Augustus 94. For other examples, see Cicero, *De diuinatione* 1.20:39; Valerius Maximus, *De dictis factisque memorabilibus* 1.7. Ext.7; Plutarch, *Alexander* 2.4. On dreams of the births of rivals, see Valerius Maximus, *De dictis* 1.7. Ext.5.

29. Suetonius, *Vitae Caesarum:* Galba 4. See also Suetonius, *Vitae Caesarum:* Vespasian 5, Julius Caesar 7, Augustus 96; Plutarch, *Alexander* 24.3–4.

30. Dio Cassius, *Historiae* 72.23.1–2; see F. Millar, *A Study of Cassius Dio* (Oxford, 1964), pp. 179–80.

31. Suetonius, *Vitae Caesarum:* Caligula 57. For other examples of the type, see Suetonius, *Vitae Caesarum:* Tiberius 74 and Domitian 23.

32. Suetonius, *Vitae Caesarum:* Claudius 37; Browne, "On Dreams" (ca. 1650), quoted in *The Oxford Book of Dreams,* ed. Stephen Brook (Oxford, 1983), p. 58; Valerius Maximus, *De dictis* 1.7; Cicero, *De diuinatione* 1.26:56.

33. Plato, *Republic* 10. 615b–d; Plutarch, *De sera numinis uindicta* 566E–F.

34. Virgil, *Aeneid* 4.350–55; Suetonius, *Vitae Caesarum:* Otho 7, Nero 46, and see also Caligula 50.

35. Lucan, *Bellum ciuile* 7.760–86. On Lucan's political opinions, see R. C. Udaeta, *Historia y politica en la Farsalia de Marco Anneo Lucano* (Madrid, 1956), and J. Brisset, *Les idées politiques de Lucain* (Paris, 1964).

36. From Cicero, *De re publica* 6.9.9–6.26.9. On the political context of Cicero's *Somnium Scipionis,* see R. Harder, *Über Ciceros "Somnium Scipionis"* (Halle, 1929), and K. Büchner, "Das *Somnium Scipionis* und sein Zeitbezug," *Gymnasium: Zeitschrift für Kultur der antike und humanistische Bildung* 69 (1962): 220–41.

37. On dreams in the Bible, see Dulaey, *Le rêve,* pp. 33–47, 231–33; E. L. Ehrlich, *Der Traum im Alten Testament,* Beihefte zur Zeitschrift für die alttestamentliche Wissenschaft, 73 (Berlin, 1953); A. Resch, *Der Traum im Heilsplan Gottes. Deutung und Bedeutung des Traums im Alten Testament* (Freiburg, 1964); A. Wikenhauser, "Die Traumgesichte des Neuen Testaments in religionsgeschichtlicher Sicht," in *Pisciculi: Studien zur Religion und Kultur des Altertums,* ed. T. Klauser and A. Rucker (Münster in Westfalen, 1939), pp. 320–33; J. Le Goff, *The Medieval Imagination,* trans. A. Goldhammer (Chicago, 1988), pp. 193–96, 229–31.

38. For the most widely known classifications, see Artemidorus, *Oneirocritica* 1.1–10; Macrobius, *Commentarii in Somnium Scipionis* 1.3.2–13; Philo, *De somniis;* Tertullian, *De anima* 47; Calcidius, *Commentarius super Timaeum* 249–56. See also A. H. M. Kessels, "Ancient Systems of Dream-Classification," *Mnemosyne* 4th ser., 22 (1969): 389–424; K. Speckenbach, "Von den troimen. Über den Traum in Theorie und Dichtung," in *"Sagen mit Sinne": Festschrift für Marie-Luise Dittrich zum 65. Geburtstag,* ed. H. Rucker and K. O. Seidel, Göppinger Arbeiten zur Germanistik, 180

(Göppingen, 1976), pp. 169–204. On the fortune of these systems in the Middle Ages, see S. Kruger, *Dreaming in the Middle Ages* (Cambridge, 1992), pp. 7–122.

39. Augustine, *Confessiones* 6.13.23. On the history of the Christian distinction between dreams and visions, see Dulaey, *Le rêve*, pp. 49–55.

40. Gregory of Nyssa, *De hominis opificio* 13.13; see Eriugena's Carolingian translation of this as *De imagine* 14, ed. M. Cappuyns, "Le 'De imagine' de Grégoire de Nysse traduit par Jean Scot Erigène," *Recherches de théologie ancienne et médiévale* 32 (1965): 229 [205–62].

41. See J. Amat, *Songes et visions. L'au-delà dans la littérature latine tardive* (Paris, 1985); Dulaey, *Le rêve*, pp. 36–68; Hanson, "Dreams and Visions in the Graeco-Roman World and Early Christianity," pp. 1421–25. See also T. Silverstein, "The Vision of Saint Paul: New Links and Patterns in the Western Tradition," *Archives d'histoire doctrinale et littéraire du Moyen Age* 34 (1959): 199–248; Dodds, *Pagan and Christian in an Age of Anxiety*, pp. 38–53; M. Himmelfarb, *Tours of Hell: An Apocalyptic Form in Jewish and Christian Literature* (Philadelphia, 1983).

42. *Passio Maximiani*, PL 8:770D4–7, and see Himmelfarb, *Tours of Hell*, pp. 123–25.

43. On Constantine's famous vision, see A. H. M. Jones, *Constantine and the Conversion of Europe*, Medieval Academy Reprints for Teaching, 4 (1948; Toronto, 1978), pp. 84–87; Dodds, *Pagan and Christian in an Age of Anxiety*, pp. 46–47; Brown, *The Making of Late Antiquity*, pp. 62–63; A. Alfoldi, *The Conversion of Constantine and Pagan Rome* (Oxford, 1948), pp. 16–24, 125–26; F. Cumont, *Lux Perpetua* (Paris, 1949), pp. 18–19; T. D. Barnes, *Constantine and Eusebius* (Cambridge, Mass., 1981), p. 42; Amat, *Songes et visions*, pp. 204–8.

44. A. Brasseur, "Le songe de Théodose le Grand," *Latomus* 2 (1938): 190–95; on the dream that saved Justin's life: Procopius, *Anecdota* 6.5–10; Liutprand, *Relatio de legatione Constantinopolitana* 39, ed. J. Becker, MGH:SRGUS (Hanover, 1915), pp. 195–96.

45. Procopius, *Anecdota* 19.1–20.12; Ammianus Marcellinus 15.3.4–6; Synesius, *De insomniis* 1.8–9, Patrologia Graeca, 66, gen. ed. J. P. Migne, 1305A [1281B–1320C]. See also W. Lang, *Das Traumbuch des Synesius von Kyrene. Übersetzung und Analyse der philosophischen Grundlagen*, Heidelberger Abhandlungen zur Philosophie und ihrer Geschichte, 10 (Tübingen, 1926).

46. On dreams in the Islamic tradition, see G. E. von Grunebaum, "The Cultural Function of the Dream as Illustrated by Classical Islam," in *The Dream in Human Societies*, pp. 3–21, and T. Fahd, "The Dream in Medieval Islamic Society," in *The Dream in Human Societies*, pp. 351–63.

47. P. Courcelle, "La vision cosmique de saint Benoît," *Revue des études augustiniennes* 13 (1967): 97–117, and Sulpice Sévère, *Vie de saint Martin*, trans. and ed. J. Fontaine, 3 vols., Sources Chrétiennes, 133–35 (Paris, 1967–69), 1:195–98.

48. Gregory the Great, *Dialogi* 4.31, ed. U. Moricca, *Gregorii Magni Dialogi libri IV*, Fonti per la storia d'italia, 57 (Rome, 1924), pp. 274–75. On the *Dialogues*, see J. M. Peterson, *The Dialogues of Gregory the Great in Their Late Antique Cultural Background*, Pontifical Institute of Mediaeval Studies, Studies and Texts, 69 (Toronto, 1984).

49. Bede, *Historia ecclesiastica gentis anglorum* 3.19, 5.12, 2.12.

50. Gregory of Tours, *Historia Francorum* 8.5, ed. B. Krusch and W. Levison in MGH:SRM I.1 (Hanover, 1951), p. 374.

51. Peter Godman, *Poets and Emperors: Frankish Politics and Carolingian Poetry* (Oxford, 1987), esp. pp. 38–39.

52. Boniface, *epistola* 10, ed. M. Tangl, MGH: *Epistolae Selectae* 1 (Berlin, 1955), p. 14, and *epistola* 73, pp. 146–55. See C. Carozzi, "La géographie de l'au-delà et sa signification pendant le haut Moyen Age," *Popoli e paesi nella cultura altomedievale* 2, Settimane di Studio del Centro Italiano di Studi sull'Alto Medioevo, 29 (Spoleto, 1983), pp. 448–51 [423–81]; J. Le Goff, *The Birth of Purgatory,* trans. A. Goldhammer (Chicago, 1984), pp. 110–11; and E. Dunninger, *Politische und geschichtliche Elemente in mittelalterlichen Jenseitsvisionen bis zum Ende des 13. Jahrhunderts* (Inaugural-Dissertation, Universität zu Würzburg, 1962), pp. 20–21.

53. Boniface, *epistola* 115, ed. Tangl, MGH: *Epistola Selectae* 1:247 [247–49]. Also see A. J. Gurevic, "Au Moyen Age: conscience individuelle et image de l'au-delà," *Annales: E.S.C.* 37.2 (1982): 255–75.

54. *Constitutum Constantini* 7–8, ed. H. Fuhrmann, MGH: *Fontes iuris germanici antiqui in usum scholarum,* 10 (Hanover, 1968), pp. 69–74; on the manuscripts and various textual traditions, see pp. 8–47. For a translation of the *Donation,* see *Carolingian Civilization: A Reader,* ed. P. E. Dutton (Peterborough, Ont., 1993), pp. 13–19. See also S. Williams, "The Oldest Text of the *Constitutum Constantini,*" *Traditio* 20 (1964): 448–51 and the edition of the text on pp. 451–61. See also E. Ewig, "Das Bild Constantins der Grossen in den ersten Jahrhunderten des abendländischen Mittelalters," *Historisches Jahrbucher* 75 (1956): 1–46; *Legenda sancti Silvestri,* ed. B. Mombrizio, vol. 2 of *Sanctuarium seu Vitae Sanctorum,* rev. ed. (Paris, 1910), p. 513.

55. The specific sequence is discussed in the *Libri Carolini* 2.13, ed. H. Bastgen, MGH:Con. 2 supplementum (Hanover, 1924), pp. 72–73 and subsequently (in 825) in *Libellus Synodalis Parisiensis* 2, MGH:Con. 2:485, and *Epitome Libelli Synodalis Parisiensis* 2, MGH:Con. 2:536–37. In the *Decretales Pseudo-Isidorianae et Capitula Angilramni,* ed. P. Hinschius (Leipzig, 1863), the *Constitutum Constantini* is found at pp. 249–54.

56. Walahfrid Strabo, *De exordiis et incrementis quarundam in obseruationibus ecclesiasticis rerum* 8, in MGH:Cap. 2:484, and Hincmar of Rheims, *De ordine palatii* 13, ed. Gross and Schieffer, p. 56. On use of the *Constitutum* by other writers, see G. Laehr, *Die konstantinische Schenkung in der abendländischen Literatur des Mittelalters bis zur Mitte des 14. Jahrhunderts,* Historische Studien, 166 (Berlin, 1926; repr. 1965), pp. 1–22.

57. See above p. 189. See Otloh, *Liber uisionum* 19, ed. P. G. Schmidt, in MGH: *Quellen zur geistesgeschichte des Mittelalters,* 13 (Weimar, 1989), pp. 95–101.

58. W. Ullmann, *The Carolingian Renaissance and the Idea of Kingship: The Birbeck Lectures 1968–9* (London, 1969), pp. 71–110; J. M. Wallace-Hadrill, *Early Germanic Kingship in England and on the Continent* (Oxford, 1971), pp. 98–100; on church-state relations and the development of the Frankish church, see Wallace-Hadrill, *The Frankish Church* (Oxford, 1983); J. L. Nelson, "Kingship and Empire," in *The Cam-*

bridge History of Medieval Political Thought, ca. 350–ca. 1450 (Cambridge, 1988), pp. 213–15 [211–51].

59. See also Hilduin, *Reuelatio Stephano papae ostensa,* ed. Waitz, in MGH:SS 15.1:2–3. This text seems to have been composed for Louis the Pious. See also A. J. Stoclet, "La *Clausula de unctione Pippini regis:* mises au point et nouvelles hypothèses," *Francia* 8 (1980): 13 [1–42].

60. *Admonitio generalis* 65, ed. Boretius, MGH:Cap. 1:58–59, also repeated in *Capitulare missorum item speciale* (802) 40, MGH:Cap. 1:104. See *Episcoporum ad Hludowicum imperatorem relatio* (829) 54 (20), ed. Boretius and Krause, MGH:Cap. 2:44. On legal condemnation of dream interpretation, see H. J. Kamphausen, *Traum und Vision in der lateinischen Poesie der Karolingerzeit,* Lateinische Sprache und Literatur des Mittelalters, 4 (Bern, 1975), pp. 32–33 and n. 77.

61. Agobard of Lyons, *De grandine et tonitruis,* ed. L. Van Acker, in *Agobardi Lugdunensis Opera Omnia,* Corpus Christianorum: Continuatio Mediaevalis, 52 (Turnhout, 1981); also ed. as *Liber contra insulsam uulgi opinionem de grandine et tonitruis,* in PL 104:147–58; Agobard, *epistola* 12, ed. Dümmler, MGH:Ep. 5:206–10; Egon Boshof, *Erzbischof Agobard von Lyon: Leben und Werk,* Kölner historische Abhandlungen, 17 (Cologne, 1969), pp. 170–78; H. Liebeschütz, "Wesen und Grenzen des karolingischen Rationalismus," *Archiv für Kulturgeschichte* 33 (1950): 17–44; P. E. Dutton, "Thunder and Hail over the Carolingian Countryside," in *Agriculture in the Middle Ages,* ed. Del Sweeney (Philadelphia, Pa., 1994). See also Hrabanus Maurus, *De magicis artibus,* PL 110:1095–110, and *epistola* 31 to Hatto, ed. Dümmler, MGH:Ep. 5:458–62; Hincmar, *De diuortio Lotharii regis et Tetbergae reginae* 15, PL 125:716C–725D; and Halitgar of Cambrai, *Liber poenitentialis,* PL 105:698–99, repeats the injunctions of the eighth-century Pseudo-Theodore against magicians. See, in general, J. B. Russell, *Witchcraft in the Middle Ages* (Ithaca, N.Y., 1972), pp. 63–100; P. Riché, "La magie à l'époque carolingienne," *Academie des Inscriptions et Belles-Lettres: Comptes Rendus* (Paris, 1973), pp. 127–38; Riché, *Daily Life in the World of Charlemagne,* trans. J. McNamara (Philadelphia, 1978), pp. 181–90; V. I. J. Flint, *The Rise of Magic in Early Medieval Europe* (Princeton, N.J., 1991).

62. On medieval dream books, see L. Thorndike, *A History of Magic and Experimental Science during the First Thirteen Centuries of Our Era,* 8 vols. (New York, 1923–58), 2:290–302; W. Suchier, "Altfranzösische Traumbücher," *Zeitschrift für französische Sprache und Literatur* 67 (1957): 129–67; A. Paradis, "Les oniromanciens et leur traités des rêves," *Aspects de la marginalité au Moyen Age,* ed. G. H. Allard (Montreal, 1975), pp. 118–27; S. R. Fischer, "Dreambooks and the Interpretation of Medieval Literary Dreams," *Archiv für Kulturgeschichte* 65 (1983): 1–20. Practical manuals on the interpretation of dreams, such as the *Dreambook of Daniel,* could be found on the shelves of Carolingian libraries: see *The "Somniale Danielis": An Edition of a Medieval Latin Dream Interpretation Handbook,* ed. L. T. Martin (Frankfurt am Main, 1981), pp. 24–25, 67–90, 169–72, 260–63; A. Önnerfors, *Mediaevalia: Abhandlungen und Aufsätze,* Lateinische Sprache und Literatur des Mittelalters, 6 (Frankfurt am Main, 1977), pp. 32–57.

63. *Codex Carolinus* 88, ed. W. Gundlach, MGH:Ep. 3 (Berlin, 1892), pp. 624–25;

see Gen. 28:12. See also T. F. X. Noble, *The Republic of St. Peter: The Birth of the Papal State 680–825* (Philadelphia, 1984), p. 283 and, on Garamann, *Codex Carolinus* 86, pp. 622–23.

64. *Actio quarta Concilii Nicaeni Secundi*, ed. J. D. Mansi, *Sacrorum conciliorum nova et amplissima collectio*, 31 vols. (Florence, 1739–98; repr. Graz, 1960), 13:33–34; Hadrian, *epistola* 2.13, ed. K. Hampe, MGH:Ep. 5:20. See also D. R. Sefton, "The Popes and The Holy Images in the Eighth Century," in *Religion, Culture, and Society in the Early Middle Ages: Studies in Honor of Richard E. Sullivan*, ed. T. F. X. Noble and J. Contreni (Kalamazoo, Mich., 1987), pp. 120–25 [117–30].

65. *Libri Carolini* 3.26, ed. H. Bastgen, MGH:Con. 2 suppl., pp. 158–61, and see Kamphausen, *Traum und Vision*, pp. 49–58. On the *Libri Carolini*, see P. Henry, "Images of the Church in the Second Nicene Council and in the *Libri Carolini*," in *Law, Church, and Society: Essays in Honor of Stephan Kuttner*, ed. K. Pennington and R. Somerville (Pittsburgh, 1977), pp. 237–52. For reflections on the controversial question of authorship, see P. Meyvaert, "The Authorship of the *Libri Carolini*. Observations Prompted by a Recent Book," *Revue Bénédictine* 89 (1979): 29–57; D. A. Bullough, *Carolingian Renewal: Sources and Heritage* (Manchester, 1991), pp. 177–86 [161–240].

66. *Libri Carolini* 3.26, ed. Bastgen, MGH:Con. 2 suppl., p. 160.

67. Gregory the Great, *Dialogi* 4.50, ed. Moricca, pp. 309–10, and Gregory the Great, *Moralia in Job* 1.8.42–43, PL 75:827A-828B. See Isidore, *Sententiae* 3.6, PL 83:669A and the appendix 1163A–D. See above p. 19.

68. *Libri Carolini* 3.26, ed. Bastgen, MGH:Con. 2 suppl., pp. 160–61; Alcuin, *epistola* 135, ed. Dümmler, MGH:Ep. 4:204, and *Commentaria in Apocalypsin* 1, PL 100:1089A5–B6. The threefold division is based on Augustine, *De genesi ad litteram* 12.36, ed. J. Zycha, CSEL 28.3.2 (Prague, 1894), pp. 433–34. On the tradition of this distinction, see Dulaey, *Le rêve*, p. 82; J. H. Taylor, "The Meaning of *Spiritus* in St. Augustine's *De genesi*, XII," *The Modern Schoolman* 26 (1948; repr. 1966): 211–18; Kamphausen, *Traum und Vision*, pp. 44–45 and nn. 109–12; Kruger, *Dreaming in the Middle Ages*, pp. 35–43.

69. Paschasius Radbertus, *Epitaphium Arsenii* 1.5, ed. Dümmler, p. 28; Heito, *Visio Wettini* 5, ed. Dümmler, MGH:PLAC 2:269; *Visio Raduini*, ed. O. Holder-Egger, *Neues Archiv* 11 (1986): 262 [262–63]. Alcuin said that Willibrord's mother "in somnis uidit oroma" ["saw visions in her sleep"]: *De uita Willibrordi Traiectensis episcopi* 2, ed. W. Levison, MGH:SRM 7:117.13. See also P. Dinzelbacher, *Vision und Visionliteratur im Mittelalter*, Monographien zur Geschichte des Mittelalters, 23 (Stuttgart, 1981), pp. 46–50.

70. Macrobius, *Commentarii in Somnium Scipionis* 3.2–11, ed. Willis, pp. 8–11. See also A. M. Peden, "Macrobius and Mediaeval Dream Literature," *Medium Aevum* 54 (1985): 59–73.

71. *Libri Carolini* 3.26, ed. Bastgen, MGH:Con. 2 suppl., p. 160.

72. Paschasius Radbertus, *Epitaphium Arsenii* 1.5, ed. Dümmler, p. 27, and see 2.23, p. 95; *Vita Richarii* 14, ed. B. Krusch, MGH:SRM 7:452–53.

73. Alcuin, *De uita Willibrordi* 2, ed. Levison, MGH:SRM 7:117. The handlist of vi-

sions compiled by Dinzelbacher, *Vision and Visionliteratur,* pp. 13–28, contains only major items and does not isolate the hagiographical dimension of the medieval dream.

74. Theodulf, *carmen* 45, ed. Dümmler, MGH:PLAC 1:544.53–55. On the lost *De somno,* see Dümmler, MGH:PLAC 1:443.

75. J. Devisse, *Hincmar, archevêque de Reims, 845–882,* 3 vols., Travaux d'histoire ethico-politique, 29 (Geneva, 1975–76), 2:822 and n. 697; Bede, *Historia ecclesiastica gentis anglorum* 5.12; Alcuin, *Versus de patribus, regibus, et sanctis Euboricensis ecclesiae,* ed. P. Godman, in Alcuin, *The Bishops, Kings, and Saints of York* (Oxford, 1982), pp. 72–80.876–1007. See also Carozzi, "La géographie de l'au-delà," pp. 454–61.

76. Alcuin, *Versus de patribus,* ed. Godman, pp. 130–32.1602–48; *Vita Alcuini,* ed. W. Arndt, MGH:SS 15.1:184–97.

77. Alcuin, *Commentaria super Ecclesiasten* (at Eccles. 5:6), PL 100:689B1–5.

78. Walahfrid Strabo, *De quodam somnio ad Erluinum,* ed. Dümmler, MGH:PLAC 2:364–65.

79. Boniface, *epistola* 10, ed. Tangl, p. 14; *Gesta Dagoberti* 9, ed. B. Krusch, MGH:SRM 2:403; Heito, *Visio Wettini* 10, ed. Dümmler, MGH:PLAC 2:270–71; Walahfrid Strabo, *Visio Wettini,* ed. Dümmler, MGH:PLAC 2:301–3, and see also pp. 317–18.400–434. For an English translation of Heito's *Visio Wettini,* see *Visions of Heaven and Hell before Dante,* ed. Eileen Gardiner (Ithaca, N.Y., 1989), pp. 65–79. Walahfrid's *Visio Wettini* has also been edited and translated (into English) by D. A. Traill, *Walahfrid Strabo's Visio Wettini: Text, Translation, and Commentary,* Lateinische Sprache und Literatur des Mittelalters, 1 (Bern, 1974), and (into German) by H. Knittel, in Walahfrid Strabo, *Visio Wettini. Die Vision Wettis* (Sigmaringen, 1986).

80. On the popularity of the *Visio Wettini,* see Traill, *Walahfrid Strabo's Visio Wettini,* pp. 16–18, and the list of manuscripts, pp. 19–20. See also the acknowledgments of its influence, PL 105:769C–771D. Alcuin, *Liber metricus de uita sancti Willibrordi* 2.34, ed. Dümmler, MGH:PLAC 1:219.28, and see p. 218.1–2. Alcuin, *epistola* 42, ed. Dümmler, MGH:Ep. 4:86, apparently trusted the visions of his student Seneca.

81. *Karolus Magnus et Leo Papa,* ed. Dümmler, MGH:PLAC 1:366–79; also ed. F. Brunhölzl, *Karolus Magnus et Leo Papa: ein Paderborner Epos Vom 799,* Studien und Quellen zur westfälischen Geschichte, 8 (Paderborn, 1966). See H. Beumann, "Das Paderborner Epos und die Kaiseridee Karls des Grossen," in *Zum Kaisertum Karls des Grossen: Beiträge und Aufsätze,* ed. G. Wolf, Wege und Forschung, 38 (Darmstadt, 1972), pp. 309–83; A. Ebenbauer, *Carmen historicum. Untersuchungen zur historischen Dichtung im karolingischen Europa* (Vienna, 1978), pp. 34–74; D. Schaller, "Das Aachener Epos für Karl den Kaiser," FS 10 (1976): 134–68, and "Interpretationsprobleme im Aachener Karlsepos," *Rheinische Vierteljahrsblätter* 41 (1977): 162 [160–79]; R. P. H. Green, "Modoin's Eclogues and the 'Paderborn Epic,'" *Mittellateinisches Jahrbuch* 16 (1981): 34–44 [43–53]; Godman, *Poets and Emperors,* pp. 82–90.

82. *Karolus Magnus et Leo Papa,* ed. Dümmler, MGH:PLAC 1:374.326–32.

83. Notker, *Gesta Karoli Magni* 1.26, ed. Haefele, MGH:SRG n.s. 12:37.

84. *Karolus Magnus et Leo Papa,* ed. Dümmler, MGH:PLAC 1:377.441–44, and see p. 374.334. See also Schaller, "Interpretationsprobleme," pp. 178–79.

85. See *Aeneid* 2.270–78 On the Virgilian motifs, see T. M. Anderson, *Early Epic Scenery: Homer, Virgil, and the Medieval Legacy* (Ithaca, N.Y., 1976), pp. 105–22; P. Godman, "The Poetic Hunt from Saint Martin to Charlemagne's Heir," in *Charlemagne's Heir: New Perspectives on the Reign of Louis the Pious (814–840),* ed. Godman and R. Collins (Oxford, 1990), pp. 565–89.

The Carolingians recognized that pagan kings had required help to understand their dreams: see Alcuin, *epistola* 135, ed. Dümmler, MGH:Ep. 4:204; *Libri Carolini* 3.26, ed. Bastgen, MGH:Con. 2 suppl., p. 160: "Legimus etiam infedilibus ac profanis quibusque regibus quaedam archana per somnia demonstrata, quae non illis reuelata sunt ullis propriorum meritorum praerogatiuis, sed ut uiri sancti, qui ea illis Spiritu sancto reuelante monstrauere, honoribus sublimarentur et suis ualerent prodesse concaptiuis." See also Petrus, *Quaestiones in Danielem,* PL 96:1349A.

86. For Theoderic, see Sedulius Scottus, *De rectoribus christianis* 8, ed. S. Hellmann, *Sedulius Scottus,* Quellen und Untersuchungen zur lateinischen Philologie des Mittelalters, 1.1 (Munich, 1906), pp. 44–45; Walahfrid Strabo, *De imagine Tetrici,* ed. Dümmler, MGH:PLAC 2:371.30–39. The Carolingians knew of Constantine's dream ("uidit per soporem") of a cross in the sky from Eusebius, *Historia ecclesiastica,* as translated by Rufinus (9.9) and from Cassiodorus, *Historia Tripertita* 1.4–5. See *Concilium Parisiense* (825) 65–67, ed. A. Werminghoff, MGH:Con. 2.2 (Hanover, 1908), pp. 502–3. See also *Gesta regis Dagoberti* 44, ed. Krusch, MGH:SRM 2:421–22. It has been suggested that Hincmar of Rheims wrote the *Gesta:* see M. Büchner, "Zur Entstehung und zur Tendenz der *Gesta Dagoberti,*" *Historisches Jahrbuch* 47 (1927): 252–74; J. M. Wallace-Hadrill, *The Long-haired Kings and Other Studies in Frankish History* (London, 1962), pp. 97–100. Charlemagne's own copy of Bede's *Ecclesiastical History* survives in Cambridge University Library, MS. Kk.5.16: see P. H. Blair and R. A. B. Mynors, *The Moore Bede* (Copenhagen, 1959), and B. Bischoff, *Mittelalterliche Studien. Ausgewählte Aufsätze zur Schriftkunde und Literaturgeschichte,* 3 vols. (Stuttgart, 1966–81), 3:160.

87. Heito, *Visio Wettini* 4, ed. Dümmler, MGH:PLAC 2:269.

88. On the political dreams of the ninth century, see C. Fritzsche, "Die lateinischen Visionen des Mittelalters bis zur Mitte des 12. Jahrhunderts," *Romanische Forschungen* 2 (1886): 276–79, [247–79] and 3 (1887): 337–45 [337–69]; M. Dods, *Forerunners of Dante: An Account of Some of the More Important Visions of the Unseen World from the Earliest Times* (Edinburgh, 1903), pp. 192–211; W. Levison, "Die Politik in den Jenseitsvisionen des frühen Mittelalters," *Festgabe Friederich von Bezold* (Bonn, 1921), pp. 81–100, repr. in Levison, *Aus rheinischer und fränkischer Frühzeit* (Düsseldorf, 1948), pp. 229–46; E. D. Nourry (under the pseudonym P. Saintyves), *En marge de la légende dorée: songes, miracles, et survivances. Essai sur la formation de quelques thèmes hagiographiques* (Paris, 1930), pp. 145–51; A. B. van Os, *Religious Visions: The Development of the Eschatological Elements in Mediaeval English Religious Literature* (Amsterdam, 1932), pp. 3–26; H. R. Patch, *The Other World According to Descriptions*

in Medieval Literature (Cambridge, Mass., 1950; repr. 1970), pp. 95–133, and 329–71 for an extensive bibliography; E. Dunninger, *Politische und geschichtliche Elemente in mittelalterlichen Jenseitsvisionen bis zum Ende des 13. Jahrhunderts* (Inaugural-Dissertation, Universität zu Würzburg, 1962); C. J. Holdsworth, "Visions and Visionaries in the Middle Ages," *History* 48 (1963): 148–50 [141–53]; B. de Gaiffier, "La légende de Charlemagne: le péché de l'empereur et son pardon," *Etudes critiques d'hagiographie et d'iconologie,* Subsidia hagiographica, 43 (Brussels, 1967), pp. 260–75; Kamphausen, *Traum und Vision;* A. C. Spearing, *Medieval Dream-Poetry* (Cambridge, 1976), pp. 14–15; Dinzelbacher, "Reflexionen irdischer Sozialstrukturen in mittelalterlichen Jenseitsschilderungen," *Archiv für Kulturgeschichte* 61 (1979): 16–34; Dinzelbacher, *Vision und Visionliteratur im Mittelalter;* M. Aubrun, "Caractères et portée religieuse et sociale des *Visiones* en Occident du VIᵉ au XIᵉ siècle," *Cahiers de civilisation médiévale: Xᵉ–XIIᵉ siècles* 23 (1980): 109–30; Le Goff, "Dreams in the Culture and Collective Psychology of the Medieval West" (1971) *Time, Work, and Culture in the Middle Ages,* trans. A. Goldhammer, (Chicago, 1980), pp. 201–4; Le Goff, *The Birth of Purgatory,* pp. 103–22; Le Goff, *The Medieval Imagination* (1985), trans. A. Goldhammer (Chicago, 1985), pp. 193–242; Le Goff, "The Learned and Popular Dimensions of Journeys in the Otherworld in the Middle Ages," pp. 19–37; Carozzi, "La géographie de l'au-delà," pp. 423–81; F. Neiske, "Vision und Totengedanke," FS 20 (1986): 137–85; M. P. Ciccarese, *Visioni dell'aldilà in Occidente: Fonti, modelli, testi* (Florence, 1987); *Visions of Heaven and Hell before Dante,* ed. Gardiner, pp. 65–79, 129–33; Dinzelbacher, *Revelationes,* Typologie des sources du Moyen Age occidental, 57 (Turnhout, 1991).

CHAPTER THREE: CHARLEMAGNE AND HIS DREAM CRITICS

1. Alcuin, *Aduersus Elipandum libri quattuor* 1.16, PL 101:251D3–6. On Alcuin's idealization of Charlemagne, see J. M. Wallace-Hadrill, *Early Germanic Kingship in England and on the Continent* (Oxford, 1971), pp. 101–6.

2. *Planctus de obitu Karoli* stanza 15, ed. Dümmler, MGH:PLAC 1:436 [435–36]. For a translation, see *Carolingian Civilization: A Reader,* ed. P. E. Dutton (Peterborough, Ont., 1993), pp. 139–40. On the author, see M. Lapidge, "The Authorship of the Adonic Verses 'ad Fidolium' Attributed to Columbanus," *Studi Medievali* 3d ser., 18.2 (1977): 290–97 [249–314]; H. Löwe, "Columbanus und Fidolius," *Deutsches Archiv* 37 (1981): 1–19; M. Herren, "A Ninth-Century Poem for St. Gall's Feast Day and the 'Ad Sethum' of Columbanus," *Studi Medievali* 3d ser., 24 (1983): 487–520.

3. Dhuoda, *Liber Manualis* 1.7, ed. Riché, p. 116; *Planctus de obitu Karoli* stanzas 7, 10, ed. Dümmler, MGH:PLAC 1:435. On Dhuoda, see P. Dronke, *Women Writers of the Middle Ages: A Critical Study of Texts from Perpetua (203) to Marguerite Porete (1310)* (Cambridge, 1985), pp. 36–54.

4. Rimbert, *Vita Anskarii* 2, ed. G. Waitz, MGH:SRGUS (Hanover, 1884), p. 20; W. Lammers, "Anscar: Visionäre Erlebnisformen und Missionsauftrag," *Vestigia Mediaevalia: augsgewählte Aufsätze zur mittelalterlichen Historiographie, Landes- und Kirchengeschichte,* Frankfurter historische Abhandlungen, 19 (Wiesbaden, 1979),

pp. 202–4 [198–218]. On Anskar as visionary, see G. Mehnert, "Ansgar als Visionär: ein Beitrag zur Geschichte der christlichen Visionen des Frühmittelalters," *Schriften des Vereins für Schleswig-Holsteinische Kirchengeschichte* 21 (1965): 44–67.

5. Rimbert, *Vita Anskarii* 3, ed. Waitz, pp. 21–24. See also H. Jankuhn, "Das Missionsfeld Ansgars," FS 1 (1967): 213–21; W. Haas, "*'Foris apostolus—intus monachus'*: *Ansgar als Mönch und 'Apostel des Nordens'*," *Journal of Medieval History* 11 (1985): 1–30; I. Wood, "Christians and Pagans in Ninth-Century Scandinavia," in *The Christianization of Scandinavia—Report of a Symposium Held at Kungälv, Sweden, 4–9 August 1985*, ed. B. Sawyer, P. Sawyer, and Wood (Alingsås, 1987), pp. 36–67.

6. Julius von Schlosser, *Schriftquellen zur Geschichte der karolingischen Kunst*, no. 949, Quellenschriften für Kunstgeschichte und Kunst-Technik des Mittelalters und der Neuzeit, 4 (Vienna, 1892), pp. 341–42.

7. See H. Schnitzler, "Das Kuppelmosaik der Aachener Pfalzkapelle," *Aachener Kunstblätter* 29 (1964): 17–44; Herbert Schrade, "Zum Kuppelmosaik der Pfalzkapelle und zum Theoderich-Denkmal in Aachen," *Aachener Kunstblätter* 30 (1965): 25–37; E. Stephany, "Das Aachener Domschatz: Versuch einer Deutung," *Aachener Kunstblätter* 42 (1972): xx–xxii; P. E. Dutton and E. Jeauneau, "The Verses of the *Codex Aureus* of Saint-Emmeram," *Studi Medievali* 3d ser., 24.1 (1983):113–17 [75–120]. See also F. Kreusch, "Kirche, Atrium und 'Porticus der Aachener Pfalz,'" in *Karl der Grosse: Lebenswerk und Nachleben*, ed. W. Braunfels, 4 vols. (Düsseldorf, 1965), 3:463–533. On the Ciampini drawing, see P. Clemen, *Die Romanische Monumentalmalerei in den Rheinlanden* (Düsseldorf, 1916), pp. 12–19; Schnitzler, "Das Kuppelmosaik," pp. 32–35; C. Heitz, *L'architecture religieuse carolingienne: Les formes et leurs fonctions* (Paris, 1980), pp. 68–77.

8. Lupus of Ferrières, *epistola* 31, ed. Levillain, *Correspondance*, 1:142.10–11.

9. Notker, *Gesta Karoli Magni* 1.31, ed. Haefele, MGH:SRG n.s. 12:42–44.

10. F. L. Ganshof, *The Carolingians and the Frankish Monarchy: Studies in Carolingian History*, trans. J. Sondheimer (Ithaca, N.Y., 1971), pp. 240–55; Dutton, "Beyond the *Topos* of Senescence: The Political Problems of Aged Carolingian Rulers," in *Aging and the Aged in the Middle Ages*, ed. M. M. Sheehan, Papers in Mediaeval Studies, 11 (Toronto, 1990), pp. 75–94. On the *uerbum regis* as law, see Ganshof, *Recherches sur les Capitulaires* (Paris, 1958). On Charlemagne's itinerary, see A. Gauert, "Zum Itinerar Karls des Grossen," in *Karl der Grosse*, 1:307–21. For criticisms of the *missi*, see Theodulf of Orléans, *Versus contra iudices*, ed. Dümmler, MGH:PLAC 1:493–517, and Ganshof, *The Carolingians and the Frankish Monarchy*, pp. 248 and 254 n. 48.

11. ARF 815, p. 141; ARF 822, p. 158; Ermold, *In honorem Hludowici* 2, ed. Faral, p. 66.829–35; Thegan, *Vita Hludowici* 13, ed. G. H. Pertz, MGH:SS 2:593; Astronomer, *Vita Hludowici* 23, ed. Pertz, MGH:SS 2:619.

12. Edward Gibbon, *The History of The Decline and Fall of the Roman Empire*, ed. J. B. Bury, 7 vols. (London, 1909–14), 5:303.

13. VKM, preface, p. 2, and Walahfrid Strabo in his prologue to the VKM, p. xxix. On the date of the VKM, see H. Löwe, "Die Entstehungszeit der Vita Karoli Einhards," *Deutsches Archiv* 39 (1983): 85–103.

14. VKM 3, pp. 5–6; VKM 18, p. 22; and see ARF 771, p. 32. The revised entry of the

ARF 771, p. 33, echoes the theme of Charlemagne's fraternal patience. Cathwulf, a contemporary observer of these events, was amazed that Charlemagne had come to power, "sine sanguinis effusione" ["without the shedding of blood"]: *Epistolae uariorum* 7, ed. Dümmler, MGH:Ep. 4:502.25.

15. Paul the Deacon, *Gesta episcoporum Mettensium*, ed. G. H. Pertz, MGH:SS 2:265.22–28, and Thegan, *Vita Hludowici* 1–2, ed. Pertz, MGH:SS 2:590–91. See also W. Goffart, "Paul the Deacon's *Gesta Episcoporum Mettensium* and the Early Design of Charlemagne's Succession," *Viator* 42 (1986): 59–93.

16. VKM 18, p. 22. The marriage had caused Charlemagne problems from the beginning, as it had outraged Pope Stephen, who feared an alliance of Franks and Lombards: see the stinging letter he wrote, *Codex Carolinus* 45, ed. Gundlach, MGH:Ep. 3:560–63. See also E. Delaruelle, "Charlemagne, Caroloman, Didier et la politique du mariage Franco-Lombard," *Revue historique* 170 (1932): 213–24; M. V. Ary, "The Politics of the Frankish-Lombard Marriage Alliance," *Archivium Historiae Pontificale* 19 (1981): 7–26. On the Lombard princess, see S. Hellmann, "Desiderata," *Neues Archiv* 34 (1908): 208–9. Notker, *Gesta Karoli Magni* 2.17, ed. Haefele, MGH:SRG n.s. 12:82.2–5, says that she was bedridden.

17. VKM 19, p. 24; and see the epitaphs for two of Charlemagne's daughters, ed. Dümmler, MGH:PLAC 1:59–60.

18. VKM 20, p. 26; ARF 792, p. 91.

19. See P. Stafford, "Sons and Mothers: Family Politics in the Early Middle Ages," in *Medieval Women*, ed. D. Baker (Oxford, 1978), pp. 99–100 [79–100]; Stafford, *Queens, Concubines, and Dowagers: The King's Wife in the Early Middle Ages* (Athens, Ga., 1983), pp. 60–61. The Poeta Saxo blamed Tassilo's wife for the contumacy of her husband: *Annales* 2, ed. Winterfeld, MGH:PLAC 4:27.346–63.

20. ARF 771, pp. 32–33; Paschasius Radbertus, *Vita Adalhardi* 7, PL 120:1511C4–10 and the fragments ed. G. H. Pertz, MGH:SS 2:525; Stafford, "Sons and Mothers," pp. 80–83, 91; Stafford, *Queens, Concubines, and Dowagers*, pp. 60–62; S. Konecny, *Die Frauen des karolingischen Königshauses* (Vienna, 1976), pp. 65–71, 81–85; S. F. Wemple, *Women in Frankish Society: Marriage and the Cloister, 500 to 900* (Philadelphia, 1981), pp. 78–79.

21. *Diuisio regnorum*, ed. Boretius, MGH:Cap. 1:126–30. For a translation, see *Carolingian Civilization: A Reader*, pp. 129–33. See W. Schlesinger, "Kaisertum und Reichsteilung zur *Diuisio regnorum* von 806" (1958), repr. in *Zum Kaisertum Karls des Grossen: Beiträge und Aufsätze*, ed. G. Wolf, Wege und Forschung, 38 (Darmstadt, 1972), pp. 117–73. We should not, therefore, accept the thesis that Charlemagne was simply driven by lust: see M. Rouche, "Charlemagne, polygame et incestueux," *L'histoire* 64 (1984): 18–24.

22. Astronomer, *Vita Hludowici* 21, ed. Pertz, MGH:SS 2:618.

23. Thegan, *Vita Hludowici* 19, ed. Pertz, MGH:SS 2:594–95.

24. See the domestic portraits of Charlemagne by Paul the Deacon, *Gesta episcoporum Mettensium*, MGH:SS 2:265; the *Epitaphium* of Queen Hildegard, ed. Dümmler, MGH:PLAC 1:58–59; and the epitaphs for three of Charlemagne's children, MGH:PLAC 1:59–60, 71–73. See also Angilbert, *Ecloga ad Carolum regem*, ed.

Dümmler, MGH:PLAC 1:360–63; Theodulf of Orléans, *carmen* 25, ed. Dümmler, MGH:PLAC 1:483–89. See also W. von den Steinen, "Karl und die Dichter," in *Karl der Grosse*, 2:65–94.

25. Hibernicus Exul, *carmen* 4, ed. Dümmler, MGH:PLAC 1:400.17–20. Alcuin, *epistola* 30, ed. Dümmler, MGH:Ep. 4:71; *epistola* 122, MGH:Ep. 4:179.22–29; *epistola* 119, MGH:Ep. 4:174.16–17; see Prov. 5:17–18.

26. Alcuin, *epistola* 241, ed. Dümmler, MGH:Ep. 4:386.29–387.1. See also Paschasius Radbertus, *Vita Adalhardi* 33, PL 120:1526C3–12 and 1528A14–B3.

27. Alcuin, *epistola* 220, ed. Dümmler, MGH:Ep. 4:364. For Charles's extensive progeny, see S. Rösch, *Caroli Magni Progenies*, vol. 1, Genealogie und Landesgeschichte, 30 (Neustadt an der Aisch, 1977).

28. Bernhard von Simson, *Jahrbücher des fränkischen Reiches unter Ludwig dem Frommen*, 2 vols. (Leipzig, 1874–76), 1:15–19; Astronomer, *Vita Hludowici* 21, MGH:SS 2:618–19.

29. At court in 814 were probably Louis's sisters Bertha, Gisela, Gertrude, Hiltrude, and Ruothild and his five nieces (the daughters of Pepin of Italy). On what Charlemagne had intended for his daughters, see *Diuisio regnorum* 17, ed. Boretius, MGH:Cap. 1:129. On the subsequent career of the princesses, see Simson, *Jahrbücher*, 1:17–19, and Rösch, *Caroli Magni Progenies*, 1:66–71.

30. Nithard, *Historiarum* 1.1, ed. Lauer, pp. 6–8.

31. *Capitulare de disciplina palatii Aquisgranensis* 1, ed. Boretius, MGH:Cap. 1:298.1–7. Pertz suggested that "igroti" was a corruption of "aegroti"; Baluze read "ignoti."

32. See Jonas of Orléans, *De institutione regia* 3.2, ed. Jean Reviron, in *Les idées politico-religieuses d'un évêque du IXe siècle: Jonas d'Orléans et son 'De institutione regia'*, L'église et l'état au Moyen Age, 1 (Paris, 1930), p. 138; Sedulius Scottus, *De rectoribus* 5, ed. Hellmann, pp. 34–36.

33. C. Carozzi, "La géographie de l'au-delà et sa signification pendant le haut Moyen Age," *Popoli e paesi nella cultura altomedievale* 2, Settimane di Studio del Centro Italiano di Studi sull'Alto Medioevo, 29 (Spoleto, 1983), pp. 423–81; Dinzelbacher, *Vision und Visionliteratur im Mittelalter*, Monographien zur Geschichte des Mittelalters, 23 (Stuttgart, 1981), pp. 90–168; A. Morgan, *Dante and the Medieval Other World*, Cambridge Studies in Medieval Literature, 8 (Cambridge, 1990), pp. 11–50. On the distinctions between purgation, purgatorial, and purgatory, see the discussion of Carozzi and J. Le Goff in *Popoli e paesi* (following Carozzi's paper), pp. 483–85, and Le Goff, *The Birth of Purgatory*, trans. A. Goldhammer (Chicago, 1984). See also U. Ebel, "Die literarischen Formen der Jenseits– und Endzeitvisionen," in *Grundriss der romanischen Literatur des Mittelalters*, vol. 6.1, *La littérature didactique, allegorique et satirique* (Heidelberg, 1968), pp. 181–215.

34. J. Ntedika, *L'évocation de l'au-delà dans la prière pour les morts: étude de patristique et de liturgie latines (IVe–VIIIes.)*, Recherches africaines de théologie, 2 (Louvain, 1971), pp. 84–135; F. Neiske, "Vision und Totengedanke," FS 20 (1986): 137–85.

35. "Aus Petersburger Handschriften," ed. W. Wattenbach, *Anzeiger für Kunde der deutschen Vorzeit* 22 (1875): 72–74. The text was originally discovered by J. Mabillon,

Acta sanctorum ordinis sancti Benedicti 4.1 (Paris, 1667), p. 667. On the tradition, see B. de Gaiffier, "La légende de Charlemagne: le péché de l'empereur et son pardon," *Etudes critiques d'hagiographie et d'iconologie,* Subsidia hagiographica, 43 (Brussels, 1967), pp. 260–75; Neiske, "Vision und Totengedanke," pp. 155–56.

36. *Visio Rotcharii,* ed. Wattenbach, p. 73.

37. See 2 Cor. 5:1; John 14:2; Gregory the Great, *Dialogi* 4.36, ed. Moricca, pp. 282–85. On the visionary images of mansions and palaces, see M. Dulaey, *Le rêve dans la vie et la pensée de Saint Augustin* (Paris, 1973), pp. 212–17, and P. Riché, "Les représentations du palais dans les textes littéraires du haut Moyen Age," *Francia* 4 (1976): 168–69 [161–71].

38. Mabillon, *Acta sanctorum,* 4.1:667, identified the author with the Rotgarius of the *Vita sancti Faronis;* F. Lot, "La légende d'Ogier le Danois," *Romania* 66 (1941): 250–53, with Count Ogier; Wattenbach, "Aus Petersburger Handschriften," p. 74, with an unknown monk of Saint-Benoît-sur-Loire (Fleury); but Gaiffier, "La légende de Charlemagne," p. 262, raised a question about the attribution to Fleury. See also Adrevald, *Miracula sancti Benedicti* 18, 20, 31, PL 124:921C–922A, 923D–924C, 935D–936A; J. M. Wallace-Hadrill, *The Frankish Church* (Oxford, 1983), pp. 356–57. For the necrologies of Reichenau, see *Das Verbrüderungsbuch Abtei Reichenau (Einleitung, Register, Faksimile),* ed. J. Autenrieth, D. Geuenich, and K. Schmid, in MGH: *Libri memoriales et necrologia. Nova series,* vol. 1 (Hanover, 1979), pp. 108.C2, 22.D4, 108.B3, 108.B1, 100.B1, 123.B4.

39. Heito, *Visio Wettini* 3, ed. Dümmler, MGH:PLAC 2:269.

40. Heito, *Visio Wettini* 11, ed. Dümmler, MGH:PLAC 2:271.

41. C. Fritzsche, "Die lateinischen Visionen," *Romanische Forschungen* 3 (1887): 337–39. See also G. Björck, *"Onar idein,"* *Eranos* 44 (1946): 308–9; G. D. Kelchner, *Dreams in Old Norse Literature and Their Affinities in Folklore: With an Appendix Containing the Icelandic Texts and Translations* (Cambridge, 1935), pp. 17–20; H. R. Ellis, *The Road to Hel: A Study of the Conception of the Dead in Old Norse Literature* (Cambridge, 1943), pp. 127–35; and, in general, N. Chadwick, "Dreams in Early European Literature," *Celtic Studies: Essays in Memory of Angus Matheson, 1912–1962,* ed. J. Carney and D. Greene (New York, 1968), pp. 33–50.

42. Wisd. of Sol. 6:6–7; M. Rouche, "The Early Middle Ages in the West," in *A History of Private Life,* vol. 1, *From Pagan Rome to Byzantium,* ed. P. Veyne, trans. A. Goldhammer, (Cambridge, Mass., 1987), pp. 489–91 [410–549].

43. Ermold, *In honorem Hludowici* 2, ed. Dümmler, MGH:PLAC 2:29–30.155–72.

44. Walahfrid Strabo,*Visio Wettini,* preface, ed. Dümmler, MGH:PLAC 2:303, and for the Charlemagne acrostic, pp. 318–19.444–61; also D. A. Traill, *Walahfrid Strabo's Visio Wettini: Text, Translation, and Commentary,* Lateinische Sprache und Literatur des Mittelalters, 1 (Bern, 1974), p. 197. On Charlemagne in this vision, see E. Dunninger, *Politische und geschichtliche Elemente in Mittelalterlichen Jenseitsvisionen bis zum Ende des 13. Jahrhunderts* (Inaugural-Dissertation, Universität zu Würzburg, 1962), pp. 61–63, and H. J. Kamphausen, *Traum und Vision in der lateinischen Poesie der Karolingerzeit,* Lateinische Sprache und Literatur des Mittelalters, 4 (Bern, 1975), pp. 141–45. See also M. Brooke, "The Prose and Verse Hagiography of Walahfrid

Strabo," in *Charlemagne's Heir: New Perspectives on the Reign of Louis the Pious (814–840)*, ed. P. Godman and R. Collins (Oxford, 1990) pp. 551–64.

45. Walahfrid Strabo, *Visio Wettini*, ed. Dümmler, MGH:PLAC 2:319.460–65.

46. Walahfrid Strabo, *Visio Wettini*, ed. Dümmler, MGH:PLAC 2:318.445. See Jer. 2:13.

47. H. Houben, "*Visio cuiusdam pauperculae mulieris*: Überlieferung und Herkunft eines frühmittelalterlichen Visionstextes (mit Neuedition)," *Zeitschrift für die Geschichte des Oberrheins* 124 [NF85] (1976): 31–42. Also edited by W. Wattenbach and W. Levison in *Deutschlands Geschichtsquellen im Mittelalter: Vorzeit und Karolinger*, 2d ed., 5 vols., rev. by H. Löwe (Weimar, 1952–73), 3:317–18. For a translation, see *Carolingian Civilization: A Reader*, pp. 179–80. See also Levison, "Die Politik in den Jenseitsvisionen des Frühen Mittelalters," *Aus rheinischer und fränkischer Frühzeit* (Düsseldorf, 1948), pp. 237–39.

48. On *agapes*, see Gaiffier, "La légende de Charlemagne," p. 262 n. 4; Neiske, "Vision und Totengedanken," p. 154. See also Gregory the Great, *Dialogi* 4.57, ed. Moricca, p. 315.

49. *Ordinatio imperii*, ed. Boretius, MGH:Cap. 1:270–73. For a translation, see *Carolingian Civilization: A Reader*, pp. 176–79. See also Ganshof, *The Carolingians and the Frankish Monarchy*, pp. 273–88. On the Bernard events, see T. F. X. Noble, "The Revolt of King Bernard of Italy in 817: Its Causes and Consequences," *Studi Medievali* 3d ser., 15 (1974): 315–26; J. Jarnut, "Kaiser Ludwig der Fromme und König Bernhard von Italien. Der Versuch einer Rehabilitierung," *Studi Medievali* 3d ser., 30 (1989): 637–48; K. F. Werner, "*Hludouicus Augustus*: Gouverner l'empire chrétien—Idées et réalités," in *Charlemagne's Heir*, pp. 34–54 [3–123].

50. Houben, "*Visio cuiusdam pauperculae mulieris*," 37–40. Heito was interested in dreams and visions, and another text was sent to him: see K. Hampe, "Eine ungedruckte Vision aus karolingischer Zeit," *Neues Archiv* 22 (1897): 628–33; the same, ed. H. Farmer in *Studia Monastica* 1 (1959): 395–97; and in *La chronique de Saint-Maixent, 751–1140*, ed. J. Verdon, Les classiques de l'histoire de France au Moyen Age, 33 (Paris, 1979), pp. 38–44. On the latter, see F. Dolbeau, "Une vision adressée à Heito de Reichenau († 836) dans *La chronique de Saint-Maixent*," *Analecta Bollandiana* 98 (1980): 404. Werner, "*Hludouicus Augustus*," pp. 44–45 n. 147, seems to assume that the author of the *Vision of the Poor Woman of Laon* was connected with Laon or Rheims, but does not cite Houben or the many features that connect this dream text with Heito and Reichenau.

51. Notker, *Gesta Karoli Magni* 2.6, ed. Haefele, MGH:SRG n.s. 12:53–58; VKM 33, p. 41; K. Brunner, *Oppositionelle Gruppen im Karolingerreich*, Veröffentlichungen des Instituts für österreichische Geschichtsforschung, 25 (Vienna, 1979), p. 76.

52. For Waldo, see Heito, *Visio Wettini* preface, ed. Dümmler, MGH:PLAC 2:267, and 10, p. 270; Walahfrid Strabo, *Visio Wettini*, ed. Dümmler, MGH:PLAC 2:305.37. For Gerold, see Heito, *Visio Wettini* 27, ed. Dümmler, MGH:PLAC 2:274; Walahfrid Strabo, *Visio Wettini*, ed. Dümmler, MGH:PLAC 2:329–30.802–26. See also K. Schmid, "Bemerkungen zur Anlage des Reichenauer Verbrüderungsbuches: Zugleich ein Beitrag zum Verständnis der *Visio Wettini*," in *Landesgeschichte und Geistesgeschichte. Festschrift*

für Otto Herding zum 65. Geburtstag, ed. K. Elm, E. Gönner, and E. Hillenbrand (Stuttgart, 1977), pp. 24–41; Schmid, "Zeugnisse der Memorialüberlieferung aus der Zeit Ludwigs des Frommen," in *Charlemagne's Heir,* pp. 517–18 [509–22].

53. See *Das Verbrüderungsbuch der Abtei Reichenau,* in MGH: *Libri Memoriales et Necrologia. Nova Series,* 1:98–99; also *Liber Confraternitatum Sancti Galli, Augiensis, Fabariensis,* ed. P. Piper, MGH: *Necrologia Germaniae* (Berlin, 1884), pp. 262–64. See S. Airlie, "The Political Behaviour of the Secular Magnates in Francia, 829–879" (Ph.D. diss., Oxford, 1985), pp. 43–56.

54. Ermold, *In honorem Hludowici* 1, ed. Faral, pp. 20–22.214–23, 46.578–87, 50.640–41, described Bego as a faithful, wise, and brave chief of Charlemagne. It is he who, in *In honorem Hludowici* 2, ed. Faral, p. 60.756–69, consoled Louis the Pious on the loss of his father. Bego married one of Louis's daughters; the emperor was saddened to hear of his death in 816, and divided his goods and titles among Bego's sons (p. 88.1134–37). For the negative Rheims view, see *Vita Rigoberti* 12, ed. W. Levison, MGH:SRM 7:59. See also L. Levillain, "Les comtes de Paris à l'époque franque," *Le Moyen Age* 51 (1941): 186–89 [137–205]; Werner, *"Hludouicus Augustus,"* pp. 44–45.

55. Freud, *The Interpretation of Dreams, Standard Edition of the Complete Psychological Works of Sigmund Freud,* trans. and ed. J. Strachey, 24 vols. (London: 1953–74), 5:570, repeats the story of a Parthian queen who ordered molten gold to be poured down the throat of the dead triumvir Crassus (53 B.C.) while saying, "Now you have what you wanted." Though Freud's exact reference is obscure, see Lucius Annaeus Florus 1.46.11 and Dio Cassius 40.27.3. Seneca, *epistola* 122.12, had said, "Multi bona comedunt" ["Many people eat their property"]. See Heito, *Visio Wettini* 22, ed. Dümmler, MGH:PLAC 2:273.

56. Northrup Frye, *Divisions on a Ground: Essays on Canadian Culture* (Toronto, 1982), p. 161. On the importance of the *secundus a rege,* see Brunner, *Oppositionelle Gruppen,* pp. 27–35.

57. P. R. McKeon, "The Empire of Louis the Pious: Faith, Politics, and Personality," *Revue Bénédictine* 90 (1980): 51 [50–62]; and see Egon Boshoff, *Erzbischof Agobard von Lyon: Leben und Werk,* Kölner historische Abhandlungen, 17 (Cologne, 1969), pp. 38–41.

58. Rudolf of Fulda, *Vita Leobae abbatissae Biscofesheimensis* 20, ed. G. Waitz, MGH:SS 15.1:130. For a translation, see *Carolingian Civilization: A Reader,* pp. 311–25.

59. Bernard and Wetti were both remembered in the Reichenau necrologies: see *Das Verbrüderungsbuch der Abtei Reichenau,* pp. 114.A2, 12.B3, 7.B3, 45.B3, 69.B4, 89.C4. On the liturgy of death, see Neiske, "Vision und Totengedanken," pp. 152–54; D. Sicard, *La liturgie de la mort dans l'église latine des origines à la reforme carolingienne* (Münster, 1978), pp. 399–418.

60. Bede, *Historia ecclesiastica* 5.12 and *Visio sancti Pauli* 19, ed. T. Silverstein, in *Visio Sancti Pauli: The History of the Apocalypse in Latin Together with Nine Texts* (London, 1935), p. 136.

61. ARF 822, p. 158; Paschasius Radbertus, *Vita Adalhardi* 51, PL 120.1534D6–1535A10. On Theodosius, penance, and the virtue of imperial humility, see Augustine, *De ciuitate dei* 5.26 and 5.24, ed. B. Dombart and A. Kalb, in Corpus Christianorum:

Series Latina, 47 (Turnhout, 1955), pp. 160–63; Jonas of Orléans, *De institutione regia* 3, ed. Reviron, pp. 138–44; T. F. X. Noble, "Louis the Pious and his Piety Reconsidered," *Revue Belge de philologie et d'histoire* 58 (1980): 312–13 [297–316]; J. L. Nelson, "Kingship, Law, and Liturgy in the Political Thought of Hincmar of Rheims," *Politics and Ritual in Early Medieval Europe* (London, 1986), pp. 135–36 [133–71].

62. *Episcoporum de poenitentia quam Hludowicus imperator professus est relatio Compendiensis,* ed. Boretius and Krause, MGH:Cap. 2:54.7; Thegan, *Vita Hludowici* 22–23, ed. Pertz, MGH:SS 2:596. See also M. de Jong, "Power and Humility in Carolingian Society: The Public Penance of Louis the Pious," *Early Medieval Europe* 1 (1992): 31–32 [29–52].

63. B. Stock, *The Implications of Literacy: Written Language and Models of Interpretation in the Eleventh and Twelfth Centuries* (Princeton, N.J., 1983), pp. 90–92.

64. Walahfrid Strabo, *Visio Wettini,* ed. Dümmler, MGH:PLAC 2:330.845–46, 332.919–21.

65. *Mittelalterliche Bibliothekskataloge Deutschlands und der Schweiz,* vol. 1, *Die Bistümer Konstanz und Chur,* ed. P. Lehmann (Munich, 1918), p. 259 [257–62]. See also R. McKitterick, *The Carolingians and the Written Word* (Cambridge, 1989), pp. 179–82.

66. Heito, *Visio Wettini* 10, ed. Dümmler, MGH:PLAC 2:270–71; E. Kleinschmidt, "Zur Reichenauer Überlieferung der *Visio Wettini* im 9. Jahrhundert," *Deutsches Archiv* 30 (1974): 199–207; J. Autenrieth, "Heitos Prosaniederschrift der *Visio Wettini*—von Walahfrid Stabo redigiert?" in *Geschichtsschreibung und geistiges Leben im Mittelalter. Festschrift für Heinz Löwe zum 65 Geburtstag,* ed. K. Hauck and H. Mordek (Cologne, 1978), pp. 172–78; Houben, "*Visio cuiusdam pauperculae mulieris,*" p. 36; *Mittelalterliche Bibliothekskataloge,* 1:265.

67. *Mittelalterliche Bibliothekskataloge,* 1:84, 87–89; McKitterick, *The Carolingians and the Written Word,* pp. 183–84; on the text of the Saint-Gall copy of the *Vision of Saint Paul,* see Silverstein, *Visio Sancti Pauli,* pp. 131–47.

68. On various manuscript collections of these ninth-century dreams, see W. Levison's discussion of the manuscripts in which the Merovingian *Visio Baronti* occurs: MGH:SRM 5 (Hanover, 1910), pp. 372–77; Dunninger, *Politische und geschichtliche Elemente,* pp. 16–17; A. M. Peden, "Macrobius and Mediaeval Dream Literature," *Medium Aevum* 54 (1985): 61–62 [59–73]; Traill, *Walahfrid Strabo's Visio Wettini,* pp. 13 and n. 5, 33.

69. Walahfrid Strabo, *Visio Wettini,* preface, ed. Dümmler, MGH:PLAC 2:301–3; the special appeal, ed. Dümmler, MGH:PLAC 2:328.762–68; Traill, *Walahfrid Strabo's Visio Wettini,* pp. 9–11; P. Godman, *Poets and Emperors: Frankish Politics and Carolingian Poetry* (Oxford, 1987), pp. 130–33.

70. Le Goff, *The Birth of Purgatory,* p. 95.

71. Jonas of Orléans, *De institutione regia* 1, ed. Reviron, pp. 134–35; 8, p. 158.

72. H. H. Anton, *Fürstenspiegel und Herrscherethos in der Karolingerzeit,* Bonner historische Forschungen, 32 (Bonn, 1968), p. 95, and Wallace-Hadrill, *Early Germanic Kingship,* p. 103. On the genre in general, see Anton, *Fürstenspiegel;* M. L. W. Laistner, *Thought and Letters in Western Europe: A.D. 500 to 900,* 2d ed. (Ithaca, N.Y.,

1957; repr. 1966), pp. 315–21; Wallace-Hadrill, "The *Via Regia* of the Carolingian Age," in *Trends in Medieval Political Thought*, ed. B. Smalley (Oxford, 1965), pp. 22–41, repr. in Wallace-Hadrill, *Early Medieval History* (Oxford, 1975), pp. 181–200.

These advice manuals were meant to shape the character of young princes. Smaragdus's *Via regia*, PL 102:933–70, was composed between 812 and 815 for Louis the Pious: see Laistner, "The Date and the Recipient of Smaragdus' *Via Regia*," *Speculum* 3 (1928): 392–97. Jonas of Orléans's *De institutione regia* was written for Pepin, son of Louis the Pious, in 834. Dhuoda's *Liber manualis* was composed in the early 840s for her young son William. Hincmar, too, wrote works for the edification of Charles the Bald's son and grandson: for Louis the Stammerer, *Ad Ludouicum regem Balbum. Novi regis instructio ad rectam regni administrationem*, PL 125:983–90, and for young Carloman, *De ordine palatii*. Note, however, that Hincmar's *De regis persona et regio ministerio*, PL 125:833–56, was written late in Charles the Bald's life and has a corrective function.

73. On Charlemagne as *pater*, see Alcuin, *carmen* 45, ed. Dümmler, MGH:PLAC 1:257.25, 258.27; *Karolus Magnus et Leo Papa*, ed. Dümmler, MGH:PLAC 1:379.504. See also K. J. Leyser, "Concepts of Europe in the Early Middle Ages," *Past and Present* 137 (1992): 25–47. On the emperor's charitable acts, for which he sought an eternal reward rather than damnation, see *Capitulare missorum generale* (802) 14, ed. Boretius, MGH:Cap. 1:94. H. Fichtenau, *The Carolingian Empire: The Age of Charlemagne*, trans. P. Munz (New York, 1964), p. 185, thought that Charlemagne had provided generously for the church in his will in order to secure prayer for his soul.

74. On these changing cultural patterns, see Godman, *Poets and Emperors*, pp. 143–48; F. Mütherich, "Book Illumination at the Court of Louis the Pious," in *Charlemagne's Heir*, pp. 594–96 [593–604].

75. See Godman, *Poets and Emperors*, pp. 172–73.

76. Gaiffier, "La légende de Charlemagne," pp. 266–75; Radbod, *De uita sanctae uirginis Christi Amelbergae*, PL 132:551C–552C; Rouche, "Charlemagne, polygame et incestueux," *L'histoire* 64 (1984): 18–24.

77. *Concilium Parisiense* (825) 2.1 (55), ed. Werminghoff, MGH:Con. 2:649; Jonas of Orléans, *De institutione regia* 3, ed. Reviron, p. 138. See Isidore, *Etymologiae* 9.3.1, ed. W. M. Lindsay, in *Isidori Hispalensis Episcopi Etymologiarum siue Originum libri XX*, 2 vols. (Oxford, 1911).

CHAPTER FOUR: LOUIS'S THEATER OF ILLUSIONS

1. Paschasius Radbertus, *Epitaphium Arsenii* 2.8, ed. Dümmler, p. 68. See also 2.9, pp. 71–73; D. Ganz, "The *Epitaphium Arsenii* and Opposition to Louis the Pious," in *Charlemagne's Heir: New Perspectives on the Reign of Louis the Pious (814–840)*, ed. P. Godman and R. Collins (Oxford, 1990), pp. 538–41 [537–50]; H. Peltier, *Pascase Radbert, Abbé de Corbie: contribution à l'étude de la vie monastique et de la pensée chrétienne aux temps carolingiens* (Amiens, 1938); W. Wehlen, *Geschichtsschreibung und Staatsauffassung im Zeitalter Ludwigs des Frommen*, Historische Studien, 418 (Lübeck, 1970), pp. 105–30.

2. Hibernicus Exul, *carmen* 5, ed. Dümmler, MGH:PLAC 1:400.12; Ovid, *Fasti* 1.225; Paschasius Radbertus, *Epitaphium Arsenii* 1.3, ed. Dümmler, p. 25.

3. Paschasius Radbertus, *Epitaphium Arsenii* 2.1, ed. Dümmler, p. 61.

4. Jonas of Orléans, *De institutione regia* 10–11, ed. Reviron, pp. 162–71; Exod. 5:7–12.

5. Einhard, *epistola* 40, ed. Hampe, MGH:Ep. 5:130.129–30.

6. F. L. Ganshof, "Louis the Pious Reconsidered" (1957), *The Carolingians and the Frankish Monarchy: Studies in Carolingian History,* trans. J. Sondheimer (Ithaca, N.Y., 1971), p. 113 and n. 5 [261–72]; P. R. McKeon, "The Empire of Louis the Pious," *Revue Bénédictine* 90 (1980): 50–51; T. F. X. Noble, "Louis the Pious and his Piety Reconsidered," *Revue Belge* 58 (1980): 307–8; Noble, "The Monastic Ideal as a Model for Empire: The Case of Louis the Pious," *Revue Bénédictine* 86 (1976): 235–50.

7. Thegan, *Vita Hludowici* 1–6, ed. Pertz, MGH:SS 2:590–91; Noble, "Louis the Pious and the Frontiers of the Frankish Realm," in *Charlemagne's Heir,* p. 341 [333–47]. For a translation of Thegan's biography of Louis, see *Carolingian Civilization: A Reader,* ed. P. E. Dutton (Peterborough, Ont., 1993), pp. 141–55. On Thegan, see E. Tremp, *Studien zu den Gesta Hludowici imperatoris des Trierer Chorbischofs Thegan,* in MGH:Schriften 32 (Hanover, 1988).

8. Astronomer, *Vita Hludowici* 21, ed. Pertz, MGH:SS 2:618; ARF 817, p. 148; Astronomer, *Vita Hludowici* 29, ed. Pertz, MGH:SS 2:623; J. M. Wallace-Hadrill, *The Frankish Church* (Oxford, 1983), p. 217; Noble, "Some Observations on the Deposition of Archbishop Theodulf of Orléans in 817," *Journal of the Rocky Mountain Medieval and Renaissance Association* 2 (1981): 30 [29–41].

9. Moduin, *carmen* 73, ed. Dümmler, MGH:PLAC 1:570–71.33–48 [569–73]; Theodulf, *carmen* 72.1, ed. Dümmler, MGH:PLAC 1:563–64.13–26; Godman, *Poets and Emperors: Frankish Politics and Carolingian Poetry* (Oxford, 1987), pp. 94–106; D. Schaller, "Vortrags– und Zirkulardichtung am Hof Karls des Grossen," *Mittellateinisches Jahrbuch* 6 (1970): 14–36, and "Poetic Rivalries at the Court of Charlemagne," *Classical Influences on European Culture (A.D. 500–1500),* ed. R. R. Bolgar (Cambridge, 1971), pp. 151–57.

10. Theodulf, *carmen* 14, ed. Dümmler, MGH:PLAC 1:468–69; Cyprian, *epistola* 10.3, ed. G. Hartel, CSEL 3.1 (Vienna, 1868), pp. 352–53, and also in MGH:PLAC 1:468 n. 2. See Paul the Deacon, *carmen* 52, stanza 19, ed. Dümmler, MGH:PLAC 1:82. On the theme of senescence, see Dutton, "Beyond the *Topos* of Senescence: The Political Problems of Aged Carolingian Rulers," in *Aging and the Aged in the Middle Ages,* ed. M. M. Sheehan, Papers in Mediaeval Studies, 11 (Toronto, 1990), pp. 77–81.

11. Theodulf, *carmen* 72.1., ed. Dümmler, MGH:PLAC 1:564–65.25–66. On Theodulf and this poem, see H. Liebeschütz, "Theodulf of Orléans and the Problem of the Carolingian Renaissance," in *Fritz Saxl, 1890–1948. A Volume of Memorial Essays from His Friends in England,* ed. D. J. Gordon (London, 1957), pp. 77–92.

12. Josh. 3:7–17; Theodulf, *carmen* 72.2, ed. Dümmler, MGH:PLAC 1:465–66.

13. Theodulf, *carmen* 72.3, ed. Dümmler, MGH:PLAC 1:567.131–32.

14. Godman, *Poets and Emperors,* pp. 106–29; K. F. Werner, "*Hludouicus Au-*

gustus: Gouverner l'empire chrétien—Idées et réalités," in *Charlemagne's Heir,* pp. 109–20.

15. G. Monod, *Etudes critiques sur les sources de l'histoire carolingienne,* vol. 1, *Les annales carolingiennes des origines à 829* (Paris, 1898), pp. 131–41; L. Malbos, "L'annaliste royale sous Louis le Pieux," *Le Moyen Age* 82 (1966): 225–33; M. McCormick, *Les annales du haut Moyen Age,* Typologie des sources du Moyen Age occidental, 14 (Turnhout, 1975).

16. ARF 823, p. 162; ARF 825, p. 167; ARF 826, pp. 170–71; ARF 827, p. 173.

17. See particularly ARF 826–27, pp. 166–67.

18. ARF 820, p. 154.

19. ARF 821–22, p. 157; ARF 823, pp. 163–64; ARF 824, pp. 164–67; ARF 825, p. 168; ARF 827, p. 173; ARF 829, pp. 176–77.

20. W. Wattenbach and W. Levison, *Deutschlands Geschichtsquellen im Mittelalter: Vorzeit und Karolinger,* 2d ed., 5 vols., rev. H. Löwe (Weimar, 1952–73), 2:253–55; McCormick, *Les annales du haut Moyen Age,* pp. 41–42; L. Halphen, in Einhard, *Vie de Charlemagne,* ed. Halphen, 4th ed. (1923; repr. Paris, 1967), pp. vii–viii, 81 n. 16; and A. Kleinclausz, *Eginhard* (Paris, 1942), pp. 235–39.

21. VKM 32, p. 36. Halphen, in Einhard, *Vie de Charlemagne,* p. 89 n. 3, believed the first part of the statement to derive from Suetonius, *Vitae Caesarum:* Caligula 57 and the last part from Claudius 46. For omens of imperial deaths, see Suetonius, *Vitae Caesarum:* Julius Caesar 81, Augustus 97, Tiberius 74, Caligula 57, Claudius 46, Nero 46, Galba 18, Vitellius 18, Vespasian 23, and Domitian 23.

The *terminus ad quem* for the VKM is set by Lupus of Ferrières's letter to Einhard (ca. 829–30) in which he refers to the work: *epistola* 1, ed. Levillain, *Correspondance,* 1:6. M. Lintzel, "Die Zeit der Entstehung von Einhards *Vita Karoli,*" *Beiträge zur Geschichte des Mittelalters. Festschrift für R. Holtzmann* (Berlin, 1933), pp. 22–42, dated the letter to 830–36. But Levillain, *Correspondance,* 1:2–10, and Ganshof, *The Carolingians and the Frankish Monarchy,* pp. 4, 11 n. 23, dated the letter to 829–30. H. Löwe, "Die Entstehungszeit der Vita Karoli Einhards," *Deutsches Archiv* 39 (1983): 85–103, has argued that the VKM was most probably composed ca. 825–26.

22. According to the royal annals, eclipses of the moon occurred on 2 September 806, 26 February and 22 August 807, 26 December 809, and 21 June and 15 December 810. Eclipses of the sun occurred on 11 February 807, 7 June and 30 November 810, and 13 May 812. The dark spot *(macula quaedam atri coloris)* seen for seven days is identifiable, since the annalist reported that on 17 March 807 Mercury appeared as a small dark spot on the sun *(in sole quasi parua macula)* and was seen for eight days.

23. ARF 817, p. 146; Halphen, in Einhard, *Vie de Charlemagne,* pp. 90–91 n. 1; Astronomer, *Vita Hludowici* 28, ed. Pertz, MGH:SS 2:621; P. R. McKeon, "817: Une année désastreuse et presque fatale pour les Carolingiens," *Le Moyen Age* 84 (1978): 5–12; Ganshof, *The Carolingians and the Frankish Monarchy,* p. 13 n. 42.

24. VKM 32, p. 36, and see the addition to ARF 813, p. 137; VKM 17, p. 20; B. von Simson, *Jahrbücher des fränkischen Reiches unter Karl dem Grossen,* 2 vols. (Leipzig, 1888), 2:510–13; Halphen, in Einhard, *Vie de Charlemagne,* p. 91 n. 3.

25. H. Fichtenau, *The Carolingian Empire: The Age of Charlemagne*, trans. P. Munz (New York, 1964), p. 179; VKM 32, pp. 36–37.

26. ARF 810, p. 132; AX 810, p. 4; *Capitulare missorum Aquisgranense primum*, ed. Boretius, MGH:Cap. 1:153; *Richolfi archiepiscopi ad Eginonem epistola*, ed. Boretius, MGH:Cap. 1:249; Agobard, *De grandine et tonitruis* 16, ed. Van Acker, pp. 14.1–15.7 (PL 104:157C4–158C3); Paschasius Radbertus, *Epitaphium Arsenii* 2.1, ed. Dümmler, p. 61; VKM, p. 36; Simson, *Jahrbücher des fränkischen Reiches unter Karl dem Grossen*, 2:438–41.

27. VKM 32, p. 37; ARF 803, p. 117, and ARF 829, p. 176. Halphen, *Vie de Charlemagne*, p. 92 n. 2, noted that in Suetonius, *Vitae Caesarum:* Augustus 97 and Caligula 57, imperial deaths were signaled by lightning bolts. Moreover, in ARF 829, pp. 176–77, it is reported that an earthquake struck Aachen and ripped most of the lead tiles from the royal chapel's roof.

28. VKM 32, p. 37; Suetonius, *Vitae Caesarum:* Augustus 97; Halphen, in Einhard, *Vie de Charlemagne*, pp. 92–93 n. 3.

29. Louis received some verses from Gerward, ed. Dümmler, MGH:PLAC 2:216, that were recorded in a manuscript of the biography: see VKM, 6th ed., ed. Waitz, p. xxix, xvii. On Gerward as Louis's librarian, see B. Bischoff, "Die Hofbibliothek unter Ludwig dem Frommen," *Mittelalterliche Studien. Ausgewählte Aufsätze zur Schriftkunde und Literaturgeschichte*, 3 vols. (Stuttgart, 1966–81), 3:172–73 [170–86].

30. ARF 826, pp. 171–72; Astronomer, *Vita Hludowici* 40, ed. Pertz, MGH:SS 2:630.

31. ARF 827, p. 174; Einhard, *Translatio et miracula sanctorum Marcellini et Petri*, ed. G. Waitz, MGH:SS 15.1:239–64. For a translation of Einhard's *Translatio et miracula*, see *Carolingian Civilization: A Reader*, pp. 198–246. See also P. J. Geary, *Furta Sacra: Thefts of Relics in the Central Middle Ages* (Princeton, N.J., 1978), pp. 52–59, 143–46; J. Fleckenstein, "Einhard, seine Gründung und sein Vermächtnis in Seligenstadt," *Ordnungen und forende Krafte des Mittelalters: Ausgewählte Beiträge* (Göttingen, 1989), pp. 84–111.

32. On the placement of altars, relics, and images in the church of Saint-Riquier, see C. Heitz, *L'architecture religieuse carolingienne: Les formes et leurs fonctions* (Paris, 1980), pp. 56–62.

33. Einhard, *epistola* 14 (April 830, referring to an illness of 829), ed. Hampe, MGH:Ep. 5:117; *Translatio et miracula* 4.6–7, ed. Waitz, MGH:SS 15.1:257–58. See M. Bondois, *La translation des saints Marcellin et Pierre: étude sur Einhard et sa vie politique de 827 à 834* (Paris, 1907), p. 90 n. 1.

34. Einhard, *epistola* 15, ed. Hampe, MGH:Ep. 5:118. On Einhard as a lay abbot, see F. J. Felten, *Äbte und Laienäbte im Frankenreich. Studien zum Verhältnis von Staat und Kirche im früheren Mittelalter*, Monographien zur Geschichte des Mittelalters, 20 (Stuttgart, 1980), pp. 283–86.

35. Einhard, *epistola* 10, ed. Hampe, MGH:Ep. 5:113–14; *Translatio et miracula* 3.13, ed. Waitz, MGH:SS 15.1:252–53; Bondois, *La translation des saints Marcellin et Pierre*, pp. 86–91.

36. *Translatio et miracula* 3.6 and 3.12, ed. Waitz, MGH:SS 15.1:250, 252.

37. *Translatio et miracula* 3.13, ed. Waitz, MGH:SS 15.1:252–53.

38. Ibid.

39. Dan. 8:27.

40. Petrus, *Quaestiones in Danielem* (Dan. 8:16), PL 96:1356B7–10. On this commentary, which is dependent upon Jerome, see M. Manitius, *Geschichte der lateinischen Literatur des Mittelalters*, 3 vols., Handbuch der Altertumswissenschaft, 9.2 (Munich, 1911; repr. 1965), 1:453.

41. Petrus, *Quaestiones in Danielem*, PL 96:1356B11–C1; Luke 1:19, 26–35.

42. Dan. 9:21–27; C. Heitz, *Recherches sur les rapports entre architecture et liturgie à l'époque carolingienne* (Paris, 1963), pp. 221–29.

43. S. Airlie, "Bonds of Power and Bonds of Association in the Court Circle of Louis the Pious," in *Charlemagne's Heir*, p. 195 [191–204].

44. Einhard, *Translatio et miracula* 3.14, ed. Waitz, MGH:SS 15.1:253. For other cases of possession, see AF 858, pp. 51–53, and Joseph of Aquitaine, *Historia translationis corporum sanctorum Ragnoberti et Zenonis* 7, PL 106:899D. The Synod of Frankfurt (794) 25, ed. Boretius, MGH:Cap. 1:76, had also stated that the previous year of famine "was filled with talk about empty harvests devoured by demons and voices of reproach were heard." On Carolingian demonology, see G. Tabacco, "Agiografia e demonologia come strumenti ideologici in età carolingia," in *Santi e demoni nell'alto medioevo occidentale (secoli v–xi)*, 2 vols., Settimane di Studio del Centro Italiano di Studi sull'Alto Medioevo, 26 (Spoleto, 1989), 1:121–53.

The demon's name is Wiggo or Wiggon as cited by Bondois and others: see Pope Gregory III, *epistola*, ed. Dümmler, MGH:Ep. 3:292. Wiggo calls himself "apud inferos ianitor." In some versions of the *Visio sancti Pauli* 20, ed. Silverstein, p. 192, there is talk of the "ostiarius inferni" and "ostiarius, minister infernalis."

45. Einhard, *Translatio et miracula* 3.12, ed. Waitz, MGH:SS 15.1:252, 3.14, p. 254.

46. See above pp. 219–22.

47. Paschasius Radbertus, *Epitaphium Arsenii* 2.1, ed. Dümmler, p. 61. See also F. L. Ganshof, "Am Voraben der ersten Krise der Regierung Ludwigs des Frommen: Die Jahre 828 und 829," FS 6 (1972): 44 [39–54].

48. See above pp. 81–82, 287 n. 3.

49. Ermold, *In honorem Hludowici* 2, ed. Faral, p. 66.840–47.

50. ARF 828, p. 176; MGH:Con. 2.2:597–98. On the records of the councils, see pp. 596–680. On the manuscript tradition of this letter, see pp. 597–99; on the element of falsification, Bondois, *La translation des saints Marcellin et Pierre*, pp. 94–97.

51. MGH:Con. 2.2:599.27–34.

52. MGH:Con. 2.2:600.24–26.

53. *Concilium Parisiense* (829) 50–53, 57, ed. Werminghoff, MGH:Con. 2.2:643–48, 653–54. See also Bondois, *La translation des saints Marcellin et Pierre*, p. 94.

54. *Concilium Parisiense* (829), prologue and 2 (69), ed. Werminghoff, MGH:Con. 2.2:606–7 and pp. 669–71; Jon. 3; 1 Kings 21:29; 2 Chron. 33. After the 820s this was to be a frequent theme. Paschasius Radbertus, *In threnos siue Lamentationes Jeremiae libri quinque* 4, PL 120:1220D9–10: "et propter iniquitates sacerdotum et principum, hinc et inde tanta crebrescunt mala."

Notes to Pages 100–103 291

55. MGH:Con. 2.2:649–51; Jonas of Orléans, *De institutione regia* 3, ed. Reviron, pp.138–44; *Concilium Parisiense* (829) prologue, ed. Werminghoff, MGH:Con. 2.2:607.44–45; and *Concilium Parisiense* (829) 1.5, MGH:Con. 2.2:612–14.

56. See Ganshof, "Am Voraben der ersten Krise der Regierung Ludwigs des Frommen," pp. 47–50.

57. Agobard, *epistola* 15, ed. Dümmler, MGH:Ep. 5:224.8–11.

58. Walahfrid Strabo, *De imagine Tetrici*, ed. Dümmler, MGH:PLAC 2:370–78. See F. von Bezold, "Kaiserin Judith und ihr Dichter Walahfrid Strabo," *Historische Zeitschrift* 130 (1923): 375–439; H. Homeyer, "Zu Walahfrid Strabos Gedicht über das Aachener Theoderich-Denkmal," *Studi Medievali* 3d ser., 12 (1971): 889–913; Godman, *Poets and Emperors*, pp. 133–45; M. Herren, "The 'De imagine Tetrici' of Walahfrid Strabo: Edition and Translation," *Journal of Medieval Latin* 1 (1991): 118–39.

59. *Diuisio regni*, ed. Boretius and Krause, MGH:Cap. 2:21–24.

60. Thegan, *Vita Hludowici* 36, ed. Pertz, MGH:SS 2:597; Astronomer, *Vita Hludowici* 44, ed. Pertz, MGH:SS 2:633; Odo Ariberti, *Narratio de morte Bernardi*, ed. M. Bouquet et al., in *Recueil des historiens des Gaules et de la France*, 24 vols. (Paris, 1738–1904), 7:286–87.

61. Astronomer, *Vita Hludowici* 44, ed. Pertz, MGH:SS 2:633. On Pepin, see R. Collins, "Pepin I and the Kingdom of Aquitaine," in *Charlemagne's Heir*, pp. 363–89.

62. Paschasius Radbertus, *Epitaphium Arsenii* 2.7, ed. Dümmler, p. 67.

63. Agobard of Lyons, *Cartula de Ludouici imperatoris poenitentia*, ed. Van Acker, pp. 323–24 (PL 104:319D–324A, esp. 321A). See also Egon Boshof, *Erzbischof Agobard von Lyon: Leben und Werk*, Kölner historische Abhandlungen, 17 (Cologne, 1969), pp. 247–53.

64. Agobard, *Libri duo pro filiis et contra Iudith uxorem Ludouici pii* (sometimes called the *Liber Apologeticus* 1 and 2), ed. G. Waitz, MGH:SS 15.1:275–79, and ed. Van Acker, in Corpus Christianorum: Continuatio Mediaevalis, 52:309–19. See also E. Ward, "Caesar's Wife: The Empress Judith," in *Charlemagne's Heir*, pp. 207–14, 226–27 [205–27]; P. Stafford, *Queens, Concubines, and Dowagers: The King's Wife in the Early Middle Ages* (Athens, Ga., 1983), pp. 18–20, 93–94; Boshof, *Erzbischof Agobard*, pp. 228–46.

65. Agobard, *Libri duo* 1.1, ed. Waitz, MGH:SS 15.1:275; and ed. Van Acker, p. 309.

66. Agobard, *Libri duo* 1.2, ed. Waitz, MGH:SS 15.1:275; and ed. Van Acker, p. 309.

67. Agobard, *Flebilis epistola de diuisione imperii Francorum inter filios Ludouici imperatoris* 3, ed. Dümmler, MGH:Ep. 5:224 [223–26]; and ed. Van Acker, pp. 247–49. On the date of this letter, see Boshof, *Erzbischof Agobard*, pp. 202–5.

68. Jonas, *De institutione regia*, preface, ed. Reviron, pp. 127–29; Einhard, *epistola* 11, ed. Hampe, MGH:Ep. 5:114–15.

69. Hrabanus, *epistola* 15, ed. Dümmler, MGH:Ep. 5:404–15; Rudolf, *Miracula sanctorum in Fuldenses ecclesias translatorum* 15, ed. G. Waitz, MGH:SS 15.1:341; AB 836, p. 18. Thegan, *Vita Hludowici* 52, ed. Pertz, MGH:SS 2:601–2, prints biblical injunctions that correspond almost exactly to Hrabanus, *epistola* 15, ed. Dümmler, MGH:Ep. 5:404.37–405.4. See also E. Sears, "Louis the Pious as *Miles Christi*: The

Dedicatory Image in Hrabanus Maurus's *De laudibus sanctae crucis,*" in *Charlemagne's Heir,* pp. 621–22 [605–28].

70. Gregory IV, *epistola,* ed. Dümmler, MGH:Ep. 5:226.4–5 [223–26]. See also Agobard, *epistola* 16, ed. Dümmler, MGH:Ep. 5:226–28.

71. Paschasius Radbertus, *Epitaphium Arsenii* 2.17, ed. Dümmler, pp. 85–86.

72. Einhard, *epistola* 14, ed. Hampe, MGH:Ep. 5:117.

73. Walahfrid Strabo, *Ad Ruadbern laicum,* ed. Dümmler, MGH:PLAC 2:388–90; AB 834, p. 13. On Ruadbern, see Wattenbach and Levison, *Deutschlands Geschichtsquellen im Mittelalter,* 3:322, and P. Godman, *Poetry of the Carolingian Renaissance* (Norman, Okla., 1985), p. 37. See also A. Önnerfors, *Mediaevalia. Abhandlungen und Aufsätze,* Lateinische Sprache und Literatur des Mittelalters, 6 (Frankfurt am Main, 1977), pp. 195–201, 391–93.

74. Walahfrid Strabo, *Ad eandem de quodam somno,* ed. Dümmler, MGH:PLAC 2:379.6–7 [379–80]. On this poem, see H. J. Kamphausen, *Traum und Vision in der lateinischen Poesie der Karolingerzeit,* Lateinische Sprache und Literatur des Mittelalters, 4 (Bern, 1975), pp. 150–54.

75. Walahfrid Strabo, *Ad eandem,* ed. Dümmler, MGH:PLAC 2:380.36–37.

76. Walahfrid Strabo, *De imagine Tetrici,* ed. Dümmler, MGH:PLAC 2:371.42–43, and see Boethius, *Philosophiae consolatio* 2.5.29, ed. Bieler, in Corpus Christianorum: Series Latina, 94 (Turnhout, 1957), p. 28. Walahfrid Strabo, *De imagine Tetrici,* ed. Dümmler, MGH:PLAC 2:378.256–57, and see Boethius, *Philosophiae consolatio* 1.4.5, ed. Bieler, p. 7.

77. Walahfrid Strabo, *De imagine Tetrici,* ed. Dümmler, MGH:PLAC 2:371.30–34, 49–51.

78. See Kamphausen, *Traum und Vision,* pp. 151–53.

79. Plutarch, *Morales* 566E. See Herodotus 5.55–56.

80. AB 839, pp. 29–30. In 853 Aethelwulf sent his four-year-old son Alfred to Rome and himself made the journey in 855: see Asser, *De rebus gestis Aelfredi* 8, 11–13, 16, ed. W. H. Stevenson, *Asser's Life of King Alfred* (Oxford, 1904), pp. 7, 9–10, 14. According to the Anglo-Saxon Chronicle, the Vikings had conducted raids on southern England in 837. See also M. J. Enright, "Charles the Bald and Aethelwulf of Wessex: the Alliance of 856 and Strategies of Royal Succession," *Journal of Medieval History* 5 (1979): 295–96 [291–302]; C. Stancliffe, "Kings who Opted Out," in *Ideal and Reality in Frankish and Anglo-Saxon Society: Studies Presented to J. M. Wallace-Hadrill,* ed. P. Wormwald with D. Bullough and R. Collins (Oxford, 1983), pp. 154–57, 170–72 [154–76].

81. J. L. Nelson, "The Annals of St. Bertin," *Politics and Ritual in Early Medieval Europe* (London, 1986), pp. 177–78 [173–94].

82. See Bede, *Historia ecclesiastica* 5.13; Exod. 32:32–33; Deut. 7:10; Luke 10:20; Phil. 4:3; Rev. 20:12–15; K. Schmid, "Zeugnisse der Memorialüberlieferung aus der Zeit Ludwigs des Frommen," in *Charlemagne's Heir,* p. 517 [509–22]; J. L. Nelson, "Literacy in Carolingian Government," in *The Uses of Literacy in Early Medieval Europe,* ed. R. McKitterick (Cambridge, 1990), p. 296 [258–96].

83. Ed. Dümmler, MGH:PLAC 1:579–81.

84. AB 839, pp. 26–28.

85. AB 830–35, pp. 1–17; Astronomer, *Vita Hludowici* 55, ed. Pertz, MGH:SS 2:641, and see 2 Sam. 19:1–4. See also J. L. Nelson, "The Last Years of Louis the Pious," in *Charlemagne's Heir*, pp. 147–59.

86. *Diuisio imperii*, ed. Boretius and Krause, MGH:Cap. 2:58; AB 839, p. 26.

87. Astronomer, *Vita Hludowici* 62–63, ed. Pertz, MGH:SS 2:647. Drogo held the title of archbishop as a personal title by virtue of his importance at the court: see J. Fleckenstein, *Die Hofkapelle der deutschen Könige*, vol. 1, *Grundlegung: Die karolingische Hofkapelle*, MGH:Schriften 16.1 (Stuttgart, 1959), pp. 55–56, 83–84, 118–22.

88. Astronomer, *Vita Hludowici* 63–64, ed. Pertz, MGH:SS 2:647–48. Hincmar of Rheims described how another man on his deathbed had spoken to demons and straightaway been carried off to hell: AB 868, p. 144. On the notion that death was a final, crucial contest with the Devil, see J. Ntedika, *L'évocation de l'au-delà dans la prière pour les morts: étude de patristique et de liturgie latines (IVᵉ–VIIIᵉs.)*, Recherches africaines de théologie, 2 (Louvain, 1971), p. 47 [46–83].

89. On the sarcophagus, see P. E. Schramm and F. Mütherich, *Denkmale der deutschen Könige und Kaiser. Ein Beitrag zur Herrschergeschichte von Karl dem Grossen bis Friedrich II, 768–1250*, Veröffentlichungen des Zentralinstituts für Kunstgeschichte in München, 2 (Munich, 1962), p. 122; J. A. Schmoll, "Das Grabmal Kaiser Ludwigs des Frommen in Metz," *Aachener Kunstblätter* 45 (1974): 75–96; R. Melzak, "Antiquarianism in the Time of Louis the Pious and Its Influence on the Art of Metz," in *Charlemagne's Heir*, pp. 629–32 [629–40].

90. Thegan, *Vita Hludowici* 20, ed. Pertz, MGH:SS 2:595–96.

91. Jonas of Orléans, *De institutione regia*, preface, ed. Reviron, p. 126, and see pp. 129–30.

CHAPTER FIVE: CIVIL WARS AND WORSE

1. Horace, *Odes* 1.2.

2. See R. Faulhaber, *Der Reichseinheitsgedanke in der Literatur der Karolingerzeit bis zum Vertrag von Verdun*, Historische Studien, 204 (Berlin, 1931, repr. 1965); U. Penndorf, *Das Problem der "Reichseinheitsidee" nach der Teilung von Verdun (843): Untersuchungen zu den späten Karolingern*, Münchener Beiträge zur Mediävistik und Renaissance-Forschung, 20 (Munich, 1974); E. Boshof, "Einheitsidee und Teilungsprinzip Ludwigs des Frommen," in *Charlemagne's Heir: New Perspectives on the Reign of Louis the Pious (814–840)*, ed. P. Godman and R. Collins (Oxford, 1990), pp. 161–89; H. Beumann, "Unitas ecclesiae—unitas imperii—unitas regni. Von der imperialen Reichseinheitsidee zur Einheit der regna," in *Nascita dell'Europa ed Europa Carolingia: un'equazione da verificare, 19–25 aprile 1979*, Settimane di Studio del Centro Italiano di Studi sull'Alto Medioevo, 27 (Spoleto, 1981), pp. 531–71; R. B. Delamare, *L'idée de paix à l'époque carolingienne* (Paris, 1939). On the notions of *imperium* and *regnum*, see J. Fried, "Der karolingische Herrschaftsverband im 9. Jh. zwischen 'Kirche' und 'Köningshaus,'" *Historische Zeitschrift* 235 (1982): 1–15 [1–43].

3. Gal. 3:28; Agobard, *Liber aduersus legem Gundobadi* 3–4, ed. Dümmler,

MGH:Ep. 5:159 [158–64]; also ed. Van Acker, pp. 20–21 [19–28]. See Paschasius Radbertus, *Epitaphium Arsenii* 2.17, ed. Dümmler, p. 85.

4. John 17:21; J. A. Cabaniss, "Agobard of Lyons," *Speculum* 26 (1951): 58–63 [50–76]; H. Liebeschütz, *Synagoge und Ecclesia: Religionsgeschichtliche Studien über die Auseinandersetzung der Kirche mit dem Judentum im Hochmittelalter*, Veröffentlichungen der deutschen Akademie für Sprache und Dichtung, Darmstadt, 55 (Heidelberg, 1983), pp. 55–94; Boshof, *Erzbischof Agobard von Lyon: Leben und Werk*, Kölner historische Abhandlungen, 17 (Cologne, 1969), pp. 102–38; and B. Blumenkranz, *Les auteurs chrétiens latins du Moyen Age sur les Juifs et le Judaisme*, Etudes juives, 4 (Paris, 1963), pp. 152–68. On the uproar over Bodo, see AB 839, pp. 27–28; AB 847, pp. 53–54.

5. H. X. Arquillière, *L'Augustinisme politique: essai sur la formation des théories politiques du Moyen Age*, L'Eglise et l'état au Moyen Age, 2 (Paris, 1934). See also F. L. Ganshof, *The Carolingians and the Frankish Monarchy: Studies in Carolingian History*, trans. J. Sondheimer (Ithaca, N.Y., 1971), pp. 41–85.

6. Ganshof, *The Carolingians and the Frankish Monarchy*, pp. 245–47; W. Schlesinger, "Kaisertum und Reichsteilung. Zur Divisio regnorum von 806," in *Zum Kaisertum Karls des Grossen: Beiträge und Aufsätze*, ed. G. Wolf, Wege und Forschung, 38 (Darmstadt, 1972), pp. 116–73; ARF 813, p. 138; K. Brunner, *Oppositionelle Gruppen im Karolingerreich*, Veröffentlichungen des Instituts für österreichische Geschichtsforschung, 25 (Vienna, 1979), pp. 97–103.

7. Nithard, *Historiarum* 2.10–3.1, ed. Lauer, pp. 68–82; J. L. Nelson, *Politics and Ritual in Early Medieval Europe* (London, 1986), pp. 204–11; E. Müller, "Der Schlachtort Fontaneum (Fontanetum) von 841," *Neues Archiv* 33 (1908): 201–11; F. Pietzcker, "Die Schlacht bei Fontenoy, 841: Rechtsformen im Krieg des frühen Mittelalters," *Zeitschrift der Savigny-Stiftung für Rechtsgeschichte*, Germanistische Abteilung, 81 (1964): 318–42. For some plates showing the layout of the field of battle, see C. Fabre, "Deux Planctus rythmiques en Latin vulgaire du IXᵉ siècle," in *La chanson de geste et le mythe carolingien. Mélanges René Louis*, 2 vols. (Saint-Père-sous-Vézelay, 1982), 1:210, 217, 219 [177–228].

8. AB 841, p. 38; AX 841, p. 11; AF 841, p. 32; Regino, *Chronicon* 841, ed. F. Kurze, MGH:SRGUS (Hanover, 1890), p. 75.2.

9. See, for instance, Hugh of Fleury, *Chronicon* 1, ed. Pertz, MGH:SS 8 (Hanover, 1848), p. 353, and Otto of Freising, *Chronica siue Historia de duabus ciuitatibus* 5.35, ed. A. Hofmeister, MGH:SRGUS (Hanover, 1912), p. 259.

10. Engelbert, *Versus de bella quae fuit acta Fontaneto*, ed. Dümmler, MGH:PLAC 2:138–39. For a translation of the poem, see *Carolingian Civilization: A Reader*, ed P. E. Dutton (Peterborough, Ont., 1993), pp. 363–65. Also ed. E. Faral, "Le poème d'Engelbert," pp. 86–98; Fabre, "Deux Planctus rythmiques," pp. 182–228; P. Godman, *Poets and Emperors: Frankish Politics and Carolingian Poetry* (Oxford, 1987), pp. 151–53.

11. Engelbert, *Versus* stanza 2, ed. Dümmler, MGH:PLAC 2:138.

12. Job 3:6–8; Engelbert, *Versus* stanzas 11–12, ed. Dümmler, MGH:PLAC 2:139.

13. *Capitula tractanda cum comitibus, episcopis et abbatibus* 9, ed. Boretius,

MGH:Cap. 1:161. See also Ganshof, *The Carolingians and the Frankish Monarchy,* p. 220.

14. AX 833, p. 8; AX 842, p. 13; AX 843, p. 13. On the *Annales Xantenses,* see H. Löwe, "Studien zu den *Annales Xantenses,*" *Deutsches Archiv* 8 (1951): 87–99 [59–99].

15. AX 841, pp. 11–12.

16. See, for instance, AX 834, p. 9; AX 838, p. 10; AX 850, p. 17.

17. Florus of Lyons, *Carmen* 28, ed. Dümmler, MGH:PLAC 2:561.41–42 [559–64].

18. Florus, *Carmen* 28, ed. Dümmler, MGH:PLAC 2:561.73–76; see also p. 561.43–72.

19. Florus, *Carmen* 28, ed. Dümmler, MGH:PLAC 2:561–62.77–88.

20. Florus, *Carmen* 28, ed. Dümmler, MGH:PLAC 2:562–63.89–120; pp. 562–64.111–66.

21. For an even clearer allusion to the Virgilian motto, see Ermold, *Ad Pippinum regem* 2, ed. Faral, p. 222.61–66. Both Ermold and Florus would have found the image reinforced by 1 Pet. 5:5.

22. Florus, *Carmen* 28, ed. Dümmler, MGH:PLAC 2:562.109–11.

23. Paschasius Radbertus, *Epitaphium Arsenii* 2.7, ed. Dümmler, p. 67.

24. Lucan, *Bellum ciuile* 1.1: "Bella . . . plus quam ciuilia." For other Carolingian citations of the phrase, see Paschasius Radbertus, *Expositio in euangelium Matthei* 11.24, PL 120:801B14–15; Synod of Ver (Dec. 844) 2, ed. W. Hartmann, MGH:Con. 3 (Hanover, 1984), p. 40.5–6; Eriugena, *epistola* 14, ed. Dümmler, MGH:Ep. 6 (Berlin, 1902), p. 158.26–27; Hincmar, *De fide Carolo regi seruanda* 5, PL 125:964B1–2; Hincmar, *Vita Remigii episcopi Remensis,* preface, ed. Krusch, MGH:SRM 3:251.13–14; and see above p. 141 for Audradus Modicus. On the popularity of the *Bellum ciuile* in the ninth century, see H. C. Gotoff, *The Transmission of the Text of Lucan in the Ninth Century* (Cambridge, Mass., 1971), pp. 1–26, 95–98.

25. Matt. 12:25; Mark 3:24–27; Luke 11:17.

26. AX 834, p. 9; Lupus, *epistola* 44, ed. Levillain, *Correspondance,* 1:186; Paschasius Radbertus, *Epitaphium Arsenii* 2.10, ed. Dümmler, p. 76.

27. Hincmar, *De fide Carolo regi seruanda* 12, PL 125:967B3–4.

28. K. Thomas, *Religion and the Decline of Magic* (New York, 1971), p. 425. See also ibid., pp. 389–432, and R. L. Kagan, *Lucrecia's Dreams: Politics and Prophecy in Sixteenth-Century Spain* (Berkeley, Calif., 1990), pp. 86–88; K. Rahner, *Visions and Prophecies,* trans. C. Henkey and R. Strachan (Freiburg, 1963), p. 99; P. Alphandéry, "Prophètes et ministère prophétique dans le moyen-âge latin," *Revue d'histoire et de philosophie religieuses* 12 (1932): 334–59.

29. Agnellus of Ravenna, *Liber Pontificalis ecclesiae Ravennatis* 165, ed. Holder-Egger, MGH: *Scriptorum rerum Langobardicarum et Italicarum, saec. vi–ix* (Hanover, 1878), p. 384; John 1:47. On Agnellus, see M. Manitius, *Geschichte der lateinischen Literatur des Mittelalters,* 3 vols., Handbuch der Altertumswissenschaft, 9.2 (Munich, 1911; repr. 1965), 1:712–14; T. S. Brown, "*Romanitas* and *Campanilismo:* Agnellus of Ravenna's View of the Past," in *The Inheritance of Historiography, 350–900,* ed.

C. Holdsworth and T. P. Wiseman, Exeter Studies in History, 12 (Exeter, 1986), pp. 107–14.

30. Agnellus, *Liber Pontificalis ecclesiae Ravennatis* 165, ed. Holder-Egger, MGH: *Scriptorum rerum Langobardicarum et Italicarum,* p. 384.44. For the entire prophecy, see ibid., 166, pp. 384–86.

31. Agnellus, *Liber Pontificalis ecclesiae Ravennatis* 171–75, ed. Holder-Egger, MGH: *Scriptorum rerum Langobardicarum et Italicarum,* pp. 388–91.

32. For some examples, see J. Hubert, J. Porcher, and W. F. Volbach, *The Carolingian Renaissance* (New York, 1970), pp. 182–84; H. Omont, "Manuscrits illustrés de l'Apocalypse dans IXᵉ et Xᵉ siècles," *Bulletin de la Société française de reproduction de manuscrits à peintures* 6 (1922): 62–95.

33. AF 847, pp. 36–37.

34. Johannes Trithemius, *Annales Hirsaugienses* 1 (Saint-Gall, 1690), ed. Hartmann, MGH:Con. 3:182.

35. AF 847, p. 37.

36. Titus 1:11. See also B.-S. Albert, "Raban Maur, l'unité de l'empire et ses relations avec les Carolingiens," *Revue d'histoire ecclésiastique* 86 (1991): 5–44.

37. See J. K. Bostock, *A Handbook of Old High German Literature,* 2d ed., rev. by K. C. King and D. R. McLintock (Oxford, 1976), pp. 135–54.

38. *Libri confraternitatum sancti Galli, Augiensis, Fabariensis,* ed. P. Piper, in MGH: *Necrologia Germaniae,* Supplementband (Berlin, 1884), p. 13, col. 14.15, p. 77, col. 235.22; L. Traube, "O Roma nobilis. Philologische Untersuchungen aus dem Mittelalter," *Abhandlungen der philosophische-philologischen Classe der königlichen bayerischen Akademie der Wissenschaften,* vol. 19 (Munich, 1892), p. 390; E. K. Rand and G. Howe, "The Vatican Livy and the Script of Tours," *Memoirs of the American Academy in Rome* 1 (1917): 25–34; A. Wilmart, "Le lectionnaire de Saint-Père," *Speculum* 1 (1926): 269–78, 450. The manuscript in question, Bibliothèque municipale de Chartres 24 (32), did not survive the aerial bombardment of the city on 26 June 1944: see *Catalogue Général des manuscrits des bibliothèques publiques de France,* vol. 53: *Manuscrits des bibliothèques sinistrées de 1940 à 1944* (Paris, 1962), pp. 2–4.

39. Audradus, *Liber reuelationum* 8, ed. L. Traube, "O Roma nobilis," p. 381. See also Hartmann, MGH:Con. 3:178; Manitius, *Geschichte der lateinischen Literatur des Mittelalters,* 1:601–3; L. Traube, MGH:PLAC 3 (Berlin, 1896), pp. 67–72; W. Mohr, "Audradus von Sens, Prophet und Kirchenpolitiker (um 850)," *Archivium Latinitatis Medii Aevi* 29 (1959) 239–67.

40. T. Gottlob, *Der abendländische Chorepiskopat,* Kanonistische Studien, 1 (Bonn, 1928), p. 122; W. Hartmann, *Die Synoden der Karolingerzeit im Frankenreich und in Italien* (Paderborn, 1989), pp. 417–18.

41. Hrabanus, *epistola* 25, ed. Dümmler, MGH:Ep. 5:431–35 [431–39]; Ebbo of Rheims, *De ministris Remensium ecclesiae,* PL 135:409B2–410B1.

42. See H. Fuhrmann, *Einfluss und Verbreitung der pseudoisidorischen Fälschungen. Von ihrem Auftauchen bis in die neuere Zeit,* Schriften der MGH, 24.1 (Stuttgart, 1972), pp. 42–43, 146–47, 160 and n. 38; W. Goffart, *The Le Mans Forgeries: A Chap-*

ter from the History of Church Property in the Ninth Century, Harvard Historical Studies, 76 (Cambridge, Mass., 1966), pp. 66–67.

43. Flodoard, *Historia Remensis ecclesiae* 3.10, ed. J. Heller and G. Waitz, MGH:SS 13 (Hanover, 1881), pp. 482.43–483.4; Hincmar, *epistola* 33, ed. E. Perels, MGH:Ep. 8.1 (Berlin, 1939), p. 11.

44. Synod of Quierzy (849), ed. Hartmann, MGH:Con. 3:196; Hincmar, *De praedestinatione dei et libero arbitrio posterior dissertatio* 2, PL 125:85C; Gottlob, *Die abendländischen Chorepiskopat,* pp. 96–97, 132–33.

45. J. Devisse, *Hincmar, archevêque de Reims, 845–882,* Travaux d'histoire ethicopolitique, 29, 3 vols. (Geneva, 1975–76), 1:50–52, 2:863; Hincmar, *epistola ad Hincmarum Laudunensem,* PL 126:503C13–14; P. R. McKeon, *Hincmar of Laon and Carolingian Politics* (Urbana, Ill., 1978), p. 92.

46. Audradus, 1st preface, ed. Traube, MGH:PLAC 3:740, also ed. Traube, "O Roma nobilis," p. 375; Audradus, *Liber reuelationum* 9, ed. Traube, in "O Roma nobilis," p. 382.

47. Audradus, 1st preface, ed. Traube, MGH:PLAC 3.2, p. 740; Audradus, *Liber reuelationum* 9, ed. Traube, in "O Roma nobilis," p. 382; Audradus, proem, ed. Traube, MGH:PLAC 3.2:741.11; Audradus, *Liber reuelationum* 8, ed. Traube, "O Roma nobilis," p. 381.

48. Lupus, *epistola* 77, ed. Levillain, *Correspondance,* 2:20–22. See also Lupus, *epistolae* 75–76, 100, ed. Levillain, *Correspondance,* 2:16–20, 120, where he confirms that he went to Rome and was well received by the pope.

49. Synod of Quierzy (849), ed. Hartmann, MGH:Con. 3:194–99; Lupus, *epistola* 80, ed. Levillain, *Correspondance,* 2:42–54, and see pp. 17–19 n. 4.

50. Audradus, *Liber reuelationum* 9, ed. Traube, in "O Roma nobilis," p. 382; Synod of Paris (Nov. 849), ed. Hartmann, MGH:Con. 3:200–201.

51. Lupus, *epistola* 78, ed. Levillain, *Correspondance,* 2:22–36. See also F. Lot and L. Halphen, *Le règne de Charles le Chauve (840–877),* vol. 1, *(840–851)* (Paris, 1909), pp. 208–13, esp. p. 209 n. 1.

52. On the predestination conflict, see D. E. Nineham, "Gottschalk of Orbais: Reactionary or Precursor of the Reformation," *Journal of Ecclesiastical History* 40 (1989): 1–18; D. Ganz, "The Debate on Predestination," in *Charles the Bald: Court and Kingdom* 2d rev. ed., ed. M. T. Gibson and J. L. Nelson (Aldershot, 1990), pp. 283–302.

53. Rigbold was the suffragan bishop of Rheims for four years after the Synod of Paris: see Synod of Quierzy (849), ed. Hartmann, MGH:Con. 3:196.6 and 16–18; Synod of Soissons (Apr. 853), ed. Hartmann, MGH:Con. 3:264.12 and 3:279.1–2.

54. Hincmar, *epistola* 37, ed. Perels, MGH:Ep. 8.1:13.37–38 [12–23]; 2 Pet. 2:1–3.

55. Audradus, preface, ed. Traube, MGH:PLAC 3.2:740. I have read "librorum" here instead of "labiorum," though the latter may recall Hos. 14:3: "reddemus uitulos labiorum nostrorum."

56. Audradus, 2d preface, ed. Traube, MGH:PLAC 3.1:741.13. Manitius, *Geschichte der lateinischen Literatur,* 1:602 n. 5, noted that the proem had the line "Is septem uitulos domini mactauit in ara," and thought, therefore, that the psalm should be 50:21

(51:19). The poems in this collection were edited in two places by Traube, MGH:PLAC 3.1:73–121, MGH:PLAC 3.2:740–45.

57. Audradus, *liber septimus,* ed. Traube, MGH:PLAC 3.1, p. 87.26–27.

58. Audradus, 2d preface, ed. Traube, MGH:PLAC 3.2, p. 741. "Omnem perfidiam extinctam" is, as Traube points out, an accusative absolute.

59. Audradus, *liber quartus.*11, ed. Traube, MGH:PLAC 3.1:116–18.287–375.

60. Audradus, 1st preface. ed. Traube, MGH:PLAC 3.2:740. What Audradus had called an *oraculum diuinum* in his first preface, he called the *mandatus sancti Petri* in *Liber reuelationum* 9, ed. Traube, "O Roma nobilis," p. 382. See also Audradus, *Liber de fonte uitae,* ed. Traube, MGH:PLAC 3.1:79.224–26.

61. Audradus, proem, ed. Traube, MGH:PLAC 3.2:741.10–15.

62. Audradus, 2d preface, ed. Traube, MGH:PLAC 3.2:741.

63. Mohr, "Audradus von Sens," pp. 239–67; P. Dinzelbacher, *Vision und Vision-literatur im Mittelalter,* Monographien zur Geschichte des Mittelalters, 23 (Stuttgart, 1981), p. 34; Ganz, "The Debate on Predestination," p. 285.

64. Alberich of Trois-Fontaines, *Chronica,* ed. P. Scheffer-Boichorst, MGH:SS 23 (Hanover, 1874), pp. 733–36. Indications of incomplete reporting are evident. Of the first vision that he reports, Alberich says "et cetera que ibi dicuntur," but he omits these other materials. Since Alberich had his own chronological framework, he eliminated parts of Audradus's own unique form of dating (see the second vision). Moreover, he seems to have radically reduced (or to have received a reduced version of) the longest vision in the collection: Audradus, *Liber reuelationum* 10–11, ed. Traube, "O Roma nobilis," pp. 383–85.

65. A. Duchesne, *Historiae Francorum scriptores a Pippino Caroli M. Imp. Patre usque ad Hugonem Capetum regem,* 5 vols. (Paris, 1636–49), 2:390–93; repr. in PL 115:23D–30A.

66. Audradus, *Liber reuelationum* 1, ed. Traube, "O Roma nobilis," p. 378. On Audradus and the *Liber reuelationum,* see also H. J. Kamphausen, *Traum und Vision in der lateinischen Poesie der Karolingerzeit,* Lateinische Sprache und Literatur des Mittelalters, 4 (Bern, 1975), pp. 146–47, and Penndorf, *Das Problem der "Reichseinheitsidee,"* pp. 94–116.

67. Audradus, *Liber reuelationum* 2, ed. Traube, "O Roma nobilis," p. 379: "rapuit eum spiritus ante dominum"; *Liber reuelationum* 4, p. 380: "rapuit me spiritus domini in excelsum"; *Liber reuelationum* 10, p. 383: "raptus in spiritu"; ibid.: "eodem anno mense sexto iterum raptus uidit." See 2 Cor. 12:2; 2 Cor. 12:4; Apoc. 12:5; Wisd. of Sol. 4:11.

68. Audradus, *Liber reuelationum* 4, ed. Traube, "O Roma nobilis," p. 379: "eram orans, ait Audradus, pro salute ecclesiarum"; *Liber reuelationum* 12, p. 386: "cumque orarem solito pro fratrum salute," "in loco quo eram orans."

69. Audradus, *Liber reuelationum* 4, ed. Traube, "O Roma nobilis," pp. 379–80. See Ps. 30 (31):23; Acts 11:5.

70. See Audradus, *Liber reuelationum* 12, ed. Traube, "O Roma nobilis," p. 386; *Liber reuelationum* 1, p. 378; *Liber reuelationum* 4, p. 380; *Liber reuelationum* 13, p. 388; *Liber reuelationum* 14, pp. 388–89.

71. Audradus, *Liber reuelationum* 6, ed. Traube, "O Roma nobilis," p. 381; *Liber reuelationum* 9, p. 382; *Liber reuelationum* 10.a, p. 383; *Liber reuelationum* 10.b, p. 383; *Liber reuelationum* 11, pp. 383–85; *Liber reuelationum* 12, p. 386.

72. Audradus, *Liber reuelationum* 6, ed. Traube, "O Roma nobilis," p. 381.

73. Gen. 32:23–42; Song of Sol. 3:7–8.

74. See above pp. 16, 19.

75. Audradus, *Liber de fonte uitae,* ed. Traube, MGH:PLAC 3.1:77.140–41; *Liber reuelationum* 13, ed. Traube, "O Roma nobilis," p. 388.

76. Lord Byron, journal of 28 Jan. 1821, ed. L. A. Marchand, in *'Born for Opposition': Byron's Letters and Journals,* vol. 8, *1821* (Cambridge, Mass., 1978), p. 37: "The Best of Prophets of the future is the past."

77. J. Lindblom, *Prophecy in Ancient Israel* (Oxford, 1962), p. 1.

78. A. Herschel, *The Prophets* (New York, 1962), p. 16.

79. R. K. Emmerson, "The Prophetic, the Apocalyptic, and the Study of Medieval Literature," in *Poetic Prophecy in Western Literature,* ed. J. Wojcik and R. J. Frontain (Rutherford, N.J., 1984), p. 45 [40–54].

80. Lindblom, *Prophecy in Ancient Israel,* p. 2, and see p. 4.

81. For the date of the Vivian Bible, see H. Kessler, *The Illuminated Bibles from Tours* (Princeton, N.J., 1977), p. 6; on the *fons uitae,* pp. 48–53. See n. 105 below.

82. Audradus, *Liber reuelationum* 11, ed. Traube, "O Roma nobilis," p. 385.32, 36; *Liber reuelationum* 12, p. 387.15. See Jer. 49:14; Prov. 13:17.

83. See Ezek. 4:5, 16:2.

84. See Audradus, *Liber reuelationum* 7, ed. Traube, "O Roma nobilis," p. 381.

85. Audradus, *Liber reuelationum* 4, ed. Traube, "O Roma nobilis," p. 380.4–5.

86. Audradus, *Liber reuelationum* 12, ed. Traube, "O Roma nobilis," p. 385.34–38. On the calculations involved in the *induciae,* see Traube, "O Roma nobilis," p. 380.

87. Joel 2:28; Acts 2:17. See Audradus, *Liber reuelationum* 1, ed. Traube, "O Roma nobilis," p. 378; Joel 2:10; Ezek. 32:7; Joel 2:32; Acts 2:21.

88. Audradus, *Liber reuelationum* 2, ed. Traube, "O Roma nobilis," p. 379.

89. Audradus, *Liber reuelationum* 2, ed. Traube, "O Roma nobilis," p. 379.11–17.

90. Audradus, *Liber reuelationum* 3, ed. Traube, "O Roma nobilis," p. 379.22–23.

91. Exod. 7:14–12:36.

92. Audradus, *Liber reuelationum* 4, ed. Traube, "O Roma nobilis," pp. 379–80; *Liber reuelationum* 14, p. 389.8–13.

93. Synod of Meaux-Paris (June 845), preface, ed. Hartmann, MGH:Con. 3:81–82; Jer. 1:14.

94. Lupus, *epistola* 48, ed. Levillain, *Correspondance,* 1:200.

95. H. Zettel, *Das Bild der Normannen und der Normanneneinfälle in westfränkischen, ostfränkischen und angelsächsischen Quellen des 8. bis 11. Jahrhunderts* (Munich, 1977), pp. 191–92.

96. Lot and Halphen, *Le règne de Charles le Chauve,* pp. 130–41; J. L. Nelson, *Charles the Bald* (London, 1992), pp. 151–53.

97. Audradus, *Liber reuelationum* 10, ed. Traube, "O Roma nobilis," p. 383, and 11, pp. 383–85. See 1 Thess. 4:17. Two versions of the vision are preserved, but Al-

berich's is much shorter and possibly edited by the chronicler. See *Liber reuelationum* II, ed. Traube, "O Roma nobilis," pp. 383–85, and Alberich, *Chronica,* ed. Scheffer-Boichorst, MGH:SS 23:735–36.

98. Audradus, *Liber reuelationum* II, ed. Traube, "O Roma nobilis," p. 383.5–7.

99. Audradus, *Liber reuelationum* II, ed. Traube, "O Roma nobilis," p. 384.3–4.

100. Audradus, *Liber reuelationum* II, ed. Traube, "O Roma nobilis," p. 385.16–17.

101. See above pp. 104–5.

102. Lupus, *epistola* 81, ed. Levillain, *Correspondance,* 2:56–64. See J. H. M. Smith, *Province and Empire: Brittany and the Carolingians* (Cambridge, 1992), pp. 151–61.

103. Lupus, *epistola* 83, ed. Levillain, *Correspondance,* 2:68. P. K. Marshall, "The Learning of Servatus Lupus," *Mediaeval Studies* 41 (1979): 516, and in Servatus Lupus, *Epistulae,* ed. P. K. Marshall (Leipzig, 1984), p. 85, connected Lupus's comment to Cicero's ironic allusion to the Ides of March: Cicero, *Epistulae ad familiares,* 10.28.1. Charles quite likely held an assembly at Tours on 11 February 851: see Lot and Halphen, *Le règne de Charles le Chauve,* p. 223 and n. 2, and he donated land to Saint-Martin's on 16 February. On the Breton events of 850–51, see J. L. Nelson, "The Reign of Charles the Bald: A Survey," in *Charles the Bald: Court and Kingdom,* pp. 8–9.

104. On the liturgy and costumes of Christmas feasts with the king, see E. H. Kantorowicz, *Laudes regiae: A Study in Liturgical Acclamations and Mediaeval Ruler Worship* (Berkeley, Calif., 1958), pp. 92–93. *Bibliothecarum et psalteriorum uersus* 3.11, ed. Traube, MGH:PLAC 3.1:251.15–30; Charles the Bald, charter no. 80, ed. G. Tessier et al., in *Recueil des actes de Charles II le Chauve, roi de France,* 3 vols. (Paris, 1943–55), 1:224–26. On Carolingian victory celebrations, see M. McCormick, *Eternal Victory: Triumphal Rulership in Late Antiquity, Byzantium, and the Early Medieval West* (Cambridge, 1986), pp. 342–84.

105. See W. Köhler, *Die karolingischen Miniaturen,* vol. 1.2, *Die Schule von Tours* (Berlin, 1933), pp. 220–31; H. L. Kessler, "A Lay Abbot as Patron: Count Vivian and the First Bible of Charles the Bald," in *Committenti e produzione artistico-letteraria nell'alto medioevo occidentale,* Settimane di Studio del Centro Italiano di Studi sull'Alto Medioevo, 39 (Spoleto, 1992), pp. 647–75; K. F. Morrison, "'Know Thyself': Music in the Carolingian Renaissance," in *Committenti e produzione,* pp. 443–44 [369–479].

106. Lupus, *epistola* 53, ed. Levillain, *Correspondance* 1:214–16; Morrison, "'Know Thyself,'" pp. 445–46.

107. See F. Mütherich and J. E. Gaehde, *Carolingian Painting* (New York, 1976), pp. 72–77, pl. 20–21.

108. *Bibliothecarum et psalteriorum uersus* 3.11, ed. Traube, MGH:PLAC 3.1:251.1–2.

109. Kessler, "A Lay Abbot as Patron," pp. 648–51, 668–75. But see also Rand and Howe, "The Vatican Livy and the Script of Tours," pp. 30–31, who suggest that in 845 Aregarius would have been over seventy.

110. Synod of Meaux-Paris (845–46) 10, ed. Hartmann, MGH:Con. 3:89–91, and 23,

3:97; F. J. Felten, *Äbte und Laienäbte im Frankenreich. Studien zum Verhältnis von Staat und Kirche im früheren Mittelalter,* Monographien zur Geschichte des Mittelalters, 20 (Stuttgart, 1980), pp. 50–51; E. Lesne, *Histoire de la propriété ecclésiastique en France,* 6 vols. (Lille, 1910–) 2.1:197–203, 245–47.

111. Lupus, *epistola* 39 (Oct. 844), ed. Levillain, *Correspondance,* 1:168.

112. AB 850, p. 59; AB 851, pp. 60–63; and see *Conuentus apud Marsnam Secundus,* ed. Boretius and Krause, MGH:Cap. 2:72–74. See Mohr, "Audradus von Sens," pp. 246–67; Penndorf, *Das Problem,* pp. 99–108. On fraternalism as an ideal promoted by church synods, see H. H. Anton, "Zum politischen Konzept: Karolingischen Synoden und zur karolingischen Brüdergemeinschaft," *Historisches Jahrbuch* 99 (1979): 110–32 [55–132].

113. Ezek. 28:1–10.

114. On Martin as the saint of a particular people, see O. Guillot, "Les saints des peuples et des nations dans l'occident des vie–xes. Un aperçu d'ensemble illustré par le cas des Francs en Gaulle," in *Santi e demoni nell'alto medioevo occidentale (secoli v–xi),* 2 vols., Settimane di Studio del Centro Italiano di Studi sull'Alto Medioevo, 36 (Spoleto, 1989), 1:232–40 [205–51].

115. Audradus, *Liber reuelationum* 12, ed. Traube, "O Roma nobilis," p. 386.1–2.

116. Synod of Soissons, ed. Hartmann, MGH:Con. 3:253–89.

117. Audradus was wrong, of course, about the status of Bishop Pardulus, who correctly identified himself at Soissons: see MGH:Con. 3:277.20.

118. Audradus, *Liber reuelationum* 12, ed. Traube, "O Roma nobilis," p. 386.4–5.

119. Audradus, *Liber reuelationum* 12, ed. Traube, "O Roma nobilis," p. 386.20–22.

120. Synod of Soissons, 3, ed. Hartmann, MGH:Con. 3:281.

121. AB 854, p. 69; Lupus, *epistola* 26, ed. Levillain, *Correspondance,* 1:126.

122. Audradus, *Liber reuelationum* 12, ed. Traube, "O Roma nobilis," p. 387. On the Synod of Sens, see Hartmann, MGH:Con. 3:300–301.

123. Audradus, *Liber reuelationum* 12, ed. Traube, "O Roma nobilis," p. 387.15–16. See also AB 853, pp. 67–68.

124. Audradus, *Liber reuelationum* 14, ed. Traube, "O Roma nobilis," pp. 388–89.

125. Thegan, *Vita Hludowici* 44, ed. Pertz, MGH:SS 2:599.22–24.

CHAPTER SIX: THE PROPERTY OF DREAMS

1. Artemidorus, *Oneirocritica* 4.17, 3.3, trans. White, *The Interpretation of Dreams,* pp. 192, 159.

2. F. Pollock and F. W. Maitland, *The History of English Law before the Time of Edward I,* 2 vols. (Cambridge, 1895), 1:34.

3. Ibid., 1:1; E. Lesne, *Histoire de la propriété ecclésiastique en France,* 6 vols. (Lille, 1910–40).

4. On the ecclesiastical and synodal concern with the theft of church property, see W. Hartmann, *Die Synoden der Karolingerzeit im Frankenreich und in Italien* (Paderborn,

1989), pp. 458–61. On the spread of a literate culture in the ninth century, see R. McKitterick, *The Carolingians and the Written Word* (Cambridge, 1989).

5. D. Herlihy, "Church Property on the European Continent, 701–1200," *Speculum* 36 (1961): 87 [81–102]; repr. in Herlihy, *The Social History of Italy and Western Europe, 700–1500: Collected Studies* (London, 1978). See also J. M. Wallace-Hadrill, *The Frankish Church* (Oxford, 1983), pp. 123–42.

6. Notker, *Gesta Karoli Magni* 1.18, ed. Haefele, MGH:SRG n.s. 12:123–24.

7. J. W. Thompson, *The Dissolution of the Carolingian Fisc in the Ninth Century,* University of California Publications, 23 (Berkeley, Calif., 1935); J. Dhondt, *Etudes sur la naissance des principautés territoriales en France (IXᵉ–Xᵉ siècle)* (Bruges, 1948), pp. 1–65, 259–69; J. Martindale, "The Kingdom of Aquitaine and the 'Dissolution of the Carolingian Fisc,'" *Francia* 11 (1983): 131–91. Herlihy, "Church Property," p. 92.

8. Published as Lupus, *epistola* 18, ed. Levillain, *Correspondance*, 1:100–102.

9. Hincmar, *epistola* 198, ed. Perels, MGH:Ep. 8.1:216.16–18. On the property problems that arose after the death of Louis the Pious, see Lesne, *Histoire*, 2.1:170–203.

10. See W. Goffart, *The Le Mans Forgeries: A Chapter From the History of Church Property in the Ninth Century,* Harvard Historical Studies, 76 (Cambridge, Mass., 1966), pp. 10–14; G. Constable, "*Nona et decima.* An Aspect of Carolingian Economy," *Speculum* 35 (1960): 225–27 [224–50].

11. *Epistola Synodi Carisiacensis ad Hludowicum regem* 15, ed. Hartmann, MGH:Con. 3:425.9–12. See also p. 425.12–18, and AB 837, p. 23.

12. Goffart, *The Le Mans Forgeries,* pp. 207–20.

13. AB 863, p. 103; Charles the Bald, charter 258, ed. G. Tessier et al., in *Receuil des Actes de Charles II le Chauve, roi de France,* 3 vols. (Paris, 1943–55), 2:81–86.

14. Lupus, *epistola* 11, ed. Levillain, *Correspondance*, 1:84. Levillain, 1:83 n.4 argued that Reginb. was probably Lupus's brother. On the politics of court and Lupus's ambitions, see also *epistolae* 16 and 27, ed. Levillain, *Correspondance*, 1:96, 128–30.

15. Lupus, *epistola* 24, ed. Levillain, *Correspondance*, 1:118–20; and *epistola* 22, *Correspondance*, 1:112.

16. Lupus, *epistolae* 35, 36, 38, ed. Levillain, *Correspondance*, 1:154–60, 166. See also F. Lot and L. Halphen, *Le règne de Charles le Chauve (840–877),* vol. 1, (840–851) (Paris, 1909), pp. 89–90 n. 4. On another enemy at court, see Lupus, *epistola* 54, ed. Levillain, *Correspondance*, 1:216–18.

17. See Lupus, *epistolae* 26, 41, 66, ed. Levillain, *Correspondance*, 1:122–28, 172–74, 242–44; *epistolae* 68, 93, 94, 96, 98, 128, ed. Levillain, *Correspondance*, 2:2–4, 100–106, 112–14, 116, 198.

18. See Lupus, *epistola* 44, ed. Levillain, *Correspondance*, 1:184. See also Lupus, *epistolae* 45, 58, 60, 61, ed. Levillain, *Correspondance*, 1:190, 226, 230–32.

19. Lupus, *epistolae* 31, 37, ed. Levillain, *Correspondance*, 1:140–46, 160–64; and *epistola* 78, *Correspondance*, 2:22–36.

20. Lupus, *epistolae* 45, 24, 34–36, ed. Levillain, *Correspondance*, 1:190, 116, 152–60.

21. Lupus, *epistola* 72, ed. Levillain, *Correspondance* 2:12. See Claudius's com-

plaint, *epistola* 6, ed. Dümmler, MGH:Ep. 4:601.16–22. On the campaign of 851, see Lupus, *epistolae* 82–83, ed. Levillain, *Correspondance*, 2:66–68.

22. Lupus, *epistola* 106, ed. Levillain, *Correspondance*, 2:138.

23. On Lupus's refusal of the abbacy of Saint-Amand, see *epistola* 67, ed. Levillain, *Correspondance*, 1:246–48.

24. See Lupus, *epistolae* 19, 32, ed. Levillain, *Correspondance*, 1:102–4, 146–50.

25. See Lupus, *epistolae* 43, 45, 47–48, ed. Levillain, *Correspondance*, 1:178–84, 186–92, 196–202; *epistola* 82, *Correspondance*, 2:266.

26. AB 833, pp. 9–10; Lupus, *epistolae* 58, 65, ed. Levillain, *Correspondance*, 1:224–28, 238–42.

27. Lupus, *epistola* 61, ed. Levillain, *Correspondance*, 1:232–34.

28. Lupus, *epistolae* 32, 36, 58, ed. Levillain, *Correspondance*, 1:148, 158, 224–26. On Adalhard's patronage, see J. L. Nelson, *Politics and Ritual in Early Medieval Europe* (London, 1986), pp. 201 n. 22, 212, 218.

29. Lupus, *epistolae* 42, 49, and 57, ed. Levillain, *Correspondance*, 1:174–78, 202–8, and 220–24.

30. Synod of Ver (844) 12, ed. Hartmann, MGH:Con. 3:42.1–2. Lupus, *epistolae* 42–43, 45, 47–49, ed. Levillain, *Correspondance*, 1:176, 180, 188, 198–200, 204–6.

31. Lupus, *epistolae* 32, 47, ed. Levillain, *Correspondance*, 1:176, 198. On the warning to Nominoë, see Lupus, *epistola* 81, ed. Levillain, *Correspondance*, 2:62.

32. Lupus, *epistola* 58, ed. Levillain, *Correspondance*, 1:226.

33. Lupus, *epistola* 43, *Correspondance*, 1:182; Synod of Ver (844) 12, ed. Hartmann, MGH:Con. 3:42–44.

34. Lupus, *epistola* 45, ed. Levillain, *Correspondance*, 1:188; *epistola* 43, *Correspondance*, 1:180–82.

35. On the return of the cell, see Lupus, *epistolae* 84–86, ed. Levillain, *Correspondance*, 2:72–76. On the date, see Levillain, *Correspondance*, 2:76–77 n. 1.

36. Lupus, *epistola* 48, ed. Levillain, *Correspondance*, 1:200–202.

37. Lupus, *epistola* 88, ed. Levillain, *Correspondance*, 2:84.

38. Lupus, *epistola* 88, ed. Levillain, *Correspondance*, 2:82–84.

39. On Charles's extensive property needs in 840–45, see Nelson, *Politics and Ritual*, pp. 223–25, 77–82.

40. Nithard, *Historiarum* 2.2, ed. Lauer, p. 42.

41. See F. Lot, "Note sur le sénéchal Alard," *Le Moyen Age* 2d ser., 12 (1908): 187–89 [185–201].

42. Lupus, *epistola* 48, ed. Levillain, *Correspondance*, 1:202.

43. Lupus, *epistola* 119, ed. Levillain, *Correspondance*, 2:180; see *epistola* 77, *Correspondance*, 2:22.

44. See Goffart, *The Le Mans Forgeries*, pp. 15–17.

45. Lupus, *epistola* 13, ed. Levillain, *Correspondance*, 1:88–90. See *Vita Maximi episcopi Trevirensis*, ed. B. Krusch, MGH:SRM 3:72–73, and Lot, "Le sénéchal Alard," p. 191, who provide conflicting evidence on the dates of Adalhard's abbacy. See also J. F. Böhmer, *Regesta imperii*, vol. 1, *Die Regesten des Kaiserreichs unter den*

Karolingern 751–918, ed. E. Mühlbacher and J. Lechner (Innsbruck, 1908; repr. Hildesheim, 1966), p. 449.

46. Lupus, *Vita Maximini* 5, ed. Krusch, MGH:SRM 3:76–77; M. L. W. Laistner, *Thought and Letters in Western Europe,* A.D. *500 to 900,* 2d ed. (Ithaca, N.Y., 1957), p. 259 n. 1. See also Wallace-Hadrill, *The Frankish Church,* pp. 311–12.

47. Lupus, *Vita Maximini* 17, ed. Krusch, MGH:SRM 3:80; Anon., *Vita sancti Maximini et uaria miracula Treverensis patrata* 12, ed. G. Henschenius and D. Papebrochius, *Acta Sanctorum . . . maii tomus septimus* (Paris, 1668; repr. 1866), p. 24a [21a–24b]. H. H. Anton, *Trier im Frühen Mittelalter,* Quellen und Forschungen aus den Gebiet der Geschichte, Neue Folge, Heft 9 (Paderborn, 1987), pp. 197, 208–9, has associated the work with the time of Weomad, who became the bishop of Trier in 762.

48. Lupus, *Vita Maximini* 17, ed. Krusch, MGH:SRM 3:80. On this vision, see M. Aubrun, "Caractères et portée religieuse et sociale des *Visiones* en Occident du VIᵉ au XIᵉ siècle," *Cahiers de civilisation médiévale: Xᵉ–XIIᵉ siècles* 23 (1980): 121 n.126.

49. Charlemagne, charter 66, ed. E. Mühlbacher, MGH: *Diplomata Karolinorum,* vol. 1 (Hanover, 1906; repr. Munich, 1979), p. 96.7–8 [95–97]; Lupus, *Vita Maximini* 21–23, ed. Krusch, MGH:SRM 3:81.

50. See *Vita Rigoberti episcopi Remensis* 4–5, ed. W. Levison, MGH:SRM 7 (Hanover, 1920), pp. 64–65, and see also Flodoard, *Historia Remensis ecclesiae* 2.11, ed. Heller and Waitz, MGH:SS 13:459; Notker, *Gesta Karoli Magni* 1.31, ed. Haefele, MGH:SRG n.s. 12:43–44; Virgil, *Aeneid* 3.613–91.

51. *Miracula Martini abbatis Vertauensis* 7, ed. B. Krusch, MGH:SRM 3:572.

52. *Miracula Martini abbatis Vertauensis* 18, ed. B. Krusch, MGH:SRM 3:575.

53. Herlihy, "Church Property on the European Continent," p. 91.

54. Hincmar, *Vita Remigii* 22, ed. Krusch, MGH:SRM 3:315–16; Flodoard, *Historia Remensis ecclesiae* 1.17, ed. Heller and Waitz, MGH:SS 13:427.

55. See Hincmar, *carmen* 8, ed. Traube, MGH:PLAC 3.2:420; Flodoard, *Historia Remensis ecclesiae* 4.30, MGH:SS 13:554. See also Philippe Depreux, "*Imbuendis ad fidem prefulgidum surrexit lumen gentibus:* La dévotion à Saint Remi de Reims aux IXᵉ et Xᵉ siècles," *Cahiers de civilisation médiévale* 35 (1992): 111–29. A drawing of the tomb (see Fig. 21) was preserved in Bernard de Montfaucon, *Les monuments de la monarchie Française . . . ,* vol. 1, *L'origine des François et la suite des rois jusqu'à Philippe I* (Paris, 1729), pl. 28. The figures on the tomb are identified by K. F. Morrison, "*Unum ex multis:* Hincmar of Rheims' Medical and Aesthetic Rationales for Unification," in *Nascita dell'Europa ed Europa Carolingia, un' equazione da verificare, 19–25 aprile 1979,* Settimane di Studio del Centro Italiano di Studi sull'Alto Medioevo, 27 (Spoleto, 1981), pp. 661–65 [583–712]. See also A. K. Porter, "The Tomb of Hincmar and Carolingian Sculpture," *Burlington Magazine* 287 (1927): 75–91. On the twelfth-century date of the tomb and its extant fragments, see A. Prache, "Les monuments funéraires des carolingiens éléves à Saint-Remi de Reims au XIIᵉ siècle," *Revue de l'Art* 6 (1969): 70–75 [68–76]; R. Hamann-Mac Lean, "Die Reimser Denkmale des französischen Königtums im 12. Jahrhundert. Saint-Remi als Grabkirche im frühen und hohen Mittelalter," in *Beiträge zur Bildung der französischen Nation im Früh- und Hochmittelalter,* ed H. Beumann, Nationes, 4 (Sigmaringen, 1983), pp. 201 [93–259].

56. Hincmar, *Vita Remigii* 32, ed. Krusch, MGH:SRM 3:336–40 and see pp. 341–47; Flodoard, *Historia Remensis ecclesiae* 1.19, ed. Heller and Waitz, MGH:SS 13:428–34. See A. H. M. Jones, P. Grierson, and J. A. Crook, "The Authenticity of the 'Testamentum s. Remigii,'" *Revue Belge de philologie et d'histoire* 35 (1957): 356–73.

57. Hincmar, *Vita Remigii* 24, ed. Krusch, MGH:SRM 3:320.28; Flodoard, *Historia Remensis ecclesiae* 1.20, ed. Heller and Waitz, MGH:SS 13:434.28–29.

58. Hincmar, *Vita Remigii* 28, ed. Krusch, MGH:SRM 3:323; Flodoard, *Historia Remensis ecclesiae* 1.20, ed. Heller and Waitz, MGH:SS 13:435.38–45.

59. Hincmar, *Vita Remigii* 28, ed. Krusch, MGH:SRM 3:325.18–24; Flodoard, *Historia Remensis ecclesiae* 1.20, ed. Heller and Waitz, MGH:SS 13:436.39–44.

60. Hincmar, *Pro ecclesiae libertatum defensione* 1, PL 125:1044B5–6.

61. Hincmar, *Pro ecclesiae libertatum defensione* 1, PL 125:1051A9–12.

62. See the summary review of Hincmar's correspondence in Flodoard, *Historia Remensis ecclesiae* 3.20, ed. Heller and Waitz, MGH:SS 13:511–13; about the correspondence with Erluin, see Flodoard, *Historia Remensis ecclesiae* 3.26, ed. Heller and Waitz, MGH:SS 13:544.31–35.

63. Hincmar, *Vita Remigii* 28, ed. Krusch, MGH:SRM 3:324; Flodoard, *Historia Remensis ecclesiae* 1.20, ed. Heller and Waitz, MGH:SS 13:436.13–17. Richuin is mentioned in Charles the Bald, charter 75, ed. Tessier, *Receuil des Actes de Charles II,* 1:213.2.

64. Hincmar, *Vita Remigii* 28, ed. Krusch, MGH:SRM 3:325.4–6.

65. See J. Bédier, *La Chanson de Roland (Commentaires)* (1927; Paris, 1968), p. 513; U. T. Holmes, "The Post-Bédier Theories on the Origins of the *Chansons de Geste,*" *Speculum* 30 (1955): 77 and n. 17a [72–81].

66. Flodoard, *Historia Remensis ecclesiae* 3.20, ed. Heller and Waitz, MGH:SS 13:511.12–14; Hincmar, *epistola* 114, ed. Perels, MGH:Ep. 8.1:57. See also J. Devisse, *Hincmar, archevêque de Reims, 845–882,* 3 vols. Travaux d'histoire ethico-politique 29 (Geneva, 1975–76), 1:281–366.

67. Flodoard, *Historia Remensis ecclesiae* 3.20, 3.21, ed. Heller and Waitz, MGH:SS 13:511, 517; Hincmar, *epistolae* 116–18, ed. Perels, MGH:Ep. 8.1:57–58.

68. Flodoard, *Historia Remensis ecclesiae* 3.20, ed. Heller and Waitz, MGH:SS 13:511; see Hincmar, *epistolae* 115, ed. Perels, MGH:Ep. 8.1:57.

69. See *Epistola Synodi Carisiacensis* 2, ed. Hartmann, MGH:Con. 3:409 [408–27]; and see Ps. 54:16 (55:15).

70. *Epistola Synodi Carisiacensis* 4, ed. Hartmann, MGH:Con. 3:410.

71. *Epistola Synodi Carisiacensis* 4, ed. Hartmann, MGH:Con. 3:411.14–17.

72. *Epistola Synodi Carisiacensis* 5, ed. Hartmann, MGH:Con. 3:411.

73. *Epistola Synodi Carisiacensis* 7, ed. Hartmann, MGH:Con. 3:413.

74. *Epistola Synodi Carisiacensis* 7–8, 12, 14, ed. Hartmann, MGH:Con. 3:414, 418, 421–23.

75. *Epistola Synodi Carisiacensis* 11, ed. Hartmann, MGH:Con. 3:419.11–13.

76. *Epistola Synodi Carisiacensis* 7, ed. Hartmann, MGH:Con. 3:414.21–415.4. On Charles Martel in hell, see W. Lesne, *Histoire* 2.1:247–49; W. Levison, "Die Politik in den Jenseitsvisionen des frühen Mittelalters," *Aus rheinischer und fränkischer Frühzeit*

(Düsseldorf, 1948), pp. 240–41; and E. Dunninger, *Politische und geschichtliche Elemente im mittelalterlichen Jenseitsvisionen biz zum Ende des 13. Jahrhunderts* (Innaugural-Dissertation, Universität zu Würzburg, 1962), pp. 18–20; U. Nonn, "Das Bild Karl Martells in den lateinischen Quellen vornehmlich des 8. and 9. Jahrhunderts," FS 4 (1970): 106–14 [70–137]; Devisse, *Hincmar,* 1:323–25; J.M. Wallace-Hadrill, "History in the Mind of Archbishop Hincmar," in *The Writing of History in the Middle Ages: Essays Presented to Sir Richard Southern,* ed. R. H. C. Davis and Wallace-Hadrill (Oxford, 1981), pp. 50–52 [43–70]; Aubrun, "Caractères," pp. 121–22.

77. *Vita Eucherii,* ed. W. Levison, MGH:SRM 7:51; *Vita Rigoberti,* ed. Levison, MGH:SRM 7:70.

78. Adrevald, *Miracula sancti Benedicti* 14, ed. Holder-Egger, MGH:SS 15.1:483–84. See also W. Goffart, "Le Mans, Saint Scholastica, and the Literary Tradition of the Translation of Saint Benedict," *Revue Benedictine* 77 (1967): 107–41.

79. Flodoard, *Historia Remensis ecclesiae* 2.12, ed. Heller and Waitz, MGH:SS 13:460. In one of the manuscripts of the AF, a reviser introduced a précis of the story of the fiery damnation of Charles Martel, taken up, as he says, from Hincmar's prologue to the *Life of Saint Remigius.* In fact, what he knew was the version in the *Epistola Synodi Carisiacensis.* See AF 738, pp. 3–4.

80. See Nonn, "Das Bild Karl Martells," pp. 111–14.

81. See Hartmann, *Die Synoden der Karolingerzeit,* p. 255.

82. Hincmar, *Vita Remigii,* preface, ed. Krusch, MGH:SRM 3:252.

83. *Epistola Synodi Carisiacensis* 7, ed. Hartmann, MGH:Con. 3:417; Ps. 82:13–17 (83:13–17).

84. A comparison of the two sentences, with their common words italicized, follows.

Heito, *Visio Wettini* 11, ed. Dümmler, MGH:PLAC 2:271: "*Cui ab angelo ductore* suo protinus *responsum est . . .* "

Epistola Synodi Carisiacensis 7, ed. Hartmann, MGH:Con. 3:415.4: "*Cui* interroganti *ab angelo* eius *ductore responsum est . . .* "

85. On the older image of Charles Martel, see Thompson, *The Dissolution of the Carolingian Fisc,* pp. 16–17; Levison, *England and the Continent in the Eighth Century* (Oxford, 1946), p. 74; Lesne, *Histoire,* 2.1:1–32. For revisions, see Goffart, *The Le Mans Forgeries,* pp. 7–10, 14–15; Wallace-Hadrill, *The Frankish Church,* pp. 132–37.

86. Eriugena, *carmen* 2.1, ed. Traube, MGH:PLAC 3.2:528.57–62. On the date of the poem, see P. E. Dutton, "Eriugena, the Royal Poet," in *Jean Scot écrivain,* ed. G. H. Allard, Cahiers d'études médiévales: cahier spécial, 1 (Montreal, 1986), pp. 63–64 [51–80]. See also M. McCormick, *Eternal Victory: Triumphal Rulership in Late Antiquity, Byzantium, and the Early Medieval West* (Cambridge, 1986), p. 373.

87. See P. Grierson, "The 'Gratia dei rex' Coinage of Charles the Bald," in *Charles the Bald: Court and Kingdom,* 2d rev. ed., ed. M. T. Gibson and J. L. Nelson (Aldershot, 1990), pp. 52–64; Eriugena, *carmen* 2.1, ed. Traube, MGH:PLAC 3.2:527.1–16.

88. Heiric, *Miracula sancti Germani* 2.8, ed. O. Holder-Egger, MGH:SS 13:403–4.

89. Hincmar, *epistola* 126, ed. Perels, MGH:Ep. 8.1:64.32–36 [63–65]. See also the treatise written in the wake of the invasion: Hincmar, *De coercendis militum rapinis,* PL 125:953–56.

90. AB 859, p. 80. On Charles the Bald's handling of property after 858, see Nelson, "The Reign of Charles the Bald: A Survey," in *Charles the Bald: Court and Kingdom,* pp. 12–13 [1–22].

91. Flodoard, *Historia Remensis ecclesiae* 3.4, ed. Heller and Waitz, MGH:SS 13:476–78.

92. Flodoard, *Historia Remensis ecclesiae* 3.4, ed. Heller and Waitz, MGH:SS 13:477.7–8. See also Charles the Bald, charter 75, ed. G. Tessier et al., *Recueil des actes de Charles II le Chauve, rol de France,* 3 vols. (Paris, 1943–55), 1:212; AB 844, p. 48.

93. See Constable, "*'Nona et decima,'*" pp. 242–44.

94. Flodoard, *Historia Remensis ecclesiae* 1.24, ed. Heller and Waitz, MGH:SS 13:444.9–38; Tessier, introductory comments, *Recueil des actes de Charles II,* 3:5 and n.7.

95. Hincmar, *De uilla Nouilliaco,* ed. O. Holder-Egger, MGH:SS 15.2 (Hanover, 1888), pp. 1167–69; Flodoard, *Historia Remensis ecclesiae* 2.17, 3.10, 17–18, 20, 26, ed. Heller and Waitz, MGH:SS 13:464.44–47, 465.7–8, 484.14–17, 510.15–16, 513.20, 544–45.

96. AB 876, p. 209; Isa. 33:1; AB 876, p. 207.

97. Flodoard, *Historia Remensis ecclesiae* 3.26, ed. Heller and Waitz, MGH:SS 13:543.

98. AB 878, pp. 222–27.

99. Hincmar, *Vita Remigii* 25, ed. Krusch, MGH:SRM 3:321–22; Flodoard, *Historia Remensis ecclesiae* 1.19, 20, ed. Heller and Waitz, MGH:SS 13:431.39–41, 435.18–25.

100. Hincmar, *Vita Remigii* 25, ed. Krusch, MGH:SRM 3:322.4–7. See also *Vita Remigii* 31, MGH:SRM 3:329.16–17.

101. See Flodoard, *Historia Remensis ecclesiae* 3.23, ed. Heller and Waitz, MGH:SS 13:528.29–31.

102. Vladimir Nabokov, "Perfection" (1932), trans. Dmitri and Vladimir Nabokov, in Nabokov, *Tyrants Destroyed and Other Stories* (New York, 1975), p. 187.

103. AB 877, pp. 216–17.

104. Hincmar, *Vita Remigii* 9, ed. Krusch, MGH:SRM 3:286–87, and see also the chapter heading, p. 255.13–24.

105. Hincmar, *Vita Remigii* 9, ed. Krusch, MGH:SRM 3:287.11–17.

106. *Visio Bernoldi,* PL 125:1115B–1120B. Though Devisse, *Hincmar,* 2:821, notes that only one twelfth-century manuscript of the work survives, we need to bear in mind that Flodoard knew a copy that must have existed in the archives of the cathedral of Rheims: Flodoard, *Historia Remensis ecclesiae* 3.3 and 18, ed. Heller and Waitz, MGH:SS 13:476, 509. There is no internal or textual support for the title supplied by Migne: *De uisione Bernoldi presbyteri.*

107. *Visio Bernoldi,* PL 125:1116B4–6.

108. *Visio Bernoldi,* PL 125:1116B3–4. See Riché, "Les représentations du palais," *Francia* 4 (1976): 168–71, and p. 230 above.

109. Flodoard, *Historia Remensis ecclesiae* 3.13, ed. Heller and Waitz, MGH:SS 13:499.32–50.

110. See Hincmar, *epistola,* PL 126:537D9–542D11; PL 126:293–95; P. R. McKeon, *Hincmar of Laon and Carolingian Politics* (Urbana, Ill., 1978), pp. 78–83.

111. Hincmar, *Schedula siue Libellus expostulationis* 33, PL 126:624A2–D13. Since Pardulus was the bishop of Laon between 849 and 856, and Aeneas was bishop of Paris between 856–57 and 870, it is not likely that that they were ever associated as bishops in any controversial synod. The figure of forty-one bishops is, however, very like the number of high prelates who would gather together at great synods like Savonnières in 859, but Hincmar himself was almost always among them. A similar number of prelates, including Pardulus, came together at Soissons in 853; Aeneas was in attendance, but as a notary of the palace: see Synod of Soissons, ed. Hartmann, MGH:Con. 3:277.20, 279.9. Thus, it may be that the *Visio Bernoldi* does not allude to a specific synodal gathering of wicked bishops.

112. *Visio Bernoldi,* PL 125:1116C11–14.

113. *Visio Bernoldi,* PL 125:1116D4–12.

114. See *Capitulare Carisiacense* 12, ed. Boretius and Krause, MGH:Cap. 2.1:358–59 [355–61]; R. McKitterick, "Charles the Bald (823–877) and His Library: The Patronage of Learning," *English Historical Review* 95 (1980): 28 [28–47].

115. Flodoard, *Historia Remensis ecclesiae* 3.18, ed. Heller and Waitz, MGH:SS 13:509.27–28.

116. Agnellus, *Liber Pontificalis ecclesiae Ravennatis* 174, ed. Holder-Egger, MGH: *Scriptorum rerum Langobardicarum et Italicarum,* p. 390.25–30; AF 876, p. 86.

117. *Visio Bernoldi,* PL 125:1117B1–1118A12; T. S. Eliot, *The Hollow Men,* in *The Complete Poems and Plays of T. S. Eliot* (London, 1969), p. 83.

118. Voncq is mentioned in the will of Remigius: Flodoard, *Historia Remensis ecclesiae* 1.19, ed. Heller and Waitz, MGH:SS 13:432.15. On Charles's donation, see Flodoard, *Historia Remensis ecclesiae* 3.10, ed. Heller and Waitz, MGH:SS 13:484.5–7; Charles the Bald, charter 393, ed. Tessier et al., *Receuil des actes de Charles II,* 2:376.

119. Charles the Bald, charter 425, ed. Tessier et al., *Receuil des actes de Charles II,* 2:452.15.

120. See Morrison, "*Unum ex multis,*" p. 622.

121. *Visio Bernoldi,* PL 125:1118D3–6.

122. *Visio Bernoldi,* PL 125:1119B1–1120A3.

123. Devisse, *Hincmar,* 2:822. Devisse thinks it difficult to believe that Hincmar had nothing to do with the composition of the *Visio Bernoldi,* but he still finds it hard to believe that Hincmar would have inserted his own name into such a dream text. Yet Devisse characterizes the *Visio* and the *Vita Remigii* as the opening compositions of the last and somewhat irrational phase of Hincmar's thought. For an interesting review of Hincmar's status as fabricator, however, see Wallace-Hadrill, *The Long-haired Kings and Other Studies in Frankish History* (London, 1962), pp. 95–105.

124. At least two manuscripts of Ambrose's work were owned by Hincmar and survive today in Rheims, Bibliothèque municipale, MSS 376 and 377: see *Catalogue général des manuscrits des bibliothèques publiques de France. Départements,* vol. 38.1, *Reims* (Paris, 1904), pp. 484–87. On Hincmar's knowledge of Ambrose, see Devisse, *Hincmar,* 3:1355–56. Sedulius Scottus said that after the Emperor Theodosius had been

rebuked and done penance, he recognized that Ambrose alone rightly deserved to be called bishop: Sedulius Scottus, *De rectoribus christianis* 12, ed. Hellmann, p. 56.23.

125. Vision literature occupies a significant place in Flodoard's works: see *Visio Gerhardi*, in *Historia Remensis ecclesiae* 3.7, ed. Heller and Waitz, MGH:SS 13:480–81; *Visiones Flothildis*, in *Les Annales de Flodoard*, ed. P. Lauer, Collection de textes pour servir à l'étude et a l'enseignement de l'histoire, 39 (Paris, 1905), pp. 170–76. Flodoard also reported that Saint Remigius had appeared to Bishop Herigar of Mainz early in the tenth century: *Historia Remensis ecclesiae* 1.20, ed. Heller and Waitz, MGH:SS 13:436.45–437.8.

126. Hincmar, *Ad Ludouicum Balbum regem. Noui regis instructio ad rectam administrationem* 1, PL 125.985A4–8 [983D–990B]; Levison, "Die Politik," p. 242.

127. Hincmar, *Ad Ludouicum Balbum regem* 9, PL 125.988D–989B.

128. Hincmar, *Ad Ludouicum Balbum regem* 9, PL 125.988C12–D1.

CHAPTER SEVEN: IN THIS MODERN AGE

1. Matthias Borbonius, in *Delitiae Poetarum Germanorum huius superiorisque aevi illustrium* . . . , ed. J. Gruterus, 6 vols. (Frankfurt, 1612), 1:685, attributed the saying (with *omnia* in place of *tempora*) to Lothar. "Omnia mutantur" comes from Ovid, *Metamorphoses* 15.165; see also Marcus Aurelius, *Meditations* 9.19. In 1577, R. Holinshed, in his *Chronicles of England, Scotland, and Ireland* 6 vols. (London, 1807–18; repr. New York, 1965), 1:302, printed the saying with *tempora*, but without attribution. John Owen reprinted the revised form: *Ioannis Audoeni Epigrammatum libri I–X*, 8.58, 2 vols., ed. J. R. C. Martyn, Textus Minores, 52 (Leiden, 1978), 2:100. The saying had considerable currency in early modern English literature: see *The Oxford Dictionary of English Proverbs* 3d ed., rev. F. P. Wilson (Oxford, 1970), p. 825b.

2. P. E. Schramm, *Herrschaftszeichen und Staatssymolik: Beiträge zu ihrer Geschichte vom dritten bis zum sechzehnten Jahrhundert*, in MGH:Schriften 13.1–3 (Stuttgart, 1954–56), 1:288–369, 3:629–727. See also J. M. Wallace-Hadrill, "A Carolingian Prince: The Emperor Charles the Bald," *Proceedings of the British Academy* 64 (1978): 155–84.

3. VKM 24, p. 29.6–10. See J. L. Nelson, *Politics and Ritual in Early Medieval Europe* (London, 1986), p. 49.

4. VKM 29, p. 33.11–14; Poeta Saxo, *Annales* 5, ed. Winterfeld, MGH:PLAC 4.1:64.377–80. Thegan, *Vita Hludowici* 19, ed. Pertz, MGH:SS 2:594, claimed that Louis the Pious came to reject this poetry which he had encountered in his younger years.

5. See Agnellus of Ravenna, *Liber Pontificalis ecclesiae Ravennatis* 94, ed. Holder-Egger, MGH: *Scriptores rerum Langobardicarum et Italicarum*, pp. 337–38.

6. Ermold, *In honorem Hludowici* 4, ed. Faral, p. 164.2143–47. For a translation, see *Carolingian Civilization: A Reader*, ed. P. E. Dutton (Peterborough, Ont., 1993), pp. 265–67. On the artistic program, see W. Lammers, "Ein karolingisches Bildprogramm in der *aula regia* von Ingelheim," in *Festschrift für Hermann Heimpel zum 70. Geburtstag am 19. September 1971*, 3 vols. (Göttingen, 1972), 3:226–89. See also K. J.

Connant, *Carolingian and Romanesque Architecture, 800 to 1200* (Middlesex, 1966), pp. 59–60, and Lawrence Nees, *A Tainted Mantle: Hercules and the Classical Tradition at the Carolingian Court* (Philadelphia, 1991), pp. 270–77.

7. A X 869 (868), pp. 26–27; Prov. 28:2. On the Cologne continuator, see H. Löwe, "Studien zu den *Annales Xantenses*," *Deutsches Archiv* 8 (1951): 59–99. This annalist, who was active between 873 and 876, shortened Gerward's annals between 852 and 860 and added his own entries to the years 861–73.

8. The issue of Lothar II's attempted divorce concerned the Cologne continuator, since his Archbishop Gunthar had been deposed for his intrigues in the matter. The entry for A X 869 (868), pp. 27–28, weaves mournful passages from Matthew and the Lamentations of Jeremiah into its description of the sorry state of the church of Cologne.

9. A X 871 (870), p. 30; A X 868 (867), p. 26; Joel 2:17.

10. A X 873 (872), p. 33; see Ps. 88:33 (89:32).

11. Eriugena, *epistola*, ed. Dümmler, M G H:Ep. 6:158.29–31.

12. Nithard, *Historiarum* 4.7, ed. Lauer, p. 144; see *Historiarum* 1, prologue, ed. Lauer, p. 2. For a translation of the work; see *Carolingian Civilization: A Reader*, pp. 333–63.

13. See Nelson, *Politics and Ritual*, pp. 226–33.

14. Notker, *Gesta Karoli Magni* 1.1, ed. Haefele, M G H:S R G n.s. 12:1. 26. See T. Siegrist, *Herrscherbild und Weltsicht bei Notker Balbus: Untersuchungen zur den Gesta Karoli*, Geist und Werk der Zeiten, 8 (Zurich, 1963), pp. 109–21; J. M. Wallace-Hadrill, *Early Germanic Kingship in England and on the Continent* (Oxford, 1971), p. 128; B. Schneidmüller, *Karolingische Tradition und frühes französisches Königtum. Untersuchungen zur Herrschaftslegitimation der westfränkisch-französischen Monarchie im 10. Jahrhundert*, Frankfurter historische Abhandlungen, 22 (Wiesbaden, 1979), pp. 23–26; H.-W. Goetz, *Strukturen der spätkarolingischen Epoche im Spiegel der Vorstellungen eines Zeitgenossischen Mönchs: eine Interpretation der 'Gesta Karoli' Notkers von Sankt Gallen* (Bonn, 1981), pp. 60–62, 70–85; D. Ganz, "Humor as History in Notker's *Gesta Karoli Magni*," in *Monks, Nuns, and Friars in Mediaeval Society*, ed. E. B. King, J. T. Schaefer, and W. B. Wadley (Sewanee, 1989), pp. 171–83.

15. Dan. 2:1–49. See D. Wells, "The Medieval Nebuchadnezzar: The Exegetical Tradition of Daniel IV," F S 16 (1982): 397–409 [308–432].

16. Edward Gibbon, *The History of the Decline and Fall of the Roman Empire*, ed. J. B. Bury, 7 vols. (London, 1909–14), 5:312.

17. V K M 25, p. 30.

18. Ekkehard IV, *Casus sancti Galli*, ed. J. von Arx, M G H:S S 2:89.

19. *Visio Karoli Magni*, ed. P. Jaffé, *Bibliotheca rerum Germanicarum* 4 (Berlin, 1868), p. 701 [701–4]. For a translation, see *Carolingian Civilization: A Reader*, pp. 423–24. See also H. Fichtenau, *The Carolingian Empire: The Age of Charlemagne*, trans. P. Munz (New York, 1964), pp. 177–78; P. Geary, "Germanic Tradition and Royal Ideology in the Ninth Century," F S 21 (1987): 274–94.

20. J. W. Dunne, *An Experiment with Time*, 3d ed. (London, 1939), p. 69.

21. *Visio Karoli Magni*, ed. Jaffé, p. 704.

22. See J. Fleckenstein, *Die Hofkapelle der deutschen Könige*, vol. 1, *Grundlegung:*

Die karolingische Hofkapelle, MGH:Schriften 16.1 (Stuttgart, 1959), pp. 176–78, 185–90, 197–200; AF 872, p. 76; *Epitaphia Moguntia* 2, ed. K. Strecker, MGH:PLAC 4.3:1037.

23. See J. K. Bostock, *A Handbook of Old High German Literature*, 2d ed., rev. by K. C. King and D. R. McLintock (Oxford, 1976), pp. 136–68; A. R. Bell, "Muspilli: Apocalypse as Political Threat," *Studies in the Imagination* 8.1 (1975): 75–104. Vatican, MS. Pal. Lat. 1447, contains a ninth-century copy of the *Heliand*: see W. M. Lindsay and P. Lehmann, "The (Early) Mayence Sciptorium," *Palaeographica Latina* 4 (1925): 20–22 [15–39].

24. Otfrid, *epistola*, ed. Dümmler, MGH:Ep. 6:166–69. For a translation, see *Carolingian Civilization: A Reader*, pp. 419–22. See also Bostock, *A Handbook of Old High German Literature*, pp. 190–212; D. Geuenich, "Die volkssprachige Überlieferung der Karolingerzeit aus der Sicht des Historikers," *Deutsches Archiv* 39 (1983): 121–30 [104–30]; B. Bischoff, "Bücher am Hofe Ludwigs des Deutschen und die Privatbibliothek des Kanzlers Grimalt," *Mittelalterlichen Studien. Ausgewählte Aufsätze zur Schriftkunde und Literaturgeschichte*, 3 vols. (Stuttgart, 1966–81), 3:190–91 [187–212]; B.-S. Albert, "Raban Maur," *Revue d'histoire ecclésiastique* 86 (1991): 32–44.

25. Notker, *Gesta Karoli Magni* 2.10, 18, ed. Haefele, MGH:SRG n.s. 12:65–66, 88–89; Regino, *Chronicon* 876, ed. F. Kurze, MGH:SRGUS (Hanover, 1890), p. 110.

26. Geary, "Germanic Tradition and Royal Ideology in the Ninth Century," pp. 278–80, 288–90.

27. Notker, *Gesta Karoli Magni* 2.11, ed. Haefele, MGH:SRG n.s. 12:68; Bischoff, "Bücher am Hofe Ludwigs des Deutschen," p. 191; Hincmar, *De uerbis Psalmi: 'Herodii domus dux est eorum,'* ed. Perels, MGH:Ep. 8.1:168–72. The psalm in question is 103:17 (104:17): see R. McKitterick, *The Carolingians and the Written Word* (Cambridge, 1989), p. 268.

28. Hrabanus, *epistola* 34, ed. Dümmler, MGH:Ep. 5:468.23–26 [467–69]. A portion of the commentary on Dan. 5 seems to be missing in the manuscript tradition. See also Bischoff, "Bücher am Hofe Ludwigs des Deutschen," pp. 187–92.

29. Ermold, *In honorem Hludowici* 2, ed. Faral, p. 66.839–40.

30. Ermold, *In honorem Hludowici* 4, ed. Faral, p. 164.2156–63.

31. See Notker, *Gesta Karoli Magni* 2.14, ed. Haefele, MGH:SRG n.s. 12:78.

32. Alcuin, *epistola* 136, ed. Dümmler, MGH:Ep. 4:205–10; *epistola* 41, ed. Dümmler, MGH:Ep. 4:84. See also Geary, "Germanic Tradition and Royal Ideology in the Ninth Century," pp. 283–87.

33. AX 852, p. 18.

34. On the Germanic custom of male initiation, see Tacitus, *Germania* 13; Astronomer, *Vita Hludowici* 6, ed. Pertz, MGH:SS 2:610; and Notker, *Gesta Karoli Magni* 2.12, ed. Haefele, MGH:SRG n.s. 12:74.

35. Notker, *Gesta Karoli Magni* 2.12, ed. Haefele, MGH:SRG n.s. 12:70–71; 2.14, MGH:SRG n.s. 12:78; and 2.18, MGH:SRG n.s. 12:88–89; Thegan, *Vita Hludowici* 44, ed. Pertz, MGH:SS 2:599.

36. See Bostock, *Handbook of Old High German Literature*, pp. 239–48; J. Carles, "Le *Ludwigslied* et la victoire à Saucourt-en-Vimeu (881)," in *La Chanson de geste et le*

mythe carolingien. Mélanges René Louis, 2 vols. (Saint-Père-sous-Vézelay, 1982), 1:101–9; D. N. Yeandle, "The Ludwigslied: King, Church, and Context," in *'mit regulu bithuungan': Neue Arbeiten zur althochdeutschen Poesie und Sprache,* ed. J. L. Flood and D. N. Yeandle, Göppinger Arbeiten zur Germanistik, 500 (Göppingen, 1989), pp. 18–79; R. Kemper, "Das Ludwigslied und die liturgischen Rechtstitel des westfränkischen Königtums," in *'mit regulu bithuungan',* pp. 1–17; McKitterick, *The Carolingians and the Written Word,* pp. 232–35. For a translation of the poem, see *Carolingian Civilization: A Reader,* pp. 482–83.

37. Liutbert, *epistola,* ed. Dümmler, MGH:Ep. 6:165–66; AF 870, p. 72.

38. Astronomer, *Vita Hludowici* 56, ed. Pertz, MGH:SS 2:642; AF 856, pp. 46–47; AB 854, p. 70.

39. VKM preface, pp. 1–2.

40. Walahfrid, prologue, VKM, pp. xxviii–xxix. Lupus, *epistola* 1, ed. Levillain, *Correspondance,* 1:4. See also Lupus, *epistolae* 9, 133, ed. Levillain, *Correspondance,* 1:72, 2:218.

41. Walahfrid, prologue, VKM, p. xxix.

42. See W. Freund, *Modernus und andere Zeitbegriffe des Mittelalters,* Neue münstersche Beiträge zur Geschichtsforschung, 4 (Cologne, 1957), pp. 46–52; W. Hartmann, "*Modernus* und *Antiquus*: zur Verbreitung und Bedeutung dieser Bezeichnungen in der wissenschaftlichen Literatur vom 9. bis zum 12. Jahrhundert," in *Antiqui und Moderni: Traditionsbewusstsein und Fortschrittsbewusstsein im späten Mittelalter,* ed. A. Zimmermann, Miscellanea Mediaevalia, 9 (Berlin, 1974), pp. 21–23; E. Gossmann, *Antiqui und Moderni im Mittelalter: eine geschichtliche Standortbestimmung,* Veröffentlichungen des Grabmann-Instituts, 23 (Munich, 1974), pp. 36–53.

43. Angelomus of Luxeuil, in his *Commentarius in Genesin,* referred to Bede as a *modernus doctor* and admired the modern efforts of men on behalf of faith: see Angelomus, *epistola,* ed. Dümmler, MGH:Ep. 5:623, and see PL 115:117B10 and 197B11. In a ninth-century catalogue, Alcuin was described as a *magister modernus*: see M. L. W. Laistner, "Some Early Medieval Commentaries on the Old Testament," *Harvard Theological Review* 46 (1953): 29–30 [27–46],repr. in *The Intellectual Heritage of the Early Middle Ages: Selected Essays by M. L. W. Laistner,* ed. C. G. Starr (New York, 1966), pp. 181–201. Notker thought that Alcuin was more learned than any other man "modernorum temporum" and that his teaching allowed the modern Gauls and Franks to equal the Romans and Greeks: see *Gesta Karoli Magni* 1.2, ed. Haefele, MGH:SRG n.s. 12:3. Hrabanus Maurus said that in this *modernum tempus* the biblical books of Judith, Tobit, and Maccabees were considered canonical and were publicly read: see Hrabanus, *epistola* 20, ed. Dümmler, MGH:Ep. 5:426.7–9, and *Commentaria in libros II paralipomenon,* PL 109:281A2–3. Eriugena counted it to the special credit of Charles the Bald that he had increased the Catholic faith through his patronage of new and modern editions of the works of the Fathers: see Eriugena, *epistola,* ed. Dümmler, MGH:Ep. 6:158. To many men of the ninth century, books themselves may have been thought of as old things, while current life and newness were associated with speech: see Thegan, *Vita Hludowici* 19, ed. Pertz, MGH:SS 2:594; AF 852, p. 42; and Einhard, *Translatio et miracula* 1.1, ed. Waitz, MGH:SS 15.1:239.

44. Paschasius Radbertus, *Epitaphium Arsenii* 2.3, 1.26, ed. Dümmler, pp. 80, 57; Hincmar, *De ordine palatii,* prologue, ed. Gross and Schieffer, MGH: *Fontes iuris germanici antiqui in usum scholarum* 3:32, 34.

45. See above pp. 63–64, 66, 181. Pope Nicholas I, *epistola* 43, ed. Perels, MGH:Ep. 6:317.38–39, referred to "praedecessores uestri, antiqui principes adhuc et moderni" in a letter of 866 to the nobles of Aquitaine.

46. AF 863, p. 56; AF 866, p. 64; AF 867, p. 66; AF 871, pp. 72–74; AF 872, p. 75; AF 873, pp. 72–73. See also R. Schieffer, "Vater und Söhne im Karolingerhause," in *Beiträge zur Geschichte des Regnum Francorum,* Beihefte der Francia, 22 (Sigmaringen, 1990), pp. 149–57 [149–64]; P. E. Dutton, "Beyond the *Topos* of Senescence: The Political Problems of Aged Carolingian Rulers," in *Aging and the Aged in the Middle Ages,* ed. M. M. Sheehan, Papers in Mediaeval Studies, 11 (Toronto, 1990), pp. 85–91.

47. AF 873, p. 77.

48. AF 873, pp. 77–78; Matt. 10:26.

49. AX 873, pp. 31–32; Dan. 13:28; Ps. 7:12.

50. *Vita sancti Rimberti* 20, ed. G. Waitz, MGH:SRGUS, pp. 96–97. See also Adam of Bremen, *Gesta Hammaburgensis* 1.40, ed. B. Schmeidler, MGH:SRGUS (Hanover, 1917), p. 44.

51. AB 871, p. 182; AF 871, p. 74; AX 872, p. 75; AB 872, p. 186.

52. J. L. Nelson, "A Tale of Two Princes: Politics, Text and Ideology in a Carolingian Annal," *Studies in Medieval and Renaissance History* n.s. 10 (1988): 128 [105–40].

53. Ernest Jones, *On the Nightmare,* 2d ed. (New York, 1951), pp. 154–89; Astronomer, *Vita Hludowici* 45 and 48, ed. Pertz, MGH:SS 2:634–35. Also see Jonas of Orléans, *De institutione regia,* letter-preface to Pepin of Aquitaine, ed. Reviron, pp. 129–30.

54. AB 873, pp. 190–91.

55. AB 873, p. 191.

56. See 2 Cor. 11:14: "Satan himself is transformed into an angel of light." See Hrabanus, *De uniuerso* 10.6, PL 111:291D6–10.

57. See K. F. Morrison, "*Unum ex multis:* Hincmar of Rheims' Medical and Aesthetic Rationales for Unification," in *Nascita dell'Europa ed Europa Carolingia, un'equazione da verificare, 19–25 aprile 1979,* Settimane di Studio del Centro Italiano di Studi sull'Alto Medioevo, 27 (Spoleto, 1981), pp. 620–22; Nelson, "A Tale of Two Princes," p. 130 n. 97.

58. John 13:27.

59. AB 870, p. 178. On Carloman, see S. Airlie, "The Political Behaviour of the Secular Magnates in Francia, 829–879" (Ph.D. diss., Oxford, 1985), pp. 184–90.

60. Hincmar, *Epistola ad episcopos prouinciae Lugdunensis De Carlomanno eiusque complicibus excommunicandis,* PL 126:278A13–14 [277C–280B].

61. AB 873, p. 189.

62. Nelson, "A Tale of Two Princes," pp. 113–15.

63. AF 873, p. 78.

64. AB 873, p. 194.

65. Lupus, *epistola* 31, ed. Levillain, *Correspondance,* 1:142. See Eccles. 33:20, 22. See Dutton, "Beyond the *Topos* of Senescence," pp. 87–88.

66. Notker, *Gesta Karoli Magni* 2.11, ed. Haefele, MGH:SRG n.s. 12:68.

67. Shakespeare, *Hamlet,* act 3, sc. 1, line 196.

68. ARF 746, p. 7; Astronomer, *Vita Hludowici* 19, ed. Pertz, MGH:SS 2:616; AF 855, p. 46, and AB 855, p. 71 (Lothar I, gravely ill, did end his life in the monastry of Prüm); VKM 33, p. 39 (in his will Charlemagne left open the possibility that he might withdraw from the world). See also C. Stancliffe, "Kings who Opted Out," in *Ideal and Reality in Frankish and Anglo-Saxon Society: Studies Presented to J. M. Wallace-Hadrill,* ed. P. Wormwald with D. Bullough and R. Collins (Oxford, 1983), pp. 154–76.

69. Notker, *Gesta Karoli Magni* 2.11, ed. Haefele, MGH:SRG n.s. 12:66.20–26.

70. AF 874, p. 82.

71. Flodoard, *Historia Remensis ecclesiae* 3.20, ed. Heller and Waitz, MGH:SS 13:513.9–12

72. Flodoard, *Historia Remensis ecclesiae* 3.18, ed. Heller and Waitz, MGH:SS 13:510.16–18.

73. AF 874, p. 82; Rom. 1:32.

74. Two sentences can be compared, with shared vocabulary italicized:

Heito, *Visio Wettini* 11, ed. Dümmler MGH:PLAC 2:271: "Cui ab angelo ductore suo protinus responsum est, *quod, quamuis multa* miranda et *laudabilia et deo* accepta *fecisset . . .* "

AF 874, p. 82: "Unde datur intelligi, *quod, quamuis* memoratus imperator *multa laudabilia et deo* placita *fecisset . . .* "

75. See above pp. 93–95.

76. See P. Kehr, "Die Kanzlei Ludwigs des Deutschen," in *Abhandlungen der Preussischen Akademie der Wissenschaften,* Philosophisch-historische Klasse, 1 (Berlin, 1932), p. 8 [3–30]; Fleckenstein, *Die Hofkapelle,* 1:171–75.

77. AF 874, p. 82. Vatican, MS Ottobon. Lat. 2531, fol. 6r. See G. Althoff and E. Freise et al., *Die Klostergemeinschaft von Fulda im früheren Mittelalter unter Mitwirkung,* ed. K. Schmid, Münstersche Mittelalter-Schriften, 8.1 (Münster, 1978), pl. 6; O. G. Oexle, "Die Überlieferung der Fuldischen Totenannalen," *Die Klostergemeinschaft von Fulda* 8.2.2:457–62 [447–504]; Neiske, "Vision und Totengedanken," FS 20 (1986): 156–57.

78. Lindsay and Lehmann, "The (Early) Mayence Sciptorium," pp. 15–39.

CHAPTER EIGHT: CHARLES THE FAT'S CONSTITUTIONAL DREAMS

1. AB 877, pp. 216–19; AV 877, p. 42.

2. AV 882, p. 52; AF 884, p. 101; AV 884, p. 56; Regino, *Chronicon* 884, ed. Kurze, MGH:SRGUS, pp. 121–22.

3. Regino, *Chronicon* 888, ed. Kurze, pp. 128–29.

4. See Flodoard, *Historia Remensis ecclesiae* 4.5, ed. Heller and Waitz, MGH:SS 13:563.8–12.

5. Abbo of Saint-Germain-des-Prés, *Bella Parisiacae urbis* 2, ed. H. Waquet, in Abbon, *Le siège de Paris par les Normands: Poème du IXᵉ siècle,* Les classiques de l'histoire de France au Moyen Age, 20 (Paris, 1942; repr. 1964), p. 90.330–42.

6. Abbo, *Bella Parisiacae urbis* 2, ed. Waquet, p. 98.442–46.

7. A F 888, p. 116.

8. Charles the Bald, *Capitula Pistensia* I, ed. Boretius and Krause, M G H:Cap. 2:305.33–34.

9. A V 888, pp. 64–65.

10. Regino, *Chronicon* 888, ed. Kurze, p. 129.

11. *Visio Raduini*, ed. O. Holder-Egger, *Neues Archiv* II (1886): 262–63; Flodoard, *Historia Remensis ecclesiae* 2.19, ed. Heller and Waitz, M G H:SS 13:471.

12. *Visio Raduini*, ed. Holder-Egger, p. 263.

13. See R. Holtzmann, *Französische Verfassungsgeschichte von der mitte des neunten Jahrhunderts bis zur Revolution*, Handbuch der mittelalterlichen und neueren Geschichte, 3 (Munich, 1910; repr. 1965), p. 119; B. Schneidmüller, *Karolingische Tradition und frühes französisches Königtum. Untersuchungen zur Herrschaftslegitimation der westfränkisch-französischen Monarchie im 10. Jahrhundert*, Frankfurter historische Abhandlungen, 22 (Wiesbaden, 1979), p. 47.

14. Flodoard, *Historia Remensis ecclesiae* 1.20, ed. Heller and Waitz, M G H:SS 13:434.44–435.17.

15. A B 862, p. 94; Flodoard, *Historia Remensis ecclesiae* 3.5, ed. Heller and Waitz, M G H:SS 13:478.43–479.29; Hincmar, *carmina* 1.2–3, 2, ed. Traube, M G H:PL A C 3.2:409–12. See also J. Devisse, *Hincmar, archevêque de Reims, 845–882*, 3 vols., Travaux d'histoire ethico-politique, 29 (Geneva, 1975–76), 2:916; L. Scheffczyk, *Das Mariengeheimnis in Frömmigkeit und Lehre der Karolingerzeit* (Leipzig, 1959), and "Die Stellung Marias im Kult der Karolingerzeit," *Maria im Kult*, Der deutschen Arbeitsgemeinschaft für Mariologie. Mariologische Studien, 3 (Essen, 1964), pp. 67–85.

16. See Flodoard, *Historia Remensis ecclesiae* 2.19, ed. Heller and Waitz, M G H:SS 13:470.1–5; 3.22, p. 527.43–45; 3.26, p. 540.28–32; 3.26, p. 541.52–542.7; 3.26, p. 543.12–13; 3.27, p. 548.10–11.

17. Flodoard, *Historia Remensis ecclesiae* 3.6–8, ed. Heller and Waitz, M G H:SS 13:479–82.

18. A B 869, pp. 162–63.

19. Flodoard, *Historia Remensis ecclesiae* 4.1, ed. Heller and Waitz, M G H:SS 13:555.12–16. On Fulk and his early career, see G. Schneider, *Erzbischof Fulco von Reims (883–900) und das Frankenreich*, Münchener Bieträge zur Mediävistik und Renaissance-Forschung, 14 (Munich, 1973), pp. 1–25; R. McKitterick, "The Carolingian Kings and the See of Rheims, 882–987," in *Ideal and Reality in Frankish and Anglo-Saxon Society: Studies Presented to J. M. Wallace-Hadrill*, ed. P. Wormwald with D. Bullough and R. Collins (Oxford, 1983), pp. 231–32 [228–49].

20. Flodoard, *Historia Remensis ecclesiae* 3.24, ed. Heller and Waitz, M G H:SS 13:537.26–28; see also 3.20, p. 513.30–35. On this correspondence, see E. Hlawitschka, *Lotharingien und das Reich an der Schwelle der deutschen Geschichte*, M G H:Schriften 21 (Stuttgart, 1968), pp. 233–34 and n. 32.

21. W. Levison, "Zur Textgeschichte der Vision Karls III," *Neues Archiv* 27 (1902): 493–502.

22. T. Silverstein, "Inferno, XII, 100–126, and the *Visio Karoli Crassi*," *Modern Language Notes* 51 (1936): 449–52.

23. See Levison, "Zur Textgeschichte der Vision Karls III," and Schneider, *Erzbischof Fulco von Rheims,* pp. 22–25.

24. See *Lamberti s. Audomari canonici Liber floridus codex autographus bibliothecae universitatis Gandavensis,* ed. A. Derolez (Ghent, 1968), fol. 191r, pp. 381, 414–15.

25. *Visio Karoli III,* ed. F. Lot in *Chronique de l'abbaye de Saint Riquier,* Collection de textes pour servir à l'étude et à l'enseignement de l'histoire, 17 (Paris, 1894), pp. 144–48; William of Malmesbury, *Gesta regum Anglorum* 2.3, ed. W. Stubbs, 2 vols. (London, 1887), 1:112–16; also separately ed. Waitz, MGH:SS 10 (Hanover, 1852), p. 458. For a translation, see *Carolingian Civilization: A Reader,* ed. P. E. Dutton (Peterborough, Ont. 1993), pp. 503–6.

26. *Visio Karoli III,* ed. Lot, p. 145; ed. Waitz, MGH:SS 10:458.11–14.

27. Bede, *Historica ecclesiastica* 5.12; see above pp. 44, 73.

28. Wisd. of Sol. 6:7.

29. *Visio Karoli III,* ed. Lot, p. 146; ed. Waitz, MGH:SS 10:458.26–28.

30. *Visio Karoli III,* ed. Lot, p. 147; ed. Waitz, MGH:SS 10:458.37–44.

31. *Visio Karoli III,* ed. Lot, p. 148; ed. Waitz, MGH:SS 10:458.53–55.

32. *Visio Karoli III,* ed. Lot, p. 148; ed. Waitz, MGH:SS 10:458.55–56.

33. Matt. 18:1–7.

34. *Visio Karoli III,* ed. Lot, p. 148; ed. Waitz, MGH:SS 10:458.60–62.

35. See L. Levillain's review of R. Poupardin, *La royaume de Provence,* in *Bibliothèque de l'Ecole des chartes* 63 (1902): 712–14; Levison, "Kleine Beiträge zu quellen der fränkischen Geschichte. IV: Die Vision Kaiser Karls III," *Neues Archiv* 27 (1902): 399–408; Poupardin, "La date de la *Visio Karoli tertii,*" *Bibliothèque de l'Ecole des chartes* 64 (1903): 284–88; Hlawitschka, *Lotharingien,* pp. 100–106; Schneidmüller, *Karolingische Tradition,* pp. 44–47.

36. See Flodoard, *Historia Remensis ecclesiae* 4.2, ed. Heller and Waitz, MGH:SS 13:559.27–28.

37. See Flodoard, *Historia Remensis ecclesiae* 4.1, ed. Heller and Waitz, MGH:SS 13:556.7–12, and see 1.3, p. 414.37–51.

38. See Flodoard, *Historia Remensis ecclesiae* 4.45, ed. Heller and Waitz, MGH:SS 13:594.50–595.25.

39. Notker, *Gesta Karoli Magni* 1.18, ed. Haefele, MGH:SRG n.s. 12:23–24. See also D. Ganz, "Humor as History in Notker's *Gesta Karoli Magni,*" in *Monks, Nuns and Friars in Mediaeval Society,* ed. E. B. King, J. T. Schaefer, and W. B. Wadley (Sewanee, 1989), pp. 171–83.

40. Regino, *Chronicon* 877, ed. Kurze, p. 113. On Boso and his family, see S. Airlie, "The Political Behaviour of the Secular Magnates in Francia, 829–879" (Ph. D. diss., Oxford, 1985), pp. 194–308; C. B. Bouchard, "The Bosonids or Rising to Power in the Late Carolingian Age," *French Historical Studies* 15 (1988): 407–14 [407–31].

41. AB 876, p. 200, and see AB 868, p. 151.

42. AB 879, p. 239. On the stereotypical nature of Ermengard's speech, see K. F. Werner, "Gauzlin von Saint-Denis und die westfränkische Reichsteilung von Amiens (März 880). Ein Beitrag zur Vorgeschichte von Odos Königtum," *Deutsches Archiv* 35

(1979): 404–5 n. 36 [395–462]; P. Stafford, *Queens, Concubines, and Dowagers: The King's Wife in the Early Middle Ages* (Athens, Ga., 1983), p. 24.

43. For a review of the opinions about the date of the piece, see Levillain, review of Poupardin, *Bibliothèque de l'Ecole des chartes* 63 (1902): 712–14; E. Ewig, "Kaiser Lothars Urenkel, Ludwig von Vienne, der präsumtive Nachfolger Kaiser Karls III," in *Das erste Jahrtausend*, ed. V. H. Elbern, 2 vols. in 3 (Düsseldorf, 1962), 1:336–43; U. Penndorf, *Das Problem der "Reichseinheitsidee" nach der Teilung von Verdun (843): Untersuchungen zu der späten Karolingern*, Münchener Beiträge zur Mediävistik und Renaissance-Forschung, 20 (Munich, 1974), pp. 122–40; Hlawitschka, *Lotharingien*, pp. 103–6; and J. Le Goff, *The Birth of Purgatory*, trans. A. Goldhammer (Chicago, 1984), p. 118; Schneider, *Erzbischof Fulco von Reims*, pp. 68–72.

44. Regino, *Chronicon* 880, ed. Kurze, p. 117. Stafford, *Queens, Concubines, and Dowagers*, pp. 76–77, challenges Regino's thesis.

45. Regino, *Chronicon* 888, ed. Kurze, p. 129, argued that the later Carolingians had been too vigorous and too successful against each other to permit the emergence of a single strong ruler. He had derived this explanation from an abridgment of the *Historiae Philippicae* of Pompeius Trogus.

46. See Regino, *Chronicon* 880 and 887, ed. Kurze, pp. 116, 127–28.

47. Notker, *Gesta Karoli Magni* 2.14, ed. Haefele, MGH:SRG n.s. 12:78. On Bernard, see Hlawitschka, *Lotharingien*, pp. 27–30.

48. Notker, *Gesta Karoli Magni* 2.12, ed. Haefele, MGH:SRG n.s. 12:74; 2.11, p. 68, and 2.14, p. 78.

49. AF 885, p. 103.

50. Regino, *Chronicon* 887, ed. Kurze, p. 127. See also E. H. Kantorowicz, "The Carolingian King in the Bible of San Paolo Fuori le Mura," *Selected Studies* (New York, 1966), p. 92.

51. Stafford, *Queens, Concubines, and Dowagers*, pp. 94–96, seems to have assumed that Richardis and Liutward had truly plotted a palace revolt and that Richardis "retired when Charles the Fat divorced her" (p. 179). What might have brought Liutward and the empress together was marital or personal advice: see J. Bishop, "Bishops as Marital Advisors in the Ninth Century," in *Women of the Medieval World: Essays in Honor of John H. Mundy*, ed. J. Kirschner and S. F. Wemple (Oxford, 1985), pp. 53–84.

52. See P. Kehr, "Aus den letzen Tagen Karls III," *Deutsches Archiv* 1 (1937): 138–46; Hlawitschka, *Lotharingien*, pp. 38–45; H. Keller, "Zum Sturz Karls III: Über die Rolle Liutwards von Vercelli und Liutberts von Mainz, Arnulfs von Kärnten und der ostfränkischen Grossen bei der Absetzung des Kaisers," *Deutsches Archiv* 22 (1966): 333–84.

53. AF 887 (Continuatio Ratisbonensis), p. 115.

54. Charles the Fat, charter 165, ed. P. Kehr, MGH: *Diplomata regum Germaniae ex stirpe Karolinorum* 2 (Berlin, 1937), p. 268.15.

55. Pope John VIII, *epistola* 110, ed. E. Caspar, MGH:Ep. 7 (Berlin, 1912–28; repr. Munich, 1978), p. 102.20; see *epistola* 94, ed. Caspar, MGH:Ep. 7:89. On Guy, see Flodoard, *Historia Remensis ecclesiae* 4.1, ed. Heller and Waitz, MGH:SS 13:555.17–556.2. See also Hlawitschka, *Lotharingien*, pp. 33–35; J. H. Lynch, *Godparents and*

Kinship in Early Medieval Europe (Princeton, N.J., 1986), pp. 164–69; Schneider, *Erzbischof Fulco von Reims*, pp. 44–45.

56. T. Reuter, *Germany in the Early Middle Ages c. 800–1056 (London*, 1991), pp. 119–20. See also Kehr, "Aus den letzen Tagen Karls III," pp. 145–46.

57. *Hludowici regis Arelatensis electio*, ed. Boretius and Krause, MGH:Cap. 2.2:377.

58. Boso, charter no. 16, ed. R. Poupardin, *Recueil des actes des rois de Provence* (Paris, 1920), p. 31 [31–33].

59. See Charles the Fat, charters 156, 165–66, ed. Kehr, MGH: *Diplomata regum Germaniae ex stirpe Karolinorum* 2 (Berlin, 1937), pp. 253, 268–70. Count Wingis had met Charles in 881 in Siena: see Charles the Fat, charter 31, ed. Kehr, MGH: *Diplomata* 2:52.21, 53.17 [52–54]. See also Kehr, "Aus den letzten Tagen Karls III," pp. 140–41.

60. See Flodoard, *Historia Remensis ecclesiae* 3.26–27, ed. Heller and Waitz, MGH:SS 13:545.16–21, 550.10–15.

61. AV 888, p. 65. See also Schneider, *Erzbischof Fulco von Reims*, pp. 39–56.

62. Flodoard, *Historia Remensis ecclesiae* 4.5, ed. Heller and Waitz, MGH:SS 13:563.25–30.

63. See Flodoard, *Historia Remensis ecclesiae* 4.2, ed. Heller and Waitz, MGH:SS 13:559.44–45, 560.7–8.

64. Flodoard, *Historia Remensis ecclesiae* 4.9, ed. Heller and Waitz, MGH:SS 13:579.39–46; *Vita Rigoberti* 12, 13, ed. Levison, MGH:SRM 7:69.22, 70.9–29. See also Schneider, *Erzbischof Fulco von Reims*, pp. 233–44.

65. Silverstein, "Inferno, XII, 100–126, and the *Visio Karoli Crassi*," pp. 449–52; *The German Legends of the Brothers Grimm*, trans. and ed. D. Ward, 2 vols. (Philadelphia, 1981), 2:92–93, no. 467.

66. AF 887, p. 116; AV 887, p. 64.

67. Regino, *Chronicon* 888, ed. Kurze, p. 129.

68. See Silverstein, *Visio sancti Pauli: The History of the Apocalypse in Latin Together with Nine Texts* (London, 1935), pp. 13–14; M. Himmelfarb, *Tours of Hell: An Apocalyptic Form in Jewish and Christian Literature* (Philadelphia, 1983), p. 124; Heito, *Visio Wettini* 6, ed. Dümmler, MGH:PLAC 2:269–70.

69. See Le Goff, *The Birth of Purgatory*, pp. 46–48, 122, 197–98. On the *refrigerium* as a place of cooling refreshment after the fires of purgatory, see J. Ntedika, *L'évocation de l'au-delà dans la prière pour les morts: étude de patristique et de liturgie latines (IVᶜ–VIIIᶜs.)*, Recherches africaines de théologie, 2 (Louvain, 1971), pp. 193–200.

70. *Visio Karoli III*, ed. Lot, pp. 147–48; ed. Waitz, MGH:SS 10:458.53. In the former we find the reading "reliquias nostrae propaginis."

71. See P. E. Schramm, *Sphaira, Globus, Reichsapfel. Wanderung und Wandlung eines Herrschaftszeichens von Caesar bis zu Elisabeth II. Ein Beitrag zum Nachleben der Antike* (Stuttgart, 1958), pp. 57–59.

72. Angelomus, *epistola*, ed. Dümmler, MGH:Ep. 5:629.20 [625–30].

73. See Schramm, *Sphaira, Globus, Reichsapfel*, p. 58; Schramm and F. Mütherich, *Denkmale der deutschen Könige und Kaiser. Ein Beitrag zur Herrschergeschichte von*

Karl dem Grossen bis Friedrich II, 768–1250, Veröffentlichungen des Zentralinstituts für Kunstgeschichte in München, 2 (Munich, 1962), p. 137.58; Mütherich, "Die Reiterstatuette aus der Metzer Kathedrale," in *Studien zur Geschichte der europäischen Plastik. Festschrift Theodor Müller* (Munich, 1965), pp. 9–16.

74. Schramm, *Sphaira, Globus, Reichsapfel,* p. 58, observed that the one symbol lacking to Odo in 888 when he was crowned king was the *globus*.

EPILOGUE: TIME TO WAKE

1. Lewis Carroll, *Through the Looking-Glass,* (1872), from *More Annotated Alice: Alice's Adventures in Wonderland and Through the Looking Glass and What Alice Found There by Lewis Carroll,* illustrations by Peter Newell, with notes by Martin Gardner (New York, 1990), p. 224.

2. O. Spengler, *The Decline of the West,* trans. C. F. Atkinson, 2 vols. (London, 1926–28), 2:88; Alcuin, *Pippini regalis et nobilissimi iuuenis disputatio cum Albino scholastico,* PL 101:975C9–10.

3. See C. Carozzi, "La géographie de l'au-delà et sa signification pendant le haut Moyen Age," *Popoli e paesi nella cultura altomedievale* 2, Settimane di Studio del Centro Italiano di Studi sull'Alto Medioevo, 29 (Spoleto, 1983), pp. 458–59.

4. See K. J. Steinmeyer, *Untersuchungen zur allegorischen Bedeutung der Träume im altfranzösische Rolandslied* (Munich, 1963).

5. *Carmina Mutinensia* 1, ed. Traube, MGH:PLAC 3.2:703.1–2.

6. Prudentius, *Hymnus ad galli cantum,* ed. Cunningham, p. 6.92. See Rom. 13:11.

Index

Aachen, 15, 50, 52–53, 59, 62, 89–90, 94, figs. 10, 12
abbacy, lay, 148–49
Abbo of Saint-Germain-des-Prés, 228
Adalhard (count), 162, 165–66
Adalhard of Corbie, 57–58, 69, 74, 83
Admonitio generalis (the capitulary), 38
adoption, 233, 238–39, 242–43
Adrevald, 62, 174–75
advice and advice manuals (*Fürstenspiegel*), 59, 78, 83, 111, 238, 285 n.72
Aelius Aristides, 26
Aeneas, 31, 47
Aeneas (bishop of Paris), 184–86, 308 n.111
Aethelbald of Mercia (king), 36
Aethelwulf (king), 107–9
Agnellus of Ravenna, 124–26, 188
Agobard of Lyons, 89, 100–103, 114–16
Alberich of Trois-Fontaines, 135, 298 n.64
Alcuin, 11, 14, 16, 18–20, 42–44, 50, 58, 137, 162, 205, 253

Alexander the Great, 5–6, 23
Altfrid (bishop of Hildesheim), 204
Amalric of Tours, 150
Ambrose, 19, 40, 192
Ammianus Marcellinus, 6
Andernach, battle of, 9, 180
Angelomus of Luxeuil, 251
Angilbert of Saint-Riquier, 13–14, 50
Annals of Fulda, 126, 207, 211–13, 215, 219, 228–29, 242
Annals of Saint-Bertin, 107–10, 149, 180, 182, 214–15, 229
Annals of Xanten, 120–21, 198, 212–13, 215
Anskar, 51–53
apocalyptic thought and imagery, 125–28, 198
Arnulf of Carinthia, 228–29, 240–42, 244–45
art, 5, 15–19, 21, 39–40, 53, 64, 110–11, 125–26, 139, 147–48, 168, 191, 195–96, 199–200, 213, 235, 251
Artemidorus of Daldis, 27–30, 157
Astronomer (biographer of Louis the Pious), 8–9, 101, 110

Attila the Hun, 8
Aubrey (the blind dreamer), 93
Audradus Modicus, 128–56, 177, 254–55, 257
Augustine, 6, 34, 42, 196
Augustus, 11–12

Barontus, vision of, 75
Bede, 35, 44, 189
bedrooms, 11–12
Bego (Pico) of Paris, 68, 71–72, 83, 148, 284 n.54
Belshazzar (king), 204–5
Benedict of Aniane, 83
Benedict of Nursia, 35
Benedict IV (pope), 239
Berengar of Friuli, 239
Bernard (count of Toulouse), 180–81
Bernard (son of Charles the Fat), 240–42
Bernard of Italy, 68–74, 226
Bernard of Septimania, 100–102, 123
Bernold, vision of, 183–93, 238, 307 n.106
Bertha (daughter of Charlemagne), 13
Bertha (noblewoman), 171, 191
Bertrada (mother of Charlemagne), 57
Blitgar, 170
Boethius, 106
Boniface, Saint, 36–38, 174
Boso, 239–44
Brittany, 145–47
Burchard (bishop of Chartres), 150–52, 154–55

calamities, 82, 87, 95, 98–99, 122
Caligula (emperor), 6, 30
Carloman (brother of Pepin the Short), 115–17, 174–75, 218
Carloman (son of Charles the Bald), 11, 215–17
Carloman (son of Louis the German), 210

Carloman (son of Louis the Stammerer), 187, 227
Carloman (son of Pepin the Short), 57, 117
Caroline Books, 37, 41–42
Centulf, 168
Ceolred of Mercia (king), 36
Chanson de Roland, 18
Charlemagne: last decade of reign, 54–58; and the papacy, 39–42, 45–49; as *pater Europae,* 78; reputation of, 196–210, 258; vigilance of, 11–15, 21; vision of, 200–210
Charlemagne and Pope Leo, 45–48
Charles (archbishop of Mainz), 207
Charles the Bald, 9–10, 14, 16, 53, 116, 142–56, 198, 207, 215–17, 226–32, 238
Charles the Fat, 203–4, 210–19, 225–51; vision of, 192, 234–37
Charles the Simple, 244–46
children, illegitimate, 57, 59, 70, 226, 240–42
Chilperic, 35–36
chorepiscopate, 128–31
Cicero, 27–28, 32
Claudius (emperor), 6, 31
Clovis (king), 181, 231–32
Cluny, monastery of, 258
Codex Aureus, of Saint-Emmeram, 16, 53, fig.11
common people, rustics, 67, 74, 93, 189, 192
Constance, 126–27
Constantine (emperor), 12, 24, 37–38, 41
Constantinius II (emperor), 35
Constantinople, 7, 35
constitutional arrangements, 57, 69–70, 103–4, 114–17, 120, 210–11, 231–32
Council of Frankfurt (873), 211–19
Council of Paris (829), 98–100

Council of Saint-Médard of Soissons
(853), 150–52, 154
Council of Sens (853), 152, 154
Count Vivian, Bible of, 139, 147–48,
figs.15, 17–20
Cuthburga (queen), 36
Cyprian, 84

Dagobert (king), 168
Danes, 228
Daniel, 25, 33, 94, 139, 200, 204–5,
208
Dante, 19, 60, 233, 247
Dark Ages, as label, 20–21
David (king), 12, 17, 176
death and dying, 225–27; of Bernard of
Italy, 70; of Bernold, 183; of Charlemagne, 50–52; of Charles the Bald,
182–83; of Charles the Fat, 228–29,
247–48; of children, 56; of Ermengard, 72; of Louis the Pious,
110–11
Desiderata, 55, 57
Desiderius (king of the Lombards), 57
devil (Satan), 95–96, 98, 110, 124, 142,
213–19
Dhuoda, 16–17, 51
Dialogues, The (Gregory the Great), 35
62–63, 75, 189
Dio Cassius, 30
disorder, orderers of: Einhard, 88–91;
Florus of Lyons, 121–23; Gerward,
121; Prudentius of Troyes, 109–10;
Theodulf of Orléans, 82–86
disorder, ordering of, 82–91, 95–96
division(s), 114–15, 123, 126, 149, 171;
within a house, 124; and tripartition,
120–22, 145, 149–50, 156
Donation of Constantine, 37–38
Donatus (nobleman), 179–80
Dreambook of Daniel, 39
dreamers: Anskar, 51–53; Aubrey, 93–
95; Audradus Modicus, 137; Bernold, 183–89; Bertha (noble-

woman), 171; Centulf, 168; English
priest, 107; Eucher (bishop of Orléans), 170–71; unnamed girl, 109;
Liutfrid (royal steward), 53; monks,
36, 39, 51; poor woman of Laon,
67–68; Raduin (monk), 230;
Rotcharius (monk), 61; Walahfrid
Stabo, 44–45, 105–7; Wetti (monk
of Reichenau), 63–67
dreamers, royal: Charlemagne, 46,
200–201; Charles Martel, 167;
Charles the Fat, 234–37; Constantine, 37; Dagobert, 45; Edwin,
35; Guntram, 35; Louis the German,
219
dream guides: angels, 61, 63–64, 66,
174; Mary the Virgin, 230; monk,
68; John the Baptist, 52; Maximin,
167; Peter, 52; unnamed, 184; white
figure, 234
dreams: ancient, 28–32; bad, 44–45,
63; Byzantine, 34–35; collective,
29–30; definitions and classifications of, 28–34, 39–43; early Christian, 32–34; early medieval, 33–36;
historical, 23–27; Merovingian and
early Carolingian, 35–38; narrative
structures of, 24–25; negative comments about, 38–45; royal, 27–28,
30–49
dreams, people in: abbots, 36; Aeneas
(bishop of Paris), 184–86; Bego
(count), 68; boys, 107; Burchard
(bishop of Chartres), 151; children,
36; common, 36; counts, 36; Ebbo
(archbishop of Rheims), 184–86,
230; Hincmar (archbishop of
Rheims), 186–87; Jesse and Othar
(noblemen), 188; John I (pope), 35;
Leo III (pope), 46; monks, 61–62,
105; Pardulus (bishop of Laon),
184–86; priests, 63; Symmachus
(nobleman), 35; vassals, 235;
women, unnamed, 63

dreams, royal figures in, 37, 235–36, 250; Bernard of Italy, 68; Ceolred, 36; Charlemagne, 51, 61, 63–64, 66–67, 201; Charles Martel, 171; Charles the Bald, 144, 186–87; Charles the Fat, 234–37; Chilperic, 35–36; Cuthburga, 36; Edwin, 35; Ermengard, 68, 72–73; Lothar, 236–37; Louis the German, 144, 219, 236; Louis II of Italy, 144, 236–37; Theoderic the Great, 35; Wiala, 36

dreams, saints and holy ones in, 44–45, 64, 108, 140, 143, 201, 221; angels, 61, 63–64, 66, 136, 142–43; archangel Gabriel, 93–94; Christ, 52, 61, 64, 140, 143, 151, 153; elders of the Apocalypse, 52; John the Baptist, 52, 168; John the Evangelist, 230; Martin, 140–41, 145, 168; Mary the Virgin, 140, 230; Maximin, 167; Paul, 37, 145; Peter, 37, 52, 134, 145, 168, 236; Remigius, 171, 181, 230, 236; white figures, 44, 234

dream symbols: animals, 39, 44–45, 63–64, 66, 145, 148, 258; ball or orb, 237, 250–51; blood, 108; books, 36, 93–94, 105–9; buildings, 107; chairs, 52, 186, 188; child, 250; churches, 107, 186–87; dragons, 174, 235; fountains, 236; genitals, 63, 235; greed, 64–65; hand of God, 39; letters, 68, 73, 105–8; metal, 71–72, 235; palaces, 43, 184–85; paradise, terrestrial, 68, 236; rocks, 68, 188, 191, 236; scorpions, 235; serpents, 235; silver and riches, 64; sword, 201; Theoderic the Great, 35; thread, 234–37, 250–51; time, 190, 201, 208; tubs, 236, 249; valleys, 234–35; walls, 44, 68, 73

dream symbols of punishment: beatings, 35–36, 62–63, 168, 171, 181; boiling metal, 68, 71–72; boiling water, 61, 235–36, 249; demons, 36, 63, 68, 140, 188, 234–35; fire, 61, 63, 188, 235; giants, 235; hooks, 234–35; laceration, 46; mountains, 45, 63, 235; Northmen, 108, 140, 142, 153; pitch, sulphur, or wax, 188, 234–35; pits, 36, 186, 234; ragged dress, 184, 186–88; volcano, 35; worms, 186

Drythelm, 44, 60, 73

Dungal of Saint-Denis, 20

Ebbo of Rheims, 101, 184–85, 191–92, 230–31

Einhard, 3, 8, 10–12, 14, 20–21, 95, 103–4, 220; *Life of Charlemagne*, 11–12, 20–21, 55–57, 88–91, 196, 208–9; *History of the Translation*, 82–83, 91–97, 221

Engelberga (empress), 239, 243–44

Engelbert (poet), 9, 118–20

Epictetus, 6

Eriugena, 176–77, 199

Erluin, 170

Ermengard (queen, daughter of Louis II), 239–47

Ermengard (queen, wife of Louis the Pious), 68, 72–73

Ermintrude (queen), 150, 154, 162

Ermold the Black, 8, 86, 98, 205

Er the Pamphylian, 28, 31

Eucher, Saint, 174, 176; vision of, 173–76, 247

Evangelienbuch (Otfrid of Weissenburg), 203

exiles, 84–86

Exul, Hibernicus, 82

Ezekiel, 139–40, 150

family, 54–58, 119, 141

Fastrada (queen), 55–58

fathers and sons, 83, 101–3, 210–19, 222, 230, 243, 249

Field of Lies, 10, 101

Flodoard of Rheims, 169–93, 230–34, 244, 246

Florus of Lyons, 121–23

Fontenoy, battle of, 9, 118–20, 122, 126, 141

Formosus (pope), 237

Freculf of Lisieux, 14

Freud, Sigmund, 24–27

Fridugis, 20, 128

Fulda, monastery of, 222–23

Fulk (the annalist), 110

Fulk of Rheims, 229–51

Gabriel (the archangel), 18, 93–95, 221–22

Galba (emperor), 30–31

George (archbishop of Ravenna), 125–26

Germanic culture, 196, 201, 203–4, 223–24

Germanic partition, 115–17

Gerward, 89, 92, 120–21, 124

Gibbon, Edward, 23, 27, 54–55, 124, 199–200

Gottschalk, 20–21, 130–31

Gratiosus (archbishop of Ravenna), 125

Gregory of Nyssa, 34

Gregory of Tours, 35

Gregory the Great (pope), 35, 41–42, 62–63, 75, 189

Grimald (court chaplain), 66, 76, 98

Grimoald of Benevento (duke), 90

Gundrada (sister of Adalhard of Corbie), 58

Guntram (king), 35–36

Guy of Spoleto, 229, 242, 244–46

Hadrian I (pope), 39–41

Hadrian III (pope), 241

Halley's Comet, 8, 82, 122, 125

Hannibal, 6

Heiric of Auxerre, 177

Heito of Basle, 65, 70–78

Heliand, 203

Helisachar (chancellor), 86

Hildegard (daughter of Louis the Pious), 9

Hildegard (queen, wife of Charlemagne), 55, 72

Hilduin of Saint-Denis, 10, 86, 91–92, 101

Hincmar of Laon, 129, 177, 185–86; tomb of, 169, fig.21

Hincmar of Rheims, 10, 37–38, 124, 129–32, 137, 142, 150–52, 159, 169–94, 204–5, 214–17, 225–27, 229–32, 237, 239, 244

historical reflection, Carolingian: on the Germans, 196–97; on the Romans, 85, 196–97, 199–200; royal, 195–96

History of the Translation (Einhard), 82–83, 91–97, 221

Hitda Codex, 15–16, fig.1

Homer, 25, 177

Hucbald of Saint-Amand, 246

Hugh (abbot of Saint-Martin), 233

Ingelheim, palace of, 197, 205

Isaiah, 139

Jacob, 137

Jeremiah, 138–39

Jerome, 24

Jews, 59, 109, 114–16, 182

Job, 119

Joel, 140, 198

John the Baptist, 52, 168

John VIII (pope), 181, 227, 242

John the Evangelist, 230

Jonas of Orléans, 77–78, 82, 99, 103, 111, 161

Joseph, 33

Judith (empress), 14, 92, 100–107, 126, 160, 164

Julian, Saint, 133–34

Julius Caesar, 32

Jung, C. G., 24, 30, 270 n.27
justice and the law, 54, 144
Justin (emperor), 34
Justinian (emperor), 7, 35

kingship, 8–9, 17–18, 21–22, 37–38,
  50, 77–80, 99, 111, 143, 177–78,
  228–29, 232, 239, 243

Laon, 9, 185–86
Le Mans, 159–60
Leo IV (pope), 129–30, 132
Leo III (pope), 45–48
Leoba, Saint, 72
Life of Charlemagne (Einhard), 11–12,
  20–21, 55–57, 88–91, 196, 208–9
Life of Eucher, 174
Life of Rigobert, 174, 246–47
light, images of, 21, 209
Liutbert (archbishop of Mainz), 203–24
Liutgard (queen), 55, 57
Liutprand of Cremona, 34
Liutward (bishop of Vercelli), 241, 243
Livy, 6–7
locusts, 198
Lothar I (emperor), 10, 117–21, 125–
  26, 144, 149–50, 195, 236–37, 246
Lothar II (king), 170, 198, 241
Louis of Provence (Louis the Blind),
  228, 236–51
Louis the German, 110, 117–21, 144,
  170–77, 198–224, 236–37, 249,
  254
Louis the Pious, 8–10, 54, 58–60, 67–
  74, 78–79, 81–112, 114–17, 143–
  44, 219–22; sarcophagus of, 100–
  11, fig. 16
Louis II (emperor), 144–45, 149, 198,
  207, 210, 222, 227, 236–50
Louis the Stammerer, 179, 187, 192–
  93, 226–27, 229
Louis III (son of Louis the Stammerer),
  187, 227

Louis the Younger (son of Louis the
  German), 210–13, 219–22
Lucan, 32, 113–14, 123–24, 141
Ludwigslied, 206
Lupus of Ferrières, 9, 21, 53, 124, 130,
  146–48, 160–67, 176, 209, 263 n.15

Macrobius, 28, 42
magic, 38
Maitland, F. W., 158
Marcellinus, Saint, 91–100, 219–22
Marcward (abbot of Prüm), 162–63
marriage, 55–59, 218, 241–44
Martel, Charles, 167–68, 178, 181–82,
  205
Martin of Tours, Saint, 35, 128, 133–
  35, 140–45, 168
Mary the Virgin, 50–52, 140, 169,
  230–32
Maurus, Hrabanus, 20, 103, 127–28,
  131, 201–2, 205
Maximin, Saint, 167
Mercurius (the count of dreams), 35
Merovingians, 9, 35–38, 116–17, 167–
  68
Michael (the archangel), 94
modernity, Carolingian thoughts about,
  208–24, 312 n.43
Moduin, 84
monasticism, 77–78, 83, 143, 146–47,
  202
Monica (mother of Augustine), 34
Morman (king), 8–9
Moses, 85, 110–11
Muhammad, 35
Muspilli, 128, 203

Nebuchadnezzar, 125, 200, 208
Nero (emperor), 6, 32
Neuillay-Saint-Front, 179
Nicholas I (pope), 185, 198, 210–11
night and darkness, 9–10, 20, 208–9
Nithard, 165, 199
nobles, 70–72, 188, 192, 235, 256

Nominoë, 146, 163

nona et decima, 159, 179

Northmen, 108, 140, 142, 146, 152–53, 173, 180, 198, 204, 206, 228, 258

Notker the Stammerer, 12, 46, 53, 158, 168, 199–200, 203–4, 218, 238, 240

obedience, filial, 103, 110, 212

Odo of Cluny, 24

Odo of Ferrières, 159, 161–62

Odo of Paris, 228–29, 244, 258

Odulf (count), 162–65

Offa (king), 58

Ordinatio imperii, 70, 104, 115–16

Otfrid of Weissenburg, 203

Othar (count), 188–89

otherworld, 36–37, 60–61, 95, 136–37, 174, 184, 191; and border between ether and air, 143; churches and, 107; houses and, 61–62; palaces and, 184; pits and, 36; purgatorial, 60, 185

Otho (emperor), 6–7, 31

Otto III (emperor), 15

Ovid, 83–84

Paderborn, 46

palaces, 10, 13, 81, 184–85, 230–31

Pardulus of Laon, 150, 184–85, 308 n.111

Paul, Saint, 62, 145, 156; vision of, 34, 64, 73, 75, 200, 249

Paul the Deacon, 55

penance, 74–76, 101, 108

Pepin (son of Charlemagne), 14, 58, 69

Pepin of Aquitaine, 86, 102, 110, 207

Pepin the Hunchback, 13, 56

Pepin the Short, 174–75, 181–82, 205

Perpetua, 34

Peter, Saint, 52, 91–100, 129, 132–34, 145, 168, 219–22, 226, 236–37, 249

Peter of Pisa, 11

Petronius, 28

Pharaoah, 23, 74, 110–11, 141

Pico (Bego), 68, 71–72

Plato, 28, 31

Plutarch, 5, 31, 106

Polybius, 124

Pompey, 32

portents, 88–91

possession, cases of, 95–96, 211–12

prayer and prayer books, 16–20, 51, 61–62, 67–68, 108, 183–84, 220–22

predestination conflict, 130–32, 161

Procopius, 7, 35

property, notions of, 157–59, 178–79; ecclesiastical, 158–60, 162–64, 169–70, 202

prophecy, 124–56

Prudentius of Troyes, 16–17, 107–10, 149, 161

queens, 55, 57–58, 72–73, 101–3

Radbertus, Paschasius, 14, 42, 81–82, 102, 123–24

Raduin, vision of, 42, 230–33

Ratleig, 93–97

Rebellion of 817, 70

reform, 54, 58–60, 65, 98–103, 210

Reginbert, 75

Regino of Prüm, 118, 227, 229, 239–40, 248

Reichenau, 15, 63–79

Reichsapfel, 251

Remigius of Auxerre, 246

Remigius of Rheims, Saint, 169–94, 236, 249–50

Revolt of 830, 100–101

Revolt of 833, 101–7

Richardis (empress), 241–43

Richarius, Saint, 43

Richildis (queen), 179, 226, 239

Rigbold (suffragan bishop of Rheims), 129–31

Rimbert (archbishop of Bremen), 51–53, 212–13

Robert (bishop of Le Mans), 160

Rotcharius, vision of, 61–63, 76, 150, 191

Royal Frankish Annals, 65, 86–89

Ruadbern (Rothbern), 104–5, 146, 154

Rudolf (abbot of Saint-Bertin), 244, 246

Rudolf of Bourges, 142

Rudolf of Fulda, 103

Saint-Benoît-sur-Loire (Fleury), 62–63

Saint-Denis, 142–43, 182

Saint-Gall, 75

Saint-Josse, cell of, 162–66

Saint-Martin of Tours, 139, 145–47, 150–52, 154

Saint-Médard of Soissons, 11, 91

satire, on estates, 192, 238

Saxon Poet, 8, 13

Scipio Aemilianus, 28, 32

Second Council of Nicaea, 40–41

Seneca, 5–7, 31

Sens, see of, 229–32

sexual sins and sinners, 37, 58–59, 214, 218, 221; adultery, 54–55, 58, 101–3, 241; by Charlemagne and his court, 54–60, 66, 78–79; concubinage, 64, 220–21; fornication, punishment for, 62–64, 66; "naughty princesses," 57–59; prostitutes, 59; sodomy, 64

Sibyl, 125

sins, 99, 107–8, 167; avarice, 37, 64–65, 148–49, 235, 238; drunkenness, 6, 12, 65; pride, 65, 144, 235; vanity in dress, 65, 126, 188

sleep: Carolingian, 7–21, 200, 258; Christ as guardian of, 7–8, 15–18; Christian, 6–8, 15–18; dangers of, 9–11; as messianic symbol, 14–15; Roman attitudes toward, 5–7

statue, equestrian, of a Carolingian king, 251, fig. 26

Stephen V (pope), 242

Stephen IV (pope), 10

storm, stilling of at sea, 15–16, fig. 1

Strabo, Walahfrid, 11, 21, 37, 44–45, 65–78, 98, 100, 104–7, 146, 209, 256

Stuttgart Psalter, 17, 19, 168, 235, figs. 3, 5, 6, 8, 13, 14, 22, 23, 25

Suetonius, 6–7, 11–12, 24–25, 30–31, 89

swords, 201–6, 218

Sylvester (pope), 37

Synesius of Cyrene, 35

Synod of Quierzy (858), 172–76

Tassilo, 57

textual communities, 70, 254, 257; Charlemagne's court, 47–48; Einhard's, 97; Mainz, 223; Reichenau, 70, 74–76; Rheims, 191–92, 246–47; Saint-Gall, 75

Thegan, 58, 74, 111, 156

Theoderic the Great, 35, 100, 106, 197

Theodora (empress), 7

Theodore (bishop of Myra), 40–41

Theodosius the Great, 34, 74

Theodulf of Orléans, 19, 41–44, 70, 83–86

Thespesius, 31, 106

Theutberga (queen), 241

Thiota, 126–28

Tiberius (emperor), 25

Trier, 167–68

unity, imperial, 114–16

Ursmar (archbishop of Tours), 147

Utrecht Psalter, 11, 17, 19, 21, 191, 235, figs. 2, 4, 7, 9, 24

Valerius Maximus, 31

Victor of Vita, 30

Virgil, 8, 25, 29, 43, 45–46, 60, 85, 123, 125, 177

visio, as label, 41–44

Vivian (count), 139, 145–49, 162

Voncq, 189

Wala (brother of Adalhard of Corbie),
74, 81, 98, 124
Waldo (abbot of Saint-Maximin of
Trier), 166
Waldrada, 241
Wenilo (archbishop of Sens), 128–33,
142, 150–52, 177
Wetti, vision of, 42, 44–45, 48, 63–65,
98, 176, 189–90, 210, 221, 235;
Heito's version of, 63–65;

Walahfrid Strabo's version of, 65–
67, 98
Wiala (queen), 36
Wiggo (demon), 3, 95–96, 99
Willibrord, 43
Wingis (count), 243
Witgar (bishop of Augsburg), 202
women: defiled, 63; and poor woman of
Laon, 68, 73–74; royal, 36, 55–59,
72–73, 100–107, 150, 238–47;
Thiota and, 126–28